Fodor's 2010

PUERTO VALLARTA

By Jane Onstott

Where to Stay and Eat for All Budgets

Must-See Sights and Local Secrets

Ratings You Can Trust

Fodor's Travel Publications   New York, Toronto, London, Sydney, Auckland
www.fodors.com

FODOR'S PUERTO VALLARTA 2010
Editor: Laura M. Kidder

By: Jane Onstott

Production Editor: Jennifer DePrima
Maps & Illustrations: David Lindroth and Mark Stroud, *cartographers*; Bob Blake, Rebecca Baer, *map editors;* William Wu, *information graphics*
Design: Fabrizio LaRocca, *creative director*; Guido Caroti, Siobhan O'Hare, *art directors*; Tina Malaney, Chie Ushio, Ann McBride, Jessica Walsh, *designers*; Melanie Marin, *senior picture editor*
Cover Photo: Tequila, Jalisco: Patrick Frilet/hemis.fr
Production Manager: Angela L. McLean

COPYRIGHT

ISBN 978–1–4000–0851–3

ISSN 1558–8718

SPECIAL SALES

This book is available at special discounts for bulk purchases for sales promotions or premiums. Special editions, including personalized covers, excerpts of existing books, and corporate imprints, can be created in large quantities for special needs. For more information, write to Special Markets/Premium Sales, 1745 Broadway, MD 6-2, New York, New York 10019, or e-mail specialmarkets@randomhouse.com.

AN IMPORTANT TIP & AN INVITATION

Although all prices, opening times, and other details in this book are based on information supplied to us at press time, changes occur all the time in the travel world, and Fodor's cannot accept responsibility for facts that become outdated or for inadvertent errors or omissions. So **always confirm information when it matters,** especially if you're making a detour to visit a specific place. Your experiences—positive and negative—matter to us. If we have missed or misstated something, **please write to us.** We follow up on all suggestions. Contact the Puerto Vallarta editor at editors@fodors.com or c/o Fodor's at 1745 Broadway, New York, NY 10019.

PRINTED IN THE UNITED STATES OF AMERICA

10 9 8 7 6 5 4 3 2 1

Be a Fodor's Correspondent

Your opinion matters. It matters to us. It matters to your fellow Fodor's travelers, too. And we'd like to hear it. In fact, we need to hear it.

When you share your experiences and opinions, you become an active member of the Fodor's community. That means we'll not only use your feedback to make our books better, but we'll publish your names and comments whenever possible. Throughout our guides, look for "Word of Mouth," excerpts of your unvarnished feedback.

Here's how you can help improve Fodor's for all of us.

Tell us when we're right. We rely on local writers to give you an insider's perspective. But our writers and staff editors—who are the best in the business—depend on you. Your positive feedback is a vote to renew our recommendations for the next edition.

Tell us when we're wrong. We're proud that we update most of our guides every year. But we're not perfect. Things change. Hotels cut services. Museums change hours. Charming cafés lose charm. If our writer didn't quite capture the essence of a place, tell us how you'd do it differently. If any of our descriptions are inaccurate or inadequate, we'll incorporate your changes in the next edition and will correct factual errors at fodors.com immediately.

Tell us what to include. You probably have had fantastic travel experiences that aren't yet in Fodor's. Why not share them with a community of like-minded travelers? Maybe you chanced upon a beach or bistro or B&B that you don't want to keep to yourself. Tell us why we should include it. And share your discoveries and experiences with everyone directly at fodors.com. Your input may lead us to add a new listing or highlight a place we cover with a "Highly Recommended" star or with our highest rating, "Fodor's Choice."

Give us your opinion instantly at our feedback center at www.fodors.com/feedback. You may also e-mail editors@fodors.com with the subject line "Puerto Vallarta Editor." Or send your nominations, comments, and complaints by mail to Puerto Vallarta Editor, Fodor's, 1745 Broadway, New York, NY 10019.

You and travelers like you are the heart of the Fodor's community. Make our community richer by sharing your experiences. Be a Fodor's correspondent.

Happy traveling!

Tim Jarrell, Publisher

CONTENTS

MAPS

Fodor's Features

WHERE TO STAY
SPAAAHH 102

WHERE TO EAT
Mexico's Gourmet Town. 139

SHOPPING
The Art of the Huichol. 166

AFTER DARK
¡Tequila! 180

OVERNIGHT EXCURSIONS
Mariachi: Born in Jalisco 223

ABOUT THIS BOOK

Our Ratings

Sometimes you find terrific travel experiences and sometimes they just find you. But usually the burden is on you to select the right combination of experiences. That's where our ratings come in.

As travelers we've all discovered a place so wonderful that its worthiness is obvious. And sometimes that place is so experiential that superlatives don't do it justice: you just have to be there to know. These sights, properties, and experiences get our highest rating, **Fodor's Choice,** indicated by orange stars throughout this book.

Black stars highlight sights and properties we deem **Highly Recommended,** places that our writers, editors, and readers praise again and again for consistency and excellence.

By default, there's another category: any place we include in this book is by definition worth your time, unless we say otherwise. And we will.

Disagree with any of our choices? Care to nominate a place or suggest that we rate one more highly? Visit our feedback center at fodors.com.

Budget Well

Hotel and restaurant price categories from ¢ to $$$$ are defined in the opening pages of chapters 4 and 5. For attractions, we always give standard adult admission fees; reductions are usually available for children, students, and senior citizens. Want to pay with plastic? **AE, D, DC, MC, V** following restaurant and hotel listings indicate if American Express, Discover, Diners Club, MasterCard, and Visa are accepted.

Restaurants

Unless we state otherwise, restaurants are open for lunch and dinner daily. We mention dress only when there's a specific requirement and reservations only when they're essential or not accepted—it's always best to book ahead.

Hotels

Hotels have private bath, phone, TV, and air-conditioning and operate on the European Plan (aka EP, meaning without meals), unless we specify that they use the Continental Plan (CP, with a continental breakfast), Breakfast Plan (BP, with a full breakfast), or Modified American Plan (MAP, with breakfast and dinner), or are all-inclusive (AI, including all meals and most activities). We always

list facilities but not whether you'll be charged an extra fee to use them, so when pricing accommodations, find out what's included.

Many Listings
- ★ Fodor's Choice
- ★ Highly recommended
- ⊠ Physical address
- ✛ Directions
- ⌖ Mailing address
- ☎ Telephone
- 🖷 Fax
- ⊕ On the Web
- ✉ E-mail
- 🎫 Admission fee
- ☉ Open/closed times
- Ⓜ Metro stations
- ⊟ Credit cards

Hotels & Restaurants
- 🏨 Hotel
- ⇗ Number of rooms
- ⌂ Facilities
- ❍I Meal plans
- ✕ Restaurant
- ⌂ Reservations
- ↘ Smoking
- 🈂 BYOB
- ✕🏨 Hotel with restaurant that warrants a visit

Outdoors
- 🏌 Golf
- ⛺ Camping

Other
- ☺ Family-friendly
- ⇨ See also
- ⊠ Branch address
- ☞ Take note

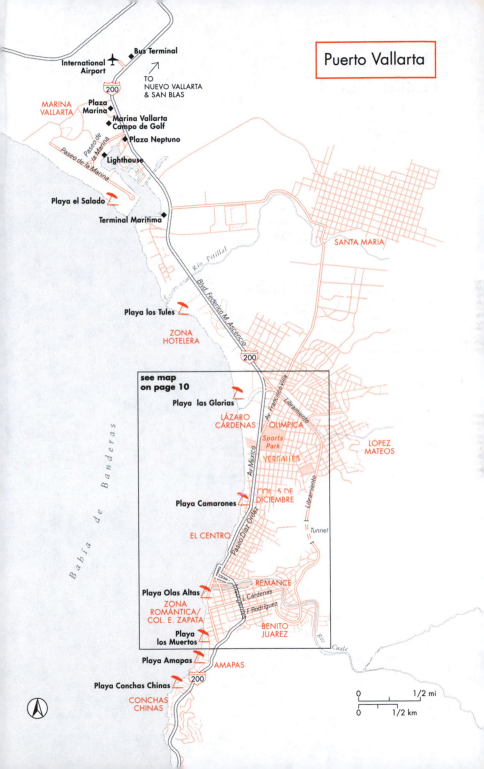

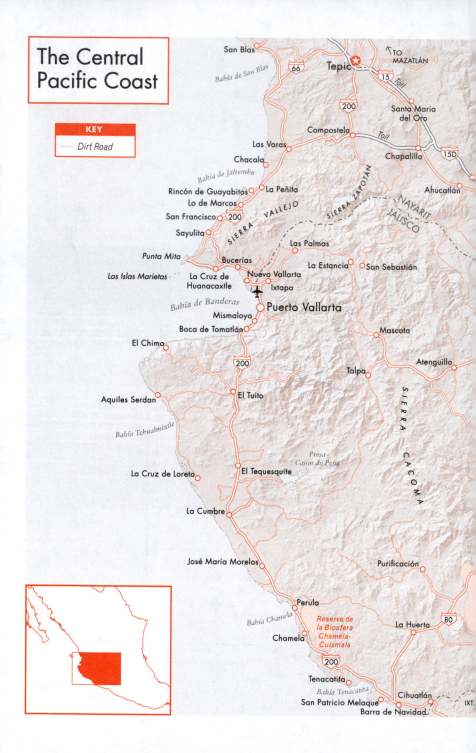

The Central Pacific Coast

KEY
----- Dirt Road

San Blas
Bahía de San Blas
66
TO MAZATLÁN
Tepic
15 Toll
200
Santa Maria del Oro
Compostela
Toll
Chapalilla
15D
Las Varas
Chacala
Ahucatlán
Bahía de Jaltemba
Rincón de Guayabitos
La Peñita
NAYARIT
JALISCO
Lo de Marcos
SIERRA ZAPOTAN
San Francisco
200
SIERRA VALLEJO
Sayulita
Las Palmas
Punta Mita
La Estancia
San Sebastián
Bucerías
Las Islas Marietas
La Cruz de Huanacaxtle
Nuévo Vallarta
Ixtapa
Bahía de Banderas
Puerto Vallarta
Mismaloya
Mascota
Boca de Tomatlán
El Chimo
200
Talpa
Atenguillo
Aquiles Serdan
El Tuito
SIERRA CACOMA
Bahía Tehualmixtle
Presa Cajón du Peña
La Cruz de Loreto
El Tequesquite
La Cumbre
José María Morelos
Purificación
Perula
80
Bahía Chamela
Reserva de la Biosfera Chamela-Cuixmala
La Huerta
Chamela
200
Tenacatita
Cihuatlán
Bahía Tenacatita
IXT.
San Patricio Melaque
Barra de Navidad

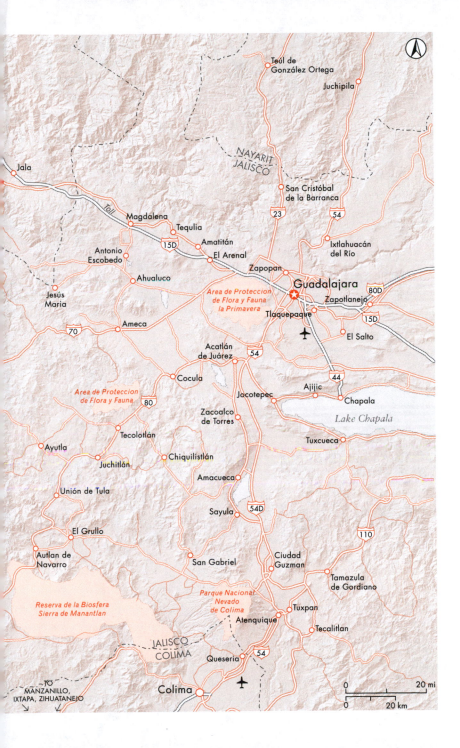

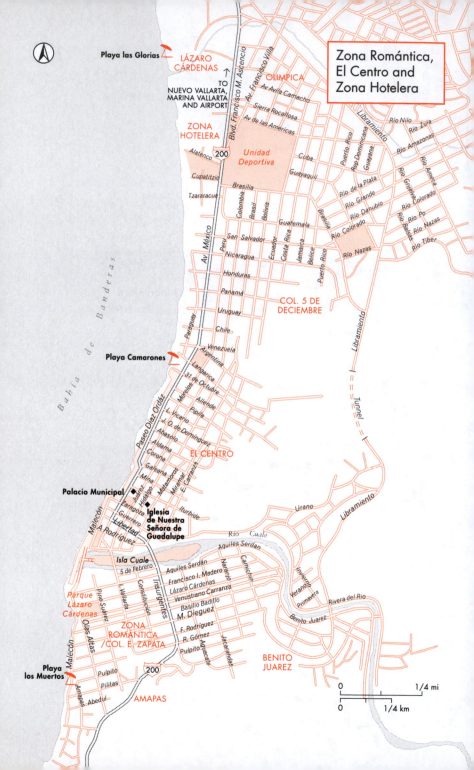

Zona Romántica, El Centro and Zona Hotelera

Playa las Glorias

LÁZARO CÁRDENAS

TO NUEVO VALLARTA, MARINA VALLARTA AND AIRPORT

OLÍMPICA

Blvd. Francisco M. Ascencio

Av. Francisco Villa

Av. Ávila Camacho

Sierra Rocallosa

Av. de las Américas

ZONA HOTELERA

Alatenco

200

Cupatitzio

Tzararacua

Unidad Deportiva

Cuba

Guayaquil

Brasilia

Puerto Rico

Rep. Dominicana

Guayana

Río de la Plata

Río Grande

Río Danubio

Río Colorado

Colombia

Brasil

Bolivia

Guatemala

Costa Rica

Jamaica

Belice

Río Nilo

Río Zula

Río Amazonas

Río Ameca

Río Grijalva

Río Colorado

Río Po

Río Balsas

Río Nazas

Río Tiber

Libramiento

Río Colorado

Río Nazas

Puerto Rico

Av. México

San Salvador

Perú

Ecuador

Nicaragua

Honduras

Panamá

Uruguay

Paraguay

Chile

COL. 5 DE DICIEMBRE

Bahía de Banderas

Venezuela

Argentina

Lanfarica

31 de Octubre

Morelos

Allende

Pípila

L. Vicario

J. O. de Domínguez

Abasolo

Aldama

Corona

Galeana

Mina

Metamoros

Miramar

E. Carranza

Iturbide

Libramiento

Tunnel

Playa Camarones

Paseo Díaz Ordaz

EL CENTRO

Palacio Municipal

Juárez

Hidalgo

Zaragoza

Guerrero

Libertad

A. Rodríguez

Malecón

Iglesia de Nuestra Señora de Guadalupe

Urano

Libramiento

Río Cuale

Aquiles Serdán

Isla Cuale

5 de Febrero

Aquiles Serdán

Francisco I. Madero

Lázaro Cárdenas

Venustiano Carranza

Basilio Badillo

M. Dieguez

F. Rodríguez

R. Gómez

Pulpito

Naranjo

Camichín

Invierno

Verano

Primavera

Benito Juárez

Rivera del Río

Parque Lázaro Cárdenas

I. Vallarta

Pino Suárez

Constitución

Insurgentes

Jacarandas

Aguacate

ZONA ROMÁNTICA /COL. E. ZAPATA

Olas Altas

Malecón

Pulpito

Pilitas

Amapas

Abedul

200

Playa los Muertos

AMAPAS

BENITO JUAREZ

0 — 1/4 mi

0 — 1/4 km

Experience Puerto Vallarta

WORD OF MOUTH

" . . . I particularly enjoyed walking along the boardwalk area in downtown, watching the street performers; the Rhythms of the Night boat cruise and dinner; the canopy zip-line tour (so much fun!) through Vallarta Adventures; and riding the buses (you just can't beat 5.5 pesos for transportation, plus you get to experience some of the locals). The things that annoyed me: the timeshare people everywhere and getting insect bites no matter what kind of repellent I used . . ."

—barnumbailey

WELCOME TO PUERTO VALLARTA

TOP REASONS TO GO

★ **Legendary restaurants:**
Eat barbecued snapper
with your feet in the sand
or chateaubriand with
a killer ocean view.

★ **Adventure and indulgence:** Ride a horse,
mountain bike or go four-
wheeling into the moun-
tains, dive into the sea,
and relax at an elegant
spa—all in one day.

★ **Natural beauty:** Enjoy
the physical beauty of
Pacific Mexico's prettiest
resort town, where cobblestone streets disappear into
emerald green hills with the
big, sparkling bay below.

★ **Authentic art:** PV's
artists and artisans—
from Huichol Indians to
expats—produce a huge
diversity of exceptional
folk treasures and fine art.

★ **Diverse nightlife:**
Whether you're old,
young, gay, straight,
mild, or wild, PV's casual
and unpretentious party
scene has something to
entice you after dark.

1 Old Vallarta. Rising
abruptly from the sea are
the hilly, cobblestoned
streets of El Centro (Downtown), lined with white-
washed homes and shops.
South of the Cuale River, the
Zona Romántica (Romantic
Zone, in Col. E. Zapata) has
PV's highest density of restaurants and shops.

2 North of Downtown.
Facing a busy avenue, the
Zona Hotelera Norte (Northern Hotel Zone) has malls,
businesses, and high-rise
hotels. The shopping centers
and deluxe hotels of Marina
Vallarta are sandwiched
between a golf course and
the city's main marina.

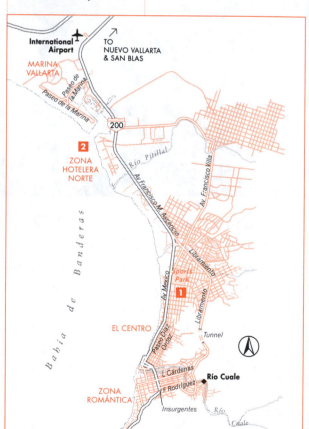

3 Nuevo Vallarta. The southernmost spot in Nayarit State, this planned resort is ideal if you want all-inclusive hotels. It has few restaurants and shops outside the Paradise Plaza mall.

4 The Southern Nayarit Coast. Exclusive Punta Mita (aka Punta de Mita) is dominated by the Four Seasons. Sayulita, San Francisco, and La Cruz de Huanacaxtle attract visitors with their small-town charm. Lovely, untouristy beaches like Playa Chacala complete the picture.

5 South of Puerto Vallarta. To Mismaloya, the hotels of the Zona Hotelera Sur hug the beach or overlook it from cliff-side aeries. Between La Cruz de Loreto and the Colima State border, the Costalegre is a mixture of luxury resorts and earthy seaside hamlets.

Dreams Hotel, Puerto Vallarta, Jalisco, Mexico

GETTING ORIENTED

The original town, Old Vallarta, sits at the center of 42-km (26-mi) Bahía de Banderas, Mexico's largest bay, in Jalisco State. From here, the Sierra Madre foothills dive into the sea. Mountain-fed rivers nourish tropical deciduous forests as far north as San Blas, in Nayarit State. South of PV the hills recede from the coast and the drier tropical thorn forest predominates south to Barra de Navidad.

PUERTO VALLARTA PLANNER

The Scene

Mexico's second-most-visited resort after Cancún, Puerto Vallarta is touristy. That said, this isn't a spring-break destination. Yes, twentysomethings party all night. But a sense of decorum and civic pride keeps things reasonably restrained. Most tour companies, restaurants, and hotels are run by locals who are happy to have you because tourism is PV's only real industry.

Fast Facts

Nickname: Foreigners call it PV or Vallarta. A *vallartense* (person from Puerto Vallarta), however, is known as a *pata salada* (salty foot).

State: PV is in the state of Jalisco, whose capital is Guadalajara.

Population: 220,368

Latitude: 20°N (same as Cancún, Mexico; Port-au-Prince, Haiti; Hanoi, Vietnam; Calcutta, India)

Longitude: 105°W (same as Regina, Saskatchewan; Denver, Colorado; El Paso, Texas)

Trivia: Two of the four quadrants in PV's official seal symbolize the tourism industry: a sailfish represents sportfishing; the hands welcome visitors.

Visitor Info

Before you visit and when you arrive, contact the **Puerto Vallarta Tourism Board & Convention and Visitors Bureau** (✉ *Local 18 Planta Baja, Zona Comercial Hotel Canto del Sol, Zona Hotelera, Las Glorias* ☎ *322/224–1175, 888/384–6822 in U.S., 01800/719–3276 in Mexico* ⊕ *www.visitpuertovallarta.com*).

The **Municipal Tourist Office** (✉ *Av. Independencia 123, Centro* ☎ *322/223–2500 Ext. 131*) is open weekdays 8–4.

The friendly folks at the **Jalisco State Tourism Office** (✉ *Plaza Marina shopping center, Local 144, Planta Alta, Marina Vallarta* ☎ *322/221–2676*), open weekdays 9–5, have information about PV and other destinations.

For information about Nayarit, contact the **Nuevo Vallarta Tourism Office** (✉ *Paseo de los Cocoteros at Blvd. Nuevo Vallarta, between Gran Velas and Maribal hotels* ☎ *322/297–1006 or 322/297–0180*).

Classes and Tours

With so many expats living here, PV and environs have lots of classes conducted in English. Low-cost courses at the Centro Cultural Cuale and other outlets put you in touch with locals as well as other English speakers.

In winter there are house and garden tours and even more cultural activities up and down the coast. A good source of information for current classes is the bimonthly, free *Bay Vallarta*, which always lists a Web page or phone number for further information.

CLASSES

You can matriculate midsession at the informal **Centro Cultural Cuale** (⊠*East end of Isla Río Cuale, Centro* ☎*322/223–0095*) for classes like painting, drawing, and acting for children and for adults. Most instructors speak some English, others are fluent. The center also sells the work of local artists and hosts cultural events. Cost of classes is nominal, and cultural events are free.

Biblioteca Los Mangos (⊠*Av. Francisco Villa 1001, Col. Los Mangos* ☎*322/224–9966*) has lots of reasonably priced art classes, and free or inexpensive monthly events, such as dance performances.

Philo's (⊠*Calle Delfin 15, La Cruz de Huanacaxtle* ☎*329/295–5068*) is the unofficial cultural center of La Cruz, north of Bucerías. Spanish classes are Tuesday and Saturday at 10:30 AM. Classes are free, but donations are expected. **AmeriSpan Unlimited** (☎*800/879–6640 in U.S. and Canada* ⊕ *amerispan.com*), based in the United States, specializes in medical and business Spanish; see the Web site for student blogs.

TOURS

Puerto Vallarta Tours (☎*322/222–4935, 866/217–9704 in U.S. or Canada* ⊕ *www.puertovallartatours. net*) runs ecotours, city and ranch tours, tequila tours, and private tours. **Vallarta Adventures** (⊠*Paseo de las Palmas 39–A, Nuevo Vallarta* ☎*322/297–1212, 888/303–2653 in U.S. and Canada* ⊠*Edifício Marina Golf, Local 13–C, Calle Mástil, Marina Vallarta* ☎*322/221–0657* ⊕ *www.vallarta-adventures.com*), has a wonderful tour that includes round-trip air transportation to the highlands, with a visit to the former mining town of San Sebastián.

When to Go

High season (aka dry season) is November through April, with the resorts being the most crowded and expensive December through Easter. If you don't mind afternoon showers, temperatures in the 80s and 90s F (20s and 30s C), and high humidity, rainy season (late June through October) is a great time to visit. Hotel rates drop by as much as 40% and there aren't any crowds.

Summer sees the best diving, snorkeling, and surfing conditions. By August the coast and inland forests are green and bursting with blooms. Afternoon rains clean the streets; waterfalls and rivers outside of town spring into action. On the downside, some businesses close shop in the hottest months, August and September, and nightlife slacks off.

Climate

The proximity of mountains to the coast increases humidity. From Puerto Vallarta north to San Blas there's jungly terrain (officially, tropical deciduous forest). South of PV, the mountains recede from the coast, making that area's thorn-forest ecosystem drier.

°F PACIFIC COAST °C

TOP EXPERIENCES

Canopy Tours

Canopy tours are action-packed rides, where, fastened to a zip line high off the ground, you fly from tree to tree. Blue sky above, ribbons of river below, and in between: a forest of treetops and a healthy shot of adrenaline.

Water Sports

Spend a day on the bay. Dive the varied landscape of Las Marietas Islands, angle for billfish, or take a boat ride for the fun of it. Look for orcas or humpbacks in winter and dolphins year-round. Swim, snorkel, or learn to surf or sail. Perhaps just build a sand castle with your kids.

Dining Out

First-time travelers come for the sun and sea, but it's PV's wonderful restaurants that create long-term fans. Dozens of top toques have restaurants here, and each November sees the International Gourmet Festival with guest chefs, recipes, and ideas from around the globe. Seaside family-owned eateries grill fish right off the boat, and tiny city cafés have great eats at bargain prices. And a number of street-side stalls are as hygienic as five-star-hotel restaurants.

Late Nights, Latino Style

Much of Vallarta is geared to the gringo palate, however, there's plenty of authentic spice for those who crave it. Enjoy a mojito at La Bodeguita del Medio, on the malecón. Dine on roast pork, black beans, and fried plantains before heading for the dance floor at around 9, when the house band comes to life. Thursday and Friday, take a taxi to J.B. Dance Club, in the hotel zone, for $4 dance lessons at 8 to 10 PM. Otherwise hang at La Bodeguita until around 11, when the Latino crowds start to arrive at J.B. for a late night of cumbia, salsa, and merengue.

Sensational Sunsets

After a day of activity, you deserve R, R, and R: rest, relaxation, and rewarding views. Sip a fancy cocktail to live music at busy Los Muertos Beach or indulge in dessert from the crow's nest at Bucerías's The Bar Above. For dramatic views from high above the sea head to Barcelona Tapas, Vista Guayabitos, or Las Carmelitas (⇨ *Chapter 5*). All serve dinner and drinks.

Hilltop Retreats

Get away from the gringo trail 4,000 feet above sea level in the mountain towns east of PV. Admire the elegant simplicity of tiny San Sebastián; in Talpa, visit the diminutive Virgin of Talpa statue, revered throughout Mexico for petitions granted. Buy keepsakes and mountain-grown coffee in shops on the square. Road access is relatively easy, but you can still charter a plane to these towns or to Mascota, where you can sample homemade *raicilla*—second cousin of tequila. Hike into tapestry hills and deep green valleys where, on a good day, you can spy PV and a ribbon of the Pacific. For an unforgettable experience (at least until your thigh muscles recover), take a horseback expedition (⇨ *Chapter 3*) into forests. Rancho Charro and Rancho Ojo de Agua have full-day excursions; the former offers multiday excursions as well, including tours to the former silver-mining towns of Mascota and San Sebastián. For those who prefer motorized horsepower, Wild Vallarta runs full-day ATV tours to San Sebastián.

THE MALECÓN

Puerto Vallarta's **malecón** is its Champs Élysées—only shorter, warmer, and less expensive. On the mile-long cement walkway bordering the sea, small groups of young studs check out their feminine counterparts; cruise-ship passengers stretch their legs; and landlocked visitors stroll before dinner. Even those who have lived here all their lives come out to watch the red sun sink into the gray-blue water beyond the bay.

Every night and weekend is a parade. Vendors sell *agua de tuba*, a refreshing coconut-palm-heart drink. Empanada, corn-on-the-cob, and fried-banana stands congregate near the Friendship Fountain and its trio of leaping bronze dolphins. Peddlers sell helium balloons and cotton candy. Clowns, magicians, and musicians entertain in the Los Arcos amphitheater.

There are also performances by *los voladores de Papantla*, the Papantla "flyers," near Los Arcos. Dressed in exquisite costumes of red-velveteen pants decorated with sequins, mirrors, embroidery, and fringe, five men climb a 98-foot pole. Four of them dive from the top of the platform as the leader "speaks" to them while balancing atop the pinnacle and playing a fife and drum. Held by a rope tied to one foot, the men wing around the pole exactly 13 times before landing on the ground. The total number of revolutions adds up to 52, a number of great ritual significance in the cosmology of the Aztecs. This traditional performance, native to Veracruz State, is held Thursday and Sunday evenings at 6 PM and 8 PM in low season and every hour on the hour from 6 PM to 9 PM in high season (December through April).

Some of PV's most endearing art is en plein air. Stretching along the sea walk is a series of bronze sculptures that are constantly touched, photographed, and climbed on. These nonstop caresses give a bright bronze luster to strategic body parts of Neptune and the Nereid, a mermaid and her man. Higher up on its pedestal, Puerto Vallarta's well-known sea-horse icon retains a more traditional (and dignified) patina.

Rotunda on the Sea, a wacky grouping of chair-people by Alejandro Colunga, is a good spot to sit and watch the sea, although around sunset, people waiting their turn to be photographed here make it hard to linger.

The three mysterious figures that compose *In Search of Reason,* by Sergio Bustamante, are just as otherworldly as the jewelry, painting, and statuettes sold in his Vallarta shops. Look for the pillow-headed figures climbing a ladder to the sky. Ramiz Barquet's *Nostalgia* is an ode to the artist's reunion with the love of his life at this very spot.

Gary Thompson, owner of Galería Pacífico, leads public sculpture walking tours mid-November through mid-April. The free two-hour tours, which don't require reservations, leave Tuesday mornings at 9:30 from the *Millennium* sculpture, next to the Hotel Rosita, after a briefing by its creator, artist Mathis Lidice. Tours end at the gallery, where sculptor Ramiz Barquet answers questions about his three sculptures featured on the tour and presents a brief demonstration of modeling in clay.

✉ *Extending south from Calle 31 de Octubre to Los Arcos outdoor amphitheater and Cuale River.*

TOP PUERTO VALLARTA ATTRACTIONS

La Iglesia de Nuestra Señora de Guadalupe

(A) The **Church of Our Lady of Guadalupe** is dedicated to the patron saint of Mexico and of Puerto Vallarta. The holy mother's image, by Ignacio Ramírez, is the centerpiece of the cathedral's slender marble altarpiece. The brick bell tower is topped by a lacy-looking crown that replicates the one worn by Carlota, short-lived empress of Mexico. The wrought-iron crown toppled during an earthquake that shook this area of the Pacific Coast in October 1995, but was soon replaced with a fiberglass version, supported, as was the original, by a squadron of stone angels. ✉ *Calle Hidalgo between Iturbide and Zaragoza, Centro* ☎ *No phone* ⏲ 7:30 AM–8 PM.

Museo Arqueológico

(B) Pre-Columbian figures and Indian artifacts are on display at the **Archeological Museum.** There's a general explanation of Western Pacific cultures and shaft tombs

and abbreviated but attractive exhibits of Aztatlán and Purépecha cultures and the Spanish conquest. ✉ *Western tip of Isla Río Cuale, Centro* ☎ *No phone* ✉ *By donation* ⏲ *Mon.–Sat. 10–7.*

Jardín Botánico de Puerto Vallarta

(C) On 20 acres of land 19 km (12 mi) south of town, the **Puerto Vallarta Botanical Gardens** feature more than 3,000 species of plants. Set within the tropical dry forest at 1,300 feet above sea level, its trails lead to a stream where you can swim; palm, agave, and rose gardens; a tree fern grotto; an orchid house; and displays of Mexican wildflowers and carnivorous plants. There's free parking and a free guided tour daily at 1 PM December through Easter. A lovely, open-sided restaurant serves a wide array of salads as well as pizza and Mexican dishes. Beverages include wine and a full bar. Go to its Web site to arrange a four-hour birding or

hiking tour, with lunch, for $85 per person. A taxi here will cost about 300 pesos, but, for less than a dollar, you can take the "El Tuito" bus from the corner of Aguacate and Venustiano Carranza streets. Another tip: slather on insect repellent before you go and bring some with you. This is the jungle, and *jejenes* (no-see-ums), mosquitoes, and other biting bugs can be counted on to attack. ⊠ *Carretera a Barra de Navidad Km 24, Las Juntas y Los Veranos* ☎ *322/223–6182* ⊕ *www. vallartabotanicalgardensac.org* 🎟 *$3* 🕘 *Tues.–Sun. 9–5.*

La Tobara

(D) Turtles sunning themselves on logs, crocodiles masquerading as logs, water-loving birds, and exotic orchids make the maze of green-brown canals that is **La Tobara** an out-of-town must for nature lovers. Launches putter along these waterways from El Conchal Bridge, at the outskirts of San Blas, about a three-hour drive from Marina Vallarta, or from the nearby village of Matanchén. After cruising along for about 45 minutes—during which you'll have taken *way* too many photos of the mangrove roots that protrude from the water and the turtles—you arrive at spring-fed freshwater pools for which the area is named. You can hang out at the restaurant overlooking the pool or play Tarzan and Jane on the rope swing. Most folks take the optional trip to a crocodile farm on the way back, stretching a two-hour tour into three hours. ⊠ *El Conchal Bridge, entrance to/exit from San Blas, San Blas* ☎ *323/101–7774* 🎟 *$9 per person; $28 for the whole boat* 🕘 *Daily 10–5.*

CRUISING TO PUERTO VALLARTA

Expanded and updated in 2007, PV's cruise ship terminal berths three full-size ships at a time and is midway between Marina Vallarta and the northern Hotel Zone, a 15-minute drive (barring traffic) from Old Vallarta. In 2008 about 275 ships called, bringing some 589,000 passengers who spent the day zinging along zip lines, riding horses into the hills, playing in the surf, or in winter, sightseeing for humpbacks and orcas in Vallarta's bay.

Companies with cruises to the Pacific Coast include Carnival, Holland America, Norwegian, Princess, and Royal Caribbean. Most depart from Los Angeles (Long Beach) or San Diego and head to Los Cabos or Mazatlán, Puerto Vallarta, Manzanillo, Ixtapa/Zihuatanejo, and/or Acapulco; some trips originate in Vancouver or San Francisco.

Carnival. Carnival is known for its large-volume cruises and template approach to its ships, two factors that probably help keep fares accessible. Boats in its Mexican fleet have more than 1,000 staterooms; the newest ship, *Splendor,* was inaugurated in 2008. Seven-night trips out of Los Angeles hit Mazatlán, Los Cabos, and Puerto Vallarta. Las Vegas–style shows and passenger participation are the norm. ☎888/227–6482 ⊕*www.carnival.com.*

Holland America. The venerable Holland America line leaves from and returns to San Diego. Its 10-day Sea of Cortez cruise calls at Puerto Vallarta as well as Cabo San Lucas, Loreto, La Paz, Mazatlán, and Topolobampo, with a chance to ride the narrow-gauge Chihuahua al Pacífico Train into the most scenic part of the Copper Canyon. The company also offers a 14-day cruise hitting Victoria and Vancouver, in British Columbia and a seven-day Riviera Mexico cruise with stops at PV, Mazatlán, and Los Cabos. ☎877/932–4259 ⊕*www. hollandamerica.com.*

Norwegian Cruise Lines. Its tagline is "whatever floats your boat," and Norwegian *is* known for its relatively freewheeling style and variety of activities and excursions. Six-day cruises are out of Los Angeles, with three nights at sea and full days in Los Cabos and PV. The seven-day trip adds a day in Mazatlán; an 11-day itinerary also has stops in La Paz and Topolobampo for a Copper Canyon train adventure. ☎800/327–7030 ⊕*www.ncl.com.*

Princess Cruises. Not so great for small children but good at keeping tweens, teens, and adults occupied, Princess strives to offer luxury at an affordable price. Its cruises may cost a little more than others, but you also get more for the money: large rooms, varied menus, and personalized service. The seven-day Riviera Mexico cruise aboard the *Sapphire Princess* starts in Los Angeles and hits Los Cabos, PV, and Mazatlán. Ten-day trips out of San Francisco add Acapulco and Ixtapa but don't stop at Mazatlán. ☎800/774–6237 ⊕*www.princess.com.*

Royal Caribbean. Royal Caribbean's seven-night cruises originate in Los Angeles and stop in Los Cabos, Mazatlán, and PV. Nine-night cruises from San Diego add a stop in Manzanillo as well as Ixtapa/Zihuatanejo. Striving to appeal to a broad clientele, the line offers lots of activities and services as well as many shore excursions. ☎800/521–8611 ⊕*www.royalcaribbean.com.*

GAY PUERTO VALLARTA

Puerto Vallarta is a gay old town. Men check each other out over drinks and suntan oil at the south end of Los Muertos beach, dangle from parachutes above the bay, buff themselves out at South Side gyms. Rainbow boys (and girls) spend a day sailing on vessels flying the multicolor flag of love and then dance 'til morning in one of the city's oversexed discos. Mexico's most popular gay destination draws crowds of "Dorothy's friends" from both sides of the Río Grande and from the Old World as well.

The Romantic Zone is the hub for rainbow bars and sophisticated, gay-friendly restaurants. Here, many foreigners have—after falling in love with Puerto Vallarta's beaches, jungly green mountains, and friendly people—relocated to PV to fulfill their ultimate fantasy in the form of bistro, bar, or B&B. International savvy (and backing) teamed up with Mexican sensibilities have produced a number of successful gay businesses.

Gay hotels offer entertainment that allows you to party on-site without having to worry about getting "home." In addition to gay properties such as Blue Chairs and Casa Cupula, hotels like Los Cuatro Vientos, in Centro, and Quinta María Cortez above Playa Conchas Chinas (⇨ *Chapter 4*) are gay-friendly.

■ TIP ➜ Gayguide Vallarta (⊕ www.gayguide vallarta.com) has lots of listings for long- and short-term condo rentals.

Clubbing may be the favorite pastime in the Romantic Zone, but there's more than one way to cruise Vallarta. Gay boat tours keep the libations flowing throughout the day, and horses head for the hills for bird's-eye views of the beach.

THE BEACH SCENE

The undisputed yet unassuming king of daytime beach action is **Blue Chairs** (⊠ *South end of Los Muertos Beach, Col. E. Zapata* ☎ *322/222–5040, 866/ 514–7969 toll-free in U.S. and Canada*). Shaded by the bright azure umbrellas that distinguish the restaurant/bar/hotel, boys from the 'hood mingle with asphalt cowboys from the Midwest.

Waiters range from snarky queens to cherubic heteros. Next door, the green umbrellas blend with the blue; at this end of the beach, though, it's pretty much gay no matter what color the umbrellas. This is PV's most popular rainbow beach scene, a magnet for first-timers as well as those sneaking away from social obligations in Guadalajara.

SPORTS AND THE OUTDOORS

Cruises

Boana Tours (⊠ *Casa Boana, Calle Amapas 325, Col. E. Zapata* ☎ *322/222–0999* ⊕ *www.boana.net*) offers a gay cruise, Saturday only, to secluded La Pizota beach, beyond Yelapa. The tour ($75 per person) leaves from Los Muertos pier; runs from 9 to 6; and includes open bar, continental breakfast, and a barbecue lunch on the beach. Snorkel gear and kayaks are available, too. To hold a spot, make a deposit

in person at Boana's office in Torre Malibu, behind Blue Chairs on Highway 200 just south of the Romantic Zone.

Diana's Tours (☎322/222–1510, 866/514–7969 in U.S. for reservations ⊕www.dianastours.com) is a booze-and-beach cruise (Thursdays and most Fridays also in high season) popular with lesbians and gays. Straights are also welcome, but minors are not. Go for the swimming, snorkeling, and lunch on the beach at Las Animas or another area beach, or for the unlimited national-brand beers and mixed drinks. Most of the time is spent on the boat. It's easiest to reserve tickets ($75) online using PayPal.

Health Clubs

On the South Side, gay-friendly **Acqua Day Spa and Gym** (⊠Constitución 450 Col. E. Zapata48350 ☎322/223–5270) has a sauna and steam room in addition to free weights and machines, massage, body treatments, and more. It's $10 per day and is closed Sunday.

Serious muscle men and women head for **Gold's Gym** (⊠Calle Pablo Picasso s/n, Plaza Las Glorias, Zona Hotelera ☎322/225–6671) with aerobics, yoga, and Pilates as well as a sauna, steam, climbing wall, and hot tub. The $10-per-day ($28 per week) price is reasonable, especially since it includes classes like yoga or Pilates. There's also free child care for toddlers to six year olds.

For women only, **Total Fitness Gym** (⊠Calle Timón 1, at marina, Marina Vallarta ☎322/221–0770) is sparkly clean and has a sauna and lots of classes: yoga, Spinning, meditation, step, dance, salsa, jazz, aerobics, and Pilates. The daily fee is $20, including classes, or $40 per week.

> ### TOTAL RELAXATION
>
> If you must break a sweat on your vacation, the best way is while experiencing a *temazcal*, an ancient Indian sweat lodge ceremony at **Terra Noble** (⊠Av. Tulipanes 595, Fracc. Lomas de Terra Noble ☎322/222–5400 or 322/223-3530 ⊕www.terranoble.com). The spa also has therapeutic massage, body treatments, and facials.

Horseback Riding

Three-hour, $45 horseback adventures with **Boana Tours** (⊠Torre Malibú, Carretera a Mismaloya ☎322/222–0999 ⊕www.boana.net) include one-way transportation to its ranch outside the city, a little more than an hour on the horse, a light lunch, and two drinks. You can take a swim in the river before returning on your own to PV. Most of the year there are two tours, at 9:15 AM and 2:15 PM, every day but Sunday.

WEDDINGS AND HONEYMOONS

Mexico is a growing wedding and honeymoon destination for Canadians and Americans. Many area hotels—from boutiques to internationally known brands—offer honeymoon packages and professional wedding planners. Although there's an obligatory civil ceremony that must accompany the Big Event, you can get married in a house of worship, on a beach, at a hotel chapel, or on a yacht or sailboat.

The Big Day

Choosing the Perfect Place. Puerto Vallarta—including resorts to the north along the Riviera Nayarit and south along the Costalegre—is one of Mexico's most popular wedding and honeymoon destinations. Many couples choose to marry on the beach, often at sunset because it's cooler and more comfortable for everyone; others chuck the whole weather conundrum and marry in an air-conditioned resort ballroom.

The luxury of enjoying your wedding and honeymoon in one place has a cost: you may find it hard to have some alone time with your sweetie with all your family and friends on hand. Consider booking an all-inclusive, which has plenty of meal options and activities to keep your guests busy. This will make it easier for them to respect your privacy and stick to mingling with you and your spouse at planned times. Among PV's best options for on-site, catered weddings are the Marriott CasaMagna, the Westin, the Villa Premiere, and Casa Velas. Le Kliff and El Dorado restaurants offer stunning views from their wedding–reception areas; Las Caletas offers unique beachfront weddings accessed by boat through Vallarta Adventures.

Wedding Attire. Some women choose a traditional full wedding gown with veil, but more popular and comfortable—especially for an outdoor wedding—is a simple sheath or a white cotton or linen dress that will breathe in the tropical heat. Some brides, of course, opt for even less formal attire: anything from a sundress to shorts or a bathing suit.

Weddings on the beach are best done barefoot, even when the bride wears a gown. Choose strappy sandals for a wedding or reception that's not on the sand; forget the notion of stockings: it's usually too hot and humid. Whatever type gown you choose, it's best to both purchase and get any alterations done before leaving home. Buy a special garment bag and hand-carry your dress on the plane. Don't let this be the one time in your life that your luggage goes missing at great personal cost.

Time of Year. Planning according to the weather can be critical for a successful PV wedding. If you're getting married in your bathing suit, you might not mind some heat and humidity, but will your venue—and your future mother-in-law—hold up under a summer deluge? We recommend substituting the traditional June wedding that's so suitable for New England and Nova Scotia with one held between late November and February or March. April through mid-June are usually dry but extremely hot and humid. Summer rains begin to fall in mid-June. Sometimes this means a light sprinkle that reduces heat and humidity and freshens the trees, other times it means a torrential downpour that immediately floods the streets. Although hurricanes are rarer along the Pacific than the Caribbean, they can threaten September through early November. For an out-

door wedding, establish a detailed backup plan in case the weather lets you down.

Finding a Wedding Planner. Hiring a wedding planner will minimize stress for all but the simplest of ceremonies. A year or more in advance, the planner will, among other things, help choose the venue, recommend a florist, and arrange for a photographer and musicians. The most obvious place to find a wedding planner is at a resort hotel that becomes wedding central: providing accommodations for you and your guests, the wedding ceremony venue, and the restaurant or ballroom for the reception. But you can also hire an independent wedding coordinator; just google "Puerto Vallarta wedding" and you'll get tons of hits. Unless you're fluent in Spanish, make sure the person who will be arranging one of your life's milestones speaks and understands English well. Ask for references, and check them.

When interviewing a planner, talk about your budget, and ask about costs. Are there hourly fees or one fee for the whole event? How available will the consultant and her assistants be? Which vendors do they use and why? How long have they been in business? Request a list of the exact services they'll provide, and get a proposal in writing. If you don't feel this is the right person or agency for you, try someone else. Cost permitting, it's helpful to meet the planner in person.

Requirements. Getting a bona fide wedding planner will obviously facilitate completing the required paperwork and negotiating the legal requirements for marrying in Mexico. Blood work must be done upon your arrival, but not more than 14 days before the ceremony. All documents must be translated by an authorized translator

from the destination, and it's important to send these documents certified mail to your wedding coordinator at least a month ahead of the wedding. You'll also need to submit an application for a marriage license as well as certified birth certificates (bring the original with you to PV, and send certified copies ahead of time). If either party is divorced or widowed, official death certificate or divorce decree must be supplied. The bride, groom, and four witnesses will also need to present passports and tourist cards.

Jalisco State has additional requirements; for this reason some couples choose to have the civil ceremony in Nayarit State (Nuevo Vallarta or anywhere north of there) and then the "spiritual" ceremony in the location of their choice. Since church weddings aren't officially recognized in Mexico, even for citizens, a civil ceremony is required in any case, thus making your marriage valid in your home country as well. Another option is to be married (secretly?) in your own country and then hold the wedding event without worrying about all the red tape.

The Honeymoon

If you've chosen a resort wedding, you and many of the guests may be content to relax on-site after the bustle and stress of the wedding itself. Puerto Vallarta has a huge variety of accommodations, from name-brand hotels with spas and multiple swimming pools to three-bedroom B&Bs in the moderate price range. Many properties have special honeymoon packages that include champagne and strawberries on the wedding night, flowers in the room, spa treatments for the bride and attendants, or other sorts of pampering and earthly pleasures.

KIDS AND FAMILIES

What better way to bond with your kids than splashing in the pool or the sea, riding a horse into the hills, or zipping through the trees on a canopy tour? Puerto Vallarta may be short on sights, but it's long on outdoor activities like these. It also has a huge range of accommodation options: everything from B&Bs that leave lunch and dinner wide open for a family on the go to all-inclusive resorts where picky eaters can be easily indulged and kids of all ages can be kept engaged by activities or kids' clubs.

Places to Stay

Resorts: Except those that exclude children entirely, most of Vallarta's beach resorts cater to families and have children's programs. The Sol Meliá is great for little kids, as it offers lots of games and activities geared toward them; there's not so much of interest to teens here. The Marriott is kid-friendly, offering children's menus at most of its restaurants and kids' clubs for the 4 to 13 set. In addition to things like Ping-Pong, tennis, and volleyball kids absolutely love liberating tiny turtle hatchlings into the sea during the summer/early fall turtle season.

At the high end of the price spectrum, Four Seasons has plenty for the kids to do, as well as golf and spa appointments for mom and dad. The protected, almost private beach here is great for the children, who also love floating on inner tubes in the ring-shape swift-water swimming pool. The children's center, with loads of cool games and computer programs, keeps kids of all ages entertained.

South of Vallarta, Dreams is a great place for an all-inclusive family vacation, with movies on the beach and loads of activities for adults and children. Kids enjoy the secluded beach (parents needn't worry about them wandering off), the giant-screen TV on the beach for movies or ball games, and the treasure hunts and weekly overnight campouts.

Old Vallarta (El Centro and Colonia E. Zapata, aka Zona Romántica) consists mainly of moderate to budget hotels. Independent families are often drawn to such properties on or near Los Muertos Beach. Playa Los Arcos, for instance, is right on the sand; Eloisa, with its inexpensive studios (with kitchenettes) and suites, is a block from the bay.

Vacation Rentals: Apartments, condos, and villas are an excellent option for families. You can cook your own food (a big money saver), spread out, and set up a home away from home, which can make everyone feel more comfortable. If you decide to go the apartment- or condo-rental route, be sure to ask about the number and size of the swimming pools and whether outdoor spaces and barbecue areas are available.

Funky Yelapa, south of PV, has only a few hotels; most people rent homes from spartan to less-spartan, via the Internet. **Boutique Villas** (☎322/209–1992 or 866/560–2281 ⊕www.boutiquevillas. com) is an excellent resource for quality condos and villas in a variety of price ranges. Even in the winter (high) season, you can get a nice two-bedroom, two-bath condo for $150 a night. Add great locations, satellite TV in every bedroom, daily maid service, and the use of washer and dryer, and the value is obvious. You can even get your own cook who will do the shopping as well.

Beaches

Los Muertos Beach is a good bet for families who want access to snacks and water-sports rentals, and there are (usually) lifeguards here, too. Families favor the north end near Playas Olas Altas (the south end is the gay beach), but there's plenty of sand and sun for all. The all-inclusive resorts of Nuevo Vallarta rent water-sports equipment for use at a long, wide beach that continues all the way to Bucerías. The scene here is very laid-back, involving more lounging than anything else.

Water Activities

If you surf, or want to learn, Sayulita is a good option. There are also many good surfing beaches off the point at Punta Mita as well as around San Blas and Barra de Navidad.

Year-round you can catch glimpses of manta rays leaping from the water and dolphins riding the wakes of bay cruises. Winter sees whale-watching expeditions on which you can spot humpbacks and orcas.

Turtle season is summer through late fall; children love to take part in liberating the tiny hatchlings. Larger resort hotels on turtle-nesting beaches often encourage guests to participate in this, and wildlife operators offer turtle tours.

There's snorkeling (though sometimes lots of little jellyfish) around Los Arcos, just south of PV; at the Marieta Islands off Punta Mita; and other beaches north and south. Divers haunt these spots, too, in addition to farther-away destinations.

PV's yachts and *pangas* (skiffs) are available for shore- or deep-water fishing excursions. Nuevo Vallarta has a much smaller fleet based at Paradise Village marina. In small towns like Mismaloya, Boca de Tomatlán, Rincón de Guayabitos, Sayulita, Tenacatita and Barra de Navidad, you contract with local fishermen on or near the beach for angling expeditions.

Land Activities

Puerto Vallarta proper has a lovely botanical garden with a river in which kids can splash. In the hills behind town, you can go on horseback, mountain-bike, ATV, dune-buggy, or canopy-tour adventures. Golf courses range from private links at Punta Mita to fun and accessible courses in Nuevo Vallarta and Marina Vallarta. There are excellent courses to the south at El Tamarindo and Barra de Navidad.

After Dark

Nightly in high season musicians, clowns, and mimes perform at PV's Los Arcos amphitheater. Walk along the *malecón* (boardwalk) en route, stopping for ice cream, to admire the sunset, or to pose for pictures beside a sculpture.

Dinner shows often offer Mexican-theme buffets, mariachi music, and, sometimes, cowboys doing rope tricks. The pirate-theme vessel *Marigalante* has both day and evening cruises that kids love. PV has four modern movie theaters with English-language movies; note, though, that animated films or those rated "G" are often dubbed in Spanish.

GREAT ITINERARIES

Each of these itineraries fills one day. Together they touch on some of PV's most quintessential experiences, from shopping to getting outdoors to just relaxing at the best beaches and spas.

Romancing the Zone

Head south of downtown to the Zona Romántica for a day of excellent shopping and dining. Stop at Isla del Río Cuale for trinkets and T-shirts; have an island breakfast overlooking the stream at the River Cafe or an excellent lunch at Le Bistro, where the romantic, neo-Continental decor and monumental architecture produce a flood of endorphins.

■ **TIP→** Most of the stores in the neighborhood will either ship your oversized prizes for you or expertly pack them and recommend reputable shipping companies.

Crossing the pedestrian bridge nearest the bay, drop nonshoppers at Los Muertos Beach. They can watch the fishermen on the small pier, lie in the sun, sit in the shade with a good book, or walk south to the rocky coves of **Conchas Chinas Beach,** which is good for snorkeling when the water is calm. Meanwhile, the shoppers head to **Calle Basilio Badillo** and surrounding streets for folk art, housewares, antiques, clothing, and accessories. End the day back at Los Muertos with dinner, drinks, and live music.

■ **TIP→** Some of the musicians at beachfront restaurants work for the restaurant, others are freelancers. If a roving musician (or six) ask what you'd like to hear, ask the price of a song.

Downtown Exploration

Puerto Vallarta hasn't much at all in the way of museums, but with a little legwork, you can get a bit of culture. Learn about the area's first inhabitants at the tiny but tidy **Museo Arqueológico** (closed Sunday), with info in English. From the museum, head downtown along the newest section of the **malecón,** which crosses the river. About four blocks north, check out the action in the main plaza and Los Arcos amphitheater. At the **Iglesia de Nuestra Señora de Guadalupe,** you can pay your respects to the patron saint of the city (and the country).

Strolling farther north along the malecón is like walking through a sculpture garden: look for the statue of a boy riding a sea horse (it's become PV's trademark), and *La Nostalgia,* a statue of a seated couple, by noted PV artist Ramiz Barquet. Three figures climb a ladder extending into the air in Sergio Bustamante's *In Search of Reason.* One of the most elaborate sculptures is by Alejandro Colunga: *Rotunda del Mar* has more than a dozen fantastic figures—some with strange, alien appendages—seated on chairs and pedestals of varying heights.

A Day of Golf and Steam

Puerto Vallarta is one of Mexico's best golfing destinations. And what better way to top off a day of play than with a steam, soak, and massage? At the southern end of the Costalegre, Tamarindo and Grand Bay Isla Navidad have courses (18 great holes and three 9-hole courses, respectively) and very good spas. The closest spas to the greens of Marina Vallarta and the Vista Vallarta are those at the Westin Regina and the CasaMagna Marriott, which has gorgeous new facilities. The El Tigre course is associated with the Paradise Village resort, whose moderately priced spa is open also to those who golf at Mayan Palace, just up the road, and

at Flamingos, at the far northern edge of Nuevo Vallarta.

■TIP➜ Ask your concierge (or look online) to find out how far ahead you can reserve, and then try for the earliest possible tee time to beat the heat. If the course you choose doesn't have a club pool, you can have lunch and hang at the pool at the resorts suggested above, or get a massage, facial, or other treatment (always reserve ahead).

A Different Resort Scene

If you've got wheels, explore a different sort of beach resort. After breakfast, grab beach togs, sunscreen, and other essentials for a day at a beach to the north of town. Before heading out, those with a sweet tooth should make a pit stop at PV's Pie in the Sky, which has excellent pie, chocolate, and other sugar fixes.

About an hour north of PV, join Mexican families on the beach at **Rincón de Guayabitos,** on attractive Jaltemba Bay. Play in the mild surf; walk the pretty, long beach; or take a ride in a glass-bottom boat to **El Islote,** an islet with a small restaurant and snorkeling opportunities. Vendors on the sand sell grilled fish and chilled coconuts and watermelon from their brightly colored stands.

On the way back south, stop in the small town of **San Francisco** (aka San Pancho), for dinner. You can't go wrong at La Ola Rica or the more sophisticated Cafe del Mar (brush the sand off your feet for that one). In high season and especially on weekend evenings, one of the two will probably have live music.

■TIP➜ Take a water taxi out for a look at El Islote island, where with luck you might spot a whale between December and March.

LIZ + RICHARD

The affair between Richard Burton and Elizabeth Taylor ignited tourism to PV, which was an idyllic beach town when they first visited in 1963. Taylor tagged along when Burton starred in *The Night of the Iguana,* shot in and around Mismaloya beach. The fiery Welsh actor purchased Casa Kimberley (Calle Zaragoza, a few blocks behind the cathedral) for Liz's 32nd birthday and connected it to his home across the street with a pink-and-white "love bridge." Taylor owned the house for 26 years and left most of her possessions behind when she sold it. Casa Kimberely later became a B&B. The property is now owned by boutique hotelier Janice Chatterton.

SNAPSHOT OF PUERTO VALLARTA

Geography

Puerto Vallarta sits at the center point of C-shape Banderas Bay. Spurs from the Sierra Cacoma run down to the sea, forming a landscape of numerous valleys. This highly fractured mountain range is just one of many within the Sierra Madre—which runs from the Rockies to South America. Sierra Cacoma sits at the juncture of several major systems that head south toward Oaxaca State. Forming a distinct but related system is the volcanic or transversal volcanic axis that runs east to west across the country—and the globe. Comprising part of the so-called Ring of Fire, this transverse chain includes some of the world's most active volcanoes. Volcán de Fuego, southeast of Puerto Vallarta in Colima State, and the giant Popocateptl, near the Gulf of Mexico, are active. Visible from PV are the more intimate Sierra Vallejo and the Sierra Cuale ranges, to the north and south respectively.

Heading down to the sea from these highlands are a number of important rivers, including the Ameca and the Mascota, which join forces not far from the coast at a place called Las Juntas (The Joining). The Ameca is a large river whose mouth forms the boundary between Jalisco and Nayarit states. The Cuale River empties into the ocean at Puerto Vallarta, dividing the city center in two. In addition to many rivers the area is blessed with seasonal and permanent streams and springs.

Banderas Bay, or Bahía de Banderas, is Mexico's largest bay, at 42 km (26 mi) tip to tip. The northern point, Punta Mita, is in Nayarit State. Towns at the southern extreme of the bay, at Cabo Corrientes (Cape Currents)—named for the frequently strong currents off its shore—are accessible only by boat or dirt roads.

The mountains backing the Costalegre are part of the Sierra Madre Occidental range. The hilly region of eroded plains has two main river systems: the San Nicolás and Cuitzmala.

Several hundred miles east of Banderas Bay, Guadalajara—capital of Jalisco State—occupies the west end of 5,400-foot Atemajac Valley, which is surrounded by mountains. Just south of Guadalajara, Lake Chapala is Mexico's largest natural lake.

Flora

The western flanks of the Sierra Madre and foothills leading down to the sea have tropical deciduous forest. At the higher levels are expanses of pine-oak forest. Many species of pines thrive in these woods, mixed in with *encinos* and *robles,* two different categories of oak. Walnut trees and *oyamel,* a type of fir, are the mainstays of the lower *arroyos,* or river basins.

Along the coast magnificent *huanacaxtle,* also called *parota* (in English, monkey pod or elephant ear tree), mingle with equally huge and impressive mango as well as kapok, cedar, tropical almond, tamarind, flamboyant, and willow. The brazilwood tree is resistant to insects, and, therefore, ideal for making furniture. *Matapalo,* or strangler fig, are common in this landscape. As its name hints, these fast-growing trees embrace others in a death grip; once the matopalo is established, the host tree eventually dies.

Colima palms, known locally as *guaycoyul,* produce small round nuts smashed for oil or sometimes fed to domestic animals. Mango, avocado, citrus, and guava are found in the wild. Imported trees and bushes often seen surrounding homes and small farms include Indian laurel, bamboo, and bougainvillea.

The coastal fringe north of San Blas is surprisingly characterized by savannas. Guinea grass makes fine animal fodder for horses and cows. Lanky coconut trees line roads and beaches. The watery "milk" is a refreshing drink, and the meat of the coconut, although high in saturated fat, can be eaten or used in many types of candy. Another drink, *agua de tuba,* is made from the heart of the palm; the trunk is used in certain types of construction. Mangroves in saltwater estuaries provide an ecosystem for crabs, crustaceans, and birds.

South of Banderas Bay, thorn forest predominates along the coastal strip, backed by tropical deciduous forest. Leguminous trees like the *tabachin,* with its bright orange flowers, have long, dangling seedpods used by indigenous people as rattles. Other prominent area residents are the acacias, hardy trees with fluffy puffballs of light yellow blooms. The dry forest is home to more than 1,100 species of cacti. The *nopal,* or prickly pear cactus abounds; local people remove the spines and grill the cactus pads or use them in healthful salads. The fruit of the prickly pear, called *tuna,* is used to make a refreshing drink, *agua de tuna.*

Fauna

Hunting, deforestation, and the encroachment of humans have diminished many once-abundant species. In the mountains far from humankind, endangered margay, jaguar, and ocelot hunt their prey, which includes spider monkeys, deer, and peccaries. More commonly seen are skunks, raccoons, rabbits, and coyote. The coatimundi is an endearing little animal that lives in family groups, often near streambeds. Inquisitive and alert, they resemble tall, slender prairie dogs. Along with tanklike, slow-moving armadillo, the sandy-brown coatimundi is among the animals you're most likely to spot without venturing too deep within the forest. Local people call the coatimundi both *tejón* and *pisote,* and often keep them as pets.

Poisonous snakes include the Mexican rattlesnake and the fer-de-lance. Locals call the latter *cuatro narices* (four noses) because it appears to have four nostrils. It's also called *nauyaca;* the bite of this viper can be deadly. There are more than a dozen species of coral snakes with bands of black, yellow, and red in different patterns. False corals imitate this color scheme to fool their predators, but unless you're an expert, it's best to err on the side of caution.

The most famous of the migratory marine species is the humpback whale, here called *ballena jorobada,* or "hunchback" whale. These leviathans grow to 51 feet and weigh 40 to 50 tons; they travel in pods, feeding on krill and tiny fish. In a given year the females in area waters may be either mating or giving birth. During their annual migration of thousands of miles from the Bering Sea, the hardy creatures may lose some 10,000 pounds, or approximately 10% of their body weight. Hunted nearly to extinction in the 1900s, humpbacks remain an endangered species.

A few Bryde whales make their way to Banderas Bay and other protected waters near the end of the humpback season, as do some killer whales (orca) and false killer whales. Bottlenose, spinner, and pantropic spotted dolphins are present pretty much year-round. These acrobats love to bow surf just under the water's surface and to leap into the air. Another

spectacular leaper is the velvety-black manta ray, which can grow to 30 feet wide. Shy but lovely spotted eagle rays hover close to the ocean floor, where they feed on crustaceans and mollusks. Nutrient-rich Pacific waters provide sustenance for a wide range of other sea creatures. Among the most eye-catching are the graceful king angelfish and the iridescent bumphead parrotfish, striped Indo-Pacific sergeants and Moorish idols, and the funny-looking guinea fowl puffer and its close relative, the equally unusual black-blotched porcupine fish.

The varied landscape of Nayarit and Jalisco states provides a tapestry of habitats for some 350 species of birds. In the mangroves, standouts are the great blue heron, mangrove cuckoo, and vireo. Ocean and shorebirds include red-billed tropic birds as well as various species of heron, egret, gulls, and frigate birds. Military macaws patrol the thorn forests, and songbirds of all stripes live in the pine-oak forests. About 40% of the birds in the Costalegre region are migratory. Among the residents are the yellow-headed parrot and the Mexican wood nymph, both threatened species.

Environmental Issues

The biggest threat to the region is deforestation of the tropical dry forest. Slash-and-burn techniques are used to prepare virgin forest for agriculture and pasturing of animals. This practice is counterproductive, as the thin soil fails to produce after the mulch-producing trees and shrubs have been stripped.

The tropical dry forests (also called tropical thorn forest) are now being deforested due to the increasing tourism and human population. Controlled ecotourism offers a potential solution, although failed projects in the area have significantly altered or drained salt marshes and mangrove swamps.

The dry forest is an extremely important ecosystem. It represents one of the richest in Mexico and also one with the highest level of endemism (plant and animal species found nowhere else). Several species of hardwood trees, including the Pacific coast mahogany and Mexican kingwood, are being over-harvested for use in the building trade. The former is endangered and the latter, threatened.

South of Puerto Vallarta in the Costalegre are two adjacent forest reserves that together form the 32,617-acre Chamela–Cuixmala Biosphere Reserve. Co-owned and managed by nonprofit agencies, private companies, and Mexico's National University, UNAM, the reserve protects nine major vegetation types, including the tropical dry forest, tropical deciduous, and semi-deciduous forests. A riparian environment is associated with the north bank of the Cuixmala River. Within the reserve there are approximately 72 species considered at risk for extinction including the American crocodile and several species of sea turtles.

Hojonay Biosphere Reserve was established by the Hojonay nonprofit organization to preserve the jaguar of the Sierra de Vallejo range and its habitat. The 157,060-acre reserve is in the foothills and mountains behind La Cruz de Huanacaxtle and San Francisco, in Nayarit State.

There are no tours or casual access to either reserve, which serve as a buffer against development and a refuge for wildlife.

The People

The population of Puerto Vallarta is overwhelmingly of mestizo (mixed Native American and white/European descent). According to the 2000 census, fewer than 1% of Jalisco residents speak an indigenous language. Compare that to nearby states: Michoacán with 3.6%; Guerrero with about 14%; and Oaxaca, where more than a third of the inhabitants converse in a native language. Those indigenous people who do live in Jalisco State are small groups of Purépecha (also called Tarascans), in the south. The Purépecha were among the very few groups not conquered by the Aztec nation that controlled much of Mesoamerica at the time of the Spanish conquest.

Although not large in number, the indigenous groups most associated with Nayarit and Jalisco states are the Cora and their relatives, the Huichol. Isolated in mountain and valley hamlets and individual *rancherías* (tiny farms) deep in the Sierra Madre, both have maintained to a large extent their own customs and culture. According to the CDI (Comisión Nacional Para el Desarrollo de los Pueblos Indígenas, or National Commission for the Development of Native Peoples), there are about 24,390 Cora in Durango, Zacatecas, and Nayarit states, and some 43,929 Huichol, mainly in Jalisco and Nayarit. Nearly 70% of the culturally related groups speak their native language.

In 1947 a group of prominent vallartenses was returning along twisty mountain roads from an excursion to Mexico City.

When the driver lost control and the open-sided bus plunged toward the abyss, death seemed certain. But a large rock halted the bus's progress, and Los Favorecidos (The Lucky Ones), as they came to be known, returned to Puerto Vallarta virtually unharmed. Their untrammeled gestures of thanks to the town's patron saint, the Virgin of Guadalupe, set the precedent for this animated religious procession. Today, all Puerto Vallartans consider themselves to be Los Favorecidos, and thus universally blessed. This optimism and good cheer are two vital components of the local persona. For those of us fortunate enough to visit, that angelic magnetism is a big part of the pull.

The Magic of Mexico

To say that Mexico is a magical place means more than it's a place of great natural beauty and fabulous experiences. Cities like Catemaco, in Veracruz, have a reputation for their *brujos* and *brujas* (male and female witches, respectively) and herbal healers (*curanderos/curanderas*). But Mexicans use these services even in modern Mexico City and Guadalajara and in tourist towns like Puerto Vallarta. Some might resort to using a curandera to reverse *mal de ojo,* the evil eye, thought to be responsible for a range of unpleasant symptoms, circumstances, disease, or even death.

A *limpia,* or cleansing, is the traditional cure for the evil eye. The healer usually passes a raw chicken or turkey egg over the sufferer to draw out the bad spirit. Green plants like basil, or branches from certain trees can also be used, drawing the greenery over the head, front, and back to decontaminate the victim. Prayer is an essential ingredient.

Some cures are of a more practical nature. Mexican herbalists, like their colleagues around the world, use tree bark, nuts, berries, roots, and leaves to treat everything from dandruff to cancer. Epazote, or wormseed, is a distinctly flavored plant whose leaves are used in cooking. As its English name implies, its medicinal task is to treat parasites.

Most folk wisdom seems to draw from both fact and, if not fiction, at least superstition. Breezes and winds are thought to produce a host of negative reactions: from colds and cramps to far more drastic ailments like paralysis. Some people prefer sweating in a car or bus to rolling down the window and being hit by the wind, especially since mixing hot and cold is something else to be avoided. Even worldly athletes may refuse a cold drink after a hot run. Sudden shock is thought by some to cause lasting problems.

Although it doesn't take a leap of faith to believe that herbal remedies cure disease and grandma's advice was right on, some of the stuff sold in shops is a bit "harder to swallow." It's difficult to imagine, for example, that the sky-blue potion in a pint-size bottle will bring you good luck, or the lilac-color one can stop people from gossiping about you. Those that double as floor polish seem especially suspect.

Whether magic and prophesy are real or imagined, they sometimes have concrete results. Conquistador Hernán Cortés arrived on the east coast of Mexico in 1519, which correlated to the year "One Reed" on the Aztec calendar. A few centuries prior to Cortés's arrival, the benevolent god-king Quetzalcoatl had, according to legend, departed the same coast on a raft of snakes, vowing to return in the year One Reed to reclaim his throne.

News of Cortés—a metal-wearing god-man accompanied by strange creatures (horses and dogs) and carrying lightning (cannons and firearms)—traveled quickly to the Aztec capital. Emperor Moctezuma was nervous about Quetzalcoatl's return and his reaction to the culture of war and sacrifice the Aztecs had created. In his desire to placate the returning god, Moctezuma ignored the advice of trusted counselors and opened the door for the destruction of the Aztec empire.

La Vida Loca

Living the good life in Mexico—specifically in and around Banderas Bay—seems to get easier year by year. Americans and Canadians are by far the biggest groups of expats. In addition to those who have relocated to make Mexico their home, many more foreigners have part-time retirement or vacation homes here. A two-bedroom property in a gated community by the sea begins at around $230,000. You could get more modest digs for less; at the upper end of the spectrum, the sky's the limit.

The sheer number of foreigners living in Puerto Vallarta facilitates adventures that were much more taxing a decade or two ago, like building a home or finding an English-speaking realtor or lawyer. Contractors and shopkeepers are used to dealing with gringos; most speak good to excellent English. The town is rich with English-language publications and opportunities for foreigners to meet up for events or volunteer work.

FESTIVALS AND EVENTS

WINTER

January

El Día de los Santos Reyes (January 6) was the day of gift-giving in Latin America until Santa Claus invaded from the North. Although many families now give gifts on Christmas or Christmas Eve, Three Kings Day is still an important celebration. The children receive token "gifts of the Magi." *Atole* (a drink of finely ground rice or corn) or hot chocolate is served along with the *rosca de reyes,* a ring-shape cake. The person whose portion contains a tiny baby Jesus figurine must host a follow-up party on Candlemass, February 2.

February

The four-day **Festival de Música San Pancho** (*San Pancho Music Festival* ☎311/258–4135) is an amalgam of the area's best regional musicians; snowbirds also participate. The free jamboree is usually held in mid- to late February. The event has featured bluegrass, blues, jazz, funk, and standards in addition to cumbia and Mexican classics. Look for flyers around town that describe events and their venues. San Pancho is about 50 minutes north of downtown Puerto Vallarta.

Charros (cowboys) from all over Mexico compete in the four-day **Campeonato Charro Nacional** (*National Charro Championship* ☎322/224–0001) at Mojoneras. In addition to men's rope and riding tricks and the female competitors, there are mariachis, a parade, and exhibitions of charro-related art. Admission is $7–$12.

SPRING

May

★ **Las Fiestas de Mayo** (*May Festivals* ☎322/223–2500) is a three-week fair with fireworks and regional crafts and foods that is more popular with locals than visitors. In Jalisco, no such festival would be complete without *charreadas* (rodeos).

SUMMER

June

June 1 is **Día de la Marina** (☎322/224–2352). Like other Mexican ports, PV celebrates Navy Day with free boat rides (inquire at the Terminal Marítima or the XII Zona Naval Militar, just to the south). Watch colorfully decorated boats depart from here to make offerings on the water to sailors lost at sea.

July and August

Barra de Navidad celebrates its patron saint, **San Antonio de Padua**, the week preceding July 13 with religious parades, mass, street parties, and fireworks. **Cristo de los Brazos Caídos** is honored August 30–September 1 in much the same way as St. Anthony.

FALL

September

The **Celebration of Independence** is held on September 15 and 16, beginning on the evening of September 15 with the traditional *Grito de Dolores*. It translates as "Cry of Pain," but also references the town of Dolores Hidalgo, where the famous cry for freedom was uttered by priest Miguel Hidalgo. Late in the evening on September 15 there are mariachis, speeches, and other demonstrations of national pride. On September 16, witness parades and charros on horseback along the length of the boardwalk.

October

An annual event since 1996, **Old Town art-Walk** (☎322/222–1982) showcases artwork at 15 galleries. The galleries stay open late, usually offering an appetizer or snack as well as wine, beer, or soft drinks. Browse paintings, jewelry, ceramics, glass, and folk art while hobnobbing with some of PV's most respected artists. If you don't have a map, pick one up from one of the perennially participating galleries, which include Galería Arte Latinoamericano, Galería Corona, Galería 8 y Más, Galería Pacífico, Galería Uno, Galería Vallarta, and Galería de Ollas. This walk is held from 6 PM to 10 PM, from the last week of October until late April.

November and December

Fodor'sChoice★ The **Festival Gourmet International** is one of PV's biggest events (⇨ *"Mexico's Gourmet Town," in Chapter 5*). Beginning in late November or early December, the public is invited to see movies of many genres, at reasonable prices, during the five-day **Vallarta Film Festival** (☎322/297–1947 or 322/297–1605 ⊕*www.vallartafilmfestival.com*). Films and seminars are held at the Cinemark Plaza Caracol (⊠ *Plaza Caracol, Zona Hotelera* ☎322/224–8927). Film-industry types come to hobnob and honor each other with awards for best director, picture, cinematographer, and actor. Mid-November through the end of April, three-hour **villa tours** (☎322/222–5466) by the International Friendship Club get you inside the garden walls of some inspiring PV homes. English-speaking guides lead groups on air-conditioned buses: Tuesday to the north shore ($50 per person), Wednesday and Thursday to the south shore ($35 per person). Tours depart promptly at 11 AM (arrive by 10:30) from the Hotel Posada Río Cuale (⊠*Calle Aquiles Serdán 242*). Lunch is included. The fee benefits local charities.

★Puerto Vallarta's most important celebration of faith—and also one of the most elaborate spectacles of the year—is **Fiestas de la Virgin of Guadalupe** (☎322/223–2500), designed to honor the Virgin of Guadalupe, the city's patron saint and the patroness of all Mexico. Exuberance fills the air as the end of November approaches and each participating business organizes its own procession. The most elaborate ones include allegorical floats and papier-mâché *matachines,* or giant dolls (for lack of a better phrase), and culminate in their own private mass. Throughout the afternoon and evening, groups snake down Calle Juárez from the north or the south, ending at the Cathedral in Old Vallarta.

Beaches

Ixtapa

WORD OF MOUTH

"If you like a little adventure, Yelapa is a neat day trip. You get in the boat from the beach so you will get a little wet. If the waves are big, its a little scary. . . . We saw a whale up close, which was very cool. Yelapa is rustic and quiet. We walked up to a waterfall and down a windy unpaved road through part of what I guess is the town to the beach. There's a couple food stands, and we drank beer and ate nachos. Make sure to buy a piece of pie from the ladies on the beach. I didn't, and later heard it's a must do!"

—hopvac

Throughout the region, from the Riviera Nayarit to the Costalegre, long, flat beaches invite walking, and reefs and offshore breaks draw divers, snorkelers, and surfers. In places, untouristy hideaways, with little to distract you beyond waves lapping the shore, may be accessible by land or by sea. Omnipresent seafood shanties are perfect vantage points for sunsets on the sand.

Although Pacific Mexico's beaches aren't the sugar-sand, crystal-water variety of the Caribbean, they're still lovely. The water here is unpolluted, and the oft-mountainous backdrop, particularly from Puerto Vallarta (PV) south to Cabo Corrientes, is majestic.

PV sits at the center of horseshoe-shape Bahía de Banderas (Banderas Bay), the second-largest bay in North America (after the Hudson). Exquisitely visible from cliff-side hotels and restaurants, the bay's scalloped coast holds myriad coves and small bays perfect for shelling, sunning, swimming, and more strenuous activities.

At Hotel Zone beaches and a few popular stretches of sand north and south of PV proper you can parasail, take boat rides, or Jet Ski; some beaches lend themselves to kayaking, boogie boarding, or snorkeling. Foothills that race down to the sea are crowded with palms and cedars, and the jungle's blue-green canopy forms a highly textured background to the deep blue ocean. Dozens of creeks and rivers follow the contours of these hills, creating estuaries, mangrove swamps, and other habitats.

South of Cabo Corrientes the mountains recede from the coast. Lovely yet lonely beaches and bays are fringed, as elsewhere in and around PV, by dry tropical thorn forest with a variety of plants. Several species of whales cruise down in winter, and turtles spawn on the beaches from late summer into fall.

BEACH REGIONS

PUERTO VALLARTA

Paralleling the Romantic Zone, Playa los Muertos is PV's most popular beach, where restaurants and bars have music; vendors sell barbecued fish on a stick; and people cruise the boardwalk. Immediately north of Los Muertos is contiguous Olas Altas Beach. The beaches in the Hotel Zone and Marina Vallarta can be lively during holidays and high season but don't have as much to offer by comparison the rest of the year. At the south end of Banderas Bay are beautiful mountain-backed *playas* accessible only by boat.

NAYARIT
NUEVO VALLARTA

One wide, flat, sandy beach stretches from the mouth of the Ameca River north for miles, past the Nuevo Vallarta hotels (including the new developments at the north end, called Flamingos) and into the town of Bucerías. The generally calm water is good for swimming and, when conditions are right, bodysurfing or boogie boarding. Activities are geared to all-inclusive-hotel guests north of Paradise Village marina. Guys on the beach rent water-sports equipment, as do most of the hotels.

RIVIERA NAYARIT

From Nuevo Vallarta north into Nayarit State, rocky headlands sandwich stretches of sand. From Bucerías to Chacala, beaches attract boogie boarders, beachcombers, and those who make their own fun. While there are fewer services than in PV, the state government is investing heavily to develop the area. Surfing is big at Punta Mita (aka Punta de Mita), where some of the best spots are only accessible by boat. Guayabitos, with its offshore island, is a vacation mecca for Mexican families and a refuge for snowbirds from Canada and the northern United States. Off the main highway, long, sandy roads lead to more isolated beaches such as Destiladeras; some of these areas are now slated for development.

GO FOR:	IN PV:	NORTH OR SOUTH OF PV:
Wildlife	Los Arcos; Playa Camarones (for whales in season); Marina Vallarta (for turtles in season)	Islas Marietas (Punta Mita); Playa Careyes and nearby beaches (turtles in season)
Snorkeling	Los Arcos; Playa Conchas Chinas	Islas Marietas; Quimixto; Playa Mora
Walking or Jogging	Playa los Muertos; Playa Camarones	Nuevo Vallarta; Bucerías; La Manzanilla; Boca de Iguanas; Playa Tenacatita; Barra de Navidad and San Patricio–Melaque (Bahía de Navidad)
Calm, Swimmable Waters	Hotel pools; Conchas Chinas	Los Ayala, Rincón de Guayabitos (Bahía de Jaltemba); Playa Chalacatepec; Punta Perula; Boca de Iguanas; Tenacatita, San Patricio–Melaque
Surfing	Olas Altas (sometimes)	Punta Mita; Sayulita; Quimixto; Barra de Navidad
Eating/Drinking with Locals	Boca de Tomatlán; Playa Camarones (but not right on the beach)	Chacala; Rincón de Guayabitos (Bahía de Jaltembo); Punta Perula; Playa Tenacatita; Colimilla (Bahía de Navidad)

SOUTH OF PUERTO VALLARTA

South of PV the beaches constitute the domain of the independent traveler and the well-heeled recluse. High-end hotels on picturesque, rock-framed beaches arrange fishing and other pastimes. Other long, sandy beaches—many on large, semi-protected bays—are frequented by fishermen and local people relaxing at seafood shanties, and allow shelling, snorkeling, fishing, and trips to offshore islands. Having a car is helpful for exploring multiple beaches, although local bus service is available.

PUERTO VALLARTA

PV beaches are varied. Downtown's main beach, Los Muertos, is a fun scene, with shoulder-to-shoulder establishments for drinking and eating under the shade. There's year-round action, although water-sports equipment rentals may be available on weekends only during the rainy season. The itinerant vendors are present year-round, however, and can be annoying. Olas Altas Beach, which runs north from Los Muertos, has the same grainy brown sand but fewer vendors and services and sometimes waves big enough to surf or boogie. North of the malecón and Hotel Rosita, more stretches of sand front minor hotels.

Hotel Zone beaches offer adults opportunities to play with aquatic toys, especially in high season. The sand here is often pocked with rocks, depending on the season and tides. The beach at Marina Vallarta, between PV and Nuevo Vallarta, is swimmable but mainly uninspired except for the beach toys and hotels that offer refreshments.

South of Vallarta proper are Conchas Chinas, a few smaller beaches, and Mismaloya. The wild beaches farther south (on the north side of Cabo Corrientes, from Las Animas to Yelapa) didn't have electricity until the 1970s or later. They tend to fill up with day-trippers between December and April but are well worth a visit.

At Los Muertos as well as beaches in the Hotel Zone and Marina Vallarta, you can find Jet Skis, parasailing, and banana-boat rides in high season (December–April) and on weekends year-round.

GETTING HERE AND AROUND

You can readily access Downtown and Hotel Zone beaches from the street. Take a bus or a cab, or drive your car. There's coveted curbside parking, or you can pay by the hour at the Benito Juárez parking structure: it's just north of the Cuale River at the malecón and Calle Rodríguez, under Parque Lázaro Cárdenas, and across from Olas Altas Beach. The Hidalgo Street parking structure, near Playa Camarones, is another option.

In Marina Vallarta the main public beach access (with on-street parking) is between the airport and Condominios Grand Bay. There's little to stop you from walking through the major hotels to the beaches, though, if you take a bus or cab to the area. There's also a parking lot between the Marival and Gran Velas hotels, by the Nuevo Vallarta tourism office.

DOWNTOWN PUERTO VALLARTA

Playa los Muertos. PV's original happenin' beach isn't particularly stunning, but as action central, it's definitely PV's most engaging beach. Facing Vallarta's South Side (south of the Río Cuale), this flat beach hugs the Zona Romántica and runs about 1½ km (1 mi) south to a rocky point called El Púlpito. ■**TIP→** The steps (more than 100) at Calle Púlpito lead to a lookout with a great view of the beach and the bay.

Joggers cruise the cement boardwalk early morning and after sunset; vendors stalk the beach nonstop, hawking kites, jewelry, and serapes as well as hair-braiding and alfresco massage. Their parade can range from entertaining (good bargainers can get excellent deals) to downright maddening. Restaurant-bars run the length of the beach; the bright blue umbrellas at the south end belong to Blue Chairs resort, the hub of PV's effervescent gay scene.

The surf ranges from mild to choppy with an undertow; the small waves crunching the shore usually discourage mindless paddling. Strapping young men occupy the lifeguard tower, but the service isn't consistent. Local people fish from the small pier at the foot of Calle Francisca Rodríguez or cast nets from waist-deep water near the beach's south end. Jet Skis zip around but stay out beyond the small breakers so aren't too distracting to bathers and sunbathers. Guys on the beach offer banana-boat and parasailing rides. **Facilities:** Lifeguards, banana-boat rides, Jet Skis, parasailing; food concessions.

Playa Olas Altas. Its name means High Waves Beach, but the only waves suitable for bodysurfing, boogie boarding, or, occasionally, surfing small waves, are near the Cuale River, at the north end of this small beach. Although Olas Altas more often refers to the neighborhood of bars and businesses near the ocean south of the Río Cuale, it is also the name of a few blocks of sand between Daiquiri Dick's restaurant and the Río Cuale. It attracts fewer sunbathers than Los Muertos, but is otherwise an extension of that beach. Facing Olas Altas Beach near Lázaro Cárdenas plaza are open-air stands selling beach accessories, small grocery stores, and beach-facing bar-restaurants. **Facilities:** Food concessions, parking (at Parque Lázaro Cárdenas).

Playa Camarones. The long, flat, brown sand of Shrimp Beach, favored by locals, parallels the malecón and the hotel Rosita as far north as the Buenaventura Hotel. It's always changing, perhaps rock-strewn in the morning and clear later when the tide goes out. In high (winter) season and holiday weekends, the beach has a lifeguard and water-sports concessions. Watch for whales in winter, too, from the P.V. Beach Club bar (whose owner has a penchant for impromptu karaoke sessions) or from the Barracuda Restaurant, next door. Although the waves are gentle, there are strange currents here, which should discourage all but strong swimmers. What you see here most often are small groups of men and boys surf casting. **Facilities:** Lifeguard (sometimes), banana-boat rides, Jet Skis, parasailing; food concessions, parking (at Parque Hidalgo).

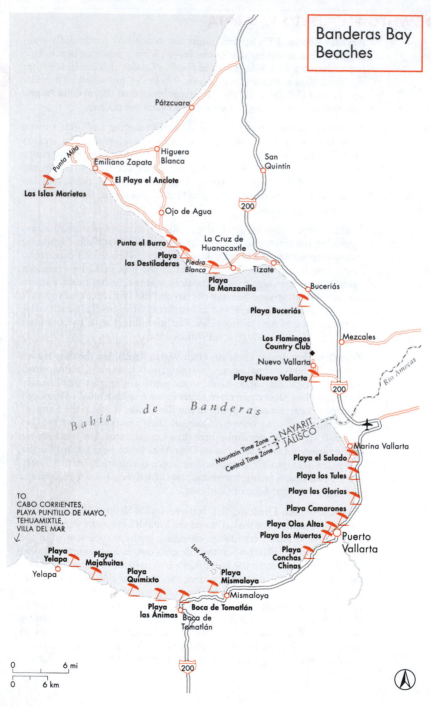

Banderas Bay Beaches

Pátzcuaro

Higuera Blanca

San Quintín

Punta Mita

Emiliano Zapata

El Playa el Anclote

Las Islas Marietas

Ojo de Agua

Punta el Burro

La Cruz de Huanacaxtle

Playa las Destiladeras

Piedra Blanca

Tizate

Playa la Manzanilla

Buceriás

Playa Buceriás

Mezcales

Los Flamingos Country Club

Nuevo Vallarta

Río Ameca

Playa Nuevo Vallarta

200

Bahía de Banderas

Mountain Time Zone — **NAYARIT**

Central Time Zone — **JALISCO**

Marina Vallarta

Playa el Salado

Playa los Tules

Playa las Glorias

Playa Camarones

TO CABO CORRIENTES, PLAYA PUNTILLO DE MAYO, TEHUAMIXTLE, VILLA DEL MAR

↓

Playa Olas Altas

Playa los Muertos

Puerto Vallarta

Playa Yelapa

Playa Majahuitas

Yelapa

Los Arcos

Playa Conchas Chinas

Playa Quimixto

Playa Mismaloya

Mismaloya

Playa las Ánimas

Boca de Tomatlán

Boca de Tomatlán

200

0 ⸻ 6 mi

0 ⸻ 6 km

NORTH OF DOWNTOWN

Zona Hotelera. The high-rise-backed Zona Hotelera beach goes by several monikers—mainly **Playa Las Glorias** but also **Playa Los Tules** around the Holiday Inn and Fiesta Americana hotels. Most people, however, just refer to each piece of beach by the hotel that it faces. Interrupted here and there by breakwaters, this fringe of gray-beige sand is generally flat but slopes down to the water. Winds and tides sometimes strew it with stones that make it less pleasant. Hit hard by Hurricane Kenna in 2002, the Sheraton, at the south end of the strip, had tons of sand deposited on its beach

> ### BEACH OF THE DEAD
>
> There are several versions of how Playa los Muertos got its name. One says that around the time it was founded, Indians attacked a mule train laden with silver and gold from the mountain towns, leaving the dead bodies of the muleteers on the beach. A version crediting pirates with the same deed seems more plausible. In 1935 anthropologist Dr. Isabel Kelly postulated that the place was an Indian cemetery.

in 2005; it is, therefore, sandier than its neighbors, although still pocked with smooth, egg-size rocks. **Facilities:** Banana-boat rides, Jet Skis, parasailing, snorkeling; food concessions.

Playa el Salado. At Marina Vallarta, Playa El Salado—facing the Grand Velas, Sol Meliá, Marriott, Mayan Palace, and Westin hotels—is pleasantly sandy. Colorful in high season with parasailers and with windsurfers rented or lent at area hotels, these beaches are actually more fun when crowded than when solitary. During fine weather and on weekends, and daily during high season, you can rent Jet Skis and pack onto colorful banana boats for bouncy tours of 10 minutes or longer. Some hotels rent small sailboats, sailboards, and sea kayaks to guests and to nonguests. In late summer and early fall, there are opportunities to view turtles. **Facilities:** Banana-boat rides, Jet Skis, kayaking, sailing, snorkeling; food concessions.

NAYARIT

At the northern end of Bahía de Banderas and farther into Nayarit state, to the north, are long, beautiful beaches fringed with tall trees or scrubby tropical forest. Only the most popular beaches like those of Nuevo Vallarta and Rincón de Guayabitos have much in the way of water-sports equipment rentals, but even the more secluded ones have stands or small restaurants serving cold coconut water, soft drinks, beer, and grilled fish with tortillas.

GETTING HERE AND AROUND

In Nuevo Vallarta, park on the street or in the lot of the tourism office, between Gran Velas and Maribal hotels. Buses arrive here as well, but the all-inclusive hotels that predominate cater to guests only, so bring your own supplies. It's a cinch to install yourself anywhere on Bucerías's long beach, with easy street-side parking. As most of the beaches north of here are off the main road, they are easiest to access by car (or taxi).

A new road (rather, the improvement of an old, narrow dirt-and-gravel road) connects Punta Mita with Sayulita, San Francisco, and points to the north. However, if your destination is north of Punta Mita, there's no need to follow the coast road to the point. Simply bear right instead of left after Bucerías, continuing on Carretera 200.

NUEVO VALLARTA TO PUNTA MITA

Nuevo Vallarta. Several kilometers of pristine, if plain, beach face the hotels of Playa Nuevo Vallarta. The wide, flat, sandy stretch is perfect for long walks: in fact, you could walk all the way to Bucerías, some 8 km (5 mi) to the north. Most of the hotels here are all-inclusives, so guests generally move between their hotel pool, bar, restaurant, and the beach in front. All-inclusive programs mean that nonguests are generally barred from the bars and restaurants. **Facilities:** Banana-boat rides, Jet Skis, parasailing; parking, toilets.

☾ **Bucerías.** Eight kilometers (5 mi) north of Nuevo Vallarta, the substantial town of Bucerías attracts flocks of snowbirds, and this has encouraged the establishment of rental apartments and good restaurants. The beach here is endless: you could easily walk along its medium-coarse beige sands all the way south to Nuevo Vallarta. Backed by businesses that give access to food and drink, it's not exactly fringed in tropical vegetation. The surf is gentle enough for swimming but also has body-surfable waves, and beginning surfers occasionally arrive with their longboards. **Facilities:** Food concessions.

☾ **Playa La Manzanilla.** On this crescent of soft, gold sand about a kilometer long, kids play in the shallow water while their parents sip cold drinks at a palapa-topped café table or dine at a seafood shack. The beach, which is somewhat protected by the Piedra Blanca headland to the north, is at the northern edge of a town called La Cruz de Huanacaxtle. Named for a cross made of superresilient wood (*huanacaxtle*, which translates to ear pod, elephant ear, or monkey ear tree), most people simply call the town "La Cruz." What was a rough little fishing village now has a 400-slip marina aptly named Marina Riviera Nayarit at La Cruz (⊕*www.marinarivieranayarit.com*). It was launched in 2008 as part of the Riviera Nayarit development plan. Several private docks are for lease; several house local fishermen, who can take you out fishing for tuna and snapper. Like it or not, homey La Cruz is growing and becoming more sophisticated. **Facilities:** Beach umbrellas, boating, fishing, inner tubes; food concessions, parking.

Destiladeras. A few miles north of Piedra Blanca headland is a 1½-km-long (1-mi-long) beach with white sand and good waves for bodysurfers and boogie boarders. There's nothing much here except for a couple of seaside *enramadas* (thatch-roof shelters) serving fillets of fish and ceviche. Part of a new development called Nahui, Hotel Capella is under construction above the beach and due to open in 2010; a golf course is also in the planning stages. At the north end of the beach **Punta el Burro** is a popular surf spot often accessed by boat from Punta Mita. **Facilities:** Food concessions, parking.

El Anclote. The most accessible beach at Punta Mita and considered to be surf central is El Anclote, whose name means "the anchorage." Just a few minutes past the gated entrance to the tony Four Seasons and St. Regis hotels, the popular beach has a string of restaurants— once simple shacks but today of increasing sophistication and price. This is a primo spot for viewing a sunset. Artificially calmed by several rock jetties and shallow for quite a way out, it's also a good spot for children and average to not-strong swimmers, but there's a long slow wave for beginning surfers, too. You can rent boards and take lessons from outfitters here. Most of the jewelry and serape sellers and fishermen looking for customers have moved—or been moved—off the beach to more official digs in buildings along the same strip or facing the Four Seasons. Accessible from El Anclote (or the adjacent town of **Corral del Risco**), more than half a dozen great surf spots pump year-round; many are accessible only by boat. Punta Mita is the northernmost point of Banderas Bay, about 40 km (25 mi) north of Puerto Vallarta. **Facilities:** Fishing, snorkeling, surfing; food concessions, parking.

Islas Marietas. Snorkelers and divers favor the fairly clear waters and abundance of fish and coral on the bay side of the Islas Marietas, about a half-hour offshore from El Anclote. In winter, especially January through March, these same islands are also a good place to spot orcas and humpback whales, which come to mate and give birth. Las Marietas is the destination for fishing, diving, and snorkeling; in addition, sea-life-viewing expeditions set out from El Anclote and Corral de Risco as well as from points up and down Banderas Bay. **Facilities:** None.

> ### BEACH BLANKET BOTHER
>
> Although it might feel rude, it's culturally permissible to simply ignore itinerant vendors, especially if you're in the middle of a conversation. However, being blatantly impolite (i.e., shouting at the vendor to take a hike) *is* rude—no matter where you're from. A wide grin and a firm "*No, gracias*," with no further eye contact, is the best response—apart from "Yes, please, I'll take it," that is!

NORTH OF BANDERAS BAY

Real estate north of the bay is booming. Mexicans are selling family holdings, jaded gringos are building private homes, and speculators from around the globe are grabbing what land they can, on and off the beach. For now, however, the Nayarit coast continues to enchant, with miles of lovely beaches bordered by arching headlands and hamlets drowsing in the tropical sun.

★ **Playa de Sayulita.** The increasingly popular town and beach of Sayulita is about 45 minutes north of PV on Carretera 200, just about 19 km (12 mi) north of Bucerías and 35 km (22 mi) north of the airport.

Despite the growth, this small town is still laid-back and retains its surfer-friendly vibe. Fringed in lanky palms, Sayulita's heavenly beach curves along its small bay. A decent shore break here is good for beginning or novice surfers; the left point break is a bit more challenging. Skiffs on the beach have good rates for surfing or fishing safaris in area waters, and you can rent surfboards and snorkeling gear. **Facilities:** Fishing, snorkeling, surfing; food concessions.

★ **Playa de San Pancho.** Ten minutes north of Sayulita is the town of San Francisco, known to most people by its nickname: San Pancho. Its beach stretches between headlands to the north and south and is accessed at the end of the town's main road: Avenida Tercer Mundo. At the end of this road, on the beach, are a slew of shaded café tables on the sand where locals and visitors congregate. You'll see men fishing from shore with nets as you walk the 1½-km-long (1-mi-long) stretch of coarse beige sand. There's an undertow sometimes but otherwise nothing to discourage reasonably strong swimmers. Small waves occasionally support longboard surfing (especially in September), but this isn't a surf spot. In fact its waves, which are too big for family splashing and too small for surfing, have probably helped maintain the town's innocence, until now. Popular with a hip crowd, San Pancho has just a few hotels but a growing number of good restaurants. **Facilities:** Food concessions, showers, toilets.

Lo de Marcos. About 8 km (5 mi) north of San Pancho, Lo de Marcos is a humble town of quiet, wide streets. It fills up on weekends and holidays with Mexican families renting the bungalow-style motel rooms that predominate. The town's main beach is flat and dark, but the sand is generally clean. There are small waves, not big enough for surfing but just right for splashing around. A small restaurant on the beach serves sodas, snacks, and the usual seafood suspects. Note that the once-popular **Playas Las Minitas** and **Los Venados** south of town proper, are closed for private development. **Facilities:** Food concessions.

Playa los Ayala. Playa los Ayala has a level beach, mild surf, and an excellent view of Isla del Coral, to which glass-bottom boats ferry passengers for about $6 per person. There are some small hotels and plenty of seaside palapas for shade and basic sustenance. On weekends, holidays, and in high season take a ride on a banana boat; most any time you can find a skiff owner to take you to Playa Frideritas or Playa del Toro, two pretty beaches for bathing that lie around the headland to the south and are accessible only by boat. You can walk, however, over the hill at the south end of the beach to a seafood restaurant on a small

---

WATER-TOY PRICES

Prices for water toys in and around Vallarta are fairly consistent:

Jet Skis: $45–$50 per half hour (one or two riders)

parasailing: $35 for a 10-minute ride

banana-boat rides: $15 for a 10-minute ride (usually four-person minimum)

Hobie Cat or small sailboat: $40–$45 per hour

2

North of the Bay Beaches

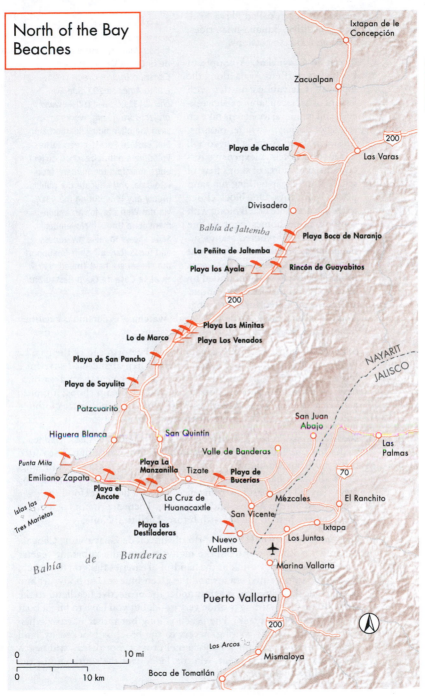

Ixtapan de le Concepción

Zacualpan

200

Playa de Chacala

Las Varas

Divisadero

Bahía de Jaltemba

Playa Boca de Naranjo

La Peñita de Jaltemba

Playa los Ayala

Rincón de Guayabitos

200

Playa Las Minitas

Lo de Marco

Playa Los Venados

Playa de San Pancho

Playa de Sayulita

NAYARIT

JALISCO

Patzcuarito

San Juan Abajo

Higuera Blanca

San Quintín

Las Palmas

Valle de Banderas

Punta Mita

Emiliano Zapata

Playa La Manzanilla

Tizate

Playa de Bucerías

70

Playa el Ancote

La Cruz de Huanacaxtle

Mézcales

El Ranchito

Islas las Tres Marietas

San Vicente

Ixtapa

Playa las Destiladeras

Nuevo Vallarta

Los Juntas

Bahía   de   Banderas

Marina Vallarta

Puerto Vallarta

200

Los Arcos

Mismaloya

0   10 mi

0   10 km

Boca de Tomatlán

scallop of beach called Playa Frideras. **Facilities:** Banana-boat rides, boating; food concessions.

⊕ ★ **Rincón de Guayabitos.** A couple of kilometers north of Ayala along the highway, Guayabitos bustles with legions of Mexican families on weekends and holidays; foreigners take up residence during the winter months. The main street, Avenida Nuevo Sol, has modest hotels, inexpensive restaurants, and scores of shops that all sell the same cheap bathing suits and plastic beach toys. One block closer to the sea are more hotels along with some vacation homes right on the sand. Colorfully painted stands on the beach sell fresh chilled fruit and coconuts; others serve up fresh seafood. This lovely beach bounded by headlands and the ocean is tranquil and perfectly suited for swimming. You can also arrange turtle and whale-watching excursions. **Facilities:** Boating, fishing, snorkeling; food concessions.

> **TURTLE RESCUE**
>
> In San Pancho, **Grupo Ecológico de la Costa Verde** (*Green Coast Ecological Group* ⊠ *Av. Latino América 102, San Pancho* ☎ *311/258–4100* ⊕ *www. project-tortuga.org*) works to save the olive ridley, leatherback, and eastern Pacific green turtles. Volunteers patrol beaches, collect eggs, maintain the nursery, tabulate data, and educate the public. (Apply any time during the year, via the Web site, for an assignment June through November.) Slide shows to raise awareness and funds (buy a T-shirt to support the cause) are held Thursday at 7 PM at La Casa de Gallo Restaurant.

La Peñita. Contiguous with Guayabitos, at the north end of the bay, La Peñita has fewer hotels and a beach that's often abandoned save for a few fishermen. Its name means "little rock." The center for area business, La Peñita has banks, shoe stores, and ice-cream shops; a typical market held each Thursday offers knock-off CDs, polyester clothing, and fresh fruits and vegetables. **Facilities:** None.

Boca de Naranjo. A few kilometers north of La Peñita, a dusty road leads to this long, secluded, sandy beach with excellent swimming. The rutted dirt road from the highway, although only about 4 km (2½ mi) long, takes almost a half hour to negotiate in most passenger cars. Enjoy great views of the coastline from one of nearly a dozen seafood shanties. Turtles nest here in August and September. There are rumors of a major development here in the near-ish future. **Facilities:** None.

Chacala. Some 30 km (19 mi) north of Rincón de Guayabitos, Chacala is another 9 km (5 mi) from the highway through exuberant vegetation. You can dine or drink at the handful of eateries right on the beach, take in the soft-scented sea air and the green-blue sea, or bodysurf and boogie board. Swimming is safest under the protective headland to the north of the cove; surfing is often very good, but you have to hire a boat to access the point break. The beach is long but rather narrow when the tide is in. At this writing, access to the beach is blocked by land that's been privatized for a major hotel project, but there's still beach access via the holistic retreat, Mar de Jade, near the south end of the bay. **Facilities:** Food concessions.

SOUTH OF PUERTO VALLARTA

While coastal Nayarit is jumping on the development bandwagon, the isolated beaches of Cabo Corriente and those of southern Jalisco—some surrounded by ecological reserves—continue to languish in peaceful abandon. Things here are still less formal, and aside from the super-posh resorts like El Careyes, Hotelito Desconocido, and Las Alamandas, whose beaches are off-limits to nonguests, words like "laid-back" and "run-down" or "very basic" still apply, much to the delight of adventurous types.

GETTING HERE AND AROUND

Catch a green bus to Conchas Chinas, Mismaloya, or Boca de Tomatlán from the southwest corner of Calle Basilio Badillo and Constitución in PV. Give the driver sufficient notice when you want to get off; pulling over along the narrow highway is challenging.

There are several ways to reach the beaches of southern Banderas Bay. Party boats (aka booze cruises) and privately chartered boats leave from Marina Vallarta's cruise-ship terminal and generally hit Las Animas, Quimixto, Majahuitas, and/or Yelapa. You can also hire a water taxi from Boca de Tomatlán ($6 one way, usually on the hour 9 AM through noon and again in early afternoon), from the pier at Los Muertos ($20 round-trip, 11 AM and in high season at 10:15 and 11 AM), or from the tiny pier next to Hotel Rosita ($20 round-trip, 11:30 AM). ■TIP→ **Note that weather and other variables can affect the water-taxi schedules.**

For maximum time at the beach of your choice and minimum frustration, head out early and relax over a soda or coffee at Boca de Tomatlán as you wait for the next available skiff to depart. Catch the 4 PM taxi from Los Muertos to Yelapa only if you're planning to spend the night; it won't return until the next day. You can hire *pangas* (skiffs) at Boca, Mismaloya, or Los Muertos. The price depends on starting and ending points, but runs about $35 per hour for up to eight passengers.

It's best to have your own car for exploring the Costalegre, as many beaches are a few kilometers—down rutted dirt roads—from the highway. However, if you want to hang out in the small but tourist-oriented towns of San Patricio–Melaque and Barra de Navidad, you don't necessarily need wheels.

SOUTHERN BANDERAS BAY

★ **Playa Conchas Chinas.** Frequented mainly by visitors staying in the area, this beach has a series of rocky coves with crystalline water. Millions of tiny white shells, broken and polished by the waves, form the sand; rocks that resemble petrified cow pies jut into the sea, separating one patch of beach from the next. These individual coves are perfect for reclusive sunbathing, and, when the surf is mild, for snorkeling around the rocks; bring your own equipment. It's accessible from Calle Santa Barbara, the continuation of the cobblestone coast road originating at the south end of Los Muertos Beach, and also from Carretera 200 near El Set restaurant. Swimming is best at the cove just north of La

Playita de Lindo Mar, below the Hotel Conchas Chinas (where the beach ends), as there are fewer rocks in the water. You can walk—be it on the sand, over the rocks, or on paths or steps built for this purpose—from Playa Los Muertos all the way to Conchas Chinas. **Facilities:** None.

Playa Mismaloya. It was in this cove that *The Night of the Iguana* was made. Visitors from the '70s remember parking their vans on the sand and eating fish plucked from the sea for week after blissful week. Unfortunately, construction of the big, tan Hotel La Jolla de Mismaloya at the north end of the once-pristine bay has stolen its Shangri-La appeal, and to add insult to injury, in 2002, Hurricane Kenna stole much of the soft beige sand. Nonetheless, the place retains a certain cachet. It also has views of the famous cove from a couple seafood restaurants on the south side of a wooden bridge over the mouth of the Río Mismaloya.

> ### SNORKELING SANCTUARY
>
> Protected area **Los Arcos** is an offshore group of giant rocks rising some 65 feet above the water, making the area great for snorkeling and diving. For reasonable fees, local men along the road to Mismaloya Beach run diving, snorkeling, fishing, and boat trips here and as far north as Punta Mita and Las Marietas or the beach villages of Cabo Corrientes. Recommended for all of these trips is Chipol's (☎ *322/228–0020*), with 23-foot skiffs and new, 75-horse-power, four-stroke motors. Restaurants and fishermen at Playa Mismaloya can also set you up.

Sun-seekers kick back in wooden beach chairs, waiters serve up food and drink on the sand, massage techs offer their (so-so) services alfresco. Chico's Dive Shop sells dive packages and boat trips and rents snorkel gear, boogie boards, Jet Skis, and double sea kayaks. Barceló La Jolla de Mismaloya has day passes for nonguests that are valid from 9 AM to 6 PM: $25 gets you use of facilities only (pool, gym, game room, an hour of kayaking); $50 gets you the full experience, including food and drink. In the afternoons locals hang out at this beach, the kids playing in the sand while the moms wait for their men to return from fishing expeditions and touring gigs. The beach is about 13 km (8 mi) south of PV. The bus drops you on the highway, and it's a 200-meter walk from there down a dirt road to the beach. The tiny village of Mismaloya is on the east side of Carretera 200. **Facilities:** Boating, diving, Jet Skis, kayaking, snorkeling; food concessions, toilets (Port-o-Potties on road to beach).

Boca de Tomatlán. This is the name of both a small village and a deep, V-shape, rocky bay that lie at the mouth ("boca" means mouth) of the Río Horcones, about 5 km (3 mi) south of Mismaloya and 17 km (10½ mi) south of PV. Water taxis leave from Boca to the southern beaches; you can arrange snorkeling trips to Los Arcos. As far as most visitors are concerned, this is mainly the staging area for water taxis with nowhere else to hang out. However, this dramatic-looking bay fringed in palm trees does have a rustic appeal. Grocery stores sell chips, Cokes, and plastic water toys for tots; a handful of informal seaside cafés cluster at the water's edge. At very low tide only, it's possible for adventurers and cheapskates to walk south from Boca to Playa Las Animas (about 40 minutes) along a small path at waters' edge. You certainly don't want to be on this path, however, when the tide begins to come in, as the rocks behind it are steep and sharp. **Facilities:** Fishing; food concessions, toilets.

Playa las Ánimas. There's lots to do besides sunbathe at this beach and town 15 minutes south of Boca de Tomatlán. Framed in oak, coconut, and pink-flowering *amapa* trees, the brown-sand beach's name means "The Souls"; a graveyard was reportedly located here many years ago. Framing the 1-km-long (½-mi-long) beach are piles of smooth, strange rocks looking an awful lot like petrified elephant poo. Because of its very shallow waters, Las Animas is often referred to as *la playa de los niños* (children's beach), and it tends to fill up with families on weekends and holidays. They come by water taxi or as part of half- or full-day bay cruises. Five or six seafood eateries line the sand; a few will lend their clients volleyballs to use on sand courts out front. You can also rent Jet Skis, ride a banana boat, or soar up into the sky behind a speedboat while dangling from a colorful parachute. **Facilities:** Banana-boat rides, boating, Jet Skis, parasailing; food concessions.

Quimixto. Between the sandy stretches of Las Ánimas and Majahuitas, and about 20 minutes by boat from Boca de Tomatlán, Quimixto has a narrow, rocky shoreline that attracts few bathers. Tour boats stop here, and their clients usually have a meal at one of the seafood eateries facing the beach. Horses by the dozens are standing by to take passengers to Quimixto Falls (about $13 round-trip). It's only slightly longer than the 25-minute ride to walk there. You can bathe at the base of the energetic falls; the pool is enclosed by sheer rock walls. Be careful of the current during the rainy season, when the water crashing into the pool tends to push swimmers toward the rock walls. Before proceeding to the falls, have a cool drink at the casual restaurant; consuming something is obligatory to gain access. During stormy weather or a full moon there's a fun, fast wave at Quimixto's reef, popular with surfers, but because of its inaccessibility, rarely crowded. **Facilities:** Horseback riding, surfing; food concessions, toilets.

Majahuitas. Between the beaches of Quimixto and Yelapa and about 35 minutes by boat from Boca de Tomatlán, this small beach is the playground of people on day tours and guests of the exclusive Majahuitas Resort. There are no services for the average José; the lounge chairs and toilets are for hotel guests only. Palm trees shade the white beach of broken, sea-buffed shells. The blue-green water is clear, and there's sometimes good snorkeling around the rocky shore. **Facilities:** None.

★ **Yelapa.** This secluded village and ½-km-long (¼-mi-long) beach is about an hour southeast of downtown PV and a half hour from Boca de Tomatlán—by boat, of course. A half-dozen seafood *enramadas* (thatch-roof huts) edge its fine, clean, grainy sand. Phones and electricity arrived in Yelapa around the turn of the 21st century. Believe it or not, it's the largest and most developed of the north Cabo Corrientes towns, with quite a few rustic rooms and houses for rent by the day, week or month. That said, **bring all the money you'll need, as there's nothing as formal as a bank.**

The beach slopes down to the water, and small waves break right on the shore. In high season and during holidays, there are water-sports outfitters. From here you can hike 20 minutes into the jungle to see the small Cascada Cola del Caballo (Horse Tail Waterfall), with a pool at its base for swimming. (The falls are often dry near the end of the dry season, especially April–early June.) A more ambitious expedition of several hours brings you to less visited, very beautiful Cascada del Catedral (Cathedral Falls). Beyond that, Yelapa is, for the most part, *tranquilisimo:* a place to just kick back in a beach chair and sip something cold. Seemingly right when you really need it, Cheggy or Agustina, the pie ladies, will show up with their homemade lime, coconut, or nut creations. **Facilities:** Boating, fishing, parasailing; food concessions.

CABO CORRIENTES

Just south of the end of Banderas Bay are the lovely beaches of pristine, wonderful Cabo Corrientes. These take an effort to visit, as well as a sturdy, high-clearance vehicle. Public transportation comes here and back once a day from the small town of El Tuito (40 km [25 mi] south of PV) along a rutted dirt-and-gravel road.

Playa Puntilla de Mayto. Thirty-eight kilometers (23 mi) down a passable road from El Tuito, this gorgeous beach is several miles long, embraced on either end by a rocky point. The sand is grainy but clean and slopes down to meet the rough to semirough surf. Despite the slope of the beach, this is a great place for a long walk or shore fishing. In late summer and fall there's a turtle camp where volunteers protect the eggs of the black and olive Ridley turtles that nest here. The Hotel Mayto has rooms at modest prices and offers massage; next door, the friendly folks of El Rinconcito have a small store and a few rooms to rent as well as four-wheelers and horses (200 pesos per hour for either). **Facilities:** ATVs, horseback riding, kayaking; food concessions.

☾ **Tehuamixtle.** Just over a mile (2 km) from Mayto, Tehuamixtle is a sheltered cove with a few basic rooms to rent. The area is known for its oysters, which you can sample fresh from the sea at an open-air restaurant facing the fishing fleet. The surf here is very gentle and lacks currents, making it popular with local children. The pristine beach invites snorkeling and diving (bring your own equipment). Fishing boats bob at one end, below the restaurant; from here, the beach curves along in a sandy brown arch to a large green headland at the other end of the cove. Tehua, as locals call it, is about the same size as Mayto: 100 people. This fishing village has only had electricity since the turn of the 21st century. There's a beach road that connects Tehua with Cruz de Loreto, about 1½ hours to the south; otherwise go out through El Tuito. **Facilities:** Fishing; food concessions

Lingering in Yelapa

If you can't tear yourself away at the end of the day (or you miss the last water taxi), consider renting one of the locally run rustic accommodations near the beach. Modest but charming in a bohemian way, Hotel La Lagunita has rooms right over the water. Rustic superchic describes La Verana hotel, a five-star property represented by Mexico Boutique Hotels. It doesn't accept walk-ins, however, and you need to make a large deposit in advance of your stay. You can arrange other accommodations by asking locals for referrals.

If you're lucky enough to be staying in Yelapa, there's plenty to do beyond the beach. Splash across the shallow lagoon or catch the water taxi to the main pier for a jungly walk past private homes and small shops; this is the Yelapa most folks never see. Turn right from the main pier, and walk to the point; turn left, and head up into the hills.

Check out the candlelit Club Yates disco on the south side of the estuary (Wednesday and Saturday nights during high season [December through Easter week] and holidays). Or ask around for one of several yoga classes, schedule a therapeutic massage with Claudia (☎ *322/209–5085* ✉ *$50*), or hire a local *pangero* (panga operator) for a trip to a secluded southern beach for swimming and a trek to a clandestine waterfall. For a simple meal in a tiny outdoor café, visit El Manguito ($$ ☎ *322/209–5061*), just a few paces from the footbridge on the north side of the stream. Order shrimp, fish, lobster, beef, or just chips and salsa. It's open daily but closes from 4:30 to 5 PM to switch gears from lunch to dinner.

But the best part of staying in Yelapa is that after the booze cruises decamp and the water taxis put in for the night, you'll have the cool and groovy place to yourself.

Villa del Mar. Four kilometers (2½ mi) beyond Tehuamixtle, Villa del Mar is a beautiful virgin beach on a broad sweep of bay. Several miles long, flat and sandy, it's great for long walks; turtles nest here in late summer and fall. At the south end of the beach, a huge estuary surrounded by coconut palms invites kayaking. The sandy streets in and around town and the beach are great for mountain biking, and local people will rent horses for a ride on the beach or into the countryside. **Facilities:** Horseback riding.

COSTALEGRE

Most people come to the Costalegre—dubbed "The Happy Coast" by Jalisco's tourism authorities—to stay at luxury accommodations on lovely, clean beaches: Hotelito Desconocido, Las Alamandas, El Careyes, and El Tamarindo. Indeed, some of the nicest beaches with services are now the private domain of *gran turismo* (government-rated five-star-plus) hotels.

Other people head to southern Jalisco State without reservations to explore the coast at their leisure. There are still some delightful, pristine, and mainly isolated beaches along the Costalegre, most with few services aside from the ubiquitous seafood *enramadas* serving fish fillets and fresh ceviche.

Whether you kick back at an elegant resort or explore the wild side, the area between Cabo Corrientes and Barra de Navidad, the latter at the southern extreme of Jalisco State, will undoubtedly delight.

GETTING HERE AND AROUND

It's optimum to explore the beaches of southern Jalisco by car, SUV, or camper. Camping is permitted on most beaches, and these are often down a long dirt road from the highway. Fill up with gas at every opportunity as gas stations are few. (If you do get into a bind, ask locals about any small stores that sell gas.) If you're in a rental car, reset the odometer and look for the kilometer signs at the side of the road. If you're driving a car marked in miles, not kilometers, the road signs are still useful, as many addresses are simply "Carretera 200" or "Carretera a Barra de Navidad" along with the marker number.

Buses leave from the **Central Camionero** (⊠ *Carretera Puerto Vallarta— Tepic [Carretera 200], Km 9, Col. Las Mojoneras* ☎ *322/290–1009*) in PV.

Playa Chalacatepec. A sylvan beach with no services lies down a rutted dirt road about 82 km (50 mi) south of El Tuito and 115 km (70 mi) south of PV. The road is negotiable only by high-clearance passenger cars and smallish RVs. The reward for 8 km (5 mi) of bone-jarring travel is a beautiful rocky point, Punta Chalacatepec, with a sweep of protected white-sand beach to the north that's perfect for swimming and bodysurfing. There's a fish camp here, so you may find some rather scraggly looking dudes on this isolated beach. Admire the tide pools at the point during low tide; take a walk along the open-ocean beach south of the point, where waves crash more dramatically, discouraging swimming. To get here, turn toward the beach at the town of José María Morelos (at Km 88). Just after 8 km (5 mi), leave the main road (which bears right) and head to the beach over a smaller track. From here it's less than a 1½ km (1 mi) to the beach. **Facilities:** None.

Playa Perula. The handful of islands just offshore of lovely Bahía de Chamela, about 131 km (81 mi) south of PV, protects the beaches from strong surf. The best place on the bay for swimming is wide, flat, **Playa Perula** (turnoff at Km 76, then 3 km [2 mi] on dirt road), in the protective embrace of a cove just below the Punta Perula headland. Fishermen there take visitors out to snorkel around the islands (about $46 for up to 10 people) or to hunt for dorado, tuna, and mackerel (about $23 per hour for one to four people); restaurants on the soft beige sand sell the same as fresh fillets and ceviche. **Facilities:** Fishing, snorkeling; food concessions.

Playa Negrita. Also on Bahía de Chamela, this lovely beach is fringed in lanky coconut palms and backed by blue foothills. There are camping and RV accommodations and plenty of opportunities for shore fishing, swimming, and snorkeling. Almost every pretty beach in Mexico has

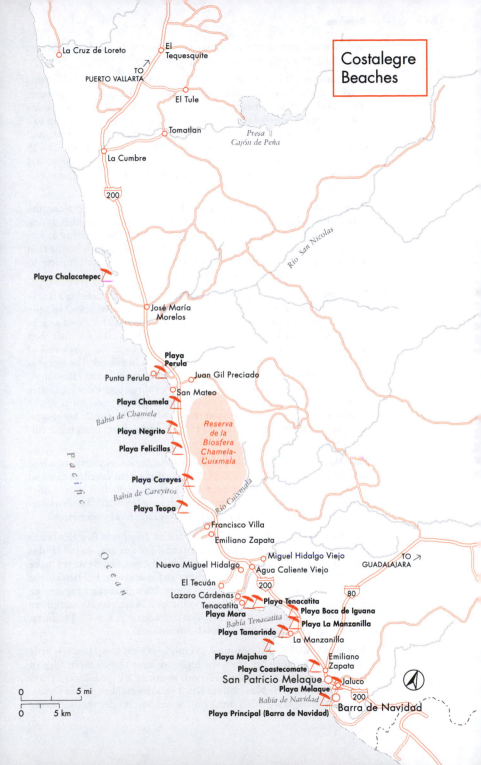

La Cruz de Loreto

El Tequesquite

TO
PUERTO VALLARTA

El Tule

Tomatlan

*Presa
Cajón de Peña*

La Cumbre

200

Playa Chalacatepec

José María
Morelos

Playa
Perula

Punta Perula

Juan Gil Preciado

San Mateo

Playa Chamela

Bahía de Chamela

Playa Negrito

*Reserva
de la
Biosfera
Chamela-
Cuixmala*

Playa Felicillas

Playa Careyes

Bahía de Careyitos

Río Cuixmala

Playa Teopa

Francisco Villa

Emiliano Zapata

Miguel Hidalgo Viejo

Nuevo Miguel Hidalgo

Agua Caliente Viejo

TO
GUADALAJARA

El Tecuán

Lazaro Cárdenas
Tenacatita

Playa Tenacatita

200

80

Playa Mora

Playa Boca de Iguana

Bahía Tenacatita

Playa La Manzanilla

Playa Tamarindo

La Manzanilla

Playa Majahua

Emiliano
Zapata

Playa Coastecomate

San Patricio Melaque

Jaluco

Playa Melaque

200

Bahía de Navidad

Barra de Navidad

Playa Principal (Barra de Navidad)

Pacific

Ocean

0   5 mi

0   5 km

Costalegre
Beaches

its own humble restaurant; this one is no exception. **Facilities:** Fishing, snorkeling; camping facilities, food concessions.

Playa Careyes. About 11 km (6½ mi) south of Bahía Chamela, this beach is named for the *careyes* (hawksbill) turtles that lay eggs here. It's a lovely soft-sand beach framed by headlands. When the water's not too rough, snorkeling is good around the rocks, where you can also fish. There's a small restaurant at the north end of the beach, and often you can arrange to go out with a local fisherman (about $25 per hour). Water-loving birds can be spotted around the lagoon that forms at the south end of the bay. **Facilities:** Birding, fishing, snorkeling; food concessions.

Playa Teopa. Here, you can walk south from Playa Careyes along the dunes, although guards protect sea turtle nests by barring visitors during the summer and fall nesting seasons. A road from the highway at Km 49.5 gains access to Playa Teopa by car; ask the guard for permission to enter this way, as you'll need to pass through private property to gain access to the beach. **Facilities:** None.

★ **Playa Tenacatita.** Named for the bay on which it lies, Tenacatita is a lovely beach of soft sand about 34 km (20 mi) north of San Patricio–Melaque and 172 km (106 mi) south of PV. Dozens of identical seafood shacks line the shore; birds cruise the miles of beach, searching for their own fish. Waves crash against clumps of jagged rocks at the north end of the beach, which curves gracefully around to a headland. The water is sparkling blue. There's camping for RVs and tents at Punta Hermanos, where the water is calm and good for snorkeling, and local men offer fishing excursions ($50–$60 for one to four people) and tours of the mangroves ($27). **Of the string of restaurants on the beach, we recommend La Fiesta Mexicana. Facilities:** Fishing, snorkeling; camping facilities, food concessions.

★ **Playa Mora.** Near the north end of Playa Tenacatita, this pretty stretch of sand has a coral reef close to the beach, making it an excellent place to snorkel. Local fishermen take interested parties out on their boats, either fishing for tuna, dorado, or bonita or searching for wildlife such as dolphins and turtles. **Facilities:** Fishing, snorkeling; food concessions.

Playa Boca de Iguanas. South of Playa Mora on Tenacatita Bay, this beach (whose name means "Mouth of the Iguanas") of fine gray-blond sand is wide and flat, and it stretches for several kilometers. Gentle waves make it great for swimming, boogie boarding, and snorkeling, but beware the undertow. Some enthusiasts fish from shore. It's a great place for jogging or walking on the beach, as there's no slope. There's an RV park here and a couple of beach restaurants. The entrance is at Km 17. **Facilities:** Snorkeling; camping facilities, food concessions.

☾ **Playa la Manzanilla.** This beautiful, 2-km-long (1-mi-long) beach is little more than a kilometer in from the highway, near the southern edge of Bahía de Tenacatita, 193 km (120 mi) south of PV and 25 km (15½ mi) north of Barra de Navidad (at Km 14). Informal hotels and restaurants are interspersed with small businesses and modest houses along the town's main street. Rocks dot the gray-gold sands and edge both ends of the wide beach; facing the sand are attractive, unpretentious vacation homes favoring a Venetian palate of ochre and brick red. The bay is calm. At the beach road's north end, gigantic, rubbery-looking crocodiles lie heaped together just out of harm's way in a mangrove swamp. The fishing here is excellent; boat owners on the beach can take you out for snapper, sea bass, and other *pescado* for $20–$25 an hour. **Facilities:** Fishing; food concessions.

Playa Melaque. Twenty-one kilometers (13 mi) south of La Manzanilla, Bahía de Navidad represents the end of the Costalegre at the border with Colima State. First up (from north to south) is **San Patricio–Melaque,** the coast's most populous town, with about 12,000 people. (It's actually two towns that have now met in the middle.) While parts of town look dilapidated or abandoned, its long, coarse-white-sand beach is beautiful and has gentle waves. Restaurants, small hotels, homes, and tall palms line the beach, which slopes down to the water. About 5 km (3½ mi) east of Barra de Navidad, which shares Navidad Bay, Melaque's beach curves around for several kilometers to end in a series of jagged rocks poking from the water. If you plop down in a seat under a shade umbrella its owner will soon show up. Pay about $5 and stay as long as you like. Fishermen here will take anglers out in search of dorado, tuna, wahoo, swordfish, mackerel, and others. ■TIP→ **The best swimming and boogie boarding is about half the length of town, in front of El Dorado restaurant. Facilities:** Banana-boat rides, boogie boarding, fishing, Jet Skis, kayaking, snorkeling, beach umbrellas.

Playa Principal (Barra de Navidad). Usually called just "Barra," this laidback little town has sandy streets and a live-and-let-live demeanor. At any time but high tide you can walk between San Patricio and Barra, a distance of about 5 km (3½ mi). It's about 4½ km (3 mi) on the highway from one town to the other. Most of Barra is comprised of two streets on a long sandbar. Calle Veracruz faces the vast lagoon and **Isla Navidad,** now home to the posh Gran Bay resort. Water taxis take folks to the Gran Bay's golf course or marina, or to the seafood restaurants of **Colimilla,** on the lagoon's opposite shore. Avenida Miguel de Legazpi faces Barra's sloping brown-sand beach and the ocean. These and connecting streets have small shops, simple but charming restaurants, and—like everywhere along Mexico's Pacific coast—a host of friendly townspeople. ■TIP→ **Surfers look for swells near the jetty, where the sea enters the lagoon. Facilities:** Boating, fishing; food concessions.

Adventure

Snorkeling

WORD OF MOUTH

"We went on a three-hour horseback ride at Rancho Charro, which I would highly recommend if you are into that sort of thing. For a reasonable price, the two of us had our own personal guide and a very rustic and scenic experience. Neither of us are experienced riders, but the horses are wonderfully gentle and took us gingerly up and down a mountain and across a river multiple times."

—bunny

For the sheer variety of activities, Puerto Vallarta is one of the best adventure-vacation destinations on Mexico's Pacific coast. The water's warm and swimmable year-round, even downright bathlike July through September. The big blue bay attracts sea turtles, humpback whales, dolphins, and a growing number of snorkelers and divers. The fishing is excellent—from deep-sea angling for marlin and sailfish to trolling near shore for roosters and red snapper.

Banderas Bay and the beaches to the north and south have waves for surfing as well as plenty of calm bays and inlets for swimming. Party boats and private yachts are great for accessing gorgeous and hard-to-reach beaches, primarily south of Vallarta along Cabo Corrientes.

The subtropical foothills are laced with streams and rivers that rush and tumble over rocks in the rainy season and dwindle but still impress at other times. Trails challenge mountain bikers and thrill dune buggy and ATV aficionados. Many family-owned ranches have horse-riding tours at reasonable prices—lasting from an hour or two to overnight forays into the Sierra Madre.

Most of the tour operators are in Puerto Vallarta. North and south of town, activities are often arranged through hotels, though there are companies springing up to meet an increasing demand. Operators generally provide transportation from strategic pickup points, usually in downtown Puerto Vallarta, Marina Vallarta, Nuevo Vallarta, and, sometimes in Conchas Chinas. To save traveling from one end of the bay to the other, try to choose an outfitter near your neck of the woods.

CRUISES

Daytime bay cruises generally begin with a quick jaunt to Los Arcos Underwater Preserve, off Mismaloya Beach. There's about a half hour for snorkeling or swimming—sometimes with legions of little jellyfish in addition to the turtles that feed on them. Cruises then proceed to Yelapa, Quimixto, or Playa las Animas, or to Islas Marietas for whale-watching (in winter), snorkeling, swimming, and lunch. Horseback riding is usually available at an additional cost (about $15).

There are plenty of tours available; our list contains some of the most popular and professional.

LOGISTICS

Buy your ticket from licensed vendors along the boardwalk at Los Muertos Beach, online, or through area tour operators. Prices are fluid; like car salespeople, the ticket sellers give discounts or jack up the price as they see fit. Full-day booze cruises cost about $40–$70 per person, including open bar, continental breakfast, snacks, and snorkeling and/or kayaks. Two-hour sunset cruises with open bar cost about $25 per person. Dinner cruises cost $55–$75. Expect to pay a small port fee (about $2) at the maritime pier in addition to the cost of the ticket.

OUTFITTERS

Cruceros Princesa. Full- and half-day trips take in the beaches of southern Bahía de Banderas with snorkeling, beach time, and lunch. Half-day cruises generally go to Los Arcos or Las Animas; full-day cruises access several different spots—such as Yelapa and Majahuitas or Los Arcos or Quimixto and Playa las Animas—as well as making jaunts to Islas Marietas for half-day whale-watching (in winter), snorkeling, swimming, and lunch. The boat *Sarape* heads to Los Arcos for 40 minutes of snorkeling and then continues to Las Animas and Quimixto. After beach time there's lunch aboard the boat on the return trip ($38). ✉*Terminal Marítima, Marina Vallarta* ☎*322/224–4777* 🌐*www.crucerosprincesa.com.mx*.

Cruceros Santamaría. Full-day tours head to Los Arcos, Las Animas, and Quimixto. You can also rent boats for large private parties. Buy tickets from booth vendors. If you order by phone staff will fax the receipts to your hotel or send them to you via the Internet. ✉*Blvd. Francisco M. Ascencio across from Sam's Club, Terminal Marítima, Marina Vallarta* ☎*322/221–2511* 🌐*www.puertovallarta.net*.

Marigalante. A really-and-truly sailing vessel that has circumnavigated the world more than once, the *Marigalante* has a pirate crew that keeps things hopping for kids and teens with fun and games. The dinner cruise, with open bar, snacks, and pre-Hispanic show, is for adults only and has some bawdy pirate humor. Women who don't want to be "kidnapped" may prefer the day cruise or another operator. Both five-hour tours cost $71. You can buy the tickets from its office or licensed vendors, but the boat takes off from Terminal Marítima, across from Sam's Club on Boulevard Francisco M. Ascencio, in Marina Vallarta. ✉*Paseo Díaz Ordáz 770, Centro* ☎*322/223–0309 or 322/223–1662* 🌐*www.marigalante.com.mx*.

★ **Vallarta Adventures.** Day or evening cruises are to Caletas Beach, the company's exclusive domain. Although the day cruise can accommodate 150 passengers, there's plenty of room to spread out: boulder-bordered coves, sandy beaches, hammocks in the shade, and jungle trails ensure that you won't feel like a cow about to be branded "tourist." The Caletas by Day cruise includes snorkeling, kayaking, hiking, and lunch (scuba or spa treatments available for additional fees). The Rhythms of the Night evening cruise includes dinner on the beach and a show at the amphitheater. Most folks love the show—men and women dressed as voluptuous natives do a modern dance to dramatic lighting and music. Tours cost $85 and $89, respectively. Kids under 8 aren't allowed on the nighttime tour. ✉*Paseo de las Palmas 39–A, Nuevo Vallarta* ☎*322/297–1212, 888/303–2653 in U.S. and Canada* ✉*Edifício Marina Golf, Local 13-C, Calle Mástil, Marina Vallarta* ☎*322/221–0657* 🌐*www.vallarta-adventures.com*.

LAND SPORTS

ATV AND DUNE BUGGY TOURS

There's an increasing number of ATV, dune buggy, and jeep tours heading to the hills around Puerto Vallarta. Most rides are to small communities, ranches, and rivers north, south, and east of town. Sharing a vehicle with a partner means a significant savings.

LOGISTICS

You need a valid driver's license and a major credit card. Wear lightweight long pants, sturdy shoes, bandanna (some operators provide one as a keepsake) and/or tight-fitting hat, sunglasses, and both sunscreen and mosquito repellent. In rainy season (July–October) it's hot and wet—ideal for splashing through puddles and streams; the rest of the year is cooler and dustier. In either season, prepare to get dirty. Four-hour tours run $80–$120; full-day trips to San Sebastián cost about $165 for one or $175 for two riders.

OUTFITTERS

Adventure ATV Jungle Treks. This company leads daily three-hour dune buggy tours ($120 for one or two riders) and ATV tours ($75 for one rider or $95 for two) that head into the hills behind Vallarta. ⊠ *Basilio Badillo 400, Col. E. Zapata* ☎ *322/223–0392.*

★ **Wild Vallarta.** Full- and half-day tours in Honda four-wheel ATVs and open-frame, five-speed buggies with VW engines cost $66 (single ATVs) to $83 (double ATV or dune buggy). The long and rugged ATV tour to San Sebastián, high in the Sierra Madre, requires some experience, but four-hour trips are fine for beginners. Consider riding two per ATV for the tequila-tasting trip, solving the drinking-and-driving conundrum if you plan to gulp rather than sip. ☎ *322/222–8928* ⊕ *www.wildvallarta.com.*

CANOPY TOURS

Canopy tours are high-octane thrill rides during which you "fly" from treetop to treetop, securely fastened to a zip line. Despite the inherent danger of dangling from a cable hundreds of feet off the ground, the operators we list have excellent safety records. If you're brave bring your camera to take photos while zipping along; just be sure the neck strap is long enough to leave your hands free.

LOGISTICS

Check with each operator regarding maximum weight (usually 250 pounds) and minimum ages for kids. ■ TIP➜ **Don't take a tour when rain threatens.** A thunderstorm isn't the time to hang out near trees attached to metal cables, and rain makes the activity scary to say the least. Even during the rainy season, however, mornings and *early* afternoons are generally sunny.

MULTISPORT OPERATORS

Ecotours (☎ *322/223–3130 or 322/222–6606* ⊕ *www.ecotours vallarta.com*). It's a downtown PV–based operator whose offerings include hiking, diving, kayaking, bird-watching, whale-watching, and turtle tours.

Natura Expeditions (☎ *322/224–0410* ⊕ *www.mexonline.com/viva. htm*). Nature-oriented excursions are the focus of this Zona Hotelera–based operator. Offerings include deep-sea fishing, scuba diving, hiking, horseback riding, and biking.

Sociedad Cooperativa Corral del Risco (☎ *329/291–6298* ⊕ *www. puntamitacharters.com*). Local fishermen at Punta Mita (aka Punta de Mita) have formed this cooperative, which offers reasonably priced fishing trips, whale-watching excursions, and snorkeling outings. All fees go directly to the guides and their families.

Tours Soltero (☎ *315/355–6777* ✎ *raystours-melaque@yahoo.com*). Canadian expat Ray Calhoun and his wife Eva rent mountain bikes, snorkeling equipment, and boogie boards ($10 per day), and lead active tours from

their base in San Patricio Melaque, a town next to Barra de Navidad. Typical excursions are snorkeling in Tenacatita with boogie boarding at Boca de Iguana, from 10 to 5 ($30), and a day trip to the state capital, Colima, which includes lunch and a stop at a typical hacienda-cum-museum ($50).

Vallarta Adventures (☎ *322/297–1212 in Nuevo Vallarta, 322/221–0657 in Marina Vallarta, 888/303–2653 in U.S. and Canada* ⊕ *www.vallarta-adventures.com*). It's a well-respected operator with 15 years' experience, two offices, dozens of tours, and a staff of some 350. It's often used by high-end hotel concierges and cruise-ship activity directors for canopy tours, hiking, sailing, dinner-show cruises, and dolphin- and whale-watching excursions.

Wildlife Connection (☎ *322/225–3621* ⊕ *www.wildlife connection.com*). Based in downtown PV, this Mexican-owned company does what its name implies: connects you with wildlife, specifically dolphins and whales on seasonal trips.

OUTFITTERS

★ **Canopy El Edén.** The daily trips to the spirited Mismaloya River and an adjacent restaurant are 3½-hour adventures ($81) that depart from the downtown office. You zip along 10 lines through the trees and above the river. To take full advantage of the lovely setting and good restaurant, take the first tour (departures are weekdays at 9, 10, 11, 12, and 1:30 and 3—sometimes less frequently in low season), and bring your swimsuit. The schedule includes about an hour to spend at the river or restaurant. If you wish to stay longer and there's room, you can return to Vallarta with a later group; otherwise take a taxi or ask the restaurant staff for a lift to the highway, where buses frequently pass. ✉ *Office: Plaza Romy, Calle Vallarta 228, Interior 1, Col. E. Zapata* ☎ *322/222–2516* ⊕ *www.canopyeleden.com*.

Canopy Tour de Los Veranos. Its rates are slightly higher than some competitors ($79), but Los Veranos has the most zip lines (14), the longest zip line (1,300 feet), the highest zip line (500 feet off the ground). It also has the most impressive scenery: crossing the Río Los Horcones half a dozen times on several miles of cables. Departures are from the office, across from the Pemex station at the south side of Puerto Vallarta, on the hour between 9 and 2, with reduced hours in low season (June through November). It's the only PV tour company that doesn't require helmets. After your canopy tour, there's time to scale the climbing wall, play in the Horcones River, eat at the restaurant, or hang out at the bar overlooking the river, but check to make sure that a ride back to town is available. ✉ *Office: Calle Francisca Rodríguez 336, Centro* ☎ *322/223–0504, 877/563–4113 from U.S.* ⊕ *www.canopy tours-vallarta.com.*

Rancho Mi Chaparrita. Luis Verdin runs a 13-zip-line tour on his family ranch. Access the ranch on his lively, healthy horses via the beach and backcountry for a complete adventure. Canopy tours are $75; a canopy tour plus the horseback ride is $95. ✉ *Manuel Rodriguez Sanchez 14, Sayulita* ☎ *329/291–3112* ⊕ *www.michaparrita.com.*

Vallarta Adventures. Although it's not the best one in town, Vallarta Adventures's canopy tour ($85) is the most convenient if you're staying in Nuevo Vallarta. You use gloved hands rather than a braking device to slow down or stop, and you must return to town right after the zip-line adventure, leaving no time for other activities. ✉ *Paseo de las Palmas 39–A, Nuevo Vallarta* ☎ *322/297–1212, 888/303–2653 in U.S. and Canada* ✉ *Edifício Marina Golf, Local 13–C, Calle Mástil, Marina Vallarta* ☎ *322/221–0657* ⊕ *www.vallarta-adventures.com.*

GOLF

"Not a bad mango in the bunch" is how one golf aficionado described Puerto Vallarta's courses. From the Four Seasons Punta Mita (prohibitively expensive for those not staying at the hotel) to the Gran Bay at Barra de Navidad, the region is a close second to Los Cabos in variety of play at a range of prices. Well-known designers are represented, including Jack Nicklaus and Tim Weiskopf.

LOGISTICS

Most of these courses offer first-class services including driving ranges and putting greens, lessons, clinics, pro shops, and clubhouses.

COURSES

★ **Marina Vallarta.** Joe Finger designed this 18-hole course; the $128 greens fee includes practice balls and a shared cart. It's the area's second-oldest course and is closest and most convenient for golfers staying in the Hotel Zone, Old Puerto Vallarta, and Marina Vallarta. Although it's very flat, it's way more challenging than it looks, with lots of water hazards. Speaking of hazards, the alligators have a way of blending into the scenery. They might surprise you, but they supposedly don't bite. ✉ *Paseo de la Marina s/n, Marina Vallarta* ☎ *322/221–0545 or 322/221–0073.*

Vista Vallarta. Some of the best views in the area belong to the aptly named Vista Vallarta. There are 18 holes designed by Jack Nicklaus and another 18 by Tom Weiskopf. The greens fee for the course, which is a few miles northwest of the Marina Vallarta area, is $194. A shared cart and tax are included. ⊠*Circuito Universidad 653, Col. San Nicolás* ☎*322/290–0030 or 322/290–0040.*

NUEVO
VALLARTA TO
BUCERÍAS

El Tigre. At the Paradise Village hotel and condo complex is this 18-hole course with 12 water features. The greens fee of $145 includes a shared cart, water, practice balls, and tax. Don't be surprised if you see a guy driving around with tiger cubs in his truck: the course's namesake and mascot is the passion of the club's director. El Tigre has a fun island par 3. ⊠*Paseo de los Cocoteros 18, Nuevo Vallarta* ☎*322/297–0773, 866/843–5951 in U.S., 800/214–7758 in Canada* ⊕*www.eltigregolf.com.*

★ **Four Seasons Punta Mita.** Nonguests are permitted to play the 195-acre, par-72, Jack Nicklaus–designed course; however, they must pay the hotel's day use fee of 50% of the room rate (approximately $300 plus 28% tax and service charge), which covers use of a guest room and hotel facilities until dark. Reservations are essential. The greens fee is $195 plus 25% tax and service and includes the golf cart. The club's claim to fame is that it has perhaps the only natural island green in golf. Drive your cart to it at low tide; otherwise hop aboard a special amphibious vessel (weather permitting) to cross the water. There are seven other oceanfront links, as well as an optional par 3, the resort's signature hole. ⊠*Punta Mita* ☎*329/291–6000* ⊕*www.fourseasons.com.*

Los Flamingos Country Club. Designed by Percy Clifford in 1978, PV's original course has been totally renovated. The 18-hole course at the northern extremity of Nuevo Vallarta has new irrigation and sprinkler systems to maintain the rejuvenated greens. The high-season greens fee is $139, including a shared cart and a bucket of balls. ⊠*Carretera a Bucerías, Km 145, 12 km (8 mi) north of airport, Nuevo Vallarta* ☎*329/296–5006* ⊕*www.flamingosgolf.com.mx.*

Mayan Palace. Nine of the 18 holes at Mayan Palace have been completely redesigned by Jack Nicklaus. At this writing renovations are ongoing; until they're finished golfers repeat play nine holes once ($79) or twice ($120). The fee includes cart, tax, use of practice range, and return transportation to hotel. Twilight fees (after 1 PM) are almost half that price, at $74 for 18 holes. ⊠*Paseo de las Moras s/n, Fracc. Nautico Turistico, Nuevo Vallarta* ☎*322/226–4000 Ext. 4600.*

Fodor'sChoice
★

El Tamarindo. About two hours south of Vallarta on the Costalegre is the area's best course. At least six of the holes play along the ocean; some are cliff-side holes with fabulous views, others go right down to the beach. On a slow day, golfers are encouraged at tee time to have a swim or a picnic on the beach during their round, or to play a hole a second time if they wish. Designed by David Fleming, the breathtaking course is the playground of birds, deer, and other wildlife. It's an awesome feeling to nail the course's most challenging hole, the 9th: a par 3 with a small green surrounded by bunkers. The greens fee is $235, including cart and tax. Resort guests get priority for tee times; call up to a week ahead to check availability. ⊠ *Carretera Melaque–Puerto Vallarta, Carretera 200, Km 7.5, Cihuatlán* ☎315/351–5032 Ext. 113.

Isla Navidad. It must have the best variety of play in the area, with three 9-hole courses of different terrain: mountain, lagoon, and ocean. Designed by Robert von Hagge, the course is beautifully sculpted, with lovely contours. Greens fees are $180 for 9 holes or $200 for 18, including driving range practice, cart, and tax. ⊠ *Isla Navidad, Barra de Navidad* ☎314/337–9006 ⊕ *www.islanavidad.com.*

HORSEBACK RIDING

Most of the horseback-riding outfits are based on family ranches in the foothill towns of the Sierra like Las Palmas. Horses are permitted on the beach in smaller towns like Sayulita and San Francisco, but not in Vallarta proper, so expect to ride into the hills for sunset-viewing there.

LOGISTICS

Outfitters pick you up either from the hotel or strategic locations north and south of town and return you to your hotel or to the pickup point. Short rides depart morning and afternoon, while longer rides are generally in the morning only, at least in winter when the sun sets earlier.

Ask at the beachfront restaurants of tiny towns like Yelapa, Quimixto, and Las Animas, south of PV, to hook up with horses for treks into the jungle. Horses are generally well cared for; some are exceptionally fit and frolicky.

OUTFITTERS

Club de Polo Costa Careyes. Though the trail rides here are expensive at $100 for 45 minutes, you know you're getting an exceptional mount. Trips leave in early morning or around sunset. ⊠ *Km 53.5, Carretera 200, Carretera a Barra de Navidad, El Careyes* ☎315/351–0320 ⊕ *www.careyes.com.*

Hacienda de Doña Engracia. Some of the large stable of horses are of Arabian stock at this ranch, which works with cruise ship excursion packagers and has, among other activities, a three-hour horseback outing ($80 per person, cheaper if you pay in pesos). After the river has receded at the end of the wet season (this dry period usually lasts from late November through June), you ride one hour to a series of three hot springs, where you spend an hour before heading back, crossing a river mid-trip. In rainy season, the tour through jungly hills is impressive but, because you often can't cross the swollen streams, it doesn't go to the hot springs. At the hacienda, you can fish in the small artificial lake, do a tequila tasting, and have lunch at the restaurant. Most people arrive as part of a cruise-ship excursion or dune buggy tour with Wild Vallarta (⇨ *ATV Tours, above*) or other adventure companies, but you can drive on your own as well. ⊠ *Carretera a las Palmas, Km 10, La Desembocada* ☎322/281–2841 ⊕ *www.haciendadonaengracia.com.*

Rancho Charro. Rancho Charro provides transportation to and from your hotel for rides to rivers and waterfalls. Choices include three-hour ($62), five-hour ($82), and all-day rides ($120). ☎322/224–0114 ⊕www.ranchoelcharro.com.

★ **Rancho Manolo.** The friendly folks at the family-owned property take you into the mountains they know so well. The usual tour is to El Edén, the restaurant-and-river property where the movie *Predator* was filmed. The three-hour trip (45 minutes each way, with 1½ hours for a meal or for splashing in the river) costs just $33. ✉*Hwy. 200, Km 12, at Mismaloya bridge, Mismaloya* ☎*322/228–0018 day, 322/222–3694 evening.*

Rancho Mi Chaparrita. This ranch has very nice, healthy horses willing to run (or walk, if you ask them politely). Ride on the beach, in the tropical forest, or a combination of the two for $25 an hour. ✉*Manuel Rodriguez Sanchez 14, Sayulita* ☎*329/291–3112* ⊕*www.michaparrita.com.*

Rancho Ojo de Agua. The horses are part Mexican quarter horse and part Thoroughbred. According to proud owner Mari González, the stock comes from the Mexican cavalry. The family-owned business conducts sunset and half-day horseback rides (three to five hours, $60 and $74), the latter including lunch and time for a swim in a mountain stream. Also available at some times of year is a full-day excursion (seven hours, most on the horse) into the Sierra Madre for an overnight ($420), which includes four meals and either tent or cabin camping. ✉*Cerrada de Cardenal 227, Fracc. Aralias, Puerto Vallarta* ☎*322/224–0607* ⊕*www.ranchojodeagua.com.*

MOUNTAIN BIKING

Although the tropical climate makes it hot for biking, the Puerto Vallarta area is lovely and has challenging and varied terrain. Major operators lead rides up river valleys to Yelapa and from the old mining town of San Sebastian (reached via plane; included in price), high in the Sierra, back to Vallarta. It's about 45 km (28 mi) of twisty downhill.

In the rainy season, showers are mainly in the late afternoon and evening, so bike tours can take place year-round. In summer and fall rivers and waterfalls are voluptuous and breathtaking. A popular ending point for rides into the foothills, they offer a place to rest, rinse off (there's lots of mud) and have a snack or meal. In dry season, it's relatively cooler and less humid. The very best months for biking are December through February: the weather is coolest and the vegetation, rivers, and waterfalls still reasonably lush after the end of the rainy season in October.

LOGISTICS

PRICES Four- to five-hour rides average $60 to $70; Yelapa costs $120 and up. The ride down from San Sebastián, including one-way plane trip, goes for around $240. Rides of more than a half day include lunch, and all include helmet, gloves, and bikes.

PICK-UP POLO

Rent a pony and join a game of polo at the **Club de Polo Costa Careyes** (⌧ *Km 53.5, Carretera 200, Carretera a Barra de Navidad, El Careyes* ☎ *315/351–0320* ⊕ *www.careyes. com*). The cost is $80 per game per player and includes horse rental, polo pro, and greens fee. Spectators are welcome, too, at no charge, to watch the various tournaments (mid-April–November). Ask about packages including accommodations, clinics (mid-February through mid-March only), and lessons. **La Patrona Polo Club** (⌧ *Ceilán 10, San Francisco* ☎ *311/258–4378* or *322/133–2601* ⊕ *polovallarta.com*) in Nayarit has matches on Saturday at 5 PM during the season (November through June). You can watch from the elegant on-site restaurant, and then enjoy entertainment and live jazz in the adjacent bar. You can also watch practice Tuesday through Friday from the stands or the restaurant.

OUTFITTERS

Eco Ride. A few streets behind Vallarta's cathedral, Eco Ride caters to intermediate and expert cyclists. Rides start at the shop and go up the Río Cuale, passing some hamlets along single tracks and dirt roads. A few rides include time at local swimming holes; the Yelapa ride ($120)—with two 10-km (6-mi) uphills and a 20-km (12-mi) downhill—returns by boat. ⌧ *Calle Miramar 382, Centro* ☎ *322/222–7912* ⊕ *www.ecoridemex.com.*

Vallarta Bikes. This family-operated PV-based outfit has custom tours of up to 10 days. More common, however, are set itineraries for beginner to advanced cyclists. A three- to four-hour beginner's ride to La Pileta ($43) is popular, as the departure point is near the town center and the destination a year-round swimming hole. This easy downhill ride includes lunch, as do all Vallarta Bikes' tours. The six-hour, 35-km (22-mi) tour to Yelapa ($143) is more physical, but the reward is lunch overlooking Yelapa's beautiful beach and returning by water taxi. Owner-guide Alejandro González leads groups whenever possible. He will certainly push you, but don't expect him to hold your hand. ⌧ *Franisco Villa 1442, Col. Los Sauces* ☎ *322/293–1142* ⊕ *www.vallartabikes.com.*

WATER SPORTS

FISHING

Sportfishing is excellent off Puerto Vallarta, and fisherfolk have landed monster marlin well over 500 pounds. Surf casting from shore nets snook, roosters, and jack crevalles. Hire a *panga* (skiff) to hunt for Spanish mackerel, sea bass, amberjack, snapper, bonito, and roosterfish on full- or half-day trips within the bay. Pangas can be hired in the traditional fishing villages of Mismaloya and Boca de Tomatlán, just south of town; in the Costalegre towns of La Manzanilla and Barra de Navidad; and in the north, at El Anclote and Nuevo Corral del Risco, Punta Mita.

Yachts are best for big-game fishing: yellowfin tuna; blue, striped, and black marlin; and dorado. Hire them for 4 to 10 hours, or overnight. Catch-and-release of billfish is encouraged. If you don't want to charter a boat, you can also join a party boat. Most sportfishing yachts are based at Marina Vallarta; only a few call home the marina at Paradise Village, in Nuevo Vallarta. The resort hotels of the Costalegre and Punta Mita arrange fishing excursions for their guests. Bass fishing at Cajón de Peña, about 1½ hours south of Vallarta, nets 10-pounders on a good day.

LOGISTICS

Most captains and crews are thoroughly bilingual, at least when it comes to boating and fishing.

LICENSES Licenses are required, however a new set of regulations requires anglers to buy their fishing licenses ahead of time via a super-confusing Internet and bank-deposit system. Since boat owners are the ones (heavily) fined if there are unlicensed anglers aboard, you can leave it to the captain to make the necessary arrangements.

PRICES Prices generally hover around $600–$650 for six hours, $600–$800 for eight hours, and $1,000–$1,200 for a 10-hour trip. A longer trip is recommended for chasing the big guys, as it takes you to prime fishing grounds like Los Bancos and Cobeteña. Pangas (skiffs) usually accommodate up to four clients and yachts, 4 to 10. Party boats start at $140 per person for an eight-hour day. Drinking water is generally included in the price; box lunches and beer or soda may be sold separately or included; sometimes it's BYOB. Pangas and superpangas, the latter with shade and a head of some sort, charge $175–$250 for four hours. You'll obviously save lots of money by going with the local guys in their often fast, but not luxurious, pangas.

OUTFITTERS

CharterDreams. Although most fisherfolk choose to leave around the smack of dawn, you set your own itinerary with this company. Excursions range from trips with one to three people in pangas for bass fishing to cruises with up to eight people aboard luxury yachts. Charter-Dreams also offers whale-watching and private sightseeing or snorkeling tours. ⊠ *Marina Las Palmas II, Locales 11 and 12, Marina Vallarta* ☎ *322/221–0690* ⊕ *www.charterdreams.com.*

Gerardo Kosonoy. For fishing excursions in and around Barra de Navidade, at the southern end of the Costalegre, contact Sr. Kosonoy. He speaks excellent English and has low hourly rates. Alternatively, you can round up another fisherman with a panga from one of the two large fishing co-ops on the lagoon side of town. There's usually at least one representative hoping for clients at the water-taxi dock. Gerardo and his compadres charge 400 pesos (just shy of $30 at this writing) per hour for one to four passengers. There's usually a three-hour minimum. For fishing close to the shore, the price can be split among up to six anglers. ☎ *315/355–5739, 315/354–2251 mobile* ✉ *hakuna kosonoy@ yahoo.com.*

★ **Fishing with Carolina.** This Canadian expat has been sending out anglers for more than 20 years. Party-boat fishing is $150; four-hour fishing expeditions on superpangas go for $250 for one to four people. You can also fish for eight hours on a 30-foot yacht ($600, up to four people); if there are eight in your party, upgrade to a 40-footer for $800. ✉ *Terminal Marítima, Marina Vallarta* ☎ *322/224–7250* ⊕ *www.fishingwithcarolina.com.*

Mismaloya Divers. Do you remember the seductive-looking divers in *Night of the Iguana?* Well, their progeny might be among the local guys of this outfit. Panga trips here go for $200 for four hours within the bay or $300 to the Marietas (five lines, all day). ✉ *Road to Mismaloya Beach, Mismaloya* ☎ *322/228–0020.*

SEASONAL CATCHES

Sailfish and dorado are abundant practically year-round. (Though dorado drop out a bit in early summer and sailfish dip slightly in spring.)

Winter: bonito, dorado, jack crevalle, sailfish, striped marlin, wahoo

Spring: amberjack, jack crevalle, grouper, mackerel, red snapper

Summer: grouper, roosterfish, yellowfin tuna

Fall: black marlin, blue marlin, sailfish, striped marlin, yellowfin tuna, wahoo

---

Reel 1 In. This operation sells rods, reels, lures, and other fishing gear and offers full-day charters (one to four passengers) for $250 to $600, depending on the size of the boat. ✉ *Hotel Alondra, Suite 17, Calle Sinaloa 16, Barra De Navidad* ☎ *No phone* ⊕ *www.reel1in.com.*

Sociedad Cooperativa Corral del Risco. The families who run this co-op were forcibly relocated from their original town of Corral del Risco due to the development of luxurious digs like the Four Seasons. The guides may not speak English as fluently as the more polished PV operators, but they know the local waters, and the fees go directly to them. Sportfishing for up to five people costs about $200 for four hours in a smaller boat or $350 for five or six hours in a superpanga. ✉ *Av. El Anclote 1, Manz. 17, Corral del Risco, Punta Mita* ☎ *329/291–6298* ⊕ *www.puntamitacharters.com.*

Vallarta Tour and Travel. Captain Peter Vines can accommodate eight fisherfolk with top-of-the-line equipment, including the latest electronics, sonar, radar, and two radios. Rates are reasonable (four hours $400, six hours $500, eight hours $600, 12 hours $800). Transportation from your hotel is included in the full-day bass-fishing expedition to Cajón de Peña. ✉ *Marina Los Palmas Local 4, in front of Dock B, Marina Vallarta* ☎ *322/294–6240, 866/682–1971 from U.S. and Canada.*

KAYAKING

Except on calm, glassy days, the open ocean is really too rough for enjoyable kayaking, and the few kayaking outfitters there are mainly offer this activity in combination with snorkeling, dolphin-watching, or

3

boating excursions to area beaches. The best places for kayaking-and-birding combos are the mangroves, estuaries, large bays, and islands of the Costalegre, south of Puerto Vallarta.

LOGISTICS

Many of the larger beachfront hotels rent or loan sea kayaks to their guests. Double kayaks are easier on the arms than single kayaks. Since the wind usually picks up in the afternoon, morning is generally the best time to paddle. Stick to coves if you want to avoid energy-draining chop and big waves. Kayaks range from $8 to $12 an hour or $23 to $35 per day. All-inclusives like Dreams, just south of Puerto Vallarta, usually don't charge their guests for kayaks.

Ecotours. Ecotours, in downtown Vallarta, has kayaking tours from Boca de Tomatlán ($70). After paddling around a rocky point you end at tiny Playa Colomitos, where there's time for snorkeling and then a snack. You'll spend 1½ to 2 hours kayaking, and, though it's fun being on the water, the scenery isn't exactly breathtaking. ⊠*Ignacio L. Vallarta 243, Col. E. Zapata* ☎*322/223–3130 or 322/222–6606* ⊕*www.ecotoursvallarta.com.*

SAILING

Although large Bahía de Banderas and towns to the north and south have lots of beautiful beaches to explore and wildlife to see, there are few sailing adventures for the public. Most boating companies don't want to rely on the wind to get to area beaches for the day's activities. The companies below are recommended for their true sailing skills and reliable vessels.

LOGISTICS

For insurance reasons, companies or individuals here don't rent bareboat (uncrewed) yachts even to seasoned sailors. Those who want to crew the ship themselves can do semi-bareboat charters, where the captain comes along but allows the clients to sail the boat.

OUTFITTERS

Casa Naval. Captain-owner Andre Schwartz has a comfortable 39-foot Beneteau Oceanis 390 called the *Symbiosis* for charters of four hours to several days. He charges $100 per hour for up to 10 passengers, with a discount of 10% for sails of four hours or more. ⊠*El Faro de la Marina, Marina Vallarta* ☎*322/100–4154 or 322/148–2203* ✉*zenigma1947@yahoo.com.*

Dos Amantes. Easygoing owners Joe and Lori Lacey will tailor a day or overnight of sailing to their clients' wishes: giving sailing tips or sailing the boat themselves, providing gourmet food, snorkeling and sunset-viewing opportunities, and most anything else. Costs are $500 to $800 for four- and eight-hour sails, respectively. ⊠*Marina Vallarta* ☎*322/140–3171 cell* ✉*dos_amantes_lacey@hotmail.com.*

Puerto Vallarta Tours. With this operator you can arrange all-day sails to Yelapa or more remote Pizota, half-day treks to Los Arcos, or private sailing charters. Prices for shared cruises range from $50 per person for a four-hour tour to Los Arcos to $77 for a full-day jaunt to Pizota. ☎322/222–4935, 866/701–3372 *from U.S. and Canada* ⊕*www.puerto vallartatours.net.*

Vallarta Adventures. Day and sunset sails during high season with these folks run about $85 per person. There are individual charters as well. ⊠*Paseo de las Palmas 39–A, Nuevo Vallarta* ☎322/297–1212, 888/303–2653 *in U.S. and Canada* ✉*Edifício Marina Golf, Local 13–C, Calle Mástil, Marina Vallarta* ☎322/221–0657 ⊕*www.vallarta-adventures.com.*

SCUBA DIVING AND SNORKELING

The Pacific waters here aren't nearly as clear as those in the Caribbean, but they are warm and nutrient-rich, which means they attract a variety of sea creatures. Many of the resorts rent or loan snorkeling equipment and have introductory dive courses at their pools.

The underwater preserve surrounding Los Arcos, a rock formation off Playa Mismaloya, is a popular spot for diving and snorkeling. The rocky bay at Quimixto, about 32 km (20 mi) south of PV and accessible only by boat, is a good snorkeling spot. *Pangeros* based in Boca, Mismaloya, Yelapa and elsewhere can take you to spots off the tourist trail.

On the north side, Punta Mita has the Marietas Islands, with lava tubes and caves and at least 10 good places to snorkel and dive, including spots for advanced divers. El Morro Islands, with their big fish lurking in the underwater pinnacles and caves, are also suitable for experienced divers.

LOGISTICS

Although it's fine all year long, June through September is the very best time for snorkeling and diving. In summer, the water is at its warmest and calmest and visibility is at its best—80 to 120 feet on a good day. You can spot gigantic manta rays, several species of eel, sea turtles, large and many species of colorful fish. In winter's less favorable conditions, some luck will yield orca and humpback whale sightings, an awesome experience.

OUTFITTERS

Chico's Dive Shop. This shop arranges PADI or NAUI certification, equipment rentals, and one- or two-tank dives. Trips to Los Arcos accommodate snorkelers ($25 per person) as well as those who want a one- or two-tank dive ($65 and $95, respectively). Book several days ahead for a night dive ($75 for one tank). From the Mismaloya shop, you can also rent kayaks ($15 per hour). ⊠*Paseo Díaz Ordáz 772, Centro* ☎322/222–1895 ✉*Mismaloya Beach, in front of Barceló La Jolla de Mismaloya, Mismaloya* ☎322/228–0248 ⊕*www. chicos-diveshop.com.*

★ **Ecotours.** This authorized equipment dealer has English-speaking PADI dive masters. Two-tank dives run $85 to $100; longer trips to Corbeteña cost $120. All two-tank trips include lunch, refreshments, and

ANNUAL SPORTING EVENTS

FEBRUARY/MARCH

The winter season brings foreign vessels and lots of racing and boating activities, beginning with the **Banderas Bay Regatta** (☎ *322/297–2222* ⊕ *www.banderas bayregatta.com*). There are cocktail parties, charity events, receptions, seminars, additional races, and boat parades. A 1,000-mi race between San Diego and Puerto Vallarta, co-hosted by the two cities' yacht clubs, begins around the third week of February and ends during March festivities. Check ⊕ *www.vallartayachtclub. com* for details.

MAY

The five-day **Annual Sports Classic** (☎ *322/226–0404 Ext. 6038, Veronica Alarcon at Sheraton Buganvilias* ⊕ *www.puertovallarta.net/news/ sports-classic-2008.php*) invites amateurs, pros, and semipros to compete in basketball, soccer, bowling, tennis,

beach volleyball, a 5K race, and an aerobics marathon. Most events take place at the Agustin Flores Contreras Stadium, Los Arcos Amphitheater, and the beach in front of the Holiday Inn.

NOVEMBER

The **Puerto Vallarta International Half Marathon** (⊕ *www.maratonval larta.com*), held in early November, gets bigger each year. There's a 5K run, too, and a big pasta dinner on the beach the day before the race.

The **International Puerto Vallarta Marlin & Sailfish Tournament** (☎ *322/225–5467* ⊕ *www. fishvallarta.com*) celebrated its 53rd anniversary in 2008. The entry fee is nearly $4,000 per boat (up to four fishermen), but the prizes and prestige of winning are great. Categories are dorado (mahimahi), tuna, marlin, and sailfish, the latter catch-and-release.

gear. ⊠*Ignacio L. Vallarta 243, Col. E. Zapata* ☎*322/223–3130 or 322/222–6606* ⊕*www.ecotoursvallarta.com.*

★ **Sociedad Cooperativa Corral del Risco.** Tours are a great deal if you have a group: two hours of snorkeling around the Marietas Islands, for up to eight people, costs just $95. ⊠*Av. El Anclote 1, Manz. 17, Corral del Risco* ☎*329/291–6298* ⊕*www.puntamitacharters.com.*

Vallarta Adventures. Vallarta Adventures accommodates nondivers (who can snorkel or kayak) as well as divers on trips that start at $95 ($105 for two tanks). It also has introductory dive classes for children and adults ($38) and open-water certification. ⊠*Paseo de las Palmas 39–A, Nuevo Vallarta* ☎*322/297–1212, 888/303–2653 in U.S. and Canada* ⊠*Edifício Marina Golf, Local 13–C, Calle Mástil, Marina Vallarta* ☎*322/221–0657* ⊕*www.vallarta-adventures.com.*

Vallarta Undersea. It's a Nayarit operation that offers PADI dive courses; runs dive trips; and sells, rents, and repairs dive equipment. It offers a couple of two-tank dives (at Majahuitas and Las Marietas) for $95; otherwise, it's $85 for a one-tank excursion to the usual dive sites. The Vallarta branch of Vallarta Undersea, which goes by the name **Pacific Scuba** (⊠*Francisco M. Ascencio 2486, Zona Hotelera* ☎*322/209–0364*

⊕*www.vallartaundersea.com*), is across the street from Peninsula Mall. ✉*Héroes de Nacozarí 152, Bucerías* ☎*329/298–2364* ⊕*www.vallarta undersea.com.*

SURFING

The main surfing areas are in the north, in Nayarit State, and include Sayulita and Punta Mita, where nearly a dozen offshore breaks for intermediate and advanced surfers are best accessed by boat. The best spots for beginners are shore breaks like those at El Anclote and Sayulita; in the south, Barra de Navidad is also appropriate for beginners.

> **WHEN TO CATCH A WAVE**
>
> Locals have lots of folk wisdom about when to catch the best waves. Some say it's best right before a good rain, others believe it's when the tide is moving toward an extreme high or low.

LOGISTICS

SEASONS Waves are largest and most consistent between June and December; the water is also warmest during the rainy season (late June–October), averaging nearly 80°F (27°C) July through September.

PRICES Surfboard rentals start at $5 an hour or $25 a day. Surfing trips run around $45 per hour, usually with a three- or four-hour minimum. Shops sell rash guards (you usually don't need a full wet suit here), boogie boards, wax, and other necessities. For good info and links check out ⊕*www.surf-mexico.com.*

OUTFITTERS

Captain Pablo. At this outfitter on the beach at Sayulita you can rent equipment or take surfing lessons with Patricia: $30 should get you to your feet (board included). Surf tours, gear included, cost $180 for four hours (up to four surfers). ✉*Calle Las Gaviotas at beach, Sayulita* ☎*329/291–2070 early morning and evenings only* ✐*pandpsouthworth@hotmail.com.*

Sininen. Sininen, on the beach at Sayulita, rents ($15 per day, $23 for 24 hours) and sells surfboards and surf paraphernalia. ✉*Calle Delfín 4–S, Sayulita* ☎*329/291–3186.*

WILDLIFE-WATCHING

Banderas Bay and the contiguous coast and inland areas are blessed with abundant species of birds and beasties. Diverse habitats from riparian forests to offshore islands are home to a wide range of native and migratory birds, including about two dozen endemic species. Beyond birds, most of the wildlife spotting is marine: whales (late November through end of March), dolphins, marine turtles, and giant manta rays, among many other species.

BIRD-WATCHING

Although there aren't many dedicated birding operators here, this region is perfect for the pastime. Vallarta has more than 350 species in a wide variety of habitats, including shoreline, rivers, marshes, lagoons, mangroves, and tropical and evergreen forests. In the mangroves, standouts are the great blue heron, mangrove cuckoo, and vireo. Ocean and shorebirds include brown and blue-footed boobies and red-billed tropic birds. Military macaws patrol the thorn forests, and songbirds of all stripes serenade the pine-oak forests.

LOGISTICS

Most people come on trips through birding clubs or organizations or hire a private birding guide. Outfitters charge $45–$60 for half-day tours and $100–$125 for full-day tours.

Ecotours. Ecotours runs three six-hour tours ($80 per person each) to different ecosystems, plus an overnight excursion to San Blas ($350). Bring plenty of insect repellent, especially in the rainy months. ⊠ *Ignacio L. Vallarta 243, Col. E. Zapata* ☎ *322/223–3130 or 322/222–6606* ⊕ *www.ecotoursvallarta.com.*

Victor Emanuel Nature Tours. This renowned operator leads several yearly small-group birding tours from Rancho Primavera, just south of PV proper. ☎ *512/328–5221, 800/328–8368 in U.S. and Canada* ⊕ *www.ventbird.com.*

Wings. It's a Tucson, Arizona–based operator that leads several week-long tours each year to the mangroves and tropical forest around San Blas, Jalisco, and Colima. ☎ *520/320–9868, 888/293–6443 in U.S. and Canada* ⊕ *www.wingsbirds.com.*

DOLPHIN ENCOUNTERS

Many folks find the idea of captive dolphins disturbing; others cherish the opportunity to interact with these intelligent creatures that communicate through body language as well as an audible code we humans have yet to decipher. Decide whether you support the idea of captive-dolphin encounters, and act accordingly. Listed below are operators with captive dolphin programs as well as one that has an open-ocean encounter. As these gregarious mammals are fond of bow-surfing, most bay-tripping boats will encounter dolphins as they motor along, providing more opportunities to see dolphins as well as leaping manta rays and other sea life.

LOGISTICS

Dolphins are abundant in the bay year-round, though not 24/7. Dolphin encounters limit the number of humans per encounter and usually allow just two visits a day. Call before you arrive or early in your stay to book.

OUTFITTERS

★ **Dolphin Discovery.** For both the Dolphin Encounter ($69) and the Dolphin Swim ($99) at Dolphin Discovery in the Sea Life Park you spend about 30 of the 45-minute experience in the water interacting with dolphins. In the Royal Dolphin Swim ($149), you still get only 30 minutes in the pool, but, with a higher ratio of cetaceans to humans, you get more face time. ⊠ *Sea Life Park, Carretera a Tepic, Km 155, Nuevo Vallarta* ☎ *322/297–0724, 866/393–5158 toll-free in U.S., 866/793–1905 toll-free in Canada* ⊕ *www.sealifeparkvallarta.com.*

☪ **Sea Life Park.** Traditionally more popular with Mexican families than foreigners, this water park has added dolphin encounters and sea lion shows to attract a wider audience. Kids love the place, regardless. They can plummet down one of 10 enormous waterslides, play on playground equipment, and indulge in junk food at the obligatory snack shops. ⊠ *Carretera a Tepic, Km 155, Nuevo Vallarta* ☎ *322/297–0724* 🖃 *$18* ☉ *Daily 10–6.*

Wildlife Connection. This Mexican-owned company uses two-motor skiffs equipped with listening equipment to find pods of dolphins in the wild blue sea. You can then jump in the water to swim with these beautiful creatures in their own environment. The most common destination is around the Marietas Islands. The cost is $65 per person for a three- to four-hour tour, including travel time; tours are conducted April through December only. There's no guarantee, however, that the dolphins will stick around for the fun. There's also a combined tour searching for whales and dolphins, $80 a pop, December through March only. ⊠ *Calle Francia 140, Dpto. 7, Col. Versalles, Puerto Vallarta* ☎ *322/225–3621* ⊕ *www.wildlifeconnection.com.*

> **CAUTION**
>
> Several organizations, including Greenpeace, the Humane Society (U.S.), and the Whale and Dolphin Conservation Society have spoken out against captive dolphin encounters, asserting that some water parks get dolphins from restricted areas and that the confined conditions at some parks put the dolphins' health at risk. Consider putting the $100-plus fee toward a snorkeling, whale-watching, or noncaptive dolphin encounter, where you can see marine life in its natural state.

HIKING

The coastal fringe and the hills behind Vallarta—with streams and rivers heading down from the mountains—are beautiful areas for exploring, but few tour operators have hiking and walking trips. If you plan an impromptu exploration, it's best to take along a local familiar with the area.

LOGISTICS

Some of the biking tour operators (⇨ *Mountain Biking, above*) will lead hiking outings as well, if you ask.

OUTFITTERS

Ecotours. Its three-hour hike around El Nogalito River ($60) includes a pit stop at a rocky, waterfall-fed pool for a dip. En route to either you'll see a small number of birds, butterflies, and tropical plants. ✉*Ignacio L. Vallarta 243, Col. E. Zapata* ☎*322/223–3130 or 322/222–6606* ⊕*www.ecotoursvallarta.com.*

Vallarta Adventures. The outdoor adventure tour ($98) combines a speedboat ride and mule trek with rappelling, hiking, and a partial canopy tour. Although hikes are generally led by knowledgeable naturalists, the emphasis is on physical activity rather than flora and fauna sightings. Participants must be 10 or over and 250 pounds or under. ✉*Paseo de las Palmas 39–A, Nuevo Vallarta* ☎*322/297–1212, 888/303–2653 in U.S. and Canada* ✉*Edifício Marina Golf, Local 13–C, Calle Mástil, Marina Vallarta* ☎*322/221–0657* ⊕*www.vallarta-adventures.com.*

3

TURTLE-WATCHING AND REPATRIATION

Mexico has seven of the world's eight sea turtle species. Three of those species live in and around Banderas Bay. The fastest growing and earliest to mature of the Pacific Coast turtles is the olive ridley, or *golfina*, which are more numerous than the Careyes and the even less frequently sighted leatherback. Researchers estimate there are one to 10 leatherbacks for every 1,000 olive ridleys in the Puerto Vallarta area.

After the female turtle creates a nest in the sand, the eggs incubate for approximately 60 days. The babies must bust out of eggs and earth on their own, and with luck they will head for the ocean under cover of night. Birds, crabs, and other wild animals are relentless predators. For every 1,000 baby turtles born, only one survives to adulthood. Fortunately the average nest holds several hundred eggs.

LOGISTICS

Tours run from summer through late fall. Wear shoes or sandals that are comfortable for walking in the sand. Bring a sweatshirt or light jacket, and plan to stay out late in the evening for most turtle repatriation programs, as that's when predators are less active. Most tours cost $46–$50 per person, last three to four hours, and combine educational programs with hands-on activities.

OUTFITTERS

Ecotours. Three-hour turtle tours August through mid-December cost $48. Depending on the time of year, you may walk the beach searching for females depositing their eggs in the sand and help remove these eggs for safekeeping. Whether or not you find egg-laying females, there are always little turtles for releasing to the wild at the end of the evening. Tours are Monday through Saturday. ✉*Ignacio L. Vallarta 243, Col. E. Zapata* ☎*322/223–3130 or 322/222–6606* ⊕*www.ecotoursvallarta.com.*

Wildlife Connection. Trained biologists lead turtle repatriation programs. During the four-hour tours you'll drive ATVs to the beach to find and collect recently deposited eggs, if possible, and then blast over to Boca de Tomates Beach to liberate tiny turtles under the relative protection of darkness. ✉*Calle Francia 140, Col. Versalles, Puerto Vallarta* ☎*322/ 225–3621* ⊕*www.wildlifeconnection.com.*

WHALE-WATCHING

Most of the boats on the bay, whether fishing boats or tour boats, also run whale-watching tours (December–mid-March). Some boats are equipped with hydrophones for listening to the whales' songs and carry trained marine biologists; others use the usual crew and simply look for signs of cetaceans. The species you're most likely to see are humpback and killer whales (a gray whale occasionally); false killer whales; and bottlenose, spinner, and pantropic spotted dolphins (yup, dolphins are whales, too!).

LOGISTICS

Whale-watching is only available December through March. Prime breeding grounds are around the Marietas Islands. The larger boats leave from Marina Vallarta, but you can hire fishermen in villages like Corral del Risco, Mismaloya, Boca de Tomatlán, Yelapa, Las Animas, Barra de Navidad, and Tenacatita for less formal, more intimate trips. The larger boats are more likely to have radio equipment useful for communicating with others about the location of whale pods. Some outfitters offer a discount if you sign up online.

OUTFITTERS

Ecotours. After a brief lecture about cetacean ecosystems, you'll board a boat equipped with hydrophones at Punta Mita for a three-hour tour. Tours are daily in season (mid-December–mid-March) and cost $75. ✉*Ignacio L. Vallarta 243, Col. E. Zapata* ☎*322/223–3130 or 322/222–6606* ⊕*www.ecotoursvallarta.com.*

Sociedad Cooperativa Corral del Risco. Two hours of whale-watching or snorkeling around the Marietas Islands, for up to 10 people, costs $114. Anyone older than six but younger than 60 also pays $2 for a wristband allowing entrance to the Marietas, a national aquatic park. You search until whales are spotted, and then have a half-hour of viewing time before returning to dry land. ✉*Av. El Anclote 1, Manz. 17, Nuevo Corral del Risco* ☎*329/291–6298* ⊕*www.puntamitacharters.com.*

Vallarta Adventures. Professional guides assist you in spotting dolphins and whales on several different types of cruises to sites on and around Banderas Bay. Sailing trips for seeking cetaceans are also an option ($89). ✉*Paseo de las Palmas 39–A, Nuevo Vallarta* ☎*322/297–1212, 888/303–2653 in U.S. and Canada* ✉*Edifício Marina Golf, Local 13–C, Calle Mástil, Marina Vallarta* ☎*322/221–0657* ⊕*www.vallarta-adventures.com.*

Wildlife Connection. The company gives whale-watching tours in season for $74. Its professional biologists are dedicated to educating the public about area wildlife. ✉*Calle Francia 140, Col. Versalles, Puerto Vallarta* ☎*322/225–3621* ⊕*www.wildlifeconnection.com.*

Where to Stay

Massage pavilion at El Tamarindo Golf Resort

WORD OF MOUTH

"Between Nuevo and PV, I'd pick PV. Nuevo is a new strip of tourist hotels; PV retains small city charm . . . 20 minutes doesn't sound like much of a drive, but you'll tire of it if you stay in Nuevo."

—Bill_H

"It's true that Nuevo isn't close to PV . . . . but [it] is closer to Bucerias, Sayulita, and San Blas. To see smaller towns, Nuevo is good! And the beaches are better."

—dar

WHERE TO STAY PLANNER

The Hotel Scene

Puerto Vallarta and its environs has a hotel for every budget and personality, from cliff-side condos with stairs winding down to the sea to classy little cottages surrounded by nature trails. There are *gran turismo* (beyond five-star) hotels and resorts up and down the coast; think beachside villa with a private plunge pool.

Some of those on the prettiest beaches are in Punta Mita (aka Punta de Mita) and the Costalegre, but you can find them also in the south hotel zone and Nuevo Vallarta, which has mainly all-inclusive hotels. Southern Nayarit State, north of PV, has a sprinkling of small hotels, guesthouses, private rentals, and bed-and-breakfasts, many of them popular with honeymooners, families, and anyone looking for more intimate digs away from large crowds.

⚠ **Overbooking is a common practice. To protect yourself, get a confirmation in writing, via fax or e-mail.**

Choosing a Hotel

If you want to walk everywhere, **Old Vallarta** (downtown, which includes Centro and the Romantic Zone) is the place to be. Centro's hilly streets provide excellent views and aerobic workouts. South of the Cuale River, the Romantic Zone has even more shops, restaurants, and Los Muertos Beach—and no hills. Most hotels here are inexpensive to moderate.

South of town, the **Zona Hotelera Sur** has many condos as well as luxury and a few moderately priced hotels—most with dramatic ocean views. Downtown is a short cab or bus ride away. The beaches and views aren't as appealing in the **Zona Hotelera Norte.** The long stretch of midrange and higher-end chains is interspersed with malls and mega-grocery stores. **Marina Vallarta,** with its luxury hotels, is close to golf courses and is a good place for biking and strolling.

Nuevo Vallarta is a planned resort on a long, sandy beach about 19 km (12 mi) north of downtown PV—about 40 minutes by car or bus when traffic complicates things. This is a good place to stay if you're content to stay put and enjoy your all-inclusive, high-rise hotel. Of interest also to Nuevo Vallarta's guests is Bucerías, as well as the towns of **southern Nayarit** (north of PV), which are offering more services in an attempt to live up to their new moniker, the Riviera Nayarit (between San Blas and Nuevo Vallarta). Several hours south of Vallarta, the **Costalegre** is a place of extremes. High-price hotels on gorgeous beaches attract celebs and honeymooners, while small towns like Barra de Navidad have modest digs and a more authentically Mexican experience—and nice beaches, too.

GRAN TURISMO

The government categorizes hotels as *gran turismo* (five-star-plus), of which only about 30 are chosen nationwide each year in addition to those five star to one star. Note that hotels might lose out on a higher rating only because they lack an amenity like air-conditioning (which isn't always needed if there are good breezes).

Apartments and Villas

When shared by two couples, a spacious villa can save you a bundle on upscale lodging and on meals. Villas often come with stereo systems, DVD players, a pool, maid service, and a/c. Prices range from $100 to $1,000 per night, with 20% discounts off-season.

At Home Abroad ☎212/421–9165 in U.S. ⊕www.athomeabroadinc.com. **Cochran Real Estate** ☎322/228–0419 in PV ⊕www.buyeragentmexico.com. **Hideaways International** ☎603/430–4433, 800/843–4433 in U.S. ⊕www.hideaways.com. **Pacific Mexico Real Estate** ☎329/298–1644 in Bucerías ⊕www.pacific mexicorealestate.com. **Villas and Apartments Abroad** ☎212/213–6435, 800/433–3020 in U.S. ⊕www.vaanyc.com. **Villas International** ☎415/499–9490, 800/221–2260 in U.S. ⊕www.villasintl.com.

Boutique Hotels

México Boutique Hotels (☎322/221–2277 or 01800/508–7923 in Mexico, 800/728–9098 in the U.S. or Canada ⊕www.mexicoboutiquehotels.com) is a private company that represents 45 intimate and unique properties—most with fewer than 50 rooms—selected for their setting, cuisine, service, and overall allure. Each is inspected annually.

Chain Hotels

Tried-and-true chains may have excellent rates, and can be good last-minute options. **Holiday Inn** ☎800/465–4329 in U.S. ⊕www.holiday-inn.com. **Inter-Continental** ☎888/424–6835 in U.S. ⊕www.ichotelsgroup.com. **Marriott** ☎888/236–2427 ⊕www.marriott.com. **Sheraton** ☎800/325–3535 in U.S. ⊕www.starwood.com/sheraton. **Westin** ☎800/937–8461 ⊕www.starwoodhotels.com/westin.

WHAT IT COSTS IN U.S. DOLLARS

¢	$	$$	$$$	$$$$
Hotels				
under $50	$50–$75	$75–$150	$150–$250	over $250

For a standard room, generally excluding taxes and service charges.

Meal Plans

AI: All-Inclusive; including all meals, drinks, and most activities. **BP:** Breakfast Plan; full breakfast. **CP:** Continental Plan; continental breakfast. **EP:** European Plan; without meals. **FAP:** Full American Plan; breakfast, lunch, and dinner. **MAP:** Modified American Plan; breakfast and dinner.

Pricing

We give high-season prices before meals or other amenities. Low-season rates usually drop 20%–30%. We always list the available facilities, but we don't specify whether they cost extra.

Less expensive hotels include tax in the quote. Most higher-priced resorts add 17% tax on top of the quoted rate; some add a 5%–10% service charge. Moderately priced hotels swing both ways. Tax and/or tips are often included with all-inclusive plans, making a $$$$ property affordable. You might be charged extra for paying with a credit card. Also note that some hotels accept credit-card payments only through PayPal.

An all-inclusive (AI) might make you reluctant to spend money elsewhere. So you don't miss out on area restaurants and activities, stay at more modest digs for part of your trip, and go AI for a day or two. Many AI hotels have day passes ($50–$75).

Finding a hotel isn't hard in PV, but choosing one is. The selection includes everything from cliff-side condos with stairs winding down to the sea to classy little cottages surrounded by nature trails. And the high-rise resorts work hard to make up in amenities and services what they lack in personality.

Lodgings are a personal choice. Some travelers want little more than a clean pillow and comfortable bed where they can rest after a long day exploring; others consider the resort hotel itself a destination. The latter look for enormous pools overlooking the ocean or multiple pools—one where kids can shriek and play, another for adults to lie quietly in the sun, and yet another for aqua aerobics or a boisterous volleyball game. Swim-up bars are popular, as are multiple bars with different personalities, from palapas on the sand to chic, sleek lobby bars with evening entertainment. Luckily, Puerto Vallarta and the beaches up and down the coast offer all of the above.

Players with cash to spend go for gran turismo (beyond five-star in Mexico's rating system): primarily coastal hotels and resorts; think beachside villas with private plunge pools and ubiquitous waiters. Some of those on the prettiest beaches are in Punta Mita and the Costalegre, but you'll find them closer to PV's center, in the Zonas Hoteleras (Hotel Zones) south and north, in Marina Vallarta, and in Nuevo Vallarta.

Now going by the moniker Riviera Nayarit, southern Nayarit State, just north of PV, has a sprinkling of small hotels, guesthouses, private rentals, and bed-and-breakfasts—many of them popular with honeymooners, families, and anyone looking for more intimate digs. Larger international chains are currently being built on Nayarit beaches as the state endeavors to cash in on PV's enormous international appeal.

Unfortunately, the region's offerings are a bit segregated. In PV, Centro and the Zona Romántica have mainly budget and moderately priced digs (with the exception of the luxurious Hacienda San Angel, overlooking but not on the beach). Just north of downtown proper are moderate to barely expensive hotels like the Buenaventura; continue north into the Zona Hotelera for condos, time-shares and high-rises like the Fiesta Americana and the Sheraton. Marina Vallarta has almost exclusively pricey, five-star resorts, while Nuevo Vallarta is the land of all-inclusives. The beaches north and south of PV and Banderas Bay are where you'll find unique B&Bs, small hotels, and some truly luxurious villas and boutique hotels.

PUERTO VALLARTA

ZONA ROMÁNTICA

¢ **Ana Liz.** Those who prefer to spend their vacation cash on eating out and shopping might consider this clean, bright, motel-like budget hotel a few blocks south of the Cuale River, behind Cine Bahía. Two floors of rooms face each other across an outdoor corridor and have tiny bathrooms but comfortable beds. Ask for a room away from the noisy street; don't ask to use the lobby phone—it's not allowed. Small-time businesspeople and backpacking Europeans stay at this extremely plain place when they come to town; they're likely drawn by the substantial discounts for monthly stays. **Pros:** best bargain in town for dedicated budget travelers; walking distance to beach, PV eateries, and mini-grocery stores; near Internet cafés and taco stands. **Cons:** zero frills, no TV. ✉ *Francisco I. Madero 429, Col. E. Zapata* ☎ *322/222–1757* 🛏 *23 rooms* ⚐ *In-room: no a/c (some), no phone* 🗖 *No credit cards* ⟊ *EP.*

$$ **Blue Chairs.** Gay guys stay here not for the rooms (they're plain) but for all that Blue Chairs offers. Horseback riding, drag and strip shows, theme nights, events, parties, booze cruises, and beach cruising all begin—and often end—right here. **Pros:** the place to enjoy nonstop evening activities, right on the gay beach, concierge service, significant low-season and online discounts. **Cons:** unexciting rooms, lackadaisical service by beachside waiters. ✉ *Almendro 4 at malecón, Los Muertos Beach, Col. E. Zapata* ☎ *322/222–5040, 888/302-3662 in U.S., 866/403-8497 in Canada* ⊕ *hotelbluechairs.com* 🛏 *24 rooms, 16 suites* ⚐ *In-room: kitchen (some). In-hotel: 2 restaurants, bars, pool* 🗖 *AE, D, DC, MC, V* ⟊ *EP.*

$$ **Casa Andrea.** One- and two-bedroom apartments in this spiffy property are truly homey. Each has a different floor plan—some have larger kitchens, but all of them are fully equipped. All also have air-conditioning, ceiling fans, and dark-wood beams that contrast with white ceilings and walls. Use the hotel's computers to check your e-mail, or curl up with a book or watch a video in the library. Coffee and pastries are served each morning on the garden patio, where guests (many of them return visitors) sit and chat. The location, a few blocks from Los Arcos and the malecón, is a real plus. With some exceptions, high-season bookings are by the week. Expect some homely but sweet rescued dogs to be wandering about. **Pros:** free Wi-Fi, great location in Zona Romántica, homey feel, good value. **Cons:** often fully booked, no credit cards accepted. ✉ *Calle Francisca Rodríguez 174, Col. E. Zapata* ☎ *322/222–1213* ⊕ *www.casa-andrea.com* 🛏 *11 apartments* ⚐ *In-room: no phone, kitchen, no TV, Wi-Fi. In-hotel: bar, pool, gym, laundry facilities, Internet terminal* 🗖 *No credit cards* ⟊ *CP.*

$ **Eloísa.** A block from the beach and overlooking Lázaro Cárdenas Park, this hotel has more of a downtown feel rather than a beachy one. Rooms are plain but clean, and there's a great city-and-mountain view from the rooftop, which has a pool and party area. Studios have small kitchenettes in one corner; suites have larger kitchens, separate bedrooms, and two quiet air-conditioners. Units with great views (Nos.

511–514) cost the same as those without, so ask for one *con vista panorámica* (with a panoramic view). **Pros:** snug studios overlook park, large pool on roof. **Cons:** no parking, mainly older a/c units. ⊠ *Lázaro Cárdenas 179, Col. E. Zapata* ☎ *322/222–6465 or 322/222–0286* ⊕ *www.hoteleloisa.com* ⟿ *60 rooms, 6 studios, 8 suites* ☖ *In-room: no phone, kitchen (some), refrigerator (some). In-hotel: restaurant, bar, pools* ▭ *MC, V* ❑ *EP.*

$–$$ 🏨 **Gaviota Vallarta.** Simple rooms in this six-story low-rise have somewhat battered colonial-style furnishings; some have tiny balconies but only a few on the top floors have a partial ocean view. The small figure-8 pool in the middle of the courtyard is exposed, but still refreshes. Choose air-conditioning and cable TV or fan only, without the *tele*, to save about $25 per night. The two-bedroom apartments are poorly designed and have stiff Mexican furnishings. For the same price you can get two standard rooms, although without the kitchen facilities. **Pros:** moderately priced rooms a block from the beach, choice of a/c or no, 20% cash discount. **Cons:** poor pool placement, unattractive furnishings, no Internet, very small parking lot. ⊠ *Francisco I. Madero 176, Col. E. Zapata* ☎ *322/222–1500* ⊕ *www.hotelgaviota.com* ⟿ *84 rooms* ☖ *In-room: no a/c (some), no phone, kitchen (some), refrigerator (some). In-hotel: restaurant, bar, pool, parking (paid)* ▭ *MC, V* ❑ *EP.*

$$ 🏨 **Hacienda Alemana.** A stay here means free champagne every day! And it isn't just the bubbly that's replenished daily in your room's pint-sized fridge, it's also the bottled water. Rooms have king-size beds, 32-inch TVs, and double-pane windows to keep out noise. The decor and furnishings are original, modern, and warm—poured-cement floors, fine wood furniture, marble sink surrounds. Regular rooms are spacious; even more spacious are the three-room suites, which are also a steal in low season and well-priced year-round. On the large patio is a biergarten and the hotel's restaurant, Café Frankfurt, which is well worth a meal or two (or three). Although this is a comfortable, classy hotel, it's better suited to self-sufficient guests as there's no front-desk staff. **Pros:** good on-site restaurant, gym, sauna and steam room, massage, DVDs and iPod stations upon request, great for couples. **Cons:** no real reception staff, so no one around after restaurant closes, possible noise from biergarten, age restrictions make it a bad choice for families. ⊠ *Calle Basilio Badillo 378, Col. E. Zapata* ☎ *322/222–2071* ⊕ *www.haciendaalemana. com* ⟿ *10 rooms* ☖ *In room: safe, kitchen (some), refrigerator, Wi-Fi. In hotel: restaurant, gym, no kids under 16* ▭ *MC, V* ❑ *BP.*

Fodor's Choice
★

$$ 🏨 **Playa Los Arcos.** This hotel is attractive because of its location: right on the beach and in the midst of Zona Romántica's restaurants, bars, and shops. Though the price is right, some longtime visitors feel both service and quality have slipped in recent years: Still, yellow trumpet vines and lacy palms draped in tiny white lights enliven the pool and the bar-restaurant, which has music nightly and a Mexican fiesta on Saturday evening. Some rooms are larger than others and have a balcony with plastic lounge chairs; balcony rooms are the same price as those without, so ask for a balcony when booking. If you're willing to cross the street, you can get an even better deal at Casa Dona Susana, whose cheaper rooms have efficient mini air-conditioners and small

Where to Stay in Zona Romántica

Ana Liz 10
Blue Chairs 1
Casa Andrea 3
Eloísa 8
Gaviota Vallarta 9

Hacienda Alemana 7
Playa Los Arcos 4
Posada de Roger 6
Tropicana 2
Yasmín 5

TVs. There's also a rooftop pool. **Pros:** great Zona Romántica location, nightly entertainment with theme-cuisine buffet. **Cons:** small bathrooms, some rooms have tired furnishings, tour group noise in high season, there are only a few of the cheaper rooms. ✉ *Av. Olas Altas 380, Col. E. Zapata* ☎ *322/222–0583, 800/648–2403 in U.S., 888/729–9590 in Canada, 01800/327–7700 toll-free in Mexico* 🌐 *www.playalosarcos.com* *158 rooms, 13 suites* *In-room: safe (some), kitchen (some). In-hotel: restaurant, bar, pool, beachfront, parking (free), no-smoking rooms* 💳 *MC, V* *AI, EP.*

MONEY CAN'T BUY HAPPINESS

Not all Los Arcos's guests are budget travelers: some better-heeled guests stay here for the easygoing ambience and the location on the beach near Zona Romántica restaurants, bars, and shops.

$ **Posada de Roger.** If you hang around the pool or the small shared balcony overlooking the street and the bay beyond, it's not hard to get to know the other guests—many of them savvy budget travelers from Europe and Canada. A shared, open-air kitchen on the fourth floor has a great view, too. Rooms are spare and vaultlike—some are downright dark. Freddy's Tucan, indoor-outdoor bar-restaurant (no dinner; $) is popular with locals—mainly for breakfast. The hotel is in a part of the Zona Romántica known for its restaurants and shops; Playa los Muertos is a few blocks away. **Pros:** great location, tinkling fountain and quiet courtyard, good bar-restaurant. **Cons:** no in-room safes, cramped rooms, get-what-you-pay-for beds. ✉ *Calle Basilio Badillo 237, Col. E. Zapata* ☎ *322/222–0836 or 322/222–0639* 🌐 *www.hotelposadaderoger.com* *47 rooms* *In-hotel: restaurant, bar, pool* 💳 *AE, MC, V* *EP.*

$$ **Tropicana.** This is a reasonably priced, well-landscaped, bright white hotel at the south end of Playa Los Muertos. Superior rooms don't cost much more than standards, and although they have more or less the same amenities, they're in a newer wing and most have better views. Suites have no separate living area but are larger than other rooms and have several different areas for sitting or playing cards, as well as a four-burner stove, blender, and fridge. The most economical rooms come without a/c, TV, or a beach view. **Pros:** great beach access, great Zona Romántica location, nice pool and landscaping. **Cons:** no bathtubs, no Internet access, wristbands required for all guests, elevator, furnishings, and paint need upgrading. ✉ *Calle Amapas 214, Col. E. Zapata* ☎ *322/226–9696* *148 rooms, 12 suites* *In room: no a/c (some), no TV (some). In-hotel: restaurant, bar, pool, beachfront, parking (free)* 💳 *MC, V* *EP.*

¢ **Yasmín.** Two-story and L-shape, this budget baby has no pool, but it's just a block from the beach and joined at the hip to Café de Olla (⇨ *Chapter 5*), the extremely popular Mexican restaurant. Small, ho-hum rooms have low ceilings, firm beds, and open closets but also floor fans and cable TV: not a bad deal for the price. About six bucks more buys you a/c. **Pros:** very inexpensive, close to Zona Romántica action, pleasant courtyard garden with café, tables, and chaise lounges. **Cons:**

dark rooms, low ceilings, no pool. ⌧*Calle Basilio Badillo, Col. E. Zapata* ☎*322/222–0087* ⤶*27 rooms* ♿*In-room: no a/c (some), no phone* ⊟*No credit cards* ⫯⦿*EP.*

CENTRO AND ENVIRONS

$$ **Buenaventura Grand Hotel & Spa.** The location on downtown's north-
�‍ ern edge is just a few blocks from the malecón, shops, hotels, and res-
taurants. The beach has gentle waves, but with brown sand and rocks,
it's not the prettiest and attracts few bathers. There's a lively pool scene;
the adults-only area facing the sea is a big part of the draw. Rooms are
cheerful, with wood furniture, bright white linens, and tastefully sub-
dued accent colors. Ocean-facing balconies are tiny, and if you sit, you
can't see a thing. Still, the sum of the whole makes up for any deficien-
cies, and the all-inclusive rate is a good deal, especially for families.
Pros: great place to socialize, concierge service, five-minute walk to the
malecón and downtown. **Cons:** balconies are small, no parking. ⌧*Av.
México 1301, Col. 5 de Diciembre* ☎*322/226–7000, 888/859–9439
in U.S. and Canada* ⊕*www.hotelbuenaventura.com.mx* ⤶*216 rooms,
18 suites* ♿*In-room: Wi-Fi. In hotel: 3 restaurants, room service, bars,
pools, spa, beachfront, laundry service, Internet terminal, Wi-Fi* ⊟*AE,
MC, V* ⫯⦿*AI, EP.*

$–$$ **Casa Dulce Vida.** Hidden four blocks off the busy malecón, this
★ '60s-era villa has apartments of various sizes filled with modern Mexi-
can art and comfortable, if well-worn, furniture. All apartments have
well-equipped kitchens—again, we're not talking sparkly here (some
fridges have rusty faces), but everything works. A few rooms have
ocean-view terraces; the largest has three bedrooms, two baths, and a
separate dining room. There's a red-tile pool and tropical gardens. In
high season the property only accepts weeklong bookings. **Pros:** home-
away-from-home feel, great value, lush landscaping and ocean breezes,
friendly staff helps book tours. **Cons:** booked for weeks and months at
a time in high season, some rooms better than others. ⌧*Calle Aldama
295, El Centro* ☎*322/222–1008* ⊕*www.dulcevida.com* ⤶*6 suites*
♿*In-room: no a/c (some), no phone (some), safe (some), kitchen, refrigerator, no TV, Wi-Fi (some). In-hotel: pool, Wi-Fi* ⊟*V* ⫯⦿*EP.*

$ **El Pescador.** Fall asleep to the sound of the waves at this modest yet
cheerful hotel that's a favorite among Mexican travelers. Balconies are
narrow but provide a view of the pool area and beach. The latter has
sand but also fist-size rocks in the tidal zone during some times of
year; the curvy, medium-size pool is a nice alternative. Bright white
and inexpensive, El Pescador is about five blocks north of the malecón
(and a sister property, Hotel Rosita). **Pros:** near malecón and downtown
action, small parking garage. **Cons:** summer storms deliver rocks on
the narrow, brown-sand beach, no ceiling fans. ⌧*Calle Paraguay 1117
at Uruguay, Col. 5 de Diciembre* ☎*322/222–1884, 888/242–9587 in
Canada, 877/813–6712 in U.S.* ⊕*www.hotelpescador.com* ⤶*103
rooms* ♿ *In-room: no a/c (some). In-hotel: restaurant, bar, pool, laundry service, Internet terminal, Wi-Fi* ⊟*MC, V* ⫯⦿*EP.*

4

HOTELS AT A GLANCE: PUERTO VALLARTA AND NAYARIT

Hotel	Worth Noting	Cost	Rooms	Restaurants	On the Beach	Dive Shop	Pools	Spa	Golf Course	Tennis Courts	Health Club/Gym	Children's Program	Location
Puerto Vallarta													
Ana Liz	bare-bones; great location	$27	23										Col. E. Zapata
Barceló	all suites; lots to do	$369	217	5	yes	yes	4	yes		1	yes	4–9	Mismaloya
Blue Chairs	gay friendly	$110	24	2	yes		1						Col. E. Zapata
Buenaventura	ideal location	$115	234	3	yes		2	yes					Col. 5 de Diciembre
Casa Andrea	homey apartments	$720/week	11	1			1				yes		Col. E. Zapata
Casa Cupola	gay friendly	$139–$225	14				1				yes		Col. Amapas
Casa Dulce Vida	spacious apartments	$70–$130	6				1						Centro
Casa Iguana All Suites	all suites; full kitchens	$81	52	2			1				yes		Mismaloya
CasaMagna Marriott	something for everyone	$229	433	4	yes		2	yes		2	yes	4–12	Marina Vallarta
Dreams	elaborate theme nights	$446	337	5	yes		3	yes			yes	4–17*	Zona Hotelera Sur*
Eloísa	request a free view	$67	74	1			2						Col. E. Zapata
El Pescador	modest Mexican favorite	$57	103	1			1						Col. 5 de Diciembre
Fiesta Americana	amazing palapa	$270	291	3	yes		1	yes			yes	4–12	Zona Hotelera Norte
Gaviota Vallarta	a block from the beach	$59–$86	84	1			1						Col. E. Zapata
Hacienda Alemana	great for couples	$136	10	1									Col. E. Zapata
Hacienda San Angel	only $$$$ downtown; elegant	$320–$620	21	1			3						Col. El Cerro
Los Cuatro Vientos	old PV spirit; good restaurant	$69	14	1			1						Centro
Majahuitas	romantic, isolated casitas	$375	8	1	yes								Cabo Corrientes Norte
Playa Conchas Chinas	great beach	$110	23	1	yes		1						Conchas Chinas
Playa Los Arcos	fab city-beach location	$115	171	1	yes		1						Col. E. Zapata
Posada de Roger	downtown; varied crowd	$65	47	1			1				yes		Col. E. Zapata
Presidente InterContinental	secluded cove	$138	120	3	yes	yes	1	yes		1	yes		Mismaloya

Quinta María Cortez	pretty beach; lots of soul	$140–$250	10		yes	1				1		Conchas Chinas
Río	24-hour computer room	$60	47	1	yes	1				1		Centro
Rosita	north end of Malecón	$87–$99	115	3	yes	1				1		Col. 5 de Diciembre
Sheraton Buganvilias	large but reliable	$155	600	6	yes	2	yes		2	yes	4–12	Zona Hotelera Norte
Sol Meliá Puerto Vallarta	great for younger kids	$265	221	1	yes	1	yes		2	yes	inf–13	Marina Vallarta
Tropicana	modest beachfront digs	$80	160	1	yes	1						Col. E. Zapata
Velas Vallarta	all suites; lots of comforts	$390	339	2	yes	2	yes		3	yes	6–12	Marina Vallarta
Westin Resort & Spa	great architecture	$85	280	2	yes	3	yes		3	yes	inf–12	Marina Vallarta
Yasmín	budget rooms w/cable	$48	27		yes	1						Col. E. Zapata
Nayarit												
Casa de Mita	excellent eats included	$485	8	1	yes	1	yes		1			Punta Mita
Casa Obelisco	great breakfasts	$225	4	1		1			1			San Francisco
Costa Azul	lots of sports and activities	$96	27	1	yes	1			1			Fracc. Costa Azul
Four Seasons Resort	excellent spa, golf	$595	168	3	yes	36	yes	yes	4	yes	5–12	Punta Mita
Grand Velas	sleek majesty	$798	269	4	yes	4	yes		1	yes	4–12	Nuevo Vallarta
Hotel Carmelitas	pretty and new	$45	10	1	yes	1			1			Bucerías
Marco's Place	basic but comfortable	$52	18	1					1			Bucerías
Marival	lots to do; all-inclusive	$220	495	6	yes	4	yes		4	yes	4–17	Nuevo Vallarta
Palmeras	large pool; block from beach	$65	21	1					1			Bucerías
Paradise Village	great for families	$145	490	4	yes	2	yes	yes	7	yes	4–11	Nuevo Vallarta
Royal Decameron	bargain, all inclusive	$136	620	7	yes	5			3			Bucerías
Villa Amor	terrific views	$110	34	1	yes	1			1			Sayulita
Villa Bella	tranquil, intimate	$180	5	1		1			1			La Cruz de Huanacaxtle
Villa Varadero	Nuevo Vallarta on a budget	$101	58	1	yes	1			1			Nuevo Vallarta
Villas Buena Vida	good swimming beach	$74	45	1	yes	2			2			Rincón de Guayabitos

$$$ ⚏**Fiesta Americana.** The dramatically designed terra-cotta building rises above a deep-blue pool that flows under bridges and beside palm oases; a seven-story palapa (which provides natural air-conditioning) covers the elegant lobby—paved in patterned tile and stone—and a large round bar. The ocean-view rooms have a modern pink-and–terra-cotta color scheme, beige marble floors, balconies, and tile baths with powerful showers. The beach is small, but bustles with activity and equipment rentals, and the breakwater forms a sheltered nook that's nice for swimming. It's in the northern Hotel Zone, about halfway between

> ### CAN I DRINK THE WATER?
>
> Most of the fancier hotels have reverse osmosis or other water filtration systems. It's fine for brushing your teeth, but play it safe by drinking bottled water (there might be leaks that let groundwater in). Note that the bottled water in your hotel room may be added to your bill when you leave, even if it appears to be free. It seems that the nicer the hotel, the costlier the water. Buy a few bottles at the corner grocery instead.

the Marina Vallarta complex and Downtown PV. **Pros:** across from Plaza Caracol, with its shops, grocery store, and cineplex, lots of on-site shops, concierge service. **Cons:** no ocean view from second and third floors, hotel is a cab or bus ride from most restaurants. ⊠*Blvd. Francisco M. Ascencio, Km 2.5, Zona Hotelera Norte* ☎*322/226–2100, 800/343–7821 in U.S.* ⊕*www.fiestaamericana.com* ⤶*288 rooms, 3 suites* ⌂*In-room: safe, Internet, Wi-Fi. In-hotel: 3 restaurants, room service, bars, pool, gym, beachfront, children's programs (ages 4–12), laundry service, Wi-Fi, parking (free), no-smoking rooms* ⊟*AE, DC, MC, V* ⦿*EP.*

$$$$ ⚏**Hacienda San Angel.** Each room is unique and elegant at this pricey boutique hotel in the hills six blocks above the malecón. Public spaces also exude wealth and privilege: 16th- through 19th-century antiques are placed throughout, water pours from fonts into Talavera tile–lined basins, mammoth tables grace open dining areas. The Celestial Room has a wondrous view of Bahía de Banderas and the cathedral's tower from its open-air, thatch-roof living room. You can call or e-mail Canada or the United States for free and enjoy live music with complimentary cocktails in the early evening. **Pros:** the only elegant lodging in downtown PV, concierge service, excellent bay views, reasonably priced airport transfers. **Cons:** scary drive up congested cobblestone streets, short but steep walk from the malecón, 5% service fee, three-night minimum summer and winter, fewer amenities than hotels of comparable price point. ⊠*Calle Miramar 336, at Iturbide, Col. El Cerro* ☎*322/222–2692, 877/815–6594 toll-free in U.S.* ⊕*www.hacienda sanangel.com* ⤶*21 rooms* ⌂*In-room: safe, DVD. In-hotel: restaurant, pools, laundry service, Internet terminal, Wi-Fi, no kids under 16* ⊟*AE, MC, V* ⦿*CP.*

$ ⚏**Los Cuatro Vientos.** This Old Vallarta original opened in 1955, and some folks have been coming here forever. That explains why most of the guests and staff seem like old friends. The Chez Elena restaurant, the unadorned rooftop bar, and the best rooms have nice views of the

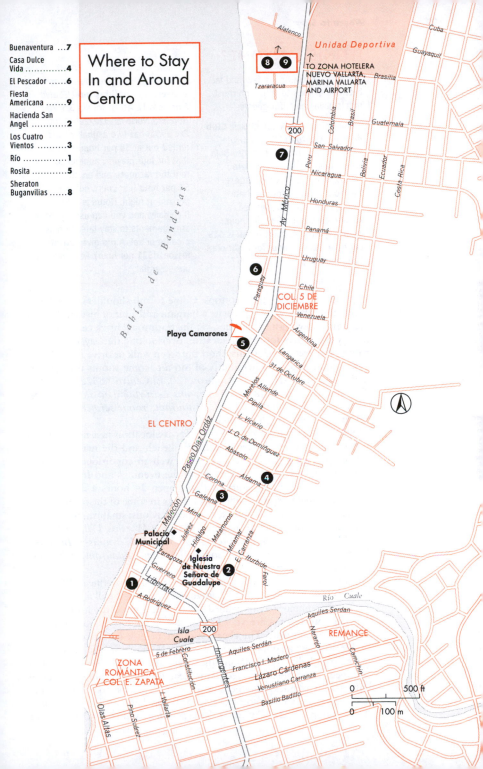

Where to Stay In and Around Centro

TENNIS, ANYONE?

Public tennis courts are few and far between in Vallarta, although most hotels have courts for guests.

Of the public tennis complexes, **Club de Tenis Canto del Sol** (⊠ *Hotel Canto del Sol, Local 18, Planta Baja, Zona Comercial, Zona Hotelera* ☎ *322/226–0123*) is the largest, with four clay and four asphalt courts; all but two are lighted. Private lessons are $33 per hour, including racquet; court rental is $13 per hour, $20 per hour for night play. Club hours are 7 AM to 10 PM (7–4 on Sunday); fees give you access to showers. The **Holiday Inn** (⊠ *Blvd. Francisco M. Ascencio, Km 3.5, Zona Hotelera Norte* ☎ *322/226–1700 Ext. 1792*) has two asphalt courts rented out at $8 per hour; it's twice that for four players; another $2 to rent the racquets, and an additional $4 per hour (per court, not per person) at night. Hours are 8 AM–8 PM daily, and you can usually make arrangements to stay later to finish a game or set. A pro gives private lessons ($21 per hour). Reservations are essential.

bay and of the city's red rooftops. Come to rub shoulders with Europeans and others who appreciate a bargain and a bit of history. Rooms are plain and without amenities, yet the traditional brick ceilings give a homey feel. **Pros:** downtown location overlooking the bay, deep, grottolike pool, free Wi-Fi. **Cons:** short but steep walk or drive from downtown, no lounge area around pool, no a/c, some rooms up multiple flights of stairs. ⊠*Calle Matamoros 520, El Centro* ☎*322/222–0161* ⊕*www.cuatrovientos.com* ➲*14 rooms* ♨*In-room: no a/c, no phone, no TV, Wi-Fi (some). In-hotel: restaurant, room service, bar, pool* ▤*MC, V* ¡⊚¡*CP (high season only).*

$ 🔠 **Río.** This budget hotel get points for its location just north of Isla Río Cuale, two blocks from both the beach and the main plaza. It gets even more points for the cheerful, well-air-conditioned little restaurant-bar with live guitar music in the evenings and for the computer room with many stations that's open 24 hours a day. On the downside are uninspired, older furnishings in some of the rooms. **Pros:** friendly staff, 24-hour Internet, near beach. **Cons:** smallish, nonprivate pool, furnishings need an upgrade. ⊠*Calle Morelos 170, El Centro* ☎*322/222–0366* ⊕*www.hotelrio.com.mx* ➲*47 rooms* ♨*In-room: kitchen (some), refrigerator (some). In-hotel: restaurant, bar, pool, Internet terminal* ▤*MC, V* ¡⊚¡*EP.*

$$ 🔠 **Rosita.** What started as a sleepy 12-room hostelry—one of PV's very first—is now a busy 115-room downtown hotel. It's still a viable budget option, mainly recommended for its location on the north end of the malecón. Rooms are very basic; expect white-tile floors and fabrics with floral prints. The cheapest quarters have no air-conditioning or TV. Request a room facing the water, as much for the view as for the natural light; rooms facing the street are dark, making them feel cramped. **Pros:** old-fashioned value near downtown, Sunday brunch buffet under 10 bucks, inexpensive Internet use. **Cons:** no bathtub, older floors and furnishings, so-so beach. ⊠*Paseo Díaz Ordaz 901, Col. 5 de Diciembre* ☎*322/223–2000* ⊕*www.hotelrosita.com* ➲*115 rooms*

In-room: no a/c (some), no TV (some). In-hotel: restaurant, bar, pool, laundry service, Wi-Fi =AE, MC, V IOIEP.

$$$ **Sheraton Buganvilias.** Juan Carlos Name, a disciple of modern-minimalist Mexican architect Luis Barragán, designed this looming high-rise near the Hotel Zone's south end and within walking distance of downtown. It's reliable, anonymous, and geared toward conventioneers and other groups. Rooms have a perky, bright, white-and–cherry red color scheme and very snug and comfortable beds with pillow-top mattresses and downy duvets. This is the closest of the major Zona Hotelera Norte hotels to downtown PV. **Pros:** excellent Sunday champagne brunch, in-room Wi-Fi cheaper than those of many megahotels, concierge service. **Cons:** slow elevators, so-so beach, faces rather unattractive boulevard. ⊠ *Blvd. Francisco Medina Ascencio 999, Zona Hotelera Norte* ☎ *322/226–0404, 800/325–3535 in U.S. and Canada* ⊕ *www.sheraton vallarta.com* ↪ *480 rooms, 120 suites* *In-room: safe, kitchen (some), Wi-Fi (some), Internet. In-hotel: 3 restaurants, room service, bar, tennis courts, pools, gym, spa, beachfront, children's programs (ages 4–12), laundry service, Internet terminal, parking (free), no-smoking rooms* =AE, MC, V IOIEP, CP.

MARINA VALLARTA

$$$ **CasaMagna Marriott.** The CasaMagna is hushed and stately in some places, lively and casual in others. Here's a classy property that nonetheless welcomes children. All of the restaurants—including a sleek Asian restaurant serving Thai, sushi, and teppanyaki and a large, pleasant sports bar—have kid's menus. The meandering grounds boast a large infinity pool as well as indigenous plant and chili gardens. Rooms have an upbeat, classy decor; each has a balcony and most have an ocean view. The Marriott chain requires smoke detectors, sprinklers, thrice-filtered water, and other beyond-the-pale safety features. Access to the amazing spa is free with the purchase of a spa service. **Pros:** lovely spa, concierge service, good Japanese restaurant. **Cons:** unimpressive beach. ⊠ *Paseo de la Marina 455, Marina Vallarta* ☎ *322/226–0000, 888/236–2427 in U.S. and Canada* ⊕ *www.casamagnapuertovallarta. com* ↪ *404 rooms, 29 suites* *In-room: safe, Wi-Fi. In-hotel: 4 restaurants, room service, bars, pools, gym, spa, beachfront, children's programs (ages 4–12), laundry service, Internet terminal, Wi-Fi, parking (free)* =AE, DC, MC, V IOIEP.

$$$$ ⊞ **Sol Meliá Puerto Vallarta.** The sprawling, all-inclusive Meliá, on the beach and close to the golf course, is popular with families and hums with activity. The breezy lobby houses an eclectic collection of Mexican art and memorabilia. The plazas beyond have still more artwork as well as garden areas, fountains, ponds and such bits of whimsy as a supersize chessboard with plastic pieces as big as a toddler. There are a huge pool, an outdoor theater with nightly shows, and elaborate children's programs and amenities—including a climbing wall and a batting cage. Rooms are havens in subdued blues, creams, and sands. Considering it's an all-inclusive only, prices are very reasonable. **Pros:** lots of activities for small children, giant pool, concierge service. **Cons:** small beach diminishes further at high tide, lots of children. ⊠*Paseo de la Marina Sur 7, Marina Vallarta* ☎*322/226–3000, 800/336–3542 in U.S.* ⊕*www.solmelia.com* ⌧*217 rooms, 4 suites* ⌂*In-room: safe, refrigerator, Wi-Fi (some). In-hotel: 6 restaurants, bars, tennis courts, pool, gym, beachfront, children's programs (ages 4 months–13 years), laundry service, Internet terminal, Wi-Fi, parking (free), no-smoking rooms* ⊟*AE, MC, V* ⍩*AI.*

$$$$ ⊞ **Velas Vallarta Suite Resort & Convention Center.** Silky sheets and cozy ★ down duvets, multiple ceiling fans, and large flat-screen TVs are a few of the creature comforts that set Velas apart from the rest. Each large living area has two comfortably wide built-in couches in colorful prints and a round dining table. Huichol cross-stitch and modern Mexican art decorate the walls. Studios and one-, two-, and three-bedroom suites have the same amenities except that the studios don't have balconies or beach views. Tall palms, pink bougainvillea, and wild ginger with brilliant red plumes surround the three enormous pools. **Pros:** large suites, concierge service, pillow menu, great specials including airport transfers and golf packages. **Cons:** small spa, annoyingly zealous time-share salespeople, high price point ⊠*Av. Costera s/n LH2, Marina Vallarta* ☎*322/221–0091 or 866/847–4609* ⊕*www.velasvallarta.com* ⌧*339 suites* ⌂*In-room: safe, kitchen, refrigerator, Wi-Fi. In-hotel: 2 restaurants, room service, bars, tennis courts, pools, gym, spa, beachfront, children's programs (ages 6–12), laundry service, Internet terminal, Wi-Fi, parking (free), no-smoking rooms* ⊟*AE, MC, V* ⍩*AI.*

$$$$ ⊞ **Westin Resort & Spa.** Hot pink! Electric yellow! Color aside, the Westin's buildings evoke ancient temples and are about as mammoth. There's not a bad sightline anywhere—whether you gaze out to the leafy courtyard or down an orange-tile, brightly painted corridor lined with Mexican art. The jarring echoes here are tempered by the rush of an enormous water feature. In the spacious, balconied rooms concrete-and-stone floors massage bare feet, and top-of-the-

WORD OF MOUTH

"We enjoyed our stay at Westin . . . . It does feel very airy almost anywhere, and the property with it's four huge meandering pools and palm trees is very inviting and lovely. The views from our deluxe oceanview room were fabulous. Things aren't on Caribbean time here; the service was very good. You'll find a much bigger expanse of beach at the Marriott, a few blocks down, but we didn't come to PV just for the beach." —Stephie

Where to Stay in Marina Vallarta

✈ Gustavo Díaz Ordaz
International Airport

Paseo de las Flores

Blvd. Francisco Medina Ascencio

Gladiola
Violetas
Clavel
Margaritas
Laureles
Orquídeas
Amapola
Jazmín
Lirios
Las Azucenas

Geranios
Amapas
Dalias
Obeliscos

**VILLAS
LAS FLORES**

Las Palmas
Canarios
Pétalos

Las Rosas

Gansos

Industrias

*Estero
"El Salado"*

Gaviotas

Albatros
Flamingos
Flamingos

Paseo
Bocanegra

Albatros

Pelicanos

Prix de
Las Garzas

● Marina Valarta
Campo De Golf

Av. Paseo de la Marina

Mástil

Popa

Proa

Quilla

**MARINA
VALLARTA**

❹

● El Faro

Av. Timón

Ancla

Vela

❸

❷

Paseo de la Marina Sur

EDUCACION

Av. Politecnico Nacional

Preparatoria

Secundaria

Blvd. Francisco Medina Ascencio

Paseo de la Marina Norte

Playa
El Salado

❶

Terminal
Maritima ◆

Av. Gob.
Prisciliano
Sánchez

Océano
Indico

Camino Viejo Aramara

*PACIFIC
OCEAN*

Av. Las Garzas

Flamingos

TO
CENTRO,
ZONA
ROMÁNTICA,
COSTALEGRE
↓

Dr. Mike
Lemus

Quetzal

Av. Las
Garzas

0 ___ 1/4 mile
0 ___ 1/4 km

line mattresses with whisper-soft duvets make for heavenly siestas. Guest quarters above the sixth floor have ocean views; those below face the 600 palm trees surrounding the four beautiful pools. **Pros:** fabulous beds and pillows, impressive architecture and landscaping, attentive but not overzealous staff, concierge service. **Cons:** small beach, fee for gym, no ocean views from lower floors. ⊠*Paseo de la Marina Sur 205, Marina Vallarta* ☏*322/226–1100, 800/228–3000 in U.S. and Canada* ⊕*www.starwoodhotels.com* ↩*266 rooms, 14 suites* &*In-room: safe, Wi-Fi. In-hotel: 2 restaurants, room service, bars, tennis courts, pools, gym, spa, beachfront, children's programs (ages infant–12), laundry service, Internet terminal, Wi-Fi, parking (free), some pets allowed, no-smoking rooms* ▭*AE, DC, MC, V* ⦿*BP.*

SOUTH ALONG BANDERAS BAY

$$$$ ⊞**Barceló La Jolla de Mismaloya.** Guests consistently give this hotel high
☾   marks, and in 2008, the AAA gave it the Four Diamond Award as
Fodor's Choice   well. Each of the classy suites has an elegant feel, with a brown-and-
★   taupe color scheme and ample terrace with a table and four chairs; the separate sitting room has a second flat-screen TV. There's even a pillow menu. The pools are surrounded by spacious patios, so there's plenty of room to find the perfect spot in the sun, whether you're on your honeymoon or with the kids. Given the elegance of the place, it's a shame to have to wear the usual wristbands required of AI guests. **Pros:** recently redecorated and remodeled, concierge service, lots of on-site dining and activity options. **Cons:** beach is smaller than it once was. ⊠*Zona Hotelera Sur, Km 11.5, Mismaloya Box 158B 48300* ☏*322/226–0660, 800/227–2356 in U.S. and Canada* ⊕*www.barcelo.com* ↩*317 suites* &*In-room: safe. In-hotel: 5 restaurants, room service, bars, tennis court, pools, gym, spa, beachfront, diving, water sports, bicycles, children's programs (ages 4–9), laundry service, Internet terminal, Wi-Fi, parking (free), no-smoking rooms (all)* ▭*MC, V* ⦿*AI.*

$$–$$$ ⊞**Casa Cupula.** This multistory, up-to-date boutique hotel has a vari-
★   ety of rooms and prices that fluctuate by season. It's a 10-minute walk down (and, later, back up) to the beach and the Romantic Zone. Most guest rooms have terraces with wonderful views of the sea and the layers of houses up and down the surrounding hills. Suites have kitchenettes, washer-dryers, separate living/sleeping quarters, and a home-theater system with speakers in the rain shower. All the rooms are classy, restrained, and individually decorated. The airy shared dining room–lounge is comfortable and welcoming; the rooftop terrace with infinity dipping pool is lovely. Gays, lesbians, their dogs, and straight friends are welcome. **Pros:** reasonably priced airport transfers, concierge service, free Wi-Fi, oh-so-comfy beds and pillows. **Cons:** aerobically challenging location, not on the beach. ⊠*Callejon de la Igualdad 129, Col. Amapas* ☏*322/223–2484, 866/352–2511 in U.S. and Canada* ⊕*www.casacupula.com* ↩*14 rooms, 6 suites* &*In-room: safe, kitchen (some), refrigerator, DVD (some), Wi-Fi. In-hotel: Restaurant, room service, bar, pool, gym, laundry service, parking (free), some pets allowed, no kids under 18* ▭*AE, MC, V* ⊗ *Closed Aug. and Sept.* ⦿*CP.*

Don't Be (Time-Share) Shark Bait

In Puerto Vallarta, time-share salespeople are as unavoidable as death and taxes. And almost as dreaded. Although a slim minority of people actually enjoy going to one- to four-hour time-share presentations to get the freebies that range from Kahlúa to rounds of golf, car rentals, meals, and shows, most folks find the experience incredibly annoying. For some it even casts a pall over their whole vacation.

The bottom line is, if the sharks smell interest, you're dead in the water. Time-share salespeople occupy tiny booths up and down main streets where tourists and cruise passengers walk. In general, while *vallartenses* are friendly, they don't accost you on the street to start a conversation. Those who do are selling something. Likewise, anyone calling you *amigo* is probably selling. The best solution is to walk by without responding, or say "No thanks" or "I'm not interested" as you continue walking. When they yell after you, don't feel compelled to explain yourself.

Some sly methods of avoidance that have worked for others are telling the tout that you're out of a job but dead interested in attending a presentation. They'll usually back off immediately. Or explaining confidentially that the person you're with is not your spouse. Time-share people are primarily interested in married couples—married to each other, that is! But our advice is still to practice the art of total detachment with a polite rejection and then ignoring the salesperson altogether if he or she persists.

Even some very nice hotels allow salespeople in their lobbies disguised as the Welcome Wagon or information gurus. Ask the concierge for the scoop on area activities, and avoid the so-called "information desk."

Time-share salespeople often pressure guests to attend time-share presentations, guilt-tripping them ("My family relies on the commissions I get," for example) or offering discounts on the hotel room and services. The latter are sometimes difficult to redeem and cost more time than they're worth. And although it may be the salesperson's livelihood, remember that this is your vacation, and you have every right to use the time as you wish.

$$ **★** **Casa Iguana All-Suites Hotel.** Palms and plants edge walkways that line the swimming pool and goldfish ponds; balconies look down on this garden scene. Suites have full kitchens, shower-only baths, and tropical-style furniture in a mellow palette. The hotel is on a cobblestone street off the highway; if you don't want to hoof it into PV, take one of the local buses that pass every 10 or 15 minutes. The beach is a five-minute walk away, at the other side of the highway; and the village of Mismaloya, with wandering chickens and even burros, is within braying distance. The stylish Boca Benta Latin Bar & Grill is on-site. **Pros:** experience village life not far from PV's bars and restaurants, on-site grocery. **Cons:** tiny gym, a cab or bus ride from nightlife, restaurants, and shops, not on beach. ⊠ *Av. 5 de Mayo 455, Mismaloya* ☎*322/228–0186* ⊕*www.casaiguanahotel.com* ⇨*49 2-bedroom suites, 3 3-bedroom suites* ⌂*In-room: kitchen (some), refrigerator (some), Wi-Fi. In-hotel:*

restaurant, room service, bar, pools, gym, spa, Internet terminal, Wi-Fi, parking (free), no-smoking rooms ☰*AE, MC, V* ⫿◯⫿ *EP, FAP.*

$$$$
☼
Fodor'sChoice
★

🏨 **Dreams.** The dramatic view of the gorgeous, rock-edged beach is just one reason that this all-inclusive is special. Theme nights go a bit beyond the usual Mexican fiestas: there are salsa dancing classes; reggae and circus nights; sports nights with ball games, hot dogs, and beer; and movies on the beach. Instead of buffet restaurants there are five à la carte eateries featuring seafood, Mexican, Asian, international, and an adults-only Italian dinner restaurant. All of the charming suites have fab views but only the newer ones have balconies, some with a hot tub. There are tons of activities for both kids and adults, and no wristbands (required at most all-inclusives to identify guests) to clash with your resort-casual clothes. **Pros:** gorgeous private beach, concierge service, easy drive or bus to downtown PV, no ugly all-inclusive wristbands. **Cons:** no-reservation restaurant system means waiting to eat during busiest seasons, standard rooms don't have balconies, pricey ✉*Carretera a Barra de Navidad (Carretera 200), at Playa Las Estacas, Zona Hotelera Sur* ☎*322/226–5000, 866/237–3267 in U.S. and Canada* ⊕*www.dreamsresorts.com* ⇖*337 suites* ⟐*In-room: safe, refrigerator, DVD. In-hotel: 5 restaurants, room service, bars, tennis courts, pools, gym, spa, beachfront, water sports, bicycles, children's programs (ages 4–17), laundry service, parking (free), no-smoking rooms* ☰*AE, D, DC, MC, V* ⫿◯⫿*AI.*

$$$$
🏨 **Majahuitas.** If travelers were animals, Majahuitas's guests would be bears, not butterflies. Eating well and resting are the two top activities. After a 20-minute boat ride you (and, hopefully, your sweetie, as this intimate place doesn't have a singles scene) arrive at a shell-strewn beach where hermit crabs scuttle about seeking larger accommodations. Eight casitas crouch amid jungly plants (and biting bugs; bring repellent) overlooking the tiny cove. Stylish guest rooms are open to the air and have low-wattage lights and tiny, solar-powered fans. It's a romantic place that also happens to be good for self-entertaining families. Older kids, type-A adults, and anyone who doesn't read will be bored. **Pros:** plenty of opportunities for "me-and-you time," short boat ride to other beaches like Yelapa and Las Animas. **Cons:** zero possibility for going out at night, party boats invade the smallish beach at midday, no Internet or phone access. ✉*Playa Majahuitas, Cabo Corrientes Norte* ☎*322/293–4506, 831/336–5036 in U.S.* ⊕*www.majahuitas-resort. com* ⇖*8 rooms* ⟐*In-room: no a/c, no phone, no TV. In-hotel: restaurant, bar, beachfront, water sports, no kids under 5* ☰*AE, MC, V* ⊘*Closed June 16–Sept.* ⫿◯⫿*FAP.*

$$
🏨 **Playa Conchas Chinas.** Studios here have functional kitchenettes, basic cookware, and somewhat thin mattresses on wood-frame beds. Each has a small tiled tub as well as a shower. The real pluses of this plain Jane are the balconies with spectacular beach views and the location above Conchas Chinas Beach, about a 20-minute walk to downtown PV along the beach. **Pros:** excellent view of rock-framed Conchas Chinas beach, a short drive or bus ride to downtown PV, good weekend breakfast buffet at nonaffiliated restaurant overlooking the beach. **Cons:** some units smell funky. ✉*Carretera a Barra de Navidad (Carretera 200),*

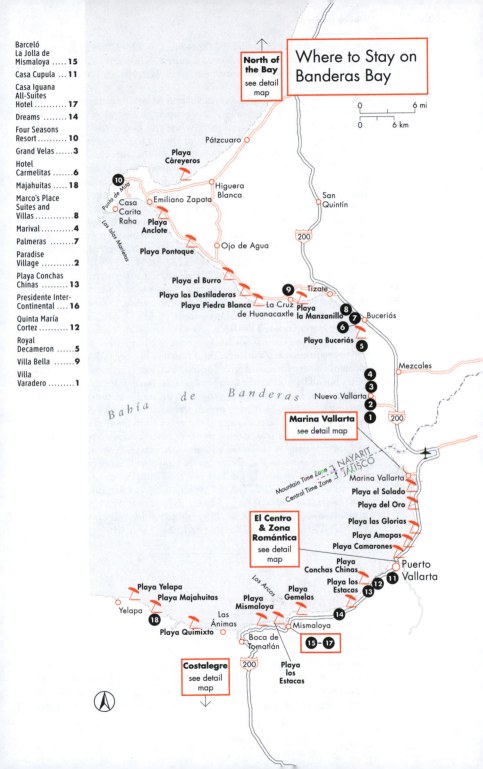

Where to Stay on Banderas Bay

0 6 mi

0 6 km

North of the Bay see detail map

Pátzcuaro

Playa Càreyeros

Higuera Blanca

San Quintín

Punto de Mita

Casa Carita Raha

Emiliano Zapata

Playa Anclote

Las Islas Marietas

Ojo de Agua

Playa Pontoque

200

Playa el Burro

Playa las Destiladeras

Playa Piedra Blanca

La Cruz de Huanacaxtle

Tizate

Playa la Manzanillo

Bucerías

Playa Bucerías

Mezcales

Nuevo Vallarta

Bahía de Banderas

Marina Vallarta see detail map

200

NAYARIT
JALISCO

Mountain Time Zone
Central Time Zone

Marina Vallarta

Playa el Salado

Playa del Oro

El Centro & Zona Romántica see detail map

Playa las Glorias

Playa Amapas

Playa Camarones

Playa Conchas Chinas

Puerto Vallarta

Playa Yelapa

Playa Majahuitas

Playa los Estacas

Yelapa

Los Arcos

Playa Gemelas

Playa Mismaloya

Las Ánimas

Playa Quimixto

Boca de Tomatlán

Mismaloya

200

Playa los Estacas

Costalegre see detail map

Km. 2.5, Conchas Chinas ☎*322/221–5763 or 322/221–5230* ⊕*www. conchaschinas.com* ➫*21 rooms, 2 suites* ⌂*In-room: safe, kitchen, refrigerator. In-hotel: restaurant, bar, pool, beachfront, Wi-Fi, parking (free)* ▤*AE, MC, V* ⏐◉⏐*EP.*

$$ 🏨 **Presidente InterContinental Puerto Vallarta Resort.** The beautiful aqua-tone cove the hotel overlooks is the property's best asset. Rooms are classy, with a minimalist look and white-tile floors and citrus-color fabrics. You'll be asked to choose from among four experiences (Joy of Life, Renewal, Romance, and Peace of Mind) that involve changing the scents, music, stones, flowers, and certain amenities in your room to set the desired tone. This marketing gimmick doesn't dramatically enhance your experience, but the packages—which may include golf, spa treatments, breakfast, and even free Wi-Fi and gym access—can. **Pros:** lovely bay great for swimming, movies (DVD) loaned free, concierge service, easy drive, bus, or taxi to downtown, 24-hour business center. **Cons:** charge for room coffee, small gym and spa. ⊠*Carretera a Barra de Navidad, Km 8.6, Mismaloya* ☎*322/228–0191, 888/424–6835 toll-free* ⊕*www.acquaesencia.com* ➫*97 rooms, 23 suites* ⌂*In-room: safe, DVD, Wi-Fi. In-hotel: 3 restaurants, room service, bars, tennis court, pool, gym, spa, beachfront, diving, laundry service, Internet terminal, Wi-Fi, parking (free), no-smoking rooms* ▤*AE, D, MC, V* ⏐◉⏐*EP.*

$$–$$$ 🏨 **Quinta María Cortez.** This B&B has soul. Its seven levels ramble up a **Fodor's Choice** steep hill at Playa Conchas Chinas, about a 20-minute walk along the ★ sand to the Romantic Zone (or a short hop in a bus or taxi). Rooms have balconies and are furnished with antiques and local art; some have kitch-enettes but all have at least a small fridge, two-burner stove, and a simple cooking area. Other draws are the efficient and welcoming staff, the fortifying breakfast (cooked to order) served on a palapa-covered patio, the nearly private beach below, and the views from the rooftop sundeck. It's popular and has few rooms, so make reservations early. Minimum stays are three nights in winter and major holidays. **Pros:** intimate, per-sonable digs, close to PV, above lovely Conchas Chinas beach. **Cons:** small property, frequently booked solid. ⊠*Calle Sagitario 126, Playa Conchas Chinas* ☎*322/221–5317, 888/640–8100 reservations* ⊕*www. quinta-maria.com* ➫*7 rooms, 3 villas* ⌂*In-room: no a/c (some), safe, kitchen (some), refrigerator, no TV. In-hotel: pool, beachfront, Internet terminal, Wi-Fi, no kids under 18* ▤*AE, MC, V* ⏐◉⏐*BP.*

NAYARIT

NORTH ALONG BANDERAS BAY

$$$$ 🏨 **Casa de Mita.** Architect-owner Marc Lindskog has created a nook ★ of nonchalant elegance, with updated country furnishings of wicker, leather, and wood; rock-floor showers without curtains or doors; and cheerful Pacific Coast architectural details. Mosquito netting lends romance to cozy, quilt-covered beds. Waves crashing onshore, their sound somehow magnified, create white noise that lulls you to sleep. In the morning, settle into a cushy chaise on your private patio to watch seabirds swim; at night watch the sunset behind Punta Mita. These simple pleasures make this hideaway a winner. It doesn't hurt that the food is truly delicious, the bar is well stocked with international labels, and it's all included in the room price. **Pros:** delicious food, nearly private beach, concierge service, personal yoga sessions. **Cons:** little nightlife in vicinity, three-night minimum stay, strict cancellation policy. ⊠*Playa Careyeros, Punta Mita, Nayarit* ☎*329/298–4114 or 866/740–7999* ⊕*www.mexicobou tiquehotels.com/casalasbrisas* ⇨*8 rooms* ⌂*In-room: no phone, safe, refrigerator, no TV, Wi-Fi. In-hotel: restaurant, bar, pool, spa, beachfront, Wi-Fi, no kids under 16* ⊟*AE, D, MC, V* ⊺⊙*|AI.*

> ## PILLOW TALK
>
> If you're picky about your pillow, Grand Velas, Four Seasons, or another top-drawer accommodation might prove to be the hotel of your dreams. Some of the swankiest hotels in the area have pillow menus with a half-dozen or more styles to choose from. Go with whisper-soft eiderdown or, if you're allergic to farm animals, 100% man-made materials.

4

$$$$ ☐ **Four Seasons Resort.** The hotel and its fabulous spa perch above a lovely beach at the northern extreme of Bahía de Banderas, about 45 minutes from the PV airport and an hour north of downtown Puerto Vallarta. Spacious rooms occupy Mexican-style casitas of one, two, and three stories. Each room has elegant yet earthy furnishings and a private terrace or balcony—many with a sweeping sea view. The Jack Nicklaus–designed championship golf course has a challenging, optional 19th island hole; the gym is first-rate; and a good variety of sporting and beach equipment is on hand. Just offshore, the Marietas Islands are great for snorkeling, diving, whale-watching, and fishing. This is the place for indulging golf and spa fantasies, or just using the luxurious, top-notch facilities. It's a great spot for kids, too, with fantastic beaches, a donut-shape pool with current where you can float in inner tubes, and an excellent kids' playroom with Internet and lots of cool games. **Pros:** beautiful beach, concierge service, yoga on the point, excellent spa, private yacht for charter. **Cons:** staff trained to be overly solicitous (you'll be saying "hola" a lot), very expensive spa treatments, not all rooms have ocean view, stringent cancellation policy. ⊠*Bahía de Banderas, Punta Mita, Nayarit* ☎*329/291–6019, 800/819–5053 U.S. and Canada* ⊕*www. fshr.com/puntamita* ⇨*141 rooms, 27 suites* ⌂*In-room: safe, refrigerator, DVD, Internet, Wi-Fi. In-hotel: 3 restaurants, room service, bars, golf course, tennis courts, pools, gym, spa, beachfront, water sports, children's programs (ages 5–12), laundry service, Internet terminal, Wi-Fi, parking (free), no-smoking rooms* ⊟*AE, MC, V* ⊺⊙*|EP, BP.*

FodorsChoice ★

☼

$$$$ ☐ **Grand Velas.** In scale and majesty, the public areas of this AAA Five Diamond property compare to other Nuevo Vallarta all-inclusives like the Taj Mahal to a roadside taco stand. Ceilings soar overhead, and the structure and furnishings are simultaneously minimalist and modern, yet earthy, incorporating stucco, rock, polished teak, and gleaming ecru marble. The spa is excellent, and the views—with the garden-shrouded pool in the foreground and the beach beyond—are striking. Rooms are sleek, with elegant furnishings and appointments. The high price

Continued on page 108

SPAAAHH

The trend of luxury spas in Mexico, and particularly in vacation hot spots like Puerto Vallarta, shows no signs of slowing. From elegant resort spas scented with essence of orange and bergamot to Aztec-inspired day spas, each has its own personality and signature treatments. Competition keeps creativity high, with an ever-changing menu of new treatments, many using native products like sage, chocolate, aloe vera, and even tequila.

Four Seasons Resort, Punta Mita

Spa Savvy

All of the spas listed here are open to nonguests, but reservations are essential. Guests of the hotel may get discounts. Spa customers can sometimes use other facilities at a resort, such as the restaurant, beach, pool, or gym. Ask when you book. Prices are generally on par with those of resort spas worldwide, but some deals are to be had, if you go with the less-expensive but still high-quality spas we lists. Or scout out hotel-spa packages and specials.

RESORT NAME	BODY TREATMENTS	SEASIDE TREATMENTS	TREATMENTS FOR TWO	FITNESS DAY PASS	HOT TUB	TEMAZCAL
CasaMagna Marriot	$75–$135	yes	yes	yes*	yes	no
Four Seasons	$100–$220	yes	yes	yes**	yes	yes
Grand Velas	$58–$178	yes	yes	$40	yes	no
Paradise Village	$46–$134	yes	no	$12–$19	yes	no
Terra Noble	$65	no	yes	no	yes	yes

* Gym free for guests, $25 for nonguests; steam, sauna, and other spa areas $15 for guests, $50 for nonguests; both areas free for guests and nonguests with purchase of spa treatment.
** Nonguests pay day-use fee to get spa treatments and use spa facilities and golf course. Fee is half the cheapest room rate (often several hundred dollars).

TOP SPOTS

New and Worth Noting

OHTLI SPA, CASAMAGNA MARRIOTT

The modern yet organic-looking Ohtli spa and its high-tech gym offer 22,000 square feet of elegant pampering. You can relax before or between treatments in the lounge, with a glass of water infused with love in the form of pink quartz crystals and messages of love in 13 languages. Come early to load up on this liquid love and to enjoy the cold pool, steam, sauna, and other elements of the separate men's and women's spa facilities.

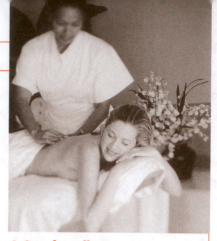

Inspiration for this tasteful, soothing spa came from indigenous cultures. Treatment rooms are adorned with Huichol art and interior gardens to maintain a spiritual and nature-oriented mood. Many of the treatments—like the coconut exfoliation with deep-tissue massage—use local ingredients. The signature exfoliation treatment contains agave, cornmeal, and sea salt.

Body Treatments & Services: Exfoliation (8 kinds); wraps (7 kinds); massage (10 kinds).

Beauty Treatments: Facials (6 kinds); manicure; pedicure; waxing; children's treatments.

Prices: Body treatments $75–$135; facials $105–$150; hair $25–$90; manicure or pedicure $30–$72; waxing $18–$60.

Packages: Mother and daughter ice cream pedicure; other packages offered seasonally. *CasaMagna Marriott Puerto Vallarta, Paseo de la Marina 5, Marina Vallarta.* ☎ *322/226-0079* ⊕ *www.marriott.com* ▭ *AE, DC, MC, V.*

A Spa for All Seasons

FOUR SEASONS PUNTA MITA APUANE SPA

Professional service is the hallmark of this exclusive spa. An inspirational experience is the Ha Waye healing waters treatment: a four-handed massage under a soothing Vichy bath complemented by aromatherapy.

Treatments are among the most expensive in the area, but everyting is top drawer. Native products are used almost exclusively; the Hakali massage, for example, employs catus pulque, which is applied to the skin using fresh cactus paddles.

Body Treatments: Exfoliation; massage (14 types); Vichy hydrotherapy; wraps and scrubs (12 types).

Beauty Treatments: Facials (7 types); manicure; pedicure; hair/scalp treatment.

Prices: Body treatments $100–$200; facials $100–$230; hair $95–$145; manicure/pedicure $75–$95; waxing $35–$88.

Packages: Couples treatments such as Like Water for Chocolate—a chocolate scrub and facial; a hot-stone massage; and servings of fruit, chocolate fondue, and champagne. *Punta de Mita, Bahía de Banderas.* ☎ *329/291-6000* ⊕ *www.fourseasons.com/puntamita.* ▭ *AE, DC, MC, V.*

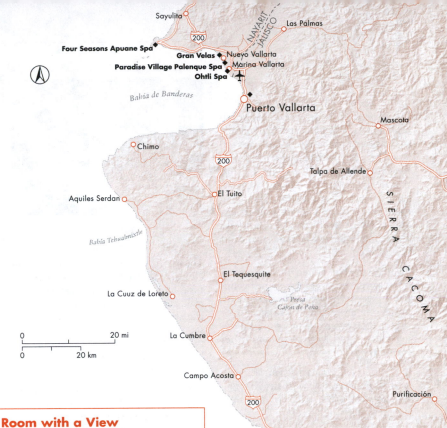

Sayulita

NAYARIT
JALISCO

Las Palmas

Four Seasons Apuane Spa

200

Gran Velas ◆ Nuevo Vallarta

Paradise Village Palenque Spa ◆ Marina Vallarta

Ohtli Spa ✈

◆ Puerto Vallarta

Bahía de Banderas

Mascota

Chimo

200

Talpa de Allende

El Tuito

Aquiles Serdan

Bahía Tchualmixtle

S
I
E
R
R
A

El Tequesquite

*El Presa
Cajón de Peña*

C
A
C
O
M
A

La Cuuz de Loreto

La Cumbre

0   20 mi

0   20 km

Campo Acosta

Purificación

200

San Mateo

Bahía Chamela

*Reserva de
la Biosfera*

La Huerta

80

Costa Careyes

El Tecuán

Bahía Tenacatita

El Tamarindo

Cihuatlán

Barra de Navidad

Room with a View

TERRA NOBLE

Your cares begin to melt away as soon as you enter the rustic, garden-surrounded property of this day-spa aerie overlooking Banderas Bay. Familiar and unpretentious, Terra Noble is more accessible pricewise than some of the area's more elegant spas. After-treatment teas are served on an outdoor patio with a great sea view. Two-hour temazcal sweat lodge rituals cleanse on three levels: physically, mentally, and spiritually. Or recharge with clay and painting classes, and Tarot readings.

Body Treatments: Reflexology; massage; several wraps and scrubs; temazcal sweat lodge; yoga/meditation.

Beauty Treatments: Facials.

Prices: Body treatments $65.

Packages: A few economical packages such as the Stress Recovery (a sea-salt body scrub, a massage, and a facial), for $145.

Av. Tulipanes 595, at Fracc. Lomas de Terra Noble, Col. 5 de Diciembre. Tel. 322/223–3530 ⊕ *www.terranoble.com.* ▭ *AE, MC, V (through PayPal only).*

MORE TOP SPOTS

Something for Every Body

PARADISE VILLAGE PALENQUE SPA

On a peninsula between the beach and marina, this modern Maya temple of glass and marble is a cool, sweet-smelling oasis with separate wings for men and women; each is equipped with private hydrotherapy tubs, whirlpools, saunas, and steam rooms. The coed gym has state-of-the-art equipment and views of the ocean, plus aerobics classes in a separate studio and an indoor lap pool.

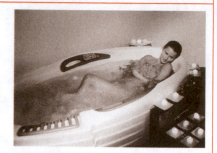

The reasonably priced therapy selections are extensive, from an anti-cellulite seaweed wrap to milk baths with honey, amaranth, and orange oil or the aromatherapy massage, employing clove, sage, bergamot, and other essential oils.

Body Treatments: Aromatherapy; facials; Reiki; exfoliation; hot-stone massage; hydrotherapy; wraps, scrubs, and body treatments (10 types); reflexology; shiatsu.

Beauty Treatments: Facials (18 types), manicure, pedicure.

Prices: Body treatments $46–$134; facials $46–$134; manicure/pedicure $39–$72; hair $39–$101; waxing $19–$61.

Packages: A wide variety of packages that allow switching treatments in an equivalent price bracket. The basic plan combines three 50-minute treatments: marine body scrub, holistic massage, and hydrating facial. *Paseo de los Cocoteros 1 Nuevo Vallarta. Tel. 322/226–6770 ⊕ www.paradisevillage. com.* ⊟ *AE, MC, V.*

Drama Queen

GRAN VELAS

The spa at Nuevo Vallarta's most elegant all-inclusive resort has dramatic architectural lines and plenty of marble, stone, teak, and tile. The 16,500-square-foot facility has 20 treatment rooms, and ample steam, sauna, and whirlpools. Lounge in the comfortable chaises near the "plunge lagoon" (with warm and cold pools) between or after treatments.

Highlights of the extensive treatments menu are the chocolate, gold, or avocado wraps; Thai massage; cinnamon-sage foot scrub; and the challenging buttocks sculpt-lift. There's even a kids spa menu with 15 treatments. Adjoining the spa is an impressive fitness facility.

Body Treatments: Reflexology; massage (18 types); shiatsu; Vichy shower; exfoliation; wraps, scrubs, baths, and body treatments (32 types).

Beauty Treatments: Facials (12+); manicure/pedicure; hair care; waxing; makeup.

Prices: Body treatments: $75–$170; facials: $75—$285; manicure/pedicure: $20–$98; hair care: $38–$98; waxing: $29–$58; makeup: $78.

Packages: Happy Bride, Just for Men, and Detox Ritual packages, plus 10% discount for three or more treatments; otherwise, no packages. *Av. de los Cocoteros 98 Sur, Nuevo Vallarta. Tel. 322/226–8000 ⊕ www.grandvelas.com.* ⊟ *AE, MC, V.*

GLOSSARY

acupuncture. Painless Chinese medicine during which needles are inserted into key spots on the body to restore the flow of *qi* and allow the body to heal itself.

aromatherapy. Massage and other treatments using plant-derived essential oils intended to relax the skin's connective tissues and stimulate the flow of lymph fluid.

ayurveda. An Indian philosophy that uses oils, massage, herbs, and diet and lifestyle modification to restore perfect balance to a body.

body brushing. Dry brushing of the skin to remove dead cells and stimulate circulation.

body polish. Use of scrubs, loofahs, and other exfoliants to remove dead skin cells.

hot-stone massage. Massage using smooth stones heated in water and applied to the skin with pressure or strokes or simply rested on the body.

hydrotherapy. Underwater massage, alternating hot and cold showers, and other water-oriented treatments.

reflexology. Massage on the pressure points of feet, hands, and ears.

reiki. A Japanese healing method involving universal life energy, the laying on of hands, and mental and spiritual balancing. It's intended to relieve acute emotional and physical conditions. Also called radiance technique.

salt glow. Rubbing the body with coarse salt to remove dead skin.

shiatsu. Japanese massage that uses pressure applied with fingers, hands, elbows, and feet.

shirodhara. Ayurvedic massage in which warm herbalized oil is trickled onto the center of the forehead, then gently rubbed into the hair and scalp.

sports massage. A deep-tissue massage to relieve muscle tension and residual pain from workouts.

Swedish massage. Stroking, kneading, and tapping to relax muscles. It was devised at the University of Stockholm in the 19th century by Per Henrik Ling.

Swiss shower. A multijet bath that alternates hot and cold water, often used after mud wraps and other body treatments.

Temazcal. Maya meditation in a sauna heated with volcanic rocks.

Thai massage. Deep-tissue massage and passive stretching to ease stiff, tense, or short muscles.

thalassotherapy. Water-based treatments that incorporate seawater, seaweed, and algae.

Vichy shower. Treatment in which a person lies on a cushioned, waterproof mat and is showered by overhead water jets.

Watsu. A blend of shiatsu and deep-tissue massage with gentle stretches—all conducted in a warm pool.

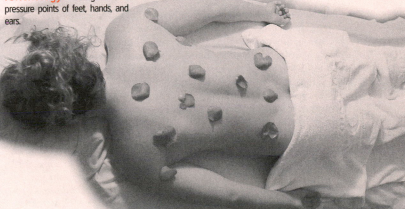

4

IN FOCUS SPAAAHH

entitles you to top-of-the-line spirits in minibars and restaurants. **Pros:** exceptionally beautiful rooms and public spaces, lovely spa, extremely long beach great for walking. **Cons:** very expensive, Nuevo Vallarta location is far from PV (but 10 minutes by car from Bucerías). ✉ *Paseo de los Cocoteros 98 Sur, Nuevo Vallarta, Nayarit* ☎ *322/226–8000, 877/398–2784 in U.S. and Canada* ⊕ *www.grandvelas.com* ↪ *269 suites* △ *In-room: safe, DVD, Wi-Fi. In-hotel: 4 restaurants, room service, bars, tennis court, pools, gym, spa, beachfront, children's programs (ages 4–12), laundry service, Internet terminal, Wi-Fi, parking (free), some pets allowed* ☰ *AE, MC, V* �‖ *AI.*

¢ ▦ **Hotel Carmelitas.** In the heart of Bucerías, this small budget hotel is as unassuming as can be, only a few years old, and well-maintained. Prettily decorated rooms with sponge-painted interiors, matching furniture of wrought iron and wood, and cheerful artwork face an L-shape corridor. All rooms are the same, with one full bed and small, clean, brightly tiled bathrooms with shower only. A periwinkle-and-mauve color scheme brightens the corridor; rooms at the back face a wider corridor with plastic tables and chairs. The single-story hotel is one block from the beach. All rooms are no-smoking. **Pros:** low price, close to beach, friendly owners have years of experience in tourist trade. **Cons:** no views, no amenities. ✉ *Francisco I. Madero 19, Bucerías, Nayarit* ☎ *329/298–0024* ✉ *hotelcarmelitas@yahoo.com* ↪ *10 rooms* △ *In hotel: no-smoking rooms* ☰ *No credit cards* �‖ *EP.*

$ ▦ **Marco's Place Suites & Villas.** Despite its name, this is a three-story motel-like property. It's also one of the few standard hotels in Bucerías, a place where the norm is small apartments and condo rentals. Rooms are small (and baths are tiny) but are cheery and bright with comfortable beds. Sit on chaise lounges by the pool or at café tables outside the first-floor rooms. The property is a block from the beach. **Pros:** bright, attractive rooms, several different outdoor spaces for reading or relaxing, even least expensive room has kitchenette. **Cons:** street parking only, cash only. ✉ *Calle Juventino Espinoza 6–A, Bucerías, Nayarit* ☎ *329/298–0865* ⊕ *www.marcosplacevillas.com* ↪ *15 rooms, 3 suites* △ *In-room: kitchen, refrigerator. In-hotel: pool* ☰ *No credit cards* �‖ *EP.*

$$$ ▦ **Marival Resort and Suites.** Come here if you're looking for an all-inclusive bargain that includes a wealth of activities. On the one hand, rooms have strong air-conditioning and amenities like hair dryers, irons, and ironing boards; on the other hand, rooms also have small tubs, cheap doors, and uninspired modern decor. There's an extra charge, inexplicably, for the use of in-room safes. Only a few units have ocean views, but there are plenty of individual palapas and lounge chairs at the beach. **Pros:** value-priced, immaculately kept grounds, premium booze brands. **Cons:** most rooms have no tub or an uncomfortable square tub, musty smell in some rooms, cheap finishing touches like plastic chairs and fake plants. ✉ *Paseo Cocoteros s/n at Blvd. Nuevo Vallarta, Nuevo Vallarta, Nayarit* ☎ *322/226–8200* ⊕ *www.gomarival.com* ↪ *373 rooms, 122 suites* △ *In-room: kitchen (some). In-hotel: 6 restaurants, room service, bars, tennis courts, pools, gym, spa, beachfront, bicycles, children's programs (ages 4–17), Internet terminal, parking (free)* ☰ *MC, V* �‖ *AI.*

$ ■**Palmeras.** A block from the beach, in an area with lots of good restaurants, Palmeras has small rooms with brightly painted interior walls and modeled-stucco sunflowers serving as a kind of headboard behind the bed. There's plenty of space to socialize around the large, clean, rectangular pool. The more expensive rooms are larger, fresher, and have a couch, satellite TV, and kitchenette; those on the second floor have a partial ocean view. Smaller, older, street-facing rooms are half the price of the newer units. **Pros:** free Wi-Fi, inexpensive older rooms for bargain hunters, newer rooms have patios and ocean view, beach towels provided. **Cons:** some rooms have odd layout. ⊠*Lázaro Cárdenas 35, Bucerías, Nayarit* ☎*329/298–1288, 647/722–4139 in U.S.* ⊕*www.hotelpalmeras.com* ⇘*21 rooms* ♿*In-room: no phone, kitchen (some), refrigerator (some), Wi-Fi. In-hotel: pool, no-smoking rooms* ▭*MC, V* ⓘⓄⒾ*EP.*

$$ ■**Paradise Village.** This Nuevo Vallarta hotel and time-share property
♺ is perfect for families, with lots of activities geared to children. Many people love it, although the property's dedication to time-share guests makes some hotel guests feel short-shrifted. Most suites have balconies with either marina or ocean views. Furnishings are attractive as well as functional, with pretty cane sofa beds in a soothing palette and well-equipped kitchens. Locals like to visit the clean, well-organized spa, which smells divine, and is noted for its massages and facials. The beach here is tranquil enough for swimming, although some small waves are suitable for bodysurfing. **Pros:** concierge service, can walk all the way to Bucerías on the beach, full kitchen in all suites, efficient a/c units, wide range of accommodations. **Cons:** big cats caged in depressing zoo, Internet room for time-share guests only, increasingly time-share oriented. ⊠*Paseo de los Cocoteros 1, Nuevo Vallarta, Nayarit* ☎*322/226–6770, 800/995–5714 Ext. 111 in U.S. and Canada* ⊕*www.paradisevillage. com* ⇘*490 suites* ♿*In-room: safe, kitchen, refrigerator, Wi-Fi. In-hotel: 4 restaurants, room service, bars, golf course, tennis courts, pools, gym, spa, beachfront, children's programs (ages 4–11), Wi-Fi, parking (free)* ▭*AE, MC, V* ⓘⓄⒾ*EP.*

$$ ■**Royal Decameron.** This high-volume hotel is at the south end of long and lovely Bucerías Beach and has manicured grounds. It also has in-house entertainment, activities, and food. Rooms are plain and not particularly modern or appealing, with laminate bathroom counters and textured stucco interior walls that have been painted over many times. Those in the older section have the best views since they were built along the water. Reservations must be made through a brick-and-mortar travel agency or one online (e.g., Expedia.com, Travelocity.com). **Pros:** excellent deal for all-inclusive (room-only and air packages, too), long beach great for walking or jogging, Spanish and dance lessons plus lots of other activities. **Cons:** so-so room decor, 35- to 45-minute drive from downtown Vallarta, limited ways to reserve rooms. ⊠*Calle Lázaro Cárdenas 150, Bucerías, Nayarit* ☎*329/298–0226, 01800/011–1111 toll-free in Mexico* ⊕*www.decameron.com* ⇘*620 rooms* ♿*In-room: safe. In-hotel: 7 restaurants, bars, tennis courts, pools, bicycles, Internet terminal, parking (free)* ▭*MC, V* ⓘⓄⒾ*AI.*

$$$ **Villa Bella.** Tropical plants give character to this privately owned property where tranquillity reigns. The hotel is on a hill above quiet La Cruz de Huanacaxtle, just north of Bucerías. Choose a garden-view room or ocean-facing suite in one of two villas that share common rooms—with TV, phone, computer with Internet access, and DVD and CD players—as well as a swimming pool and gardens. Other pretty shared spaces include a dining area and kitchen, and second-story terraces off some of the suites. It's a short drive to earthy La Cruz, a very Mexican village with a brand-new marina. **Pros:** free airport pickup before 6 PM with at least three-night stay, lap pool, free cocktail (or two) Monday through Saturday between noon and 4 PM, large breakfast with Mexican specialties. **Cons:** up a steep road, best for those with a car, little nightlife in immediate area, three-night minimum stay in high season. ✉ *Calle del Monte Calvario 12, La Cruz de Huanacaxtle 63732, Nayarit* ☎ *329/295–5161 or 329/295–5154, 877/273–6244 toll-free in U.S., 877/513–1662 toll-free in Canada* 🌐 *www.villabella-lacruz.com* *5 suites* *In-room: no a/c (some), no phone, kitchen (some), no TV (some). In-hotel: restaurant, bar, pool, Internet terminal, Wi-Fi, no-smoking rooms* *MC, V* *BP.*

GET YOUR ZZZ'S

Some accommodations in coastal Nayarit and Jalisco are along the main highway with its heavy traffic. And resort hotels often have lobby bars in the middle of an open-air atrium leading directly to rooms, or rooftop discotheques, or outdoor theme nights with live music. When you book, request a room far from the noisiest part of the hotel, and repeat your request politely when you check in.

$$ **Villa Varadero.** Kids under 10 stay and eat for free with the all-inclusive plan at this small, aging, four-story hotel in Nuevo Vallarta. Other pluses are the wide beach with gentle surf and the chummy bar with its billiards salon, dartboards, dominoes, chess, and other games. The use of bikes, kayaks, and boogie boards is free for AI guests; there's a charge for use by EP guests. Only a few of the compact, well-maintained units have tubs, decor is standard, and furniture cheap and aging. Rooms in new tower same cost as old ones. **Pros:** least expensive all-inclusive in Nuevo Vallarta, two kids under six stay and eat free, AI is little more than EP. **Cons:** worse-for-wear furnishings and room amenities, only one-bedroom suites have balconies. ✉ *Retorno Nayarit, Lotes 83 and 84, Manzana XIII, Nuevo Vallarta, Nayarit* ☎ *322/297–0430, 800/238–9996 toll-free in U.S., 877/742–6323 toll-free in Canada* 🌐 *www.villavaradero.com.mx* *29 rooms, 29 suites* *In-room: safe (some), kitchen (some), refrigerator. In-hotel: restaurant, bars, pools, beachfront, bicycles, laundry service, Internet terminal, parking (free)* *AE, MC, V* *AI, EP.*

NORTH OF BANDERAS BAY

$$$ **Casa Obelisco.** The vibe is warm and romantic, the cozy-chic rooms—endowed with original paintings, folk art, and super-comfortable king beds with pillow-top mattresses and mosquito nets—are perfect for

An Over-the-Top Stay

You don't have to be a rock star to rent one of Vallarta's most beautiful homes, but a similar income or a never-ending trust fund might help.

Just beyond Destiladeras Beach at the north end of Banderas Bay, **Casa Canta Rana** (⊕ *www.casacantarana. com)* provides stunning views of the coast from inside a gated community. Indoor-outdoor living and dining spaces have bay and island views. Decorated with tasteful, seductively subdued furnishings, two of the three-bedroom suites share a tall palapa roof; the master suite has an indoor-outdoor shower and private patio. A maid, gardener, and pool boy are included. Additional staff, airport transfer, and other services are provided at additional cost. For the nanny, pilot, or bodyguard on your payroll, there's a separate apartment with bedroom, kitchen, and bath. High-season (November–April) rate is $1,450 per night, usually with a four-night minimum.

What could be better than a former president's property on land chosen for its almost incomprehensibly beautiful vistas of the sea? Built on an 87,836-square-foot site selected by former President Luis Echeverría, **Villa Vista Mágica** is on a highly forested point between Sayulita and San Francisco, Nayarit. The circular, 10-suite

property comes with a cook who will prepare three meals a day, as well as cocktails or party snacks as you wish. The WaveRunners and two Suburbans are also at your disposal. This fabulous place costs a mere $42,000 a week (more during holidays). To rent this—or a less-pricey property where you'll feel equally special and pampered—contact **Boutique Villas** (☎ *322/209–1992, 866/560–2281 from U.S.* ⊕ *www.boutiquevillas.com).*

Twenty years ago the private heaven of simple fisherfolk and their families, the spearhead-shape point at the northern point of Banderas Bay is today home to the gated, low-density community **Punta Mita** (☎ *329/291-6500, 888/647–0979 in U.S.* ⊕ *www.puntamita.com.mx).* Here you find the Four Seasons and St. Regis resorts, as well as two private Jack Nicklaus golf courses, beach clubs, spas, and shops. Within the 1,500-acre retreat, the Four Seasons and other brands rent luxury villas whose high-season rates range from $4,000 to $10,000-plus per night. Floor plans vary but there's consistency in the large outdoor living spaces; air-conditioned common areas and bedrooms with natural-hue, high-quality furnishings; and attentive staff members, including your own full-time chef.

4

spooning and honeymooning. Ambition here means drinks by the pool, walks on the beach, and trips into town or down to Sayulita (5 km [3 mi] south). Each ocean-facing patio (some private, some shared) has either a hammock or table with *equipale* (pigskin) chairs. American owners provide opinions and information about the area. Breakfasts are varied and expansive. Kahlua, the well-behaved doodle dog, is a boon to pet-starved guests. **Pros:** attentive hosts, bountiful, varied breakfasts, newer construction. **Cons:** down long, bumpy road from town, street parking only. ⊠ *Calle Palmas 115, Fracc. Costa Azul, San Francisco, Nayarit* ☎ *311/258–4316* ⊕ *www.casaobelisco.com* 🛏 *4 rooms* ⚭ *In-room: no* *phone, no TV. In-hotel: bar, pool, no kids under 16* ▤*No credit cards* ⊘ *Closed July–Sept.* ⦿*BP.*

$$ 🛅**Costa Azul.** What makes this
🕙 place attractive are the many activities offered: horseback riding, kayaking, hiking, surfing (with lessons), and excursions to the Marietas Islands or La Tobara mangroves near San Blas. The all-inclusive plan includes activities, but since the food is mainly mediocre and San Pancho has a number of excellent restaurants, the European Plan is recommended. Although the sandy beach faces the open ocean, it curves around to a spot that's safer for swimming. **Pros:** great place to bond with kids of all ages, nice beach, planned outdoor activities. **Cons:** mediocre food, some guests have complained of disorganized and unhelpful staff members, hotel maintenance isn't what it used to be. ✉*Carretera 200, Km 118, Fracc. Costa Azul, San Francisco, Nayarit* ☎*311/258–4000, 800/365–7613 toll-free in U.S.* ⊕*www.costaazul. com* ⇱*24 rooms, 3 villas* ⚐*In-room: no phone, kitchen (some), refrigerator (some), no TV. In-hotel: restaurant, bars, pool, beachfront, water sports, laundry service, Wi-Fi, parking (free)* ▤*AE, D, DC, MC, V* ⦿*AI, EP, FAP.*

$$ 🛅**Villa Amor.** What began as a hilltop home has slowly become an
★ amalgam of unusual, rustic-but-luxurious suites with indoor and outdoor living spaces. The higher up your room, the more beautiful the view of Sayulita's coast. The trade-off for such beauty? A long walk up a seemingly endless staircase and the dearth of room phones make contacting the front desk frustrating. Accommodations, managed by different owners, range from basic to honeymoon suites with terraces and plunge pools. Details like recessed color-glass light fixtures, Talavera sinks in bathrooms, brick ceilings, wrought-iron table lamps, art in wall niches, and colorful cement floors add a lot of class. The property overlooks a rocky cove where you can fish from shore; a beautiful sandy beach is a few minutes' walk. The staff lends out kayaks, boogie boards, and sometimes snorkeling gear. **Pros:** nice location across bay from Sayulita's main beach, staff arranges tours and tee times. **Cons:** tons of stairs, no room phones, open-to-the-elements rooms can have creepy crawlies. ✉*Playa Sayulita, Sayulita, Nayarit* ☎*329/291–3010* ⊕*www. villaamor.com* ⇱*34 villas* ⚐*In-room: no a/c (some), no phone, kitchen (some), refrigerator, no TV. In-hotel: restaurant, bar, water sports, bicycles, laundry service, parking (free)* ▤*MC, V* ⦿*CP.*

$ 🛅**Villas Buena Vida.** On beautiful Rincón de Guayabitos Beach, this property has three-story units, breeze-ruffled palms, and manicured

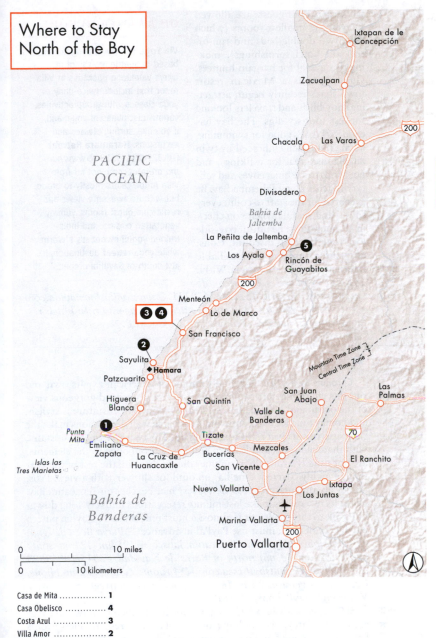

Where to Stay North of the Bay

Ixtapan de le Concepción

Zacualpan

Chacala   Las Varas

200

PACIFIC OCEAN

Divisadero

Bahía de Jaltemba

La Peñita de Jaltemba

Los Ayala

5

Rincón de Guayabitos

200

Menteón

3 4   Lo de Marco

San Francisco

2

Sayulita

Patzcuarito

◆ **Hamara**

Higuera Blanca

San Quintín

San Juan Abajo

Las Palmas

Mountain Time Zone
Central Time Zone

Valle de Banderas

1

Punta Mita

Tizate

Islas las Tres Marietas

Emiliano Zapata

La Cruz de Huanacaxtle

Bucerías

Mezcales

70

El Ranchito

San Vicente

Nuevo Vallarta

Ixtapa
Los Juntas

Bahía de Banderas

Marina Vallarta

Puerto Vallarta

0   10 miles
0   10 kilometers

4

walkways. Four guests are allowed in even the smallest rooms (which have two double beds and run-of-the-mill hotel furnishings), making this a deal for bargain hunters. Guayabitos is a Mexican resort town that's recently begun attracting snowbirds and travelers looking for less touristy digs. The bay has calm surf that's good for swimming, a long flat beach embraced by twin headlands (great for walking), and boat trips to the quiet coves and solitary beaches along Jaltemba Bay. Be prepared for the staff to count every spoon and spatula when you check in and out. **Pros:** beautiful bay-side location, 5% cash discount. **Cons:** uninspired furnishings, unreliable Internet access in rooms via Wi-Fi. ✉ *Retorno Laureles 2, Rincón de Guayabitos, Nayarit* ☎327/274–0231 ⊕ *www.villasbuenavida.com* ☞ *36 rooms, 9 suites* ♢ *In-room: kitchen, refrigerator. In-hotel: restaurant, pools, laundry facilities* ▭ *MC, V* ⫶○⫶ *EP.*

> **OM AWAY FROM HOME**
>
> **Via Yoga** (⊕ www.viayoga.com), based in Seattle, Washington, offers weeklong packages at Villa Amor that include twice-daily yoga classes with group activities, various disciplines of yoga, and, if you like, surfing classes and excursions. **Haramara Retreat** (☎ 329/291–3558 ⊕ www.haramararetreat.com), not far from Villa Amor, caters mostly to groups but with its awesome views and rustic-chic guest rooms, yummy vegetarian cuisine, and India-trained yogini owner, it's a worthwhile yoga-retreat destination. It's just south of Sayulita proper.

COSTALEGRE

$$ ⊞ **Coconuts By the Sea.** A friendly couple of American expats own and
★ run this charming cliff-top hideaway with a drop-dead-gorgeous view of the ocean and Boca de Iguana Beach below. The furniture is stylish, and homey touches like lamps and fish-theme wall decorations make the snug apartments just right for holing up. The two apartments upstairs, with thatched roofs and kitchen and living room open to the elements, are not usually available in summer due to the rain; the rest of the year they're highly coveted. One has an outdoor shower with a view. **Pros:** homey apartments, great sea views, very nice beaches on Tenacatita Bay. **Cons:** its few rooms make last-minute reservations unlikely, long down-hill walk to the beach, car is almost a must unless you're staying put; to pay by credit card, must use PayPal in advance ✉ *Playa Boca de Iguanas, 6 Dolphin Way, Bahía Tenacatita, Jalisco* ♣ *195 km (121 mi) south of PV, 21 km (13 mi) north of Barra de Navidad* ☎315/100–8899 cell ⊕ *www.coconutsbythesea.com* ☞ *4 rooms* ♢ *In-room: no phone, kitchen, refrigerator, Wi-Fi. In-hotel: pool, parking (free)* ▭ *AE, MC, V (through PayPal only)* ⫶○⫶ *EP.*

$$$$ ⊞ **El Careyes Beach Resort.** On a gorgeous bay framed by flowering veg-
★ etation, El Careyes is a boldly painted village of a resort. Guest rooms have large windows and private patios or balconies; suites have outdoor hot tubs. Colorful furnishings and artwork create a sophisticated Mexican palette. The full-service spa has fine European beauty and body treatments; a deli sells fine wines, prosciutto, and other necessities of

the good life. A full range of water-sports equipment awaits you at the beach, and there are dune buggies and kayaks, too. There are more dining options in the area than at other Costalegre resorts, making a rental car a plus. It's a short walk to pretty Playa Rosa and a short drive to Bahía Tenacatita. **Pros:** large spa menu, unique architecture, on a beautiful cove. **Cons:** few computers make it hard to check e-mail, only one on-site restaurant, 5% service charge. ⊠*Carretera a Barra de Navidad (Carretera 200), Km 53.5, Careyes, Jalisco* ✛*161 km (100 mi) south of PV, 55 km (34 mi) north of Barra de Navidad* ☎*315/351–0000* ⊕*www. elcareyesresort.com* ⤳*22 rooms, 29 suites, 3 multibedroom casitas*

⌂*In-room: safe, kitchen (some), refrigerator (some), DVD. In-hotel: restaurant, room service, bar, tennis courts, pool, gym, spa, beachfront, water sports, bicycles, laundry service, Internet terminal, Wi-Fi, parking (free)* ▤*AE, MC, V* ⫯*EP.*

$$$$ **El Tamarindo Beach & Golf Resort.** More than 2,000 acres of ecological reserve and jungle surround this magical resort along 16 km (10
Fodor's Choice mi) of private coast. The architecture fuses Mediterranean-style elements with local building materials; world-renowned Ricardo Legorreta was one of the architects. Many villas have outdoor living rooms. All have dark-wood floors; king-size beds; wet bars; ample bathrooms; and patios with plunge pools, hammocks, and chaise lounges. Sofas are upholstered in rich textured fabrics. At night the staff lights hundreds of candles around the villas to create a truly enchanting setting. The golf course is excellent. **Pros:** concierge service, individual plunge pools, CD and DVD players in each room, yoga and Pilates classes (in high season). **Cons:** 10% service fee on top of 17% sales and hotel taxes, spa isn't full service (i.e., no sauna or steam). ⊠*Carretera Melaque–Puerto Vallarta (Carretera 200), Km 7.5, Cihuatlán, Jalisco* ✛*204 km (127 mi) south of PV, 12 km (7 mi) north of Barra de Navidad* ☎*315/351–5031, 01800/823–3037 toll-free in Mexico, 866/717–4316 from U.S. or Canada* ⊕*www.mexicoboutiquehotels.com/thetamarindo* ⤳*29 villas, 3 4-bedroom houses* ⌂*In-room: safe, no TV. In-hotel: restaurant, room service, bar, gym, spa, golf course, tennis court, pool, beachfront, diving, water sports, bicycles, laundry service, Internet terminal, Wi-Fi, parking (free)* ▤*AE, MC, V* ⫯*EP.*

$$$$ **Hotelito Desconocido.** Although every inch of the place is painted, tiled, or otherwise decorated with bright Mexican colors and handicrafts, the effect is distinctive rather than fussy. Perhaps that's because rooms and suites incorporate local building styles and materials, including plank

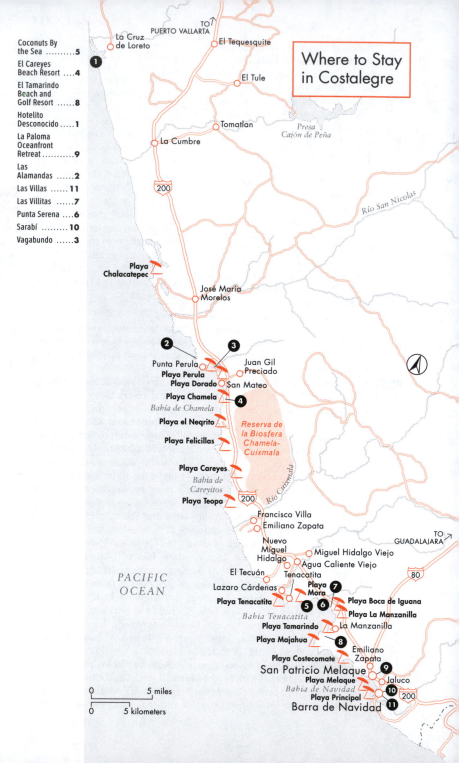

TO
PUERTO VALLARTA

La Cruz de Loreto

El Tequesquite

El Tule

1

Tomatlan

Presa Cajón de Peña

La Cumbre

200

Río San Nicolas

Where to Stay in Costalegre

Playa Chalacatepec

José María Morelos

2 **3**

Punta Perula

Playa Perula

Juan Gil Preciado

Playa Dorado San Mateo

Playa Chamela

Bahía de Chamela **4**

Playa el Negrito

Reserva de la Biosfera Chamela-Cuixmala

Playa Felicillas

Playa Careyes

Bahía de Careyitos

Río Cuixmala

Playa Teopa

200

Francisco Villa

Emiliano Zapata

TO
GUADALAJARA

PACIFIC OCEAN

Nuevo Miguel Hidalgo

Miguel Hidalgo Viejo

Agua Caliente Viejo

El Tecuán

Tenacatita

80

Lazaro Cárdenas

Playa Mora **7**

5 **6**

Playa Boca de Iguana

Playa Tenacatita

Playa La Manzanilla

Bahía Tenacatita

La Manzanilla

Playa Tamarindo

Playa Majahua **8**

Emiliano Zapata

Playa Costecomate

9

San Patricio Melaque

Playa Melaque

Jaluco

10

Bahía de Navidad

Playa Principal

200

Barra de Navidad **11**

0   5 miles

0   5 kilometers

floors, reed mats, bamboo walls, and palm-frond roofs. They're cooled by battery-powered fans and lighted by lanterns, candles, and low-wattage lamps. Rustic but lovely bathrooms bring the outdoors in through large open windows. Signal for morning coffee by running up the red flag. On a long stretch of beach, this isolated hotel is an idyllic escape for its clientele: about 60% American, 25% European, and 100% laidback. **Pros:** isolated, unique, and charming; concierge service. **Cons:** rustic-chic it is, affordable it isn't; isolated; pricey meal plan. ⊠ *Playón de Mismaloya s/n, Cruz de Loreto, Jalisco ✛97 km (60 mi) south of PV, 119 km (74 mi) north of Barra de Navidad* ☎*322/281–4010, 800/851–1143 in U.S., 01800/013–1313 toll-free in Mexico* ⊕*www. hotelito.com* ⬦*16 rooms, 8 suites* &*In-room: no a/c, no phone, no TV. In-hotel: 2 restaurants, bar, pool, spa, beachfront, water sports, bicycles, Internet terminal, parking (free)* ▤*AE, MC, V* ⎮⊙⎮*BP, FAP.*

4

$$ 🚩**La Paloma Oceanfront Retreat.** Rates are reasonable considering the small studio apartments have everything home does, and four of them face the beach (where the waves are often good for boogie boarding). Each room is configured differently, but all are bright and cheerful, with private patios and paintings by the owner (she gives lessons in high season). There's a large pool and patio facing the ocean. In high season, there's a one-week minimum stay. **Pros:** beside a beautiful bay, long beach perfect for walking and jogging. **Cons:** one-week minimum stay in high season; to pay by credit card, must use PayPal in advance. ⊠ *Av. Las Cabañas 13, San Patricio–Melaque ✛6 km (4 mi) north of Barra de Navidad* ☎ *315/355–5345* ⊕*www.lapalomamexico.com* ⬦*13 studio apartments* &*In-room: no a/c (some), no phone, kitchen, refrigerator, DVD (some). In-hotel: restaurant, pool, Internet terminal, Wi-Fi, parking (free)* ▤*AE, MC, V (through PayPal only)* ⎮⊙⎮*CP.*

$$$$ 🚩**Las Alamandas.** Personal service and exclusivity lure movie stars and royalty to this low-key resort in a thorn-forest preserve about 1½ hours from both PV and Manzanillo. Suites are filled with folk art; their indoor-outdoor living rooms have modern furnishings with deliciously nubby fabrics in bright, bold colors and Guatemalan-cloth throw pillows. Request a TV, DVD, and movie from the library for an evening in; there's little else to do at night. There's lots more to do in the daytime, however, including picnics anywhere on the property and boat rides on the Río San Nicolás. There's a 15% service charge and a two-night minimum; the average stay is seven nights. If you have to ask the price, you can't afford it. **Pros:** stargazing from rooftop bar, stunning yet cozy architecture, one-hour horseback ride included, concierge service. **Cons:** open-style bungalows not pleasant in rainy season, with mosquitoes and high humidity, not close to any restaurants or nightlife, riptides. ⊠ *Carretera 200, Km 85, Quemaro ✛83 km (52 mi) south of PV, 133 km (83 mi) north of Barra de Navidad* ☎*322/285–5500 or 888/882–9616* ⊕*www.mexicoboutiquehotels.com/lasalamandas* ⬦*14 suites* &*In-room: refrigerator, DVD. In-hotel: restaurant, room service, bars, tennis court, pool, gym, spa, beachfront, water sports, bicycles, laundry service, Internet terminal, parking (free)* ▤*AE, MC, V* ⎮⊙⎮*EP, FAP.*

$$ 🚩**Las Villas.** Aside from the luxurious and costly Grand Bay Isla Navidad and the behemoth Hotel Alondra, Barra de Navidad has only

HOTELS AT A GLANCE: COSTALEGRE

Hotel	Worth Noting	Cost	Rooms	Restaurants	On the Beach	Dive Shop	Pools	Spa	Golf Course	Tennis Courts	Health Club/ Gym	Children's Programs	Location
Coconuts by the Sea	fab beach views	$125	4				1						Bahía Tenacatita
El Careyes Beach Resort	impeccable decor	$252	55	1	yes		1	yes			yes		Careyes
El Tamarindo	stunning good taste	$625	32	1	yes	yes	1	yes	yes	2	yes		Cihuatlán
Hotelito Desconocido	rustic-chic idyll	$410	24	2	yes		1	yes	yes	1			Cruz de Loreto
La Paloma	well-equipped studios	$700/week	13	1	yes		1						San Patricio–Melaque
Las Alamandas	ultra-exclusive	$390	14	1	yes		1	yes		1	yes		Quemaro, C
Las Villas	well situated	$96	8		yes								Barra de Navidad
Las Villitas	lovely bay	$144	46		yes		1						Bahía Tenacatita
Punta Serena	adults-only oasis	$240	24	1			1	yes		3	yes		Bahía Tenacatita
Sarabi	cheap and cheerful	$28–$32	14								yes		Barra de Navidad
Vagabundo	far from crowds	$42–$52	21	1			1						Punta Perula

Buying a Time-Share

If you return to PV frequently, a time-share might make sense. Here are some tips for navigating the shark-infested waters:

■ Cruise the Internet before your vacation. Check out resale time-shares in the area, which makes it easier to determine the value of what's offered.

■ Worthwhile time-shares come with the option of trading for a room in another destination. Ask what other resorts are available.

■ Time-share salespeople get great commissions and are very good at

their jobs. Be brave, be strong, and only sign on the dotted line if it's what you really want. Remember there are plenty of good vacation deals out there that require no long-term commitment.

■ Buyer's Remorse? If you buy a time-share and get buyers' remorse, be aware that most contracts have a five-day "cooling-off period." Ask to see this in writing before you sign the contract; then you can get a full refund if you change your mind.

4

basic hotels with few rooms, and most aren't a particularly good value compared to similar hotels elsewhere. This hotel with a domed brick ceiling, comfortable beds, and remote control a/c is among the best choices. The two largest rooms have two twin beds as well as a king, plus a DVD player and a mini-refrigerator. **Pros:** well-situated near mom-and-pop groceries and restaurants, right on the beach, discounts Tuesday–Thursday and for six-night stay. **Cons:** basic rooms, no credit cards accepted, no room phones. ⊠*Calle López de Legazpi 127, Barra de Navidad, Jalisco* ☎*315/355–5354, 01800/980–7060 toll-free in Mexico* ⊕*www.lasvillitas.com.mx* ➭*9 rooms* ⚏*In-room: no phone, DVD (some), refrigerator (some). In-hotel: beachfront, Wi-Fi* ⊟*No credit cards* ¶⊙|*EP.*

$$ 🏨 **Las Villitas Club & Marina.** Las Villitas is a wonderful place to kick back on one of Pacific Mexico's most beautiful bays: Tenacatita. Each of the small bungalows has a small sitting room with two single beds doubling as couches and a separate bedroom with a king-size bed. Rooms are cheerfully painted and have large glass doors that make it easy to take in the beach views; bathrooms have tubs rather than just showers. You can borrow a kayak for a jaunt into the bay. Ask for discounts on stays Monday through Thursday in low season. **Pros:** right on the beach, beautiful bay, doors and windows are screened. **Cons:** little nearby; for TV junkies, no cable signal here. ⊠*Playa Tenacatita, Calle Bahía de Tenacatita 376, Bahía Tenacatita, Jalisco* ⊕*183 km (114 mi) south of PV, 37 km (23 mi) north of Barra de Navidad* ☎*315/355–5354, 01800/980–7060 toll-free in Mexico* ⊕*www.lasvillitas.com.mx* ➭*6 rooms, 10 bungalows* ⚏*In-room: no phone, kitchen (some), refrigerator (some), DVD (some). In-hotel: pool, beachfront* ⊟*MC, V* ¶⊙|*EP.*

$$$ 🏨 **Punta Serena.** Guests come from New York and Italy to this adults-
★ only oasis of calm. Perched on a beautiful headland, "Point Serene" enjoys balmy breezes and life-changing views from the infinity hot tub. The beach far below and pool are clothing optional. Spa treatments

are inventive: roses and red wine promote moisturizing; carotene and honey contribute to a glowing tan; and the Mayan Wrap connects you herbally to the glowing god within. Shamans leads a temazcal (ritual healing steam ceremony) twice weekly, and activities like horseback riding, tennis (three courts), and nonmotorized water sports at the adjacent Blue Bay hotel are included in the price. Additionally, rooms have lovely furnishings and decor and shared or private terraces, some with fab beach views. **Pros:** gorgeous views, intriguing spa treatments, complimentary horseback ride and mangrove cruise. **Cons:** isolated, limited menu, cobblestone walkways and hills make walking difficult for some folks. ☒ *Carretera Barra de Navidad–Puerto Vallarta (Carretera 200), Km 20, Tenacatita, Jalisco* ✛ *196 km (122 mi) south of PV, 20 km (12 mi) north of Barra de Navidad* ☎ *315/351–5427 or 315/351–5020* ⊕ *www.puntaserena.com* ⌨ *12 rooms, 12 suites* ⌂ *In-room: safe, kitchen (some). In-hotel: restaurant, bar, pool, gym, spa, beachfront, laundry service, Internet terminal, parking (free); no kids under 21* ▤ *AE, MC, V* ⏍ *AI.*

¢ ▦ **Sarabi.** The snug little rooms a block from the beach are indeed a bargain. Those with kitchenettes are still very affordable and have white-tile breakfast bar, four-burner stove, small refrigerator, and plenty of utensils. There's very little difference in the nightly rate between these and those that have a/c but not a kitchenette. For the best deal, opt for a room with a fan only. Two floors of rooms face the small parking lot. **Pros:** owner managed, clean and tidy, close to the beach, well-priced. **Cons:** no telephone, no Internet. ☒ *Av. Veracruz 196, Centro, Barra de Navidad* ☎ *315/355–8223* ⊕ *www.hotelsarabi.com* ⌨ *14 rooms, 3 bungalows* ⌂ *In room: No a/c (some), no phone, kitchen (some), refrigerator (some). In hotel: parking (free)* ▤ *No credit cards* ⏍ *EP.*

¢ ▦ **Vagabundo.** Chamela Bay, 79 km (49 mi) south of PV, is an excellent place off the gringo trail for swimming, fishing, or exploring offshore islands. Simple rooms surround a swimming pool in this motel-like, quiet, two-story hotel a block from the beach at Punta Pérula. "Bungalows" have separate bedrooms and well-equipped kitchen–dining areas; the latter don't win any beauty contests but do have a table with four chairs, stove, refrigerator, and cooking and serving utensils. The hotel owner speaks excellent English. **Pros:** beautiful Chamela Bay within walking distance, well-stocked kitchenettes. **Cons:** no Internet service, on the highway, not the beach, little charm. ☒ *Calle Independencia 100, Chamela Bay, Punta Pérula, Jalisco* ✛ *79 km (49 mi) south of PV, 137 km (85 mi) north of Barra de Navidad* ☎ *315/333–9736* ⌨ *16 rooms, 5 bungalows* ⌂ *In-room: kitchen (some), refrigerator (some). In-hotel: pool, laundry service* ▤ *No credit cards* ⏍ *EP.*

Where to Eat

Food with a view.

WORD OF MOUTH

"Trio is the best and the most consistent restaurant in Puerto Vallarta—period. The exquisite food, personalized service and the warm and artsy ambience are the reasons why I always return to this restaurant. The prices and value for money are great, too!"

—BonSaveur

WHERE TO EAT PLANNER

Quick Take

Puerto Vallarta's restaurants are to die for, but what a misuse of earthly delights that would be. Variety, quality, and innovation are the norm whether you dine in a beachfront café or a candlelit restaurant. The best places buy fresh fish daily—and it's a great bargain. Vallarta's already superior restaurants overachieve during mid-November's 10-day Festival Gourmet International.

Foodie Hot Spots

PV's biggest concentration of restaurants is in the Zona Romántica, many in Colonia Emiliano Zapata. Once called Restaurant Row, Calle Basilio Badillo now has as many shops as restaurants, but on the surrounding streets eateries continue to crop up. Centro has its fair share of choice places, too. All in all, gourmets will be happiest here in Old Vallarta, where an appetizer, sunset cocktail, or espresso and dessert isn't more than a $3 cab ride away.

Marina Vallarta's worthwhile eateries are mainly in the resorts and surrounding the marina. Bucerías has good restaurants in the center of town. In Punta Mita (aka Punta de Mita), the restaurant scene is diversifying to bring more than ceviche and fish fillets to the palapas at El Anclote.

Meals

PV restaurants cater to visitors with multicourse dinners, but traditionally, *comida* (late lunch) is the big meal of the day, usually consisting of soup and/or salad, bread or tortillas, a main dish, side dishes, and dessert. C*ena* (dinner) is lighter; in fact, many people just have milk or hot chocolate and a sweet roll, or tamales.

Desayuno (breakfast) is served in cafés (coffee shops) and small restaurants. Choices might be hefty egg-and-chorizo or -ham dishes, enchiladas, or *chilaquiles* (fried tortilla strips covered in tomato sauce, shredded cheese, and meat or eggs). Tacos and quesadillas are delicious for breakfast; some of Vallarta's best taco stands set up shop by 9 AM.

Beer and Spirits

Jalisco is far and away Mexico's most important tequila-producing state. Mexican beers range from light beers like Corona and Sol to medium-bodied, golden beers like Pacífico and the more robust Bohemia, to dark beauties Negra Modelo and Indio.

Mealtimes

Mexican mealtimes are generally as follows. Upon rising: coffee, and perhaps *pan dulce* (sweet breads). Schedule permitting, Mexicans love to eat a hearty *almuerzo*, a full breakfast, at about 10. *Comida*, typically between 2 and 5 PM, is the main meal. *Cena* is between 8 and 9 PM.

Restaurants have long hours in PV, though seafood shacks on the beach often close by late afternoon or sunset. Outside the resorts of PV, restaurants may close by 7 or 8 PM. Also, southern Nayarit is on Mountain Standard Time (an hour earlier than PV), but some restaurants in the area follow Central Time (as in PV). Always check that your restaurant is open for a later dinner and find out how it sets its clock.

Unless otherwise noted, restaurants in this guide are open daily for lunch and dinner.

Food Glossary

Here some of the dishes you're likely to find on area menus or in our reviews below. *Buen provecho!*

arrachera: skirt steak

carne asada: thin cut of flank or tenderloin (sometimes not *that* tender), grilled or broiled and usually served with beans, rice, and guacamole

carnitas: bites of steamed, fried pork served with tortillas and a variety of condiments

chilaquiles: pieces of corn tortillas fried and served with red or green sauce; good ones are crispy, not soggy, and topped with chopped onions and *queso cotija:* a crumbly white cheese

chile en nogada: a green poblano chili stuffed with a semi-sweet meat mixture and topped with walnut sauce and pomegranate seeds; the Mexican national dish, it's often served in September in honor of Independence Day

chile relleno: batter-fried green chili (mild to hot) stuffed with cheese, seafood, or a sweetish meat mixture; served in a mild red sauce

menudo: tripe stew

pozole: a rich pork- or chicken-based soup with hominy; a plate of accompanying condiments usually includes raw onions, radishes, cilantro, oregano, sliced cabbage, and tostadas

tostada: a crispy fried tortilla topped with beans and/or meat, cheese, and finely chopped lettuce or cabbage; or, the corn tortilla by itself, which is served with foods like ceviche and pozole

WHAT IT COSTS IN U.S. DOLLARS

¢	$	$$	$$$	$$$$
Restaurants				
under $6	$6–$12	$13–$19	$20–$25	over $25

Restaurant prices are for a median main course for the principal meal, usually dinner, excluding tax and service.

Reservations and Dress

Reservations are a good idea. In low season, getting a table is usually a snap. But it's always wise to call ahead and make sure the place hasn't been reserved for a party.

The most elegant restaurants simply request that men wear T-shirts with sleeves. The Mexicans are usually the best dressed, but even they forego jacket and tie for a nice button-down and slacks. If you enjoy looking like a million bucks, don't despair: looking good is always in style. The maitre d' will take notice.

Paying

Credit cards are widely accepted at pricier restaurants. More modest restaurants might accept cash only, and are leery of traveler's checks. Small eateries that do accept credit cards sometimes give a "discount" for cash (i.e., they charge a small fee for credit card use).

Tips on Tipping

Servers count on 10%–15%. In more humble establishments, tips are taken more casually than in the more prestigious restaurants. But in any case, we suggest tipping 15% for good service, a bit less for a flawed performance, and a bit more if the tab is ridiculously low.

5

PUERTO VALLARTA

ZONA ROMÁNTICA

$ ✗**Andale.** Although many have been drinking, rather than eating, at
AMERICAN   this local hangout for years, the restaurant serves great burgers, fries,
herb-garlic bread, black-bean soup, and jumbo shrimp, as well as daily
lunch and nightly drink specials at the chummy bar. The interior is cool,
dark, and informal; two rows of mini-tables line the sidewalk outside.
Service is generally attentive, although that doesn't mean the food will
arrive promptly. Plus-size patrons should beware the munchkin-size
toilet stalls. ⊠*Av. Olas Altas 425, Col. E. Zapata* ☎*322/222–1054*
☐*MC, V.*

¢   ✗**A Page in the Sun.** This corner café in the middle of Olas Altas is
CAFÉ   always full of coffee drinkers playing chess or reading newspapers and
paperback books purchased here. Items like the turkey and avocado
sandwich with all the fixings and carrot cake with cream-cheese frosting
are true comfort foods. The good coffee and location in the heart of the
Romantic Zone, a block from Playa Los Muertos, are bonuses. ⊠*Olas
Altas 399, Col. E. Zapata* ☎*322/222–3608* ☐*No credit cards.*

$$ ✗**Archie's Wok.** Dishes at this extremely popular pan-Asian restaurant
ASIAN   include Thai garlic shrimp, *pancit* (Filipino stir-fry with pasta), and
Singapore-style (lightly battered) fish. There are also lots of vegetar-
ian dishes. The spinach and watercress salad with feta, pecans, and a
hibiscus dressing is healthful, refreshing, and perfect for a late lunch
(the restaurant opens only after 2 PM). Ceilings are high, and the decor is
Asian tropical: dark wood, lacy potted palms, and Indonesian étagères.
Thursday through Saturday from 7:30 to 10:30 PM, the soothing harp
music of well-known local musician D'Rachel is the perfect accompani-
ment to your meal. ⊠*Calle Francisca Rodríguez 130, Col. E. Zapata*
☎*322/222–0411* ♨*Reservations not accepted* ☐*MC, V* ♥*Closed
Sun. and Sept.*

$ ✗**Café de Olla.** Repeat visitors swear by the enchiladas and carne asa-
MEXICAN   das at this earthy restaurant. It's also one of the few places in town
where you can get a margarita made of raicilla (green-agave firewater
as opposed to tequila). A large tree extends from the dining-room floor
through the roof, local artwork adorns the walls, and salsa music often
plays in the background. Note that as soon as Café de Olla opens for
the season, it fills up and seems to stay full: you may need to wait for a
table, especially at breakfast and dinner. If you despair of waiting, the
taco shop next door is very good. ⊠*Calle Basilio Badillo 168–A, Col.
E. Zapata* ☎*322/223–1626* ♨*Reservations not accepted* ☐*No credit
cards* ♥*Closed Tues. and Sept. 15–Oct. 15.*

¢   ✗**The Coffee Cup.** Coffee is sold in all its various presentations, includ-
CAFÉ   ing freshly ground by the kilo; there's even decaf. You can munch on
cookies, sandwiches, wraps, burritos, and breakfast breads, or get a
licuado (smoothie) made with fresh fruit and milk. There's a book
exchange, and you can use the single computer to access the Internet
or send e-mails until a waiting customer's glare chases you off. Note
that this place isn't affiliated with the Coffee Cup in Marina Vallarta.

Where to Eat in Zona Romántica

EL CENTRO

REMANCE

BENITO JUAREZ

EMILIANO ZAPATA

AMAPAS

ZONA ROMÁNTICA

Bahía de Banderas

Playa Olas Altas

Playa los Muertos

Streets labeled: Libramiento, Invierno, Verano, Primavera, Benito Juárez, Rivera del Río, Río Cuale, Camichín, Francisco I. Madero, Lázaro Cárdenas, Venustiano Carranza, Aquiles Serdán, Naranjo, Jacarandas, Basilio Badillo, M. Diéguez, F. Rodríguez, R. Gómez, Pulpito, Aguacate, Insurgentes, Constitución, Ignacio Vallarta, Pino Suárez, 5 de Febrero, Isla Cuale, Encino, A. Rodríguez, Libertad, Guerrero, Morelos, Malecón, Olas Altas, Amapas, Pilitas, Abedul

1/4 mile
1/4 km

⊠*Calle Rodolfo Gómez 146–A, Col. E. Zapata* ☎*322/222–8584* ▭*No credit cards* ⊘*No dinner Sun. Nov.–Apr.*

$$
ECLECTIC
Fodor's Choice
★

✗**Daiquiri Dick's.** Locals come over and over for breakfast (the home-made orange-almond granola is great), visitors for the good service and consistent Mexican and world cuisine. The lunch-dinner menu has fabulous appetizers, including superb lobster or shrimp tacos with a drizzle of béchamel sauce and perfect, tangy jumbo-shrimp wontons. On the menu since the restaurant opened almost 30 years ago is Pescado Vallarta, or grilled fish on a stick. The tortilla soup is popular, too. Start with a signature daiquiri; move to the extensive wine list. The open patio dining room frames a view of Playa Los Muertos, creating a beautiful, simple scene to enjoy while you sip that drink. ⊠*Av. Olas Altas 314, Col. E. Zapata* ☎*322/222–0566* ▭*MC, V* ⊘*Closed Sept. and Tues. May–Aug.*

$
MEXICAN

✗**El Brujo.** It's on a noisy street corner, and service ranges from reason-ably attentive to begrudging, but the seriously good food and generous portions mean that this is still an expat (and gay) favorite. The *molca-jete*—a sizzling black pot of tender flank steak, grilled green onion, and soft white cheese in a delicious homemade sauce of dried red peppers—is served with a big plate of guacamole, refried beans, and made-at-the-moment corn or flour tortillas. ⊠*Venustiano Carranza 510, at Naranjo, Col. Remance* ☎*322/223–2036* ⊗*Reservations not accepted* ▭*MC, V* ⊘*Closed Mon., 2 wks in late Sept.–early Oct.*

$$
ECLECTIC

✗**El Repollo Rojo.** Better known as the Red Cabbage (its English name), this restaurant is by—but doesn't overlook—the Cuale River. It's hard to find the first time out, but it's worth the effort for the international comfort food. Homesick Canadians fill up on chicken with mashed potatoes, gravy, and cranberry sauce, while Italians indulge in pasta with fresh tomatoes; there are even a few Russian dishes. Frida's Dinner includes an aperitif of tequila followed by cream of peanut soup, white or red wine, *chile en nogada* (a mild chili decorated with colors of the Mexican flag), a main dish from the Yucatán or Puebla, and flan for dessert. Romantic ballads fill the small space, and the walls are crowded with movie posters and head shots of international stars. Here's the quandary: some patrons rave about the service, and others lambaste it. ⊠*Calle Rivera del Río 204–A, El Remance* ☎*322/223–0411* ▭*No credit cards* ⊘*No lunch. Closed Sept. and Sun. May–Oct.*

$
ECLECTIC
☽

✗**Fidensio's.** One of the best reasons to come to this seaside bar-restau-rant is to let the tide lick your toes and the sand caress shoeless feet as you eat and have a beer or a mixed drink under a palapa-shaded chair at the ocean's edge. The burgers, nachos, tuna sandwiches, and fresh fish fillets are fine if unexciting; otherwise the food has gone downhill. Many

BREAKFASTS OF CHAMPIONS

In PV, **Café de Olla** and Memo's Pancake House are favorites, as is **Fredy's Tucan**. **La Palapa** and **Daiquiri Dick's** serve breakfast at the beach, and **Langostino's** has casual, ocean-side morning fare. In Bucerías, head to **Famar** for an excellent Mexican breakfast. In the Costalegre, try **Casa de la Abuela** for excellent coffee and jazzy tunes or **El Dorado** for a full breakfast at the beach.

expats come for breakfast. Service is relaxed and friendly, not overbearing or phony. It closes at sunset. ⊠*Pilitas 90, Los Muerto Beach, Col. E. Zapata* ☎*322/222–5457* ▭*No credit cards* ⊘*No dinner.*

¢ ✗**Fredy's Tucan.** Even in low season Fredy's, next door to the Hotel Roger, is full of Mexican families, friends, and businesspeople. Your mug of excellent coffee will be refilled without having to beg; service is professional and friendly.

CAFÉ

Breakfast is the meal of choice; the lunch menu is abbreviated. Eat on the covered patio or inside, where big plate-glass windows let you keep an eye on busy Basilio Badillo Street. You can get a fruit smoothie or a stiff drink from the bar. ⊠*Basilio Badillo 245,Col. E. Zapata* ☎*322/223–0778* ⚱*Reservations not accepted.* ▭*No credit cards* ⊘*No dinner.*

$$ ✗**Kaiser Maximilian.** Viennese and Continental entrées dominate the menu, which is modified each year when the restaurant participates in PV's culinary festival. One favorite is herb-crusted rack of lamb served with horseradish and pureed vegetables au gratin; another is venison medallions in chestnut sauce served with braised white cabbage and steamed vegetables. The adjacent café (open 8 AM–midnight) has sandwiches, excellent desserts, and 20 specialty coffees—all of which are also available at the main restaurant. Because a stream of street peddlers is anathema to fine dining, eat in the charming, European-style dining room, where handsome black-and-white-clad waiters look right at home amid dark-wood framed mirrors, brightly polished brass, and lace café curtains. ⊠*Av. Olas Altas 380, Col. E. Zapata* ☎*322/223–0760* ▭*AE, MC, V* ⊘*Closed Sun.*

CONTINENTAL

★

$ ✗**Langostino's.** Right on the beach just north of the pier at Playa Los Muertos, Langostino's is a great place to start the day with a heaping helping of Mexican rock, cranked up to a respectable volume. The house favorite at this professional and pleasant place is surf and turf, and the three seafood combos are a good value. The kids can play on the beach while you linger over coffee or suds. ⊠ *Calle Manuel M. Dieguez, at Los Muertos Beach, Col. E. Zapata* ☎*322/222–0894* ▭*No credit cards.*

SEAFOOD

$$$$ ✗**La Palapa.** This large, welcoming, thatch-roof place is open to the breezes of Playa Los Muertos and filled with wicker chandeliers, art-glass fixtures, and lazily rotating ceiling fans. The menu meanders among international dishes with modern presentation: roasted stuffed chicken breast, pork loin, seared yellowfin tuna drizzled in cacao sauce. The seafood enchilada plate is divine. It's pricey, but the beachfront location and, in the evening, the low lights and Latin jazz combo (8 to 11 PM nightly) keep people coming back. Breakfast here (daily after 8 AM) is popular, as is Sunday brunch. ⊠*Calle Púlpito 103, Playa Los Muertos, Col. E. Zapata* ☎*322/222–5225* ▭*AE, D, MC, V.*

ECLECTIC

5

$$
ITALIAN
★
✗La Piazzeta. Locals come for the Naples-style pizza, cooked in a brick oven and with a crust that's not too thick, not too thin. There's also great pasta and a good variety of entrées, like the cream-based salmon with caviar and lemon or the broccoli with fettuccine in cream sauce, served piping hot. For appetizers try the top-heavy (*con molto tomate*) bruschetta or steamed mussels with lemon, parsley, and butter. Most folks sit on the large patio, there's also an intimate dining room. The personal attention of the owner, Mimmo, guarantees repeat business. It's open 4 to midnight. ⊠ *Calle Rodolfo Gómez 143 at Olas Altas, Col. E. Zapata* ☎ *322/222–0650* ▤ *MC, V* ⊘ *Closed Sun. No lunch.*

WORD OF MOUTH

"[La Palapa had a] very nice atmosphere . . . you can see and hear the waves crashing. . . . I ordered the shrimp dish with crusted Parmesan and sweet potatoes, and my brother got the tuna. Both were excellent. There was a nice wine list and several good desserts. The service was attentive and not too slow. I'd recommend it for a romantic evening or a nice dinner with friends. However . . . if Mexican is what you want, you'd be happier elsewhere." —Corinn45

¢
AMERICAN
☺
✗Memo's Pancake House. If your child can't find something he or she likes on the Pancake House menu, you might have an alien on your hands. There are 12 kinds of pancakes—including the Oh Henry, with chocolate bits and peanut butter—and eight kinds of waffles. Other breakfast items include *machaca* (shredded beef) burritos, chilaquiles, and eggs Florentine, but these tend to be perfunctory: pancakes and waffles are your best bet. The large dining room bursts with local families on weekends and homesick travelers daily. It can get noisy, and service tends to slip when Memo is out of town. The back patio—draped in pothos and serenaded by birds—is pretty but is like a greenhouse when the day heats up. Everything shuts down at 2 PM. ⊠ *Calle Basilio Badillo 289, Col. E. Zapata* ☎ *322/222–6272* ⚖ *Reservations not accepted* ▤ *No credit cards* ⊘ *No dinner.*

$
PICNIC
☺
✗Picnic. Come before 8 PM for the comfort food: cheeseburgers and chips (a dollar more to replace these with a small handful of fries) and grilled chicken with salad and rice or beans. The abbreviated menu also has hot dogs, grilled cheese sandwiches, chicken salad, veggie burgers, and a super-lemony cheesecake that's served cold. There's a small selection of beer, wine, and spirits, too. Luis, the friendly owner, was the chef at the now-defunct Chiles and brought along the recipes. The decor is fresh and fun: picnic baskets hold silverware, and tablecloths are gingham. ⊠ *Calle Púlpito 154, Col. E. Zapata* ☎ *322/223–2353* ⚖ *Reservations not accepted* ▤ *No credit cards* ⊘ *Closed Sun. and Aug. to Sept.*

CENTRO AND ENVIRONS

$$
SPANISH
★
✗Barcelona Tapas Bar. One of the few places in town with both great food and an excellent bay view, Barcelona has traditional Spanish tapas like *patatas alioli* (garlic potatoes), spicy garlic shrimp, and grilled

mushrooms. In addition to traditional paella, there's also a seafood version. To start you off, attentive waiters bring a free appetizer and delicious homemade bread. The six-course tasting menu lets you try soup, salad, and dessert as well as tapas—choose your own or follow the chef's suggestions. The restaurant is air-conditioned in summer; the rest of the year the windows are taken off to let the breezes in. You pay for that patio view by having to walk up a few dozen stairs. ⊠ *Matamoros at 31 de Octubre, Centro* ☎ *322/222–0510* ⚓ *Reservations essential* ▭ *AE.*

NATURAL THIRST-BUSTER

The guy on the malecón or in the main plaza with a giant gourd and a handful of plastic cups is selling *agua de tuba*, a refreshing, pleasant, yet innocuous drink made from the heart of the coconut palm. It's stored in a gourd container called a *huaje*, and served garnished with chopped walnuts and apples.

$$$ ✗ **Café des Artistes.** Several sleek dining spaces make up Café des Artistes, ECLECTIC the liveliest of which is the courtyard garden with modern sculpture. The main restaurant achieves a contemporized Casablanca feel with glass raindrops and tranquil music. Thierry Blouet's Cocina de Autor (closed Sunday and September) is a limited-seating restaurant pairing four- to six-course tasting menus with appropriate wines. Decor is restrained, with a waterfall garden behind plate glass taking center stage. Many diners end the night at the clubby cigar bar, but it's open to anyone, as is Constantini Wine Bar, which offers some 50 vintages by the glass as well as distilled spirits, appetizers, and live music most every night of the week. ⊠ *Av. Guadalupe Sánchez 740, Centro* ☎ *322/222–3229* ▭ *AE, MC, V* ⊘ *No lunch.*

$$ ✗ **Chez Elena.** Frequented in its heyday by Hollywood luminaries and ECLECTIC the who's who of PV, this downtown restaurant still has a loyal following. The patio ambience is simple, but the wholesome food is satisfying, and portions are generous. House specialties include fajitas and Yucatan-style pork. Elena's is also known for its killer, handcrafted margaritas and its flaming coffee drinks. ⊠ *Calle Matamoros 520, Centro* ☎ *322/222–0161* ▭ *MC, V* ⊘ *Closed June–Sept. No lunch.*

¢ ✗ **Comedor de Sra. Heladia.** Take off the rose-color glasses and see the real MEXICAN Old Vallarta. A short walk up from the malecón is this neighborhood dining room that serves construction workers and locals. It's in a typical one-story Vallarta house of whitewashed brick with a red-tile roof and a burnished-cement floor. The lady of the house serves breakfast 8 to 11 AM and two or three entrées between 1 and 5 or 6 PM. Choices like meatballs in tomato sauce, pork chops, or pigs feet are usually accompanied by rice, beans, homemade salsa, and a basket of hot tortillas. There's no menu, and you'll need to communicate in basic Spanish. ⊠ *Calle Aldama, at Matamoros, Centro* ☎ *322/223–9612* ⚓ *Reservations not accepted* ▭ *No credit cards* ⊘ *Closed Sun. No dinner.*

$$ ✗ **Cueto's.** Teams of engaging waiters, all family members, squeeze past SEAFOOD the trio that croons romantic tunes throughout the day to refill beer glasses, remove empty plates, or bring more fresh tostadas and hot, crusty garlic bread. But don't fill up on nonessentials, as the casseroles—with crab, clams, fish, shrimp, or mixed seafood—are so delicious you won't want to leave even one bite. (The cream-based versions are the most successful.) Have a complimentary margarita with dinner or a free digestif later on. Cueto's is a few blocks behind the Unidad Deportivo complex of soccer fields and baseball diamonds. ✉ *Calle Brasilia 469, Col. 5 de Diciembre* ☎ *322/223–0363* 🚫 *No credit cards.*

$$ ✕ **El Andariego.** A few blocks past the north end of the malecón is this
MEXICAN lively Mexican restaurant. Paintings of the city brighten the walls; at night the lighting is subdued and the mood is romantic. Many of the traditional breakfasts are the stick-to-your ribs variety. Lunch and dinner menus are different, but the cost is about the same. Expect numerous salads, pasta dishes, a good variety of chicken and beef dishes, and seafood and lobster prepared to your taste. Enjoy live music (electric guitar versions of "Proud Mary," or mariachi music) nightly between 5 and 11 PM. There's free wireless Internet in both restaurant and bar. ✉ *Av. México 1358, at El Salvador, Col. 5 de Diciembre* ☎ *322/222–0916* ⊕ *www.elandariego.com.mx* 🚫 *MC, V.*

$$ ✕ **El Arrayán.** The oilcloth table covers, enameled tin plates, exposed
MEXICAN rafters, and red roof tiles of this patio-restaurant conjure up nostalgia
Fodor's Choice for the quaint Mexican home of less frenetic times. Here you can find
★ the things *abuelita* (grandma) still loves to cook, with a few subtle variations. Highlights are chicken breasts stuffed with zucchini blossoms, chipotle-chili shrimp with a citrus sauce, and tender pork in a sauce of orange and arrayán—the fruit after which the restaurant is named. For dessert try caramel flan or a light pumpkin-caramel ice. ✉ *Calle Allende 344, at Calle Miramar, Centro* ☎ *322/222–7195* 🚫 *MC, V* ⊗ *Closed Tues. and Aug. No lunch.*

¢ ✕ **El Campanario.** Fans swirl the air, doors are open to the street, and
MEXICAN cheerful oilcloths cover wooden tables at this no-frills spot across from the cathedral. Egg dishes and chilaquiles are served 9–11 AM, and an inexpensive daily lunch menu is served 2–5 PM. About $5 gets you soup, a main dish, drink, homemade tortillas, and dessert. Office workers come in for takeout or drift in between 6 and 10 PM for tacos, *tortas* (Mexican-style sandwiches on crispy white rolls), or pozole. A recipe for the latter is given—along with a positive dining review—in a framed *Los Angeles Times* article from the 1980s. ✉ *Calle Hidalgo 339, Centro* ☎ *322/223–1509* 🚫 *No credit cards* ⊗ *Closed Sun., and often between 5 and 6 PM.*

$$ ✕ **La Bodeguita del Medio.** Near the malecón's north end, this restaurant
CARIBBEAN with a fun-loving atmosphere has a bit of a sea view from its second-floor dining room and a Caribbean flavor. Specials vary by season; if possible, try the roast pork, the Cuban-style paella, or the pork loin in tamarind sauce; order rice, salad, or fried plantains separately. Like its Havana namesake, La Bodeguita sells Cuban rum and cigars, and the live music—like the cuisine—is pure *cubano*. During the day comrades hunch over their computers to take advantage of the free Wi-Fi; a sextet performs most nights until past midnight. Try the Havana specialty drink mojito: a blend of lime juice, sugar, mineral water, white rum, and muddled fresh mint leaves. ✉ *Paseo Díaz Ordáz 858, Centro* ☎ *322/223–1585* 🚫 *AE, MC, V.*

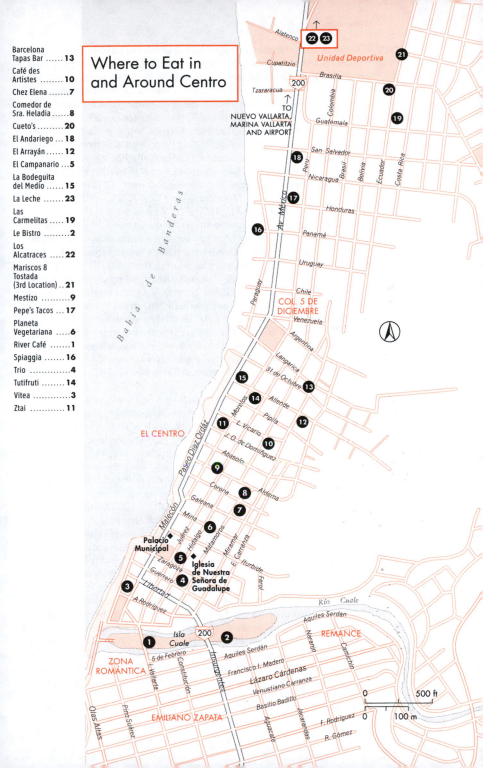

Where to Eat in and Around Centro

$$$$ ✗**La Leche.** If Chef Alfonso Cadena wasn't so cool (he looks like a refined,
ECLECTIC   former rock star because he is one!), then La Leche's main dining room,
an all-white rotunda lined with shelves of milk cans, could come off as
a gimmicky. But each night as Cadena personally presents a different
menu on a chalkboard, his "blank canvass" dining space becomes the
perfect backdrop for a unique meal. For instance, a delicate seafood
bisque, unveiled in whimsical ceramic tureens, might precede an exquisite mahi-mahi in a citrus reduction that provides the perfect balance of
sweet and sour. Servers are attentive and friendly but leave ample time
between courses, so be prepared for an enjoyable but lengthy evening.
Reservations aren't required but are a good idea. ⊠ *Blvd Francisco
Medina Ascencio., Zona Hotelera Norte* ☎322/293–0900 ⊕*www.
lalecherestaurant.com* ▤*AE, MC, V* ⊘*No lunch.*

$$$ ✗**Las Carmelitas.** Hawks soar on updrafts above lumpy, jungle-draped
MEXICAN   hills. The town and the big blue bay are spread out below in a breath-
taking, 200-degree tableau. Under the palapa roof of this small, open
restaurant romantic ballads play as waiters start you off with guaca-
mole, fresh and cooked salsas, chopped cactus pad salad, and tostadas.
Seared meats—served with grilled green onions and tortillas made on
the spot—are the specialty, but you can also order seafood stew or
soups. The restaurant opens at 1 PM. Don't despair about the 100-peso-
per-person fee you pay to enter (apparently to discourage lookie-loos);
it will be deducted from your tab. Or avoid the hassle altogether—the
fee is waived for those who have made reservations. ⊠*Camino a la
Aguacatera, Km 1.2, Fracc. Lomas de Terra Noble* ☎322/303–2104
▤*No credit cards.*

$$$ ✗**Le Bistro.** Start off with a soup of Mexican or Cuban origin and then
ECLECTIC   move on to one of the international main dishes: cream of wild spinach
soup or mushroom-sherry soup, crepes, duck with blackberry sauce,
herbed Cornish hen, or sea scallops with jicama coleslaw. The restaurant is draped in ferns and tropical plants and overlooks the Cuale
River; carved-stone columns, zebra chairs, and wicker settees are among
the sophisticated touches. At breakfast, the tinkling of the piano keys
is a lovely counterpoint to the melody the river makes as it rushes over
rocks below. ⊠*Isla Río Cuale 16–A48300* ☎322/222–0283 ⊕*www.
lebistro.com.mx* ▤*AE, MC, V* ⊘*Closed Sun. and mid-Aug.–Sept.*

$ ✗**Los Alcatraces.** For a breakfast of chilaquiles that are crisp, not soggy,
MEXICAN   come to "The Calla Lilies." *Café de olla,* real Mexican coffee simmered
with cinnamon and *panela* (unrefined brown sugar), is served in a keep-
warm carafe; crumbly white cheese is brought from a ranch in the nearby
hills. All meals are economical, especially the combo plate: a quesadilla,
chiles rellenos, arrachera beef, rice, beans, and a taco. Weekdays, a fixed-
price lunch for under $5 consists of soup, main dish, beans, and fruit
drink. This is a good, authentic-Mexican option for people staying in
the Hotel Zone. ⊠*Blvd. Federico M. Ascencio 1808, Col. Olímpica*
☎322/222–1182 ▤*No credit cards* ⊘*No dinner weekends.*

$$$ ✗**Mestizo.** Vegetarians won't find much on this traditional Mexican menu,
MEXICAN   but can concoct a meal of spinach, beet, and jicama salad; squash blos-
som soup; and *antojitos,* or grilled, corn-based snacks. Carnivores can
feast on grilled goat with cactus, chicken with *huitlacoche* (corn fungus),

beef medallions, or red snapper fillet with a mild poblano cream sauce. The garden setting, under a spreading arrayan tree at a restored old home, couldn't be prettier or imbue a more authentic ambience. And the *danzón* music reminiscent of Old Mexico music salons only adds to the charm. ✉*Calle Abasolo 233, Centro* ☎*322/222–1333* ⊕*www.mestizovallarta.com* ⊟*AE, MC, V* ⊘*Closed Sun. and May–mid-Oct.*

$ ✗**Pepe's Tacos.** No longer the be-all
MEXICAN and end-all of taco consumption in PV, Pepe's still can't be beat at 5 AM, when most sensible taco-makers are asleep. It's an open-door dive across from the Pemex station at the north end of Old Vallarta. Expect plastic tablecloths, sports on several TVs, and 11 different types of quesadil-las—from standard cheese in a flour tortilla to the "Japanese" version with beef, sausage, pineapple, and mushrooms. You can order tacos by the set or individually (choose your meat grilled or barbecued over charcoal) for about a dollar each. The menu also has pork or Hawaiian barbecue sandwiches. The bar has all the basics: rum, tequila, beer. ✉*Honduras 173, between Avs. Peru and Mexico, Col. 5 de Diciembre* ☎*322/223–1703* ⊟*No credit cards* ⊘*Closed Mon. No lunch.*

$ ✗**Planeta Vegetariana.** Those who stumble upon this hog-less heaven
VEGETARIAN can partake of the tasty meatless carne asada and a selection of main
⟳ dishes that changes daily. Choose from at least three delicious main
★ dishes, plus beans, several types of rice, and a soup at this buffet-only place. Though the selection of overdressed salads is good, the greens tend to be wilted or soggy. A healthful fruit drink, coffee, or tea, and dessert is included in the reasonable price. Eggs are not used; items containing milk products are labeled as such. It's about a block north of the cathedral, downtown. ✉*Iturbide 270, Centro* ☎*322/222–3073* ⊟*No credit cards.*

$$$ ✗**River Cafe.** At night, candles flicker at white-skirted tables with com-
ECLECTIC fortable cushioned chairs, and tiny white lights sparkle in palm trees surrounding the multilevel terrace. This riverside restaurant is recommended for breakfast and for the evening ambience. Attentive waiters serve such international dishes as seafood fettuccine and vegetarian crepes; the wild-mushroom soup and fried calamari with aioli sauce are especially recommended. If you're not into a romantic dinner, belly up to the intimate bar for a drink and—Friday and Saturday evenings—to listen to live jazz. Breakfast is served daily after 9 AM. ✉*Isla Río Cuale, Local 4, Centro* ☎*322/223–0788* ⊟*AE, MC, V.*

STREET-FOOD SMARTS

Many think it's madness to eat "street food," but when you see professionals in pinstripes thronging to roadside stands, you've got to wonder why. Stands can be just as hygienic as restaurants, as they are actually tiny exhibition kitchens. Make sure the cook doesn't handle cash, or takes your money with a plastic-gloved hand. Plates sheathed in disposable plastic wrap solve the "washing-up-in-a-bucket" dilemma, and most stands have a place for customers to wash their hands. Ask locals for recommendations, or look for a stand bustling with trade.

5

■**TIP→** A waiter would never consider bringing you your check before you ask for it; that would be rude. When you want the bill, make the universal one-hand-writing-on-the-other gesture. It works every time.

$$$
ECLECTIC

✗**Spiaggia.** Overhead lights impart a golden glow to this open, beach-front restaurant with cushy, linen-strewn tables. After dark, the harbor lights can be seen from the big, simple deck covered by a giant white pavilion. A flautist adds to the romance Thursday through Sunday at dinner hour; during other times, a sound track dominated by robust female singers enhances the perky and modern mood. Try the grilled veggies, the charcoal-grilled "cowboy" steak, and, for dessert, the extra-creamy white-chocolate parfait. Note that this place is also open for breakfast. ⊠ *Calle Uruguay 109, Col. 5 de Diciembre* ☎*322/223–3722* ▭*AE, MC, V* ⊘*Closed Mon.*

$$$
ECLECTIC
Fodor's Choice
★

✗**Trio.** Conviviality, hominess, and dedication on the parts of chef-owners Bernhard Güth and Ulf Henriksson have made Trio one of Puerto Vallarta's best restaurants—hands-down. Fans, many of them members of the local artsy crowd, marvel at the kitchen's ability to deliver perfect meal after perfect meal. Popular demand guarantees rack of lamb with fresh mint and, for dessert, the warm chocolate cake. The kitchen often stays open until nearly midnight, and during high season the restaurant opens the back patio, second floor, and rooftop terrace. Waiters are professional yet unpretentious; either the sommelier or the maitre d' can help you with the wine. But the main reason to dine here is the consistently fabulous food at great value. ⊠*Calle Guerrero 264, Centro* ☎*322/222–2196* ▭*AE, MC, V* ⊘*No lunch.*

¢
MEXICAN

✗**Tutifruti.** If you find yourself near the main square at lunchtime, consider having a taco at this little stand. While we can't exactly call this *fast* food, the quesadillas and machaca (shredded beef) burritos are delicious; you can also get a sandwich or burger. Consider sharing, because the portions are large. For breakfast, order up a fruit smoothie. If you're lucky, you might get one of the few stools at the tiled counter. ⊠*Calle Allende 200, between Av. Juaréz and Av. Guadalupe Sánchez, Centro* ☎*322/222–1068* ▭*No credit cards* ⊘*Closed Sun. No dinner.*

$$
BISTRO
★

✗**Vitea.** When chefs Bernhard Güth and Ulf Henriksson, of Trio, needed a challenge, they cooked up this delightful seaside bistro. So what if your legs bump your partner's at the small tables? This will only make it easier to steal bites off her plate. The decor of the open, casual venue is as fresh as the food. Appetizers include the smoked salmon roll with crème fraîche and the spicy shrimp tempura; crab manicotti and other entrées are light and delicious. Half portions are available, or make a meal of the bistro's soups, sandwiches, and appetizers. It's a nice place for breakfast overlooking the goings-on along the malecón. Service here isn't as crisp and professional as that at Trio. ⊠*Libertad 2, near south end of Malecón, Centro* ☎*322/222–8703* ▭*MC, V* ⊘*Closed 1 wk in late Sept.*

$$$
ECLECTIC

✗**Ztai.** Lounge music emanates from the cool, dark, modern interior and into the appealingly spare outdoor garden shaded by bamboo and fig trees. The food is quite good, and portions are large. Try the fresh and oh-so-lightly-fried calamari, the fruity shrimp ceviche, duck tacos, or the tender filet mignon. Asian flavors spice up the seafood recipes, while the meat dishes lean toward Continental cuisine. After dinner you can recline with a chaser on one of the beds, sofas, or bar stools of Ztai's upstairs lounge. ⊠ *Calle Morelos 737, Centro* ☎ *322/222–0364* ⊕ *www.ztai.com* ⊟ *AE, MC, V* ☉ *No lunch.*

MARINA VALLARTA

¢

DELICATESSEN

✕**The Coffee Cup.** Early-risers and those heading off on fishing charters will appreciate the daily 5 AM opening time, and closing time isn't until 10 PM. The café, which is filled with wonderful art for sale, has fruit smoothies and coffee in many manifestations, including frappés of Oreo cookie and cream-cheese carrot cake. Have a breakfast bagel (served all day), wrap, deli sandwich, or homemade dessert. ⊠ *Condominios Puesto del Sol, Local 14–A, at marina, Marina Vallarta* ☎ *322/221–2517* ⊟ *MC, V.*

WORD OF MOUTH

"[The Coffee Cup] is a great little place in the marina to get a morning cup of Joe, free Internet access, and a free five-minute call to the States. The breakfast bagel sandwiches hit the spot."
—rossharis

5

¢

MEXICAN

★

✕**La Taquiza.** Here's a tip: stop by this local's den on your way to the airport (it's just across the street), and get food to go. Dollar, Budget, and Thrifty rental-car storefronts surround this bright and shiny hole-in-the-wall. You can order food, drop off your rental car, and then get a shuttle to the airport. Or eat in at the brightly polished green Formica tables (with matching chairs). The tasty lime drink, lunch specials, pinto bean soup, and the house specialty—tacos—are served in or on old-fashioned red pottery plates, bowls, and mugs. ⊠ *Blvd. Federico M. Ascencio 4594, Col. Villa Las Flores* ☎ *322/209–1138* ⊟ *No credit cards* ☉ *Closed Sun. No dinner.*

$

SEAFOOD

★

✕**Mariscos 8 Tostadas.** The odd menu translations at these restaurants are a clear indication that the clientele is local. For instance, the tuna sashimi appears as *atun fresco con salsa rasurada,* or "tuna cut thick with shaved sauce," which is followed by "alone if there was fishing"—meaning that it's only available if the fish was caught that day. Speaking of the tuna: here it's thicker (though not too thick) than that in U.S. sushi houses and is served in a shallow dish with soy sauce, micro-thin cucumber slices, sesame seeds, green onions, chili powder, and lime. The ceviche couldn't be fresher. There's a small storefront subsidiary in the parking lot at Plaza Marina; the original venue, behind Blockbuster Video in the Hotel Zone, has full seafood plates alongside its ceviches, tacos, and appetizers. Portions are generous. ⊠ *Calle Quilla at Calle Proa, Local 28–29, Marina Vallarta48310* ☎ *322/221–3124* ⊟ *No credit cards* ☉ *No dinner* ⊠ *Calle Río Guayaquil 413, at Calle Ecuador, Col. Versalles (Zona Hotelera)* ⊹ *Behind Blockbuster Video store* ☎ *322/222–7691* ⊟ *No credit cards* ☉ *Closed Sun. and 2 wks in Sept. No dinner.*

$$$

ITALIAN

✕**Porto Bello.** Yachties, locals, and other return visitors attest that everything on the menu here is good. And if you're not satisfied, the kitchen will give you something else without quibbling. Undoubtedly that's what makes Marina Vallarta's veteran restaurant one of its most

Where to Eat in Marina Vallarta

Gustavo Diaz Ordaz International Airport

6

Paseo de las Flores

VILLAS LAS FLORES

Villas: Gladiola, Clavel, Violetas, Amapola, Orquidas, Jazmin, Margaritas, Laureles, Las Azucenas, Lirios, Geranios, Amapas, Obeliscos, Dalias, Las Palmas, Canarios, Pétalos, Las Rosas

5 Plaza Marina

Blvd. Francisco Medina Ascencio

Gansos

Industrias

Marina Valarta Campo De Golf

Estero "El Salado"

Paseo Bocanegra

Albatros

Flemingos

Flemingos

Albatros

Pelicanos

Gaviotas

Priv. de las Garzas

Plaza Neptuno

Popa

MARINA VALLARTA

Av. Paseo de la Marina

Mástil

Timón

El Faro

Proa

4   **3**

Quilla

2

Ancla

Vela

Isla Iguana

EDUCACION

Av. Politecnico Nacional

Preparatoria

Blvd. Francisco Medina Ascencio

Secundaria

Paseo de la Marina Sur

Paseo de la Marina Sur

Playa El Salado

PACIFIC OCEAN

Terminal Maritima

1

Av. Gob. Prisciliano Sánchez

Oceano Indico

Camino Viejo Aramara

Av. Las Garzas

Flamingos

Av. Las Garzas

Quetzal

TO CENTRO, ZONA ROMANTICA, COSTALEGRE ↓

Dr. Mike Lemus

0 ————— 1/4 mile

0 ————— 1/4 km

popular. The dining room is diminutive and air-conditioned; the patio overlooking the marina is more elegant, with a chiffon ceiling drape and white ceiling fans. Since there are no lunch specials, and the Italian menu is the same then as at dinner, most folks come in the evening. ✉ *Marina del Sol, Local 7, Marina Vallarta* ☎ *322/221–0003* ⊕ *www.portobellovallarta.com* ▭ *MC, V.*

$$ ✗ **Tino's.** Vine-covered trees poke through the roof of the breeze-blessed, SEAFOOD covered outdoor eatery overlooking a placid lagoon. The Carvajal fam-★ ily has worked hard to make the Nuevo Vallarta branch a favorite; the Punta Mita branch lets you dine near a pretty beach, while the original Pitillal location takes you back in time to Vallarta's roots. Tino's is full even midweek, mainly with groups of friends or businesspeople leisurely discussing deals. A multitude of solicitous, efficient waiters proffer green-lipped mussels meunière; crab enchiladas; oysters; and the regional specialty, fish *sarandeado* (rubbed with herbs and cooked over a wood fire). Concha de Tino is a dish with seafood, bacon, mushrooms, and spinach prettily presented in three seashells. ✉ *2a Entrada a Nuevo Vallarta, Km 1.2, Las Jarretaderas* ☎ *322/297–0221* ▭ *MC, V* ✉ *Av. El Anclote 64, El Anclote, Punta Mita* ☎ *329/291–6473* ✉ *Av. 333 at Calle Revolución, Pitillal* ☎ *322/225–2171 or 322/224–5584* ▭ *MC, V.*

SOUTH ALONG BANDERAS BAY

$$ ✗ **Boca Bento.** This comely restaurant, which moved in 2008 from the FUSION heart of the Romantic Zone to the Casa Iguana hotel in Mismaloya, is open daily for breakfast, lunch, and dinner. Dishes fuse Latin American and Asian elements. The feeling is simultaneously Eastern and modern, with contemporary music and artwork. Try the rib-eye steak, pork ribs with a honey-chili glaze, or the cross-cultural mu shu carnitas with hoisin sauce. ✉ *Av. 5 de Mayo 455, Mismaloya* ☎ *322/222–9108* ⊕ *www.bocabento.com* ▭ *AE, MC, V* ⊘ *Closed Sept.*

$$ ✗ **La Playita de Lindo Mar.** Open to the ocean air, the wood-and-palm-ECLECTIC front restaurant looks right at home on Conchas Chinas Beach. And ★ there are wonderful views of waves crashing on or lapping at the shore. Enjoy breakfast or an expansive, inexpensive Sunday brunch buffet (come before 11 AM for the best selection). Select from crepes, frittatas, omelets, and *huevos Felix (*eggs scrambled with fried corn tortillas, served with a grilled cactus pad, beans, and grilled serrano chilies). Lunch and dinner choices include grilled burgers and chicken, shrimp fajitas, and lobster thermidor. If you're driving, look for the sign on Carretera a Mismaloya; you can park in the small lot near the beach or in the hotel lot and take the elevator down to the beach. ✉ *Carrertera a Barra de Navidad 2.5, Playa Conchas Chinas, at Hotel Lindo Mar* ☎ *322/221–5511* ▭ *MC, V.*

NAYARIT

ALONG BANDERAS BAY

$
CAFÉ
✕**The Bar Above.** This little place above Tapas del Mundo defies categorization. It's a martini bar without a bar (the owners, Buddy and Jorge, prefer that people come to converse with friends rather than hang out at a bar) that also serves dessert. Order from the day's offerings, maybe molten chocolate soufflé—the signature dish—or a charred pineapple bourbon shortcake. Lights are dim, the music is romantic, and there's an eagle's view of the ocean from the rooftop nest. ⊠*Corner of Av. Mexico and Av. Hidalgo, 2 blocks north of central plaza, Bucerías* ☎*329/298–1194* ▭*No credit cards* ⊗*No lunch. Closed Sun. and June–Oct.*

$$
STEAK
✕**Brasil Nuevo Vallarta.** This steak house is in Nuevo Vallarta's large, comprehensive mall has café seating on the corridor. Cuts of meat are easy to come by, but unimaginative use of herbs and spices (or lack thereof) makes each morsel taste surprisingly similar. Lunch is served only after 2 PM. ⊠*Paradise Village Mall, 2nd fl., Nuevo Vallarta* ☎*322/297–1164* ▭*AE, MC, V.*

$
SEAFOOD
✕**Columba.** Yearn for manta ray stew? Crave fresh tuna balls? Simply must have shark soup? The recipes here are geared to the local palate; if you're an adventurous eater with a hankering for fresh, strangely prepared (a lot of things are minced beyond recognition) seafood dishes, give Columba a try. It's on the road to the fishermen's beach in Cruz de Huanacaxtle. As a backup plan, have an appetizer here, then head for one of the other picks in Bucerías. This restaurant closes at 6:30 or 7 PM, and serves only beer and sodas as beverages. It has the least expensive lobster around. ⊠*Calle Marlin 14, at Calle Coral, Cruz de Huanacaxtle* ☎*329/295–5055* ▭*No credit cards* ⊗*Closed Mon. and wk after Easter.*

$$
SEAFOOD
✕**Dugarel Plays.** Do they mean "Dugarel's Place"? No matter, of Bucerías's many beachfront eateries, this one gets extra points for longevity, attentive service, good views north and south along the bay, and the best breezes. The menu isn't extensive: there are several beef plates and Mexican dishes, and a larger assortment of fresh fish and seafood served with the usual rice and toasted bread, as well as veggies. Be sure to ask for the guacamole; it's great, but it's not on the menu. ⊠*Av. del Pacífico s/n, Bucerías* ☎*329/298–1757* ▭*No credit cards.*

$
MEXICAN
✕**Famar.** We queried Bucerías expats and locals alike, and this unassuming restaurant got just about everyone's vote. Breakfast in the noisy front room includes chilaquiles, waffles, and omelets. It's more peaceful on the back patio, where the top picks are beef fajitas and shrimp Famar: the chef's secret recipe, containing shrimp, bacon, cheese, and salsa. Consistency and friendly, familial service is the name of the game. ⊠*Héroes de Nacozari 105, Bucerías* ☎*329/298–0113* ▭*No credit cards* ⊗*Closed Sun.*

$$$
ARGENTINE
✕**La Porteña.** Restaurants are a hard sell in all-inclusive-dominated Nuevo Vallarta. This one seems to have survived. The setting, an L-shape covered patio with kids' play equipment in the center, is Mexican, but the

Continued on page 145

MEXICO'S GOURMET TOWN

Mar Plata restaurant

PV merges cooking styles and ingredients from all over the world

After huge cities like Guadalajara and Mexico City, Puerto Vallarta beats anywhere in the country for sheer number of excellent restaurants. Many talented chefs, drawn to this area by its natural beauty, have fallen in love with the place and opened restaurants, contributing to the varied world cuisine. Metaphorically duking it out, they create confits, reductions, tapanades, and tempuras. You, the visitor, are the clear winner, able to indulge in spring rolls or Filipino pancit, great pizza, melt-in-your-mouth beef carpaccio, and wonderful seafood dishes made with sea bass and tuna, shrimp, and shellfish plucked from local waters.

Competition creates excellence. "The high season is only five months long," says chef Bernhard Güth. "You have to be creative and good year-round to survive." PV doesn't have a signature cuisine—instead, it merges cooking styles and ingredients from all over the world. Traditional Mexican dishes are plentiful, but more often upscale restaurants use these as a springboard for their own specialties, infusing European techniques and classical recipes with new life. The most elegant restaurants present dishes so beautifully that you might dread the thought of disassembling these works of art.

TOP RESTAURANTS AND CHEFS

Stars among Puerto Vallarta's many fine chefs and restaurants, these trailblazers march to a different drummer.

Trio

Conviviality, hominess, and dedication on the parts of the chef-owners have made Trio one of Puerto Vallarta's best restaurants, hands-down. Fans, many of them members of PV's artsy crowd, marvel at the kitchen's ability to deliver perfect meal after perfect meal. Popular demand guarantees rack of lamb with fresh mint and for dessert, the warm chocolate cake.

Vitea

The chefs at Trio opened this oceanfront bistro in 2005— which all but guaranteed its success. In addition to the great oceanfront location and upbeat Caribbean soundtrack, Vitea charms with its wide range of Mediterranean-inspired, contemporary sandwiches, soups, small plates, and full entrées—all at accessible prices.

THE DUO AT TRIO AND VITEA When you ask patrons why they love Trio, they almost universally mention the personal attention of high-energy but low-key owner–chef **Bernhard Güth** and his colleague, **Ulf Henriksson**. Güth says "Our mission here is to hug all of our clients, mentally, to make them feel more than welcome."

TOP: Fish Dish from Trio
ABOVE: Bernhard Güth &
Ulf Henriksson

Daiquiri Dick's

Visitors come often more than once during a vacation for the excellent service and consistent and innovative Mexican and world cuisine. The menu has fabulous appetizers and fish. Start with a signature daiquiri; move to the lingering wine list. Twin patios face the sea—one covered, one not.

THE COLLABORATORS The fish on a stick has been around since Dick's was a palapa on the beach. But most of the stellar recipes originated with departed chef Rafael Nazario, and are now expertly executed by talented Mexican chef **Ignacio Uribe**. During high season, Seattle chef **Hnoi Latthitham** joins Uribe, adding sizzle and spice from her native Thailand.

Daiquiri Dick's fish on a stick

La Ola Rica

Presentation is artful, portions generous, and the decor—a cross between whimsical and chic—is as yummy as the food. Owners Gloria Honan and Triny Palomera Gil scour the coast each day for fresh ingredients, fish, and bread, and preside over the restaurant each night to make sure the food's as good as it can be.

SELF-MADE CHEF In 1996 **Gloria Honan** and her partner were selling espresso from a lopsided wooden table and inviting potential clients to sign up for a meal. But when the pasta primavera proved wildly successful, they opened La Ola Rica in Triny's family home. Their expertise is self-taught. Gloria says, "Finding out what you are capable of and pushing yourself to hold high standards is a very rewarding experience."

Gloria Honan (chef-owner) and her partner, Triny Palomero Gil, co-owner

Mark's Bar & Grill

Standout dishes at this Bucerías restaurant include the homemade bread and pizza, great salads, and such entrées as macadamia-crusted fish fillets and lobster ravioli. The restaurant is cozy but chic, with glassware from Tonalá, special-order lamps from Guadalajara, and a red tile roof peaking through exposed beams. Vie for the back patio, open to the stars.

NATURAL TALENT Creative New Zealand transplant **Jan Benton** spent happy childhood hours digging potatoes, shaking walnuts from trees, and roaming for wild mushrooms. Her appreciation for wholesome, natural foods shows in her cuisine, of which Jan says: "Everything has its own reason to be on the plate. You'll not find a repeat flavor."

Still Life No. 1: Mussels

Café des Artistes

In Thierry Blouet's kitchen Mexican ingredients and European techniques produce such stellar dishes as cream of prawn and pumpkin soup, artichoke-and-potato terrine, and grilled tenderloin served with Camembert and smoky chipotle chile sauce.

THE MASTER Well-spoken, confident **Thierry Blouet** was given the title of Master Chef of France in 2000. Born in the Philippines to French parents, Chef Blouet describes his cooking as French cuisine with Mexican—and to a lesser extent, Asian—ingredients and spices. He is also president and co-founder of PV's Gourmet Festival, and in 2008 inaugurated a seafood restaurant, also called Café des Artistes, at the boutique Hotel des Artistes in Punta Mita.

Dessert as sculpture

THE DISH ON THE DISHES

Lobster taco, Daiquiri Dick's

Puerto Vallarta has dozens of wonderful restaurants, and diligent research has produced the following list of some of the most exciting plates this gourmet town has to offer.

AMAZING APPETIZERS

Daiquiri Dick's **lobster tacos** are divine, and its shrimp wonton's wonderful melange of flavors dance a merengue in your mouth. At Trio, try the **anise-infused Portobello mushrooms** with vegetable vinaigrette. La Ola Rica has delightful **garlic mushrooms** and the sweetest **coconut shrimp** around.

SEAFOOD, MEXICAN-STYLE

The **mixed-seafood enchiladas** at La Palapa are wonderful, the best thing on the menu. Daiquiri Dick's **fish on a stick,** called Pescado Vallarta, has been pleasing crowds for nearly 30 years.

A-LIST ASIAN

Archie's Wok is the best place on the bay for multi-ethnic Asian cuisine, including Filipino, Thai, and Chinese. Favorite dishes are the **spicy Thai noodles** and **pancit** (Filipino noodle stir-fry). It's also great for vegetarians, with several wonderful stir-fried veggie dishes.

CHOCOLATE A-GO-GO

Indulge in a delicious **chocolate fondue** served with nutmeg ice cream at Café des Artistes. Trio's **warm chocolate cake** is legendary in PV. Make a pit stop at Xocodovia (⇨*Chapter 6*), for some of the most delicious truffles in La Zona Romántica or Bucerías, for a bag of crunchy **chocolate chip cookies** for the road. You could also sit down for an addictive **chocolate brownie** *beso* (kiss), so rich it goes best with strong, black coffee.

IT'S ALL IN THE ATMOSPHERE

FOOD WITH A VIEW

Get a magnificent view of the city and bay, and a varied menu of excellent Spanish tapas at **Barcelona Tapas.**

DECADENT DECOR

Greco-Roman meets the tropics modern at **Le Bistro.** One of Vallarta's original gourmet restaurants, recently revitalized, has river-view dining among stone pillars and stands of towering bamboo.

Café des Artistes has a magical, multilevel garden of ferns and figs, mangos and palms. Open to the ocean, **Vitea** is a casually

Kaiser Maximilian

hip bistro with clever and chic glass-and-metal furnishings. Two rows of tables outdoors facing the beach and boardwalk impart a European flavor. If a traditional European atmosphere appeals, repair to **Kaiser Maximilian** with dark gleaming wood, lace café curtains, and lots of polished brass. **Mar Plata** is saved from looking industrial by innovative installations, fixtures, and antiques.

EPICUREAN EVENTS

Chocolate fondant with tomato and basil sorbet and white chocolate and raspberry sauce, Café des Artistes

INTERNATIONAL GOURMET FESTIVAL

Puerto Vallarta's dining scene owes its success in part to its annual gourmet festival, which has brought it international attention since 1994. During the 10–day food fling each November, chefs from Africa, Europe, South America, and the United States bring new twists on timeless classics. Starting with an elegant chef's cocktail reception, the festival continues with a full table of events. Each of the more than two dozen participating restaurants invites a guest chef to create special menus with wine pairings. Local and guest chefs teach cooking classes and seminars. The culmination is a gala dinner with live music, fireworks, and naturally, an over-the-top gourmet meal. ☎ 322/222–3229 Café des Artistes, ⊕ www.festivalgourmet.com.

RESTAURANT WEEK

Most everyone in Vallarta works his or her tail off during the December to Easter high season. When *vallartenses* can finally take a breath—and then give a collective sigh of relief—they reward themselves with some reasonably priced nights out at the destination's best restaurants during this two-week (despite its name) event in Mayo. Each participating restaurant offers prix-fixe meals (with choices among appetizers, entrées, and desserts) for either 159 or 259 pesos. ☎ 322/221–0106.

TACO PRIMER

In this region, a taco is generally a diminutive corn tortilla heated on an oiled grill filled with meat, shrimp, or batter-fried fish. If your server asks "¿Preparadita?", he or she is asking if you want it with cilantro and onions. Add-your-own condiments are salsa mexicana (chopped raw onions, tomatoes, and green chilies), liquidy guacamole, and pickled jalapeño peppers. Some restaurants include chopped nopal cactus and other signature items.

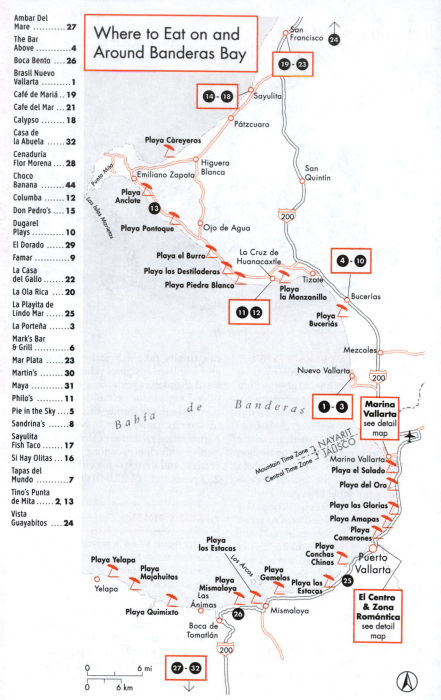

Where to Eat on and Around Banderas Bay

San Francisco

19 - 23

24

14 - 18

Sayulita

Pátzcuaro

Playa Càreyeros

Higuera
Blanca

San
Quintín

Punta Mita

Emiliano Zapata

Playa
Anclote

Las Islas Marietas

13

Playa Pontoque

Ojo de Agua

200

San

Playa el Burro

La Cruz de
Huanacaxtle

4 - 10

Playa las Destiladeras

Playa Piedra Blanca

Tizaté

Bucerías

Playa
la Manzanillo

11 12

Playa
Buceriás

Mezcales

Nuevo Vallarta

200

1 - 3

**Marina
Vallarta**
see detail
map

Bahía   de   Banderas

NAYARIT
JALISCO

Mountain Time Zone

Central Time Zone

Marina Vallarta

Playa el Salado

Playa del Oro

Playa las Glorias

Playa Amapas

Playa
los Estacas

Playa
Camarones

Playa
Conchas
Chinas

Playa
Gemelas

**Puerto
Vallarta**

Playa Yelapa

Playa
Majahuitas

Los Arcos

Playa los
Estacas

25

Yelapa

Playa
Mismaloya

**El Centro
& Zona
Romántica**
see detail
map

Playa Quimixto

Las
Ánimas

26

Mismaloya

Boca de
Tomatlán

200

0   6 mi

27 - 32

0   6 km

food is pure Argentine. Every cut of meat is grilled over mesquite, from the steaks to Angus prime rib (both imported from Texas). The adventurous yet tasty *chinculinas* (tender tripe appetizers) and chorizo turnovers certainly are authentic. Rice, veggies, and other sides must be ordered separately. Italian dishes and a few non-Argentine things like salmon and chicken dishes are also available. Come for a late lunch (it opens only after 2 PM) or dinner. ⊠*Blvd. Nayarit Pte. 250, Nuevo Vallarta* ✛*Between highway to Bucerías and El Tigre golf course* ☎*322/297–4950* ▤*AE, MC, V* ⊘*Closed Mon.*

TIME IS OF THE ESSENCE

The state of Nayarit (Nuevo Vallarta and points north) is in the Mountain Standard Time zone, while Jalisco (Marina Vallarta to Barra de Navidad) is on Central Standard Time. But because tourism in Bucerías and Nuevo Vallarta has always been linked to that of Puerto Vallarta, many Nayarit businesses run on Jalisco time. When making dinner reservations or checking restaurant hours, ask whether the place runs on *hora de Jalisco* (Jalisco time) or *hora de Nayarit*.

$$$ ✕**Mark's Bar & Grill.** You can dine
BISTRO alone at the polished black-granite
★ bar without feeling too lonely, or catch an important ball game. But seemingly a world away from the bar and TV is the charming restaurant known for its delightful decor and excellent cuisine. Both are best appreciated on the back patio, open to the stars. Menu standouts include the homemade bread and pizza, the salads, and the macadamia-crusted fresh fish fillets with mushroom ragout. The lamb is flown in from New Zealand; scallops, oysters and mussels from Baja; and the black Angus beef from Monterrey. Mixed organic lettuces, chives, and basil come from the lady down the street. The restaurant is elegant yet warm and inviting, with a golden glow over everything and roving musicians. Order wine by the glass from the extensive list. ⊠*Av. Lázaro Cárdenas 56, Bucerías* ☎*329/298–0303* ▤*MC, V* ⊘*No lunch.*

$ ✕**Philo's.** Ambitious Philo does it all: breakfast, lunch (except in low
ECLECTIC season), dinner. It's a bar with live music Thursday–Saturday after 8:30 PM; a meeting place for local fund-raisers and events; and a community center with a computer, Spanish classes, and a pool table. And if you were wondering, the food is good. Options include pizza, sandwiches, burgers, and barbecued chicken and ribs. Philo's special pizza has goat cheese, sun-dried tomatoes, onion, and pineapple—and it delivers (including to boats in the new marina)! ⊠*Calle Delfín 16, La Cruz de Huanacaxtle* ☎*329/295–5068* ▤*MC, V* ⊘*May–Oct.: no lunch, closed Sun. and Mon; Nov.–Apr.: closed Mon.*

¢ ✕**Pie in the Sky.** Although the cars on the highway can be noisy, the
CAFÉ lure of deliciously decadent mini-cheesecakes, pecan tarts, and crunchy
★ chocolate cookies exerts a strong gravitational pull. The signature dessert here is the *beso*, a deep chocolate, soft-center brownie. Cakes, including gorgeous wedding cakes, are decorated by Zulem, a fine artist who excels with frosting as her medium. Sit a spell and take advantage of the free Wi-Fi. ⊠*Héroes de Nacozari 202, Bucerías* ☎*329/298–0838* ⊠*Lázaro Cárdenas 247, at I. Vallarta, Col. E. Zapata* ☎*322/223–8183* ▤*AE, MC, V.*

$$
MEDITERRANEAN
✕**Sandrina's.** Canadian owner Sandy is as colorful as her wonderful art, which graces this locals' favorite. Dine on the back patio at night amid dozens of candles and tiny lights. The varied menu has plenty of salads and pasta dishes as well as such Mediterranean fare as chicken souvlaki and Greek-style chicken and pita bread with hummus or tzatziki. Order an espresso, delicious doctored coffee, or dessert from the bakery counter in the front, which opens at 9 AM. The main restaurant opens after 3:30 PM (Jalisco time). ⊠*Av. Lázaro Cárdenas 33, Bucerías* ☎*329/298–0273* ⊕*www.sandrinas.com* ▤*MC, V* ⊗*No lunch. Closed Tues. and 2 wks in Sept.*

> ### TACO NIGHTS
>
> Friday through Sunday nights in La Cruz de Huanacaxtle are Taco Nights (6 to 10 or 11). At the home of the Díaz Gómez family (Calle Huachinango, two blocks north of traffic circle), locals and travelers socialize over delicious carne asada tacos, or quesadillas with freshly made flour or corn tortillas, excellent homemade salsas, and homemade flan for dessert. Bring your own beer or indulge in *horchata* or *agua de jamaica*, made, respectively, of rice and hibiscus plant.

$
ECLECTIC
✕**Tapas del Mundo.** Here, worldly recipes of this and that are served in small plates perfect for sharing. Sit at one of three long bars around the open kitchen. Nosh on a hot pot of shrimp with guajillo chilies served with homemade tortillas, breaded olives, Anaheim chilies stuffed with goat cheese, or Oriental beef strips. Be apprised of the wonderful margaritas. The Bar Above, upstairs (⇨*above*), sells desserts, coffee, and mixed drinks. ⊠*Corner of Av. Mexico and Av. Hidalgo, 2 blocks north of central plaza, Bucerías* ☎*329/298–1194* ▤*No credit cards* ⊗*Closed June–Sept. No lunch.*

NORTH OF BANDERAS BAY

$$$
ECLECTIC
✕**Cafe del Mar.** Chefs Eugene of Singapore and Amandine, a Belgian-Mexican, artfully blend Asian, Mediterranean, and Mexican cuisines to create beautiful seafood and chicken dishes. The varied and excellent appetizers and desserts are especially recommended. The setting itself is romantic and sophisticated. Tiny white lights and soft music accompany individual tables down the side of a hill to a vine-drenched trellis at the bottom. There's usually a guitarist serenading during Friday dinner; the restaurant is open for lunch as well. ⊠*Av. China 9, San Francisco* ☎*311/258–4251* ▤*No credit cards* ⊗*Closed Wed. and Aug. and Sept.*

$
CAFÉ
✕**Café de María.** Friendly owner María Ines oversees the production—slow but steady—of your attractively presented fruit bowl with yogurt; spinach salad with sesame seeds and mandarin oranges; or, mimosa or Bloody Mary. Coffee and a scoop of ice cream or slice of carrot cake are also options. The prices here are similar to those you'd find in the United States, as are the lovely, clean bathrooms. Two rooms of this renovated former home overlook the street about a block from the town's main beach. It seems most popular for breakfast, but, in high season, the kitchen's open until 9 PM. ⊠*Av. Tercer Mundo 6 56, San Francisco*

☎*311/258–4439* ▭*No credit cards* ☾*Closed Wed.; closed Sept.–mid-Oct. No dinner June–Aug.*

$$
ECLECTIC

✗**Calypso.** This second-story restaurant overlooks the town plaza from beneath a big palapa roof. Locals rave about the deep-fried calamari served with spicy cocktail and tangy tartar sauces; it's an appetizer that's large enough for several people to share. Portions in general are generous. There are good pasta dishes, including the house special with basil and sun-dried tomatoes. The Cobb salad has tons of blue cheese; the Caesar and Chinese-chicken salads are also good. ✉*Av. Revolución 44, across from plaza, Sayulita* ☎*329/291–3704* ▭*MC, V* ☾*Closed Sun. No dinner June–Oct.*

> **DAILY SPECIALS**
>
> To save money, **look for the fixed-menu lunch** called either a *comida corrida* or a *menú del día*, served from about 1 to 4 in restaurants throughout Mexico, especially those geared to working-class folks.

$
AMERICAN
☺

✗**Choco Banana.** One of Sayulita's pioneer restaurants has really gotten spiffy, adding tile mosaic accents and generally beautifying its terrace restaurant. The Wi-Fi doesn't hurt, either. BLTs and burgers, omelets and bagels, and chicken with rice and chai tea are some of what you'll find here. Service isn't fast, in keeping with laid-back Sayulita's surfer attitude. This perennial favorite is almost always full of people eating and loafing; there's a kids' menu for the truly young. It closes at 6 PM (2 PM on Sunday). ✉*Calle Revolución at Calle Delfin, on plaza, Sayulita* ☎*329/291–3051* ▭*No credit cards* ☾*No dinner Sun.*

$$
CONTINENTAL

✗**Don Pedro's.** Sayulita institution Don Pedro's has pizzas baked in a wood-fire oven, prepared by European-trained chef and co-owner Nicholas Parrillo. Also on the menu are consistently reliable seafood dishes and tapenade. The mesquite-grilled filet mignon is just about the best around; it comes with baby vegetables, mashed potatoes, and pita bread. The pretty second-floor dining room, with the better view, is open when the bottom floor fills up, usually during the high season (November to May). Call to find out about live music at dinner during the week—sometimes salsa, sometimes flamenco. This is a good spot for breakfast, too, after 8 AM. ✉*Calle Marlin 2, at beach, Sayulita* ☎*329/291–3090* ⊕*www.donpedros.com* ▭*MC, V* ☾*Closed Sept.*

$$
ECLECTIC

✗**La Casa del Gallo.** If a hole-in-the-wall could be out-of-doors, this would be it. Frankly, it looks best by candlelight. But folks don't come for the decor; they come for the fab filet mignon, great fish and shrimp, and good pizza. Thursday at 7 PM there's a "save the sea turtles" presentation. The affable owner, Gallo, is also a musician who plays tunes (often blues or acoustic guitar) whenever possible after 8 PM (most often Thursday through Sunday in low season). As nightlife is an exception rather than a rule in San Pancho, locals have made this their after-dark hangout. ✉*Av. Tercer Mundo 7, San Francisco* ☎*311/258–4135* ▭*No credit cards* ☾*Closed Tues. No lunch.*

$$
ECLECTIC
Fodor'sChoice
★

✗**La Ola Rica.** The food is good. *Really* good. Somehow chef and co-owner Gloria Honan (with Triny Palomera Gil) makes garlic-sautéed mushrooms into a minor miracle on toast. The cream of poblano-chili soup is simply to die for: not too spicy, but wonderfully flavorful. And these are just the starters. The restaurant is understandably popular, and reservations are encouraged. Locals come for the coconut shrimp, lemon chicken, and medium-crust pizzas; everyone laps up the lovely margaritas. The two owners opened a beachside restaurant, La Playa de La Ola Rica, across from Palapas Iguanas in April 2009. It serves burgers, fresh fish fillets, salads, and other casual fare. ⊠*Av. Tercer Mundo s/n, San Francisco* ☎*311/258–4123* ▤*MC, V* ☉*Closed Sun.; no lunch. Also closed Sun.–Wed. June, July, and Aug.–Oct. and closed Sat. June and July.*

$$$$
CONTINENTAL

✗**Mar Plata.** Grandiose yet romantic, these impressive second-story digs have a celestial seasoning of stars on the ceiling in the form of tin lamps from Guadalajara. Dark-blue and deep terra-cotta walls juxtapose nicely; the huge space is saved from looking industrial by innovative installations and fixtures. Co-owner and chef Amadine's recipes wed traditional Argentine meats with updated Continental cuisine in a happy transcontinental marriage. Portions are smallish, and entrées exclude sides. There's live music Sunday and occasional flamenco shows or tango classes. ⊠*Calle de Palmas 130, Col. Costa Azul, San Francisco* ☎*311/258–4424* ⊕*www.marplata.com.mx* ▤*MC, V* ☉*Closed Mon. and Aug. and Sept. No lunch.*

$
SEAFOOD

✗**Sayulita Fish Taco.** Attentive if leisurely service, a central location, and low prices make this a natural choice for banishing the munchies. The ability to select both the size and nature of the dish (choose, for example, fish, veggies, chicken, or shrimp prepared as a taco, burrito, "bowl" or "shoe box" size) is another plus. The owners added a second story in 2008, an excellent place to keep their 150 different labels of tequila. ⊠*Jose Mariscal 13, Sayulita* ☎*329/291–3272* ▤*No credit cards* ☉*Closed Sun. and mid-Aug.–end of Sept.*

$
MEXICAN
♻

✗**Si Hay Olitas.** This simply decorated, open-front restaurant near tiny Sayulita's main plaza is the one most often recommended by locals for dependable Mexican and American fare. Order a giant burrito, vegetarian platter, burger, grilled chicken, or a seafood combo. There's a little of everything to choose from, and it's open for breakfast. The setting is casual, and the menu has plenty of things that children will like. ⊠*Av. Revolución 33, Sayulita* ☎*329/291–3203* ▤*No credit cards.*

$$
MEXICAN

✗**Vista Guayabitos.** Portions are large, and the cooking seems to have improved with time. Order a full Mexican meal or just a shrimp or fish taco and a beer or cocktail. Shrimp is prepared in a handful of ways; for kids there are hamburgers (or shrimp burgers) and fries or quesadillas. Enjoy lovely views of a solitary beach, an uninhabited island, and the beaches of Guayabitos. The hawk's-eye ocean view is especially wonderful around sunset. ⊠*Carretera a Los Ayala, Km 1.5, Rincón de Guayabitos* ☎*327/274–2589* ▤*MC, V.*

COSTALEGRE

$$
CONTINENTAL

✕**Ambar Del Mare.** A French woman from Provence brings a welcome addition to Barra's circumspect culinary scene, along with good thin-crust pizzas, escargot, crepes, and other tasty French and Italian fare. Of the many pasta dishes, the lasagna, cannelloni, and ravioli use pasta made from scratch. The restaurant's compact size and good tunes, along with the small bar in the middle and the few tables looking out over the beach, give it a bistro feel. ⊠ *Calle López de Legazpi 158, by Hotel Alondra, Barra de Navidad* ☎ *315/355–8169* ▭ *No credit cards* ⊘ *Closed Tues.–Thurs. May–Nov. No lunch.*

¢
AMERICAN

✕**Casa de la Abuela.** The amiable and service-oriented owner, Miguel, makes this one of the town's top choices for breakfast, snacks, or a light lunch. Listen to rock and jazz on the great sound system as you sip cappuccino and munch on the assortment of homemade Mexican cookies that comes with it. Refills of the good American-style coffee are a given ungrudgingly. Besides omelets, chilaquiles, fresh juices, and other breakfast food, Miguel and his family serve snacks like guacamole and chips, and burgers and fries for lunch. ⊠ *Av. Miguel López de Legazpi 150, Barra de Navidad* ☎ *No phone* ▭ *No credit cards* ⊘ *Closed Mon. No dinner.*

¢
MEXICAN
★

✕**Cenaduría Flor Morena.** Some folks say the enchiladas here are the best they've ever eaten. And others call this place a "local institution." Everyone pretty much agrees that this hole-in-the-wall on the main square is the best place around to get good, inexpensive pozole, tamales, and tacos. ⊠ *Facing main plaza below Catscan bar, San Patricio–Melaque* ☎ *No phone* ▭ *No credit cards* ⊘ *Closed Mon. and Tues. No lunch.*

$
SEAFOOD

✕**El Dorado.** This is the best place in town for seafood; the ocean view from under the tall, peaked, palapa roof isn't bad either. Besides seafood there's grilled chicken with baked potato, beef tips with rice and beans, soups, quesadillas, great guacamole, and fries. It's open all day (8 AM until 10 PM) and serves everyone from white-collar business types to families and friends meeting for lunch, to tourists cleaned up for an evening out. After your meal, kick your shoes off and take a walk on the beach. ⊠ *Calle Gómez Farias 1, San Patricio–Melaque* ☎ *315/355–5239* ▭ *MC, V.*

$
MEXICAN

✕**Martin's.** This second-floor, palapa-roof restaurant is the most reliable in town for food and good cheer, and for hours of operation, too, as it's open year-round. There are Mexican- and American-style breakfasts, fajitas and shrimp for lunch and dinner, and sporadic serenades. This is as much a place for socializing as for eating; at the bar you can quaff champagne, cognac, martinis, or wine. There's usually live jazz, flamenco, or Latin music from 8 PM to midnight on Monday in high season. ✉ *Calle Playa Blanco 70, La Manzanilla* ☎ *315/351–5106* ⊟ *No credit cards* ⊘ *Closed Tues. Apr.–mid-Dec.; closed Sept. 19–Oct. 1.*

$$
ECLECTIC
★
✕ **Maya.** Two Canadian women have teamed up to bring sophistication to San Patricio–Melaque's dining scene. East meets West in contemporary dishes such as tequila-lime prawns and corn, chorizo, and Gouda-cheese fritters with a smoked jalapeño aioli. Favorite entrées include Szechuan prawns and prosciutto-wrapped chicken. The hours of operation are complex and subject to change; it's best to check the Web site or confirm by phone. There's often live music including jazz or blues. ✉ *Calle Alvaro Obregón 1, Villa Obregón, San Patricio–Melaque* ☎ *315/102–0775 cell* ⊕ *www.restaurantmaya.com* ⊟ *No credit cards* ⊘ *Closed Sun. and Mon. in Nov.; closed mid-May–Oct. No lunch.*

Shopping

Huichol bowls

WORD OF MOUTH

"Shopping in town you can do on your own. Basilo Badillo and the Olas Altas area on the south side, and along the Malécon and on the parallel streets of Juarez and Morelos in El Centro are good areas for shops."

—Cabron

It's hard to decide which is more satisfying: shopping in Puerto Vallarta, or feasting at its glorious restaurants. There's enough of both to keep a bon vivant busy for weeks. But while gourmands return home with enlarged waistlines, gluttonous shoppers need an extra suitcase for the material booty they bring home.

Puerto Vallarta's highest concentration of shops and restaurants shares the same prime real estate: Old Vallarta. But as construction of hotels, time-shares, condos, and private mansions marches implacably north up the bay, new specialty stores and gourmet groceries follow the gravy train. To the south, the Costalegre is made up primarily of modest seaside towns and self-contained luxury resorts, and shopping opportunities are rare.

More than a half-dozen malls line "the airport road," Boulevard Francisco M. Ascencio, which connects downtown with the hotel zone and Marina Vallarta. There you'll find folk art, resort clothing, and home furnishing stores amid supermarkets, and in some cases bars, movie theaters, and banks.

A 15% value added tax (locally called IVA, officially the *impuesto al valor agregado*) is levied on most larger purchases. (Note that it's often included in the price, and it's usually disregarded entirely by market vendors.) As a foreign visitor, you can reclaim this 15% by filling out paperwork at a kiosk in the Puerto Vallarta airport and other major airports around the country. That said, most visitors find the system tedious and unrewarding and avoid it altogether. Here's how it works: you must make purchases at approved stores and businesses, and your merchandise must total $115 or more. Even if you plan to pay with cash or a debit card, you must present a credit card at the time of purchase and obtain a receipt and an official refund form from the merchant. Tax paid on meals and lodgings won't be refunded.

SMART SOUVENIRS

ARTS AND CRAFTS

Puerto Vallarta is an arts and crafts paradise, particularly if you're fond of ceramics, masks, fine art, and Huichol folk art. Indeed, there are several shops in and around Puerto Vallarta that specialize in or carry a good selection of Huichol works, including Galería Tanana, Peyote People, the Huichol Collection, Galería Huichol, and Hikuri (⇨ *"The Art of the Huichol," below*). You'll also find stylish clothing; vivid handwoven and embroidered textiles from Oaxaca and Chiapas; and comfortable, family-size hammocks from Yucatán State. Handmade or silk screened, blank greeting cards make inexpensive and lovely framed prints.

GLASS AND PEWTER

Glassblowing and pewter were introduced by the Spanish. A wide range of decorative and utilitarian pewter items is produced in the area. The glassware selection includes distinctive deep-blue goblets and chunky, emerald-green-rimmed drinking glasses. All are excellent buys.

JEWELRY

Many PV shop owners travel extensively during the summer months to procure silver jewelry from Taxco, north of Acapulco. *(For more information ⇨ "One Man's Metal.")*

POTTERY

After Guadalajara and its satellite towns Tlaquepaque and Tonalá—which produce ceramics made using patterns and colors hundreds of years old—Puerto Vallarta is the best place in the region to buy pottery, and at reasonable prices. PV shops also sell Talavera (majolica or maiolica) pottery from Puebla.

UNUSUAL GIFTS

For less-than-obvious souvenirs, go traditional and consider a *molinillo*, a carved wooden beater for frothing hot chocolate; you can find these at street vendors or traditional markets for about $1.50. A set of 10 or so *tiras de papel* (string of colored tissue-paper cuts) in a gift shop will only set you back about $2. Handmade huaraches (traditional sandals) are hard to break in (get them wet and let them dry on your feet), but last for years.

TIPS AND TRICKS

Better deals are often given to cash customers—even though credit cards are nearly always accepted—because stores must pay a commission to the credit-card companies. U.S. dollars are almost universally accepted, although most shops pay a lower exchange rate than a bank (or ATM) or *casa de cambio* (money exchange). You may have to pay 5% to 10% more on credit-card purchases.

Bargaining is expected in markets and by beach vendors, who may ask as much as two or three times their bottom line. Occasionally an itinerant vendor will ask for the real value of the item, putting the energetic haggler into the awkward position of offering far too little. One vendor says he asks *norteamericanos* "for twice the asking price, since they always want to haggle." The trick is to know an item's true worth by comparison shopping. It's not common to bargain for already inexpensive trinkets like key chains or quartz-and-bead necklaces or bracelets.

Shop early. Though prices in shops are fixed, smaller shops may be willing to bargain if they're really keen to make a sale. Anyone even slightly superstitious considers the first sale of the day to be good luck, an auspicious start to the day. If your purchase would get the seller's day started on the right foot, you might just get a super deal.

HOURS OF OPERATION

Most stores are open daily 10–8 or even later in high season. A few close for siesta at 1 PM or 2 PM, then reopen at 4 PM. Perhaps half of PV's shops close on Sunday; those that do open usually close up by 2 or 3 in the afternoon. Many shops close altogether during the low season (August or September through mid-October). We've noted this whenever possible; however, some shops simply close up for several weeks if things get excruciatingly slow. In any case, low season hours are usually reduced, so call ahead during that time of year.

WALKING AND GAWKING

On Wednesday evenings during high season (November–April), the PV art community hosts Old Town artWalk (⇨ Chapter 1). Participating galleries welcome lookie loos as well as serious browsers between 6 PM and 10 PM; most provide at least a cocktail. Look for signs in the windows of participating galleries, or pick up a map at any of them ahead of time.

WATCH OUT Watch that your credit card goes through the machine only once, so that no duplicates of your slip are made. If there's an error and a new slip needs to be drawn up, make sure the original is destroyed. Another scam is to ask you to wait while the clerk runs next door ostensibly to use another business's phone or to verify your number—but really to make extra copies. Don't let your card leave a store without you. While these scams aren't common in Puerto Vallarta and we don't advocate excessive mistrust, taking certain precautions doesn't hurt.

Don't buy items made from tortoiseshell or any sea turtle products: it's illegal (Mexico's turtle species are endangered or threatened, and these items aren't allowed into the United States, Canada, or the United Kingdom anyway). Cowboy boots, hats, and sandals made from the leather of endangered species such as crocodiles may also be taken from you at customs, as will birds, or stuffed iguanas or parrots. Both the U.S. and Mexican governments also have strict laws and guidelines about the import–export of antiquities. Check with customs beforehand if you plan to buy anything unusual or particularly valuable.

Although Cuban cigars are readily available, American visitors aren't allowed to bring them into the United States and will have to enjoy them while in Mexico. However, Mexico produces some fine cigars from tobacco grown in Veracruz. Mexican cigars without the correct Mexican seals on the individual cigars and on the box may be confiscated.

SHOPPING IN SPANISH

bakery: *panadería*	**health-food store:** *tienda naturista*
bookseller: *librería*	**jewelry store:** *joyería*
candy store: *dulcería* (often sells piñatas)	**market:** *mercado*
	notions store: *mercería*
florist: *florería*	**stationery store:** *papelería*
furniture store: *mueblería*	**tobacconist:** *tabaquería*
grocery store: *abarrotes*	**toy store:** *juguetería*
hardware store: *ferretería*	**undergarment store:** *bonetería*

PUERTO VALLARTA

ZONA ROMÁNTICA

ART

Fodor'sChoice ★ **Galleria Dante.** Classical, contemporary, and abstract works by more than 50 Mexican and international artists are displayed and sold in this 6,000-square-foot gallery—PV's largest—and sculpture garden. ⊠ *Calle Basilio Badillo 269, Col. E. Zapata* ☎ *322/222–2477.*

BOOKS AND PERIODICALS

A Page in the Sun. Folks read books they've bought or traded at this outdoor café, and there are almost always people playing chess. The large selection of tomes is organized according to genre and then alphabetized by author. ⊠ *Calle Olas Altas 399, Col. E. Zapata* ☎ *322/222–3608.*

CANDY

Fodor'sChoice ★ **Xocodiva.** Exquisite truffles and molded chocolates are all stylishly arranged on immaculate glass shelves at this classic Canadian chocolatier. The chocolate itself is European; among the different mousse fillings are some New World ingredients, including lime, coconut, cinnamon, Kahlúa, espresso, and a few dozen more. During holidays, out come the molded Santas and Day of the Dead skulls, some packaged as pretty gifts. ⊠ *Calle Rodolfo Gómez 111, Col. E. Zapata, between Amapas and Olas Altas* ☎ *322/113–0352* ⊕ *www.xocodiva.com* ☉ *Closed Sun. and some evenings July–early Oct.*

CERAMICS, POTTERY, AND TILE

★ **Mundo de Azulejos.** Buy machine- or handmade tiles starting at about $1 each at this large shop. You can get mosaic tile scenes (or order your own design), a place setting for eight, hand-painted sinks, or any number of soap dishes, cups, saucers, plates, or doodads. Around the corner and run by family members, Mundo de Cristal (⇨ *below*) has more plates and tableware in the same style. ⊠ *Av. Venustiano Carranza 374, Col. E. Zapata* ☎ *322/222–2675* ⊕ *www.talavera-tile.com.*

Talavera Etc. Buy reproductions of tiles from Puebla churches and small gift items or choose made-to-order pieces from the catalog. In addition

6

to being closed on Sunday, the shop is closed during lunch and for two weeks in September. ⊠ *Av. Ignacio L. Vallarta 266, Col. E. Zapata* ☎ 322/222–4100 ⊘ *Closed Sun.*

CLOTHING

Etnica Boutique. This shop has a well-edited collection of cotton and linen dresses, shawls, purses, hats, sandals, and jewelry. A few items from Indonesia are mixed in with things from different regions of Mexico and Central America. ⊠ *Av. Olas Altas 388, Col. E. Zapata* ☎ 322/222–6763.

★ **La Bohemia.** Some of the elegant clothing sold here was designed by the equally elegant owner, Toody. You'll find unique jewelry, accessories, and the San Miguel shoe—the elegant yet comfortable footwear designed for walking on cobblestone streets like those of San Miguel and Puerto Vallarta. ⊠ *Calle Constitución, at Calle Basilio Badillo, Col. E. Zapata* ☎ 322/222–3164 ⊠ *Plaza Neptuno, Av. Francisco M. Ascencio, Km 7.5, Marina Vallarta* ☎ 322/221–2160 ⊘ *Closed Sun.*

Mar de Sueños. Classy Italian threads, including the stylish La Perla brand, are on offer here. The selection of linen blouses and exquisitely cut linen pants is perfect for PV's sultry climate. Or choose from Lycra tops, sexy silk lingerie, and several lines of bathing suits. Everything is top-notch and priced accordingly. ⊠ *Calle Basilio Badillo 277-B, Zona Romántica* ☎ 322/222–7362 ⊘ *Closed Sun.*

☼ **Myskova Beachwear Boutique.** Myskova has its own extensive line of sexy bikinis, plus cover-ups, nylon slacks, and some items for children (sunglasses, bathing suits, flip-flops). There's a small line of jewelry, and Brazilian flip-flops for adults in a rainbow of colors. The shop is open daily until 10 PM. ⊠ *Calle Basilio Badillo 278, Col. E. Zapata* ☎ 322/222–6091.

Fodor's Choice
★ **Rebeca's.** You can browse its large selection of beachwear daily until late. Look for shorts, pseudo-Speedos, and bathing trunks for men, and sandals, fashionable flip-flops, attractive tankinis, lots of bikinis, and a few one-piece suits for women. Most of the goods are manufactured in Mexico. ⊠ *Olas Altas 403, Col. E. Zapata* ☎ 322/222–2320.

Serafina. This is the place to go for over-the-top ethnic clothing; stamped leather purses from Guadalajara; belt buckles from San Miguel; and clunky necklaces and bracelets of quartz, amber, and turquoise. It also sells wonderful tchotchkes. The shop doubled in size in 2008, taking over the adjacent store. ⊠ *Calle Basilio Badillo 260, Col. E. Zapata* ☎ 322/223–4594 ⊘ *Closed Sun.*

TRUE MEXICAN TALAVERA

Talavera, those blue-on-white ceramics, is named for the Spanish town where it originated. Authentic Mexican Talavera is produced in Puebla and parts of Tlaxcala and Guanajuato. The glazing process follows centuries-old "recipes." Look on the back or bottom of the piece for the factory name and state of origin. Manufacturers throughout Mexico produce Talavera-style pieces, which should sell for much less.

★ **Sirenas.** It's affiliated with Serafina and geared to women with eclectic tastes. Creative sisters from Tamaulipas State create chic and unusual, exuberant fantasy jewelry. Colorful clutches and makeup bags made from recycled packaging are an innovation from Mexico City. At this writing, the shop is filled with tight-fitting ribbed T-shirts edged in sequins and an assortment of ethnically inspired yet edgy and contemporary blouses and skirts from Indonesia and elsewhere. ✉ *Basilio Badillo 252B, Col. E. Zapata* ☎ *322/223–1925* ⊘ *Closed Sun.*

> **EXPAT HUMOR**
>
> The co-owner of Lucy's CuCú Cabana is Gil Gevens, who pens quirky epistles, often at his own expense, or the expense of other expats, about life in Puerto Vallarta. Gil writes regularly for the weekly English-language paper *Puerto Vallarta Tribune,* and you can buy his tongue-in-cheek books around town or at Lucy's.

FOLK ART AND CRAFTS

★ **Lucy's CuCú Cabana.** Here you can shop for inexpensive, one-of-a-kind folk art from Guerrero, Michoacán, Oaxaca, and elsewhere. Note that Lucy closes during lunch. ✉ *Calle Basilio Badillo 295, Col. E. Zapata* ☎ *322/222–1220* ⊘ *Closed Sun. and Sept.–mid-Oct.*

México Místico. Across from Plaza Lázaro Cárdenas you can buy custom or ready-made stained glass with traditional motifs such as hummingbirds, bearded irises, lighthouses, and angelfish. Less traditional motifs include the Harley-Davidson logo. ✉ *Lazaro Cardenas 175, Col. E. Zapata* ☎ *322/223–1021* ⊘ *Closed Sun.*

Mundo de Cristal. Come for the glassware from Jalisco and Guanajuato states in sets or individually. Also available are Talavera place settings and individual platters, pitchers, and decorative pieces. Look in the back of the store for high-quality ceramics with realistic portrayals of fruits and flowers. You can have your purchase packed, but shipping is left to you. ✉ *Av. Insurgentes 333, at Calle Basilio Badillo, Col. E. Zapata* ☎ *322/222–1426* ⊘ *Closed Sat. afternoon and Sun.*

Mundo de Pewter. Relatives of the owners of Mundo de Cristal and Mundo de Azulejos (⇨ *above*) own this shop, which is wedged in between the other two stores. Attractive, lead-free items in modern and traditional designs are sold here at reasonable prices. The practical, tarnish-free pieces can go from stovetop or oven to the dining table and be no worse for wear. ✉ *Av. Venustiano Carranza 358, Col. E. Zapata* ☎ *322/222–0503.*

GROCERY STORE

Gutiérrez Rizo. The most convenient market to the Romantic Zone has an ample liquor section, American-brand cereals, canned food, condiments and ground-to-order coffee. Naturally it's a bit more expensive than its mega-size chain competitors. ✉ *Av. Constitución 136, between 5 de Febrero and Aquiles Serdan, Col. E. Zapata* ☎ *322/222–1367.*

6

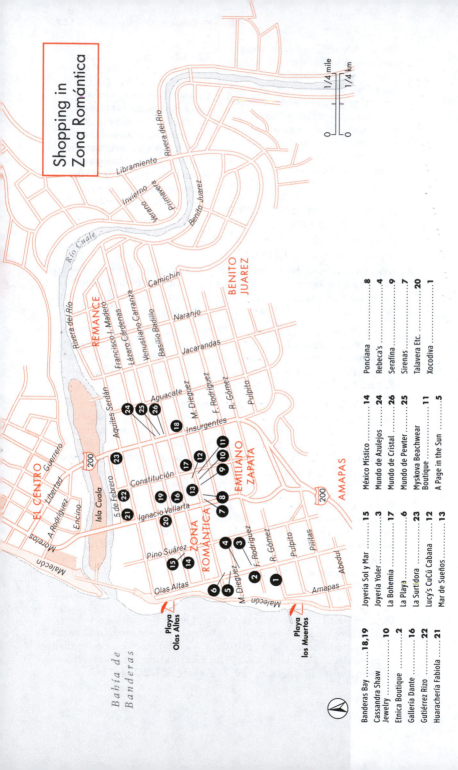

Shopping in Zona Romántica

HOME FURNISHINGS

★ **Banderas Bay.** The American owners, who also own Daiquiri Dick's restaurant (⇨ *Chapter 5*), travel around the country for months in search of antiques, collectibles, handicrafts, and unique household items. About two-thirds of the merchandise is new. The shop will pack and ship your purchases. ⊠ *Lázaro Cárdenas 263, Col. E. Zapata* ☎ *322/223–4352* ⊠ *Constitución 319A, Col. E. Zapata* ☎ *322/223–9871* ☉ *Closed Sun.*

Ponciana. You can find things here that you won't find at other stores, like porcelain replicas of antique dolls or an old reliquary transformed into wall art. Leaving room for creative license means that some "antiques" here may only have a few original parts (say, a cupboard that only has original doors). Also look for tablecloths and place mats from Michoacán, place settings, arty statuettes, matchboxes decorated with Frida Kahlo and Mexican movie themes, and other decorative items. ⊠ *Basilio Badillo 252–A, Col. E. Zapata* ☎ *322/222–2988.*

ALL THAT GLITTERS ISN'T SILVER

There's a great selection of Mexican silver in PV, but watch out for "German silver" (aka *alpaca* or *chapa*): an alloy of iron, zinc, and nickel. Real silver is weightier, and is marked "925" (indicating a silver content of at least 92.5%) for sterling and "950" (at least 95% silver content) for finer pieces. When size permits, the manufacturer's name and the word "Mexico" should also appear.

JEWELRY

Fodor's Choice **Cassandra Shaw Jewelry.** It's hard to ignore the huge, chunky rings, ★ bracelets, and necklaces here. In the back of the shop are more delicate items of pure silver set with various stones in artful ways. All are unusual. There's a small selection of hats, handbags, tunics, and other items, and, up the spiral staircase, the owner's oil paintings, mainly nonrepresentational portraits. ⊠ *Basilio Badillo 276, Col. E. Zapata* ☎ *322/223–9734.*

Joyería Sol y Mar. This shop has more or less the same selection of fine silver jewelry and knickknacks (key chains, bottle openers, and so on) from Taxco as its competition. But the friendly staff and good prices set this small shop facing Lázaro Cárdenas Park apart from the pack. ⊠ *Av. Lázaro Cárdenas 197, Col. E. Zapata* ☎ *322/222–7972.*

Joyería Yoler. Manager Ramon Cruz proudly shows off the store's collection of the Los Castillo family's silver jewelry made with lost-wax casting as well as hammering and burnishing techniques, small silver pitchers with lapis lazuli dragonfly handles, napkin rings, abalone pillboxes, and other lovely utilitarian pieces. The merchandise—which includes an extensive yet not overwhelming array of silver and semiprecious-stone jewelry—is nicely arranged in the ample shop. ⊠ *Calle Olas Altas 391, Col. E. Zapata* ☎ *322/222–8713 or 322/222–9051.*

6

LEATHER, SHOES, AND HANDBAGS

★ **Huarachería Fabiola.** Longtime visitors to Puerto Vallarta will remember this shop. Buy huaraches off the rack or order custom sandals for men or women. Most styles can be made in one to three days. There are limited hours (roughly 10–2) on Sunday, and credit cards aren't accepted. ⊠ *Av. Ignacio L. Vallarta 145 at Calle A. Serdán, Col. E. Zapata* ☎ *322/222–9154.*

CENTRO AND ENVIRONS

ART

★ **Art Gallery Millan.** It's a breath of fresh air in the gallery scene, with cheeky oils by Eduardo Eguía, sculpture by Benito Arciniegas, and affordable, fun ceramic cyclist statuettes created by Rodo Padilla. ⊠ *Calle Aldama 209, Centro* ☎ *No phone* ⊕ *www.artgallerymillan.com.*

Galería Arte Latinoamericana. This gallery sells contemporary art, primarily paintings. There are representative Indian portraits by Marta Gilbert and chunky village scenes—a cross between the Flintstones and Chagall—by Celeste Acevedo. ⊠ *Calle Josefa O. de Domínguez 15, 5 s* ✛ *Between Juárez and Morelo, Centro* ☎ *322/222–4406* ☺ *Closed Sun.*

Galería Corona. Corona is a small shop with some sculpture and art jewelry as well as ethereal and painterly portraits and landscapes in various genres. ⊠ *Calle Corona 164, Centro* ☎ *322/222–4210* ⊕ *www.galeria-corona.com* ☺ *Closed Sun. and Aug.–late Oct.*

Galería 8 y Más. It started with eight Guadalajara artists and has expanded under new ownership to 45 artists from or residing in Jalisco. The large old building has glass, bronze, chalk, and oil paintings. ⊠ *Calle Miramar 237, Centro* ☎ *322/222–7971* ⊠ *Calle Corona 186, Centro* ☎ *322/223–9970* ⊕ *www.artismexico.com* ☺ *Closed Sun. and Sept.*

Galería Pacífico. Open since 1987, Pacífico features the sculpture of Ramiz Barquet, who created the bronze *Nostalgia* piece on the malecón. Brewster Brockmann paints contemporary abstracts; Marco Alvarez, Alejandro Mondria, and Alfredo Langarica are other featured artists. ⊠ *Calle Aldama 174, Centro* ☎ *322/222–1982* ⊕ *www.galeria pacifico.com.*

Sergio Bustamante. Internationally known Sergio Bustamante—the creator of life-size brass, copper, and ceramic animals, mermaids, suns, and moons—has a team of artisans to execute his never-ending pantheon of creative and quirky objets d'art, such as pots shaped like human torsos that sell for more than US$1,000. Paintings, purses, shoes, and jewelry are sold here as well. It's across the street from the statue by the same artist, on the malecón. ⊠ *Av. Juárez 275* ✛

At Calle Corona, Centro ☎*322/223–1405* ✉ *Paseo Diaz Ordaz 542, Centro* ☎*322/297–1030* ☎*322/222–5480* ⊕*www.sergiobustamante. com.mx.*

BOOKS AND PERIODICALS

★ **Librería de Cristal.** Cristal has more than 50 magazine titles in English, plus a small but respectable selection of English-language fiction. ✉*31 de Octubre 127, Centro* ☎*322/222–7106.*

CANDY

Fodor's Choice **Dulces Típicos Mexicanos.** Passersby are yanked almost involuntarily into
★ the shop by the eye-popping displays, and the stock of candies and cookies from around the republic create a strong sense of nostalgia in Mexicans. Shop for coconut cookies by the bag, sugar-encrusted nuts and seeds by weight, or bars of sweet *ate* or *membrillo* in a variety of tropical flavors. ✉*Av. Juárez 1449 at Calle Mina, Centro* ☎*322/223–0707* ⊙ *Closed Sun.*

CERAMICS, POTTERY, AND TILE

Alfarería Tlaquepaque. This is a large store with a ton of red-clay items traditional to the area—in fact, their predecessors were crafted before the 1st century AD. After a recent dip in quality, there's been a return to more worthwhile pieces (both rustic pottery and glazed ceramic pieces in traditional styles) at reasonable prices. ✉*Av. México 1100, Col. 5 de Diciembre* ☎*322/223–2121.*

Galería de Ollas. The 300 or so potters from the village of Juan Mata Ortiz add their touches to the intensely—sometimes hypnotically—geometric designs of their ancestors from Paquimé. At this shop pieces range from about $60 to $10,000, with an average of about $400. Stop in during artWalk, or have a look at its great Web site. ✉*Calle Corona 176, Centro* ☎*322/223–1045* ⊕*www.galeriadeollas.com* ⊙ *Closed Sun.*

■ **TIP→** Before you buy rustic ceramic plates, bowls, and cups, ask if there's lead in the glaze, unless you plan to use them for decoration only and not for food service.

★ **Majolica Antica.** According to knowledgeable shop owner Antonio Cordero, majolica is also called Talavera or tin-glazed pottery. You get a certificate of origin with each piece of beautiful ornamental tile, utilitarian pitcher, plate, or place setting. The shop is open until 7 PM during the week and until 3 PM on Saturday. ✉*Calle Corona 191, Centro* ☎*322/222–5118* ⊙ *Closed Sun.*

CIGARS

La Casa del Habano. The Cuban cigars for sale here start at $3.50 each and top out at $44 for a Cohiba Millenium 2000. You can smoke your stogie downstairs in the casual lounge while sipping coffee or a shot of liquor. ✉*Aldama 170, Centro* ☎*322/223–2758* ⊙ *Closed Sun.*

■ **TIP→** If you're bringing any Mexican cigars back to the United States, make sure they have the correct Mexican seals on both the individual cigars and on the box. Otherwise, they may be confiscated.

Shopping In and Around Centro

TO
NUEVO VALLARTA,
MARINA VALLARTA
AND AIRPORT

200

Chile

29

COL. 5 DE
DICIEMBRE

Venezuela

Paraguay

Argentina

30 - 33

Playa
Camarones

*Bahía de
Banderas*

Langarica

31 de Octubre

28

Malecón

200

26

27

25

Allende

Pipila

EL CENTRO

Paseo Díaz Ordáz

Morelos

24

23

L. Vicario

J. O. de-Domínguez

20

Abasolo

21

22

18

19

17

Aldama

12

16

13

15

Huichol Collection

14

Corona

11

Galeana

Mina

10

Malecón

Juárez

Hidalgo

Matamoros

Miramar

E. Carranza

Iturbide

Palacio
Municipal

9

Iglesia de
Nuestra
Señora de
Guadalupe

6

7

Zaragoza

8

Peyote People

Guerrero

Farol

5

4 3

A. Rodríguez

Libertad

Morelos

Malecón

2

Río Cuale

1

Isla Cuale

Río Cuale

ZONA
ROMÁNTICA

5 de Febrero

Constitución

Insurgentes

Aquiles Serdán

Francisco I. Madero

Aguacate

Vacarandas

I. Vallarta

0 ___ 440 yards
0 ___ 400 meters

200

EMILIANO ZAPATA

CLOTHING

Curvas Peligrosas. Here it's all about beachwear, particularly nice bathing suits. The emphasis is on plus sizes, but you can find some items that are as small as size 12. Choose from Jantzen, Longitude, Miracle Suits, and other quality brands. The shop also has cute cover-ups and skirts. ☒*Av. Juárez 178, Centro* ☎*322/22–5978.*

★ **D'Paola.** The large and somewhat unusual selection here includes pashminas, purses, and shawls as well as lots of muslin clothing. You'll find 32 different lines and plenty of plus sizes. We'd guess that any woman patient enough to search the massive inventory will find something to her taste: there's that much variety. Complement your clothing purchases with a signature piece of jewelry—perhaps a chunky necklace with giant stones or one made of strands and strands of tiny beads. There's a small section of men's clothing, too. ☒*Calle Agustín Rodriguez 289, Centro* ☎*322/223–2742* ☷*Closed Sun.* ☒ *Paradise Plaza, Local 11, Nuevo Vallarta* ☎*322/297–1030.*

☷ **La Surtidora.** At first glance the items in this long-established shop seem mainly matronly, but plowing through the racks will unearth fashionable cocktail dresses, trendy tops and T-shirts, plus men's guayaberas and slacks. The location near the bridge in Colonia E. Zapata has the larger selection; it also has shoes (high heels to flip-flops) and children's clothing. ☒*Morelos 256, at Guerrero, Centro* ☎*322/222–1439* ☒*Av. 5 de Febrero at Insurgentes, Col. E. Zapata* ☎*322/222–0355.*

☷ **Oahu.** One of the best places in Puerto Vallarta to shop for children's casual wear not only has things like pint-size Hawaiian shirts but also water gear like board shorts and rash guards. It's also a good place for men's surf and casual wear, including well-made flip-flops and high-quality T-shirts. ☒*Calle Juárez 314, Centro* ☎*322/223–1058.*

DEPARTMENT STORE

☷ **LANS.** At this multilevel department store for men, women, and children, look for Perry Ellis khakis and Levi's, Lee, and Dockers shirts and trousers, and jeans. The store also sells housewares; purses and Swatch watches; Samsonite luggage; ladies' perfume and makeup (Chanel, Gucci, Estée Lauder); and men's undies. ☒*Calle Juárez 867, at Pípila, Centro* ☎*322/226–9100* ☒*Plaza Caracol, near Soriana supermarket, Blvd. Francisco M. Ascencio 2216, Zona Hotelera* ☎*322/226–0204.*

FOLK ART AND CRAFTS

Alas de Aguila. In addition to pewter there's a wide selection of Talavera-style objects—from soap holders and liquid-soap dispensers to pitchers, platters, and picture frames—in a variety of patterns. Quality is middle-of-the-road; prices are excellent. ☒*Av. Juárez 547, at Calle Corona, Centro* ☎*322/222–4039* ☷*Closed Sun.*

El Instituto de la Artesanía Jalisciense. This shop promotes Jalisco State's handicrafts, selling burnished clay bowls signed by the artist, blown glass, plates and bowls from Tonalá, and other items at fair prices. That said, Bustamante knockoffs and Huichol pieces in less-than-traditional themes (smiley faces not being one of the Huichols' typical motifs) are indications that quality is slipping. Still, there's a representative sampling of the state's ceramics, blue and red glassware, and *barro bruñido*: clay pieces finished by burnishing only. It's catercorner from La Plaza de Armas, and is open 9 to 9 daily. ⊠*Calle Juárez 284, Centro* ☎*322/222–1301.*

Galería Indígena. The assortment of handicrafts here is huge: Huichol yarn paintings and beaded bowls and statuettes, real Talavera ceramics from Puebla, decorative pieces in painted wood, and many other items. ⊠*Av. Juárez 628, Centro* ☎*322/223–0800.* **Querubines.** An old house that once belonged to Jesús Langarica, PV's first mayor, is the setting for this shop selling woven goods from Guatemala and southern Mexico. Items include tablecloths, napkins, place mats, and *rebozos* (stoles) made of rayon, silk, and cotton. The structure's stone, cement, and brick floors make interesting backdrops for painted gourds from Michoacán, carved gourds from the Costa Chica (northern Oaxaca coast), and Talavera pottery. ⊠*Av. Juárez 501–A, at Calle Galeana, Centro* ☎*322/223–1727.*

JEWELRY

Alberto's. This family-run shop has been in business for three generations. The inventory, which was quite disappointing when we last visited, has been revived with the introduction of lovely one-of-a-kind pieces designed by the new talent, young designer Emerson. ⊠*Av. Juárez 185, Centro* ☎*322/222–8317* ⊘*Closed Sun.*

Jades Maya. You can spend as little as $5 or as much as $5,000 on anything and everything jade here. The shop is open daily until 10 PM in high season. In addition to jewelry made from the 20 different colors of jade, there are replicas of ancient Maya masks. ⊠*Leona Vicario 226-A, Centro* ☎*322/222–0371* ⊕*www.jadesmaya.com.*

★ **Joyería El Opalo.** It's a bright spot in a nearly abandoned mall that has stayed afloat through its cruise ship contacts. Silver jewelry ranges in price from $3 per gram for simpler pieces to $30 a gram for the lighter, finer-quality, more complex pieces. There's high-grade "950" silver jewelry in addition to the usual 0.925 sterling silver. Look for gold settings as well. Most of the semiprecious stones—amethyst, topaz, malachite, black onyx, and opal in 28 colors—are of Mexican origin. The diamond-cut necklaces are magnificent. ⊠*Local 13–A, Plaza Genovesa, Col. Las Glorias* ☎*322/224–6584.*

★ **Joyas Finas Suneson.** Some of Mexico's finest designers create the unusual silver jewelry and objets d'art that are sold here. Most items have modern rather than traditional motifs. ⊠*Calle Morelos 593, Centro* ☎*322/222–5715* ⊘*Closed Sun.*

LEATHER, SHOES, AND HANDBAGS

Rolling Stone. It's good for custom-made boots, sandals, and shoes in a wide variety of leathers. But the help is often unhelpful, letting customers wait while they attend to other duties—real or imagined. ⊠*Paseo Diaz Ordáz 802, Centro* ☎*322/223–1769.*

MALL

Plaza Caracol. Caracol is lively and full on weekends and evenings, even when others are dead. Its anchors are the Soriana (formerly Gigante) supermarket and the adjacent LANS department store. Surrounding these are tiny stores dispensing electronics, ice cream, and fresh flowers. This is also a good place for manicures and haircuts. Adding to the commercial center's appeal is the six-theater CineMark cinema. ⊠ *Blvd. Francisco M. Ascencio, Km 2.5, across from Fiesta Americana hotel, Zona Hotelera* ☎*322/224–3239.*

MARKETS

Mercado de Artesanías. Flowers, piñatas, produce, and plastics share space in indoor and outdoor stands with souvenirs and lesser-quality crafts. Upstairs, locals eat at long-established, family-run restaurants. ⊠*Calle Agustín Rodríguez, between Calles Matamoros and Miramar, at base of bridge* ☎*No phone.*

Mercado Isla Río Cuale. Small shops and outdoor stalls sell an interesting mix of wares at this informal and fun market. Harley-Davidson kerchiefs, Che paintings on velvet, and Madonna icons compete with the usual synthetic lace tablecloths, shell and quartz necklaces, and silver jewelry amid postcards and key chains. The market is partially shaded by enormous fig and rubber trees and serenaded by the rushing river; a half-dozen cafés and restaurants provide sustenance. ⊠*Dividing El Centro from Colonia E. Zapata, access at Calle Morelos, Calle I. Vallarta, Calle Matamoros, Calle Constitución, Calle Libertad, Av. Insurgentes, and the malecón* ☎*No phone.*

WINE, BEER, AND SPIRITS

La Playa. Yes, it has tequila. But it also has wines from Chile, California (Gallo), and Spain; imported vodka and other spirits; and the cheapest beer around. ⊠*Blvd. Francisco M. Ascencio, Km 1.5, across from IMSS (Mexican Social Security Agency), Zona Hotelera* ☎*322/224–7130* ⊠*Calle Morelos at Calle Pípila, Centro* ☎*322/223–1818* ⊠*Olas Altas 246 at Basilio Badillo, Col. E. Zapata* ☎*322/222–5304.*

MARINA VALLARTA

ART

Galería Em. This shop sells art glass, stained glass, and glass sculpture. It also has a small selection of eccentric jewelry made by local artists. By appointment only, you can commission a piece at the **Galería Em workshop** (⊠ *Blvd. Francisco M. Ascencio 2758, Marina Vallarta* ☎*322/332–1728).* ⊠*Marina Las Palmas II, Local 17, Marina Vallarta* ☎*322/221–2228* ☉*Closed Sun. and 2–5 PM Sept. and Oct.*

CLOTHING

Boutique Osiris. The inventory may wax and wane a bit, but at its best this shop has a nice selection of simple gauze, cotton, and linen clothing for day or evening wear, although it's more practical than formal or fancy. ⊠*Plaza Marina, Local F–6, Marina Vallarta* ☎*322/221–0732.*

Continued on page 171

The intricately woven and beaded designs of the Huichols' art are as vibrant and fascinating as the traditions of its people, best known as the "Peyote People" for their traditional and ceremonial use of the hallucinogenic drug. Peyote-inspired visions are thought to be messages from God and are reflected in the art.

THE ART OF THE HUICHOL

Like the Lacandon Maya, the Huichol resisted assimilation by Spanish invaders, fleeing to inhospitable mountains and remote valleys. There they retained their pantheistic religion in which shamans lead the community in spiritual matters and the use of peyote facilitates communication directly with God.

Huichol is pronounced wee-CHOL; the people's name for themselves, however, is Wirarika (we-RAH-ri-ka), which means "healer."

Roads didn't reach larger Huichol communities until the mid-20th century, bringing electricity and other modern distractions. The collision with the outside world has had pros and cons, but art lovers have only benefited from their increased access to intricately patterned woven and beaded goods. Today the traditional souls that remain on the land—a significant population of perhaps 6,000 to 8,000—still create votive bowls, prayer arrows, jewelry, and bags, and sell them to finance elaborate religious ceremonies. The pieces go for as little as $5 or as much as $5,000, depending on the skill and fame of the artist and quality of materials.

Bead-covered wooden statuette

UNDERSTANDING THE HUICHOL

When Spanish conquistadors arrived in the early 16th century, the Huichol, unwilling to work as slaves on the haciendas of the Spanish or to adopt their religion, fled to hard-to reach mountains and valleys of the Sierra Madre. They lived there, disconnected from society, for nearly 500 years. Beginning in the 1970s, roads and electricity made their way to tiny Huichol towns. The reintroduction to society has come at a high price: at least one ill-advised government project encouraged Huichol farmers to sell their land, and with it, their traditional lifestyle, in favor of a city existence. Today, about half of the population of perhaps 12,000 continues to live in ancestral villages and *rancheritas* (tiny individual farms).

THE POWER OF PRAYER

Spirituality and prayer infuse every aspect of Huichol life. They believe that without their prayers and offerings the sun wouldn't rise, the earth would cease spinning. It is hard, then, for them to reconcile their poverty with the relative easy living of "free-riders" (Huichol term for nonspiritual freeloaders) who enjoy fine cars and expensive houses thanks to the Huichols efforts to sustain the planet. But rather than hold our reckless materialism against us, the Huichol add us to their prayers.

Huichol yarn artist at work

THE PEYOTE PEOPLE

Visions inspired by the hallucinogenic peyote plant are considered by the Huichol to be messages from God, and to help in solving personal and communal problems. Indirectly, they provide inspiration for their almost psychedelic art. Just a generation or two ago, annual peyote-gathering pilgrimages were done on foot. Today the journey is still a man's chief obligation, but they now drive to the holy site at Wiricuta, in San Luis Potosi State. Peyote collected is used by the entire community—men, women, and children—throughout the year.

SHAMANISM

A Huichol man has a lifelong calling as a shaman. There are two shamanic paths: the path of the wolf, which is more aggressive, demanding, and powerful (wolf shamans profess the ability to morph into wolves); and the path of the deer, which is playful—even clownish—and less inclined to prove his power. A shaman chooses his own path.

Huichol craftsmen, Cabo San Lucas

SMART SHOPPING TIPS

Huichol art, sun face

BEADED ITEMS: The smaller the beads, the more delicate and expensive the piece. Beads with larger holes are fine for stringed work, but if used in bowls and statuettes cheapen the piece. Items made with iridescent beads from Japan are the priciest. Look for good-quality glass beads, definition, symmetry, and artful use of color. Beads should fit together tightly in straight lines, with no gaps.

YARN "PAINTINGS": Symmetry is not necessary, although there should be an overall sense of unity. Thinner thread results in finer, more costly work. Look for tightness, with no visible gaps or broken threads. Paintings should have a stamp of authenticity on the back, including artist's name and tribal affiliation.

PRAYER ARROWS: Collectors and purists should look for the traditionally made arrows of brazilwood inserted into a bamboo shaft. The most interesting ones contain embroidery work, or tiny carved icons, or are painted with copal symbols indicative of their original, intended purpose, for example protecting a child or ensuring a successful corn crop.

WHERE TO SHOP

SUPPORTING HUICHOL TRADITIONS

Families that continue to work the land may dedicate a few hours a day to crafts, working to maintain their ceremonies, not to pay the cable bill. Buying directly from them can ensure a higher degree of artistry: the Huichol who make art to supplement farming work more slowly and with less pressure than their city-dwelling brethren. Shopping at stores like Peyote People and Hikuri supports artisans who live in their ancestral villages and practice the ancient traditions.

Peyote People treats the Huichol as a people, not a product. At their downtown Vallarta shop, the owners—a Mexican-Canadian couple—are happy to share with customers their wealth of info about Huichol art and culture. They work with just a few farming families, providing all the materials and then paying for the finished product. ⊠ *Calle Juárez 222, Centro* ☎ *322/222-2303.*

Hikuri Near the north end of Banderas Bay, is run by a British couple that pays asking prices to their Huichol suppliers and employs indigenous men in the adjoining carpentry and screen-printing shops. The men initially have little or no experience, and the jobs give them a leg up to move on to more profitable work. The excellent inventory includes fine yarn paintings. ⊠ *Calle Coral 66A, La Cruz de Huanacaxtle* ☎ *329/295-5071.*

The Huichol Collection
Native artisans working on crafts and wearing their stunning and colorful clothing draw customers in. The shop has an excellent inventory, with some museum-quality pieces. Though the merchandise is genuine, the shop is also venue for timeshare sales—albeit with a soft sales pitch. ⊠ *Paseo Diaz Ordaz 732, Centro* ☎ *322/223-0661* ⊠ *Morelos 490, Centro* ☎ *322/223-2141.*

Galería Huichol sells yarn paintings, beaded bowls and statuettes, and some smaller items like beaded jewelry and Christmas ornaments. ⊠ *Paradise Plaza, 2nd fl., Nuevo Vallarta* ☎ *322/297-0342*

TRADITION TRANSFORMED

The art of the Huichol was, for centuries, made from undyed wool, shells, stones, and other natural materials. It was not until the 1970s that the Huichol began incorporating bright, zingy colors, without sacrificing the intricate patterns and symbols used for centuries. The result is strenuously colorful, yet dignified.

YARN PAINTINGS
Dramatic and vivid yarn paintings are highly symbolic, stylized visions of life.

MASKS AND ANIMAL STATUETTES
Bead-covered wooden or ceramic masks and animal statuettes are other adaptations made for outsiders.

PRAYER ARROWS
Made for every ceremony, prayer arrows send petitions winging to God.

VOTIVE BOWLS
Ceremonious votive bowls, made from gourds, are decorated with bright, stylized beadwork.

WOVEN SHOULDER BAGS
Carried by men, the bags are decorated with traditional Huichol icons.

For years, Huichol men as well as women wore BEADED BRACELETS; today earrings and necklaces are also made.

Diamond-shape GOD'S EYES of sticks and yarn protect children from harm.

HOW TO READ THE SYMBOLS

Spiders that come out at dawn are thought to welcome the rising sun.

The **deer** is the animal manifestation of the god Kahumari, who intercedes in heaven on earthlings' behalf.

Anything with **horns** or **antlers** symbolizes communion and oneness with God.

Yarn painting

■ The trilogy of **corn, peyote,** and **deer** represents three aspects of God. According to Huichol mythology, peyote sprang up in the footprints of the deer. Depicted like stylized flowers, peyote represents communication with God. Corn, the Huichol's

Corn symbol

staple food, symbolizes health and prosperity. An image drawn inside the root ball depicts the essence of God within it.

■ The **double-headed eagle** is the emblem of the omnipresent sky god.

Peyote

■ A **nierika** is a portal between the spirit world and our own. Often in the form of a yarn painting, a nierika can be round or square.

■ **Salamanders** and **turtles** are associated with rain; the former provoke the clouds. Turtles maintain underground springs and purify water.

■ A **scorpion** is the soldier of the sun.

Scorpion

■ The Huichol depict raindrops as tiny **snakes**; in yarn paintings they descend to enrich the fields.

Snakes

Jose Beníctez Sánchez, (1938—) may be the elder statesman of yarn painters and has shown in Japan, Spain, the U.S., and at the Museum of Modern Art in Mexico City. His paintings sell for upward of $3,000 a piece.

Caprichoso. Sizes here range from XS to 2X, and it's the only PV store to stock the Oh My Gauze line of women's resort wear. Also look for Dunes, Juanita Banana, and unusual clothing by Chalí, with cutout, painted flowers. Most of the inventory is cotton, including a smaller selection of clothing for men. ⊠*Plaza Neptuno, Av. Francisco M. Ascencio, Km 7.5, Marina Vallarta* ☎*322/221–3067.*

> ## DO WEAR THEM OUT
>
> *Huaraches* are woven leather sandals that seem to last several lifetimes. Traditionally worn by peasants, they're now sold by fewer shops, but in a slightly larger assortment of styles. Once broken in—and that takes a while—this classic, sturdy footwear will be a worthwhile addition to your closet.

☪ **Gecko.** This is the place to go in Marina Vallarta for beach togs for kids and teens. The selection of any one type of item isn't large, but there are bikinis, sunglasses, flip-flops, nice ball caps, and T-shirts. Board shorts and rash guards are stocked for surfers and wannabes. ⊠ *Condominios Puesto del Sol, Marina Vallarta* ☎*322/221–2165.*

★ **María de Guadalajara.** It's DIY chic here: you choose the colorful, cotton, triangular sash of your liking, miraculously transforming pretty-but-baggy dresses into flattering and stylish frocks. The color palette is truly inspired. The selection for men is limited. ⊠*Puesta del Sol condominiums, Local 15–A, Marina, Marina Vallarta* ☎*322/221–2566* ⊠*Calle Morelos 550, Centro* ☎*322/222–2387* ⊕*www.mariadeguadalajara.com.*

DEPARTMENT STORE

Liverpool. Locals were giddy about this department store anchoring 73,000 square feet of shopping on two floors at Plaza Galerías—until they caught a look at the price tags. This and the surrounding shops are mainly visited by cruise-ship passengers and Mexican out-of-towners looking for everything from sporting goods to clothing to housewares. Plaza Galerías has two escalators; restaurants; parking; a 12-theater cinema; and a fast-food court with the ubiquitous McDonald's, Dominos Pizza, Chili's, and Starbucks (it also has the most slippery polished stone flooring known to man). ⊠*Av. Francisco M. Ascencio 2920, Plaza Galerías, Marina Vallarta* ☎*322/226–2200.*

JEWELRY

La Brisa. La Brisa is one of several silver stores owned by the same family. All have fair prices and no pressure; this one also sells Talavera pottery. ⊠*Condominios Puesta del Sol, Local 11–B, Marina Vallarta* ☎*322/221–2516.*

LEATHER

Tony's Place. This shop facing the private marina offers a nice selection of boots, shoes, purses, belts and wallets in different types of leather, including pigskin, cow, shark, alligator, and ostrich. ⊠*Royal Pacific, Loc. 117 at Marina Vallarta, Marina Vallarta* ☎*322/221–0156* ☻*Closed Sun.*

6

Shopping in Marina Vallarta

Gustavo Díaz Ordaz International Airport

Paseo de las Flores

Blvd. Francisco Medina Ascencio

⑫

Clavel
Violetas
Gladiola
Margaritas
Jazmín
Laureles
Amapola
Orquídeas
Las Azucenas
Lirios
Geranios
Amapas
Dalias
Obeliscos
Las Palmas
Canarios
Pétalos
Las Rosas

VILLAS LAS FLORES

⑩ ⑪

Plaza Marina

Gansos

Industrias

Estero "El Salado"

Gaviotas

Priv. de las Garzas

Marina Valarta Campo De Golf

⑦ · ⑨

Popa

Plaza Neptuno

Paseo Bocanegra
Albatros
Flamingos
Flamingos
Pelícanos
Albatros
Flamingos

MARINA VALLARTA

Av. Paseo de la Marina

Mástil

El Faro

③
②
⑥ ④

Timón

⑤

Ancla

Proa

Quilla

①

Paseo de la Marina Norte

Paseo de la Marina Sur

Vela

EDUCACION

Av. Politecnico Nacional

Preparatoria

Secundaria

Playa El Salado

🏖

Isla Iguana

PACIFIC OCEAN

Blvd. Francisco Medina Ascencio

Av. Gob. Prisciliano Sánchez

Terminal Maritima

Océano Índico

Camino Viejo Aramara

Av. Las Garzas

Quetzal

Flamingos

Av. Las Garzas

TO CENTRO, ZONA ROMANTICA, COSTALEGRE
↓

Dr. Mike Lemus

0 ——— 1/4 mile
0 ——— 1/4 km

One Man's Metal

In less than a decade after William Spratling arrived in the mining town of Taxco—275 km (170 mi) north of Acapulco—he had transformed it into a flourishing silver center, the likes of which had not been seen since colonial times. In 1929 the writer-architect from New Orleans settled in the then-sleepy, dusty village because it was inexpensive and close to the pre-Hispanic Mexcala culture that he was studying in Guerrero Valley.

In Taxco—Mexico's premier "Silver City"—marvelously preserved white-stucco, red-tile-roof colonial buildings hug cobblestone streets that wind up and down the foothills of the Sierra Madre. Taxco (pronounced tahss-ko) is a living work of art. For centuries its silver mines drew foreign mining companies. In 1928 the government made it a national monument.

For hundreds of years Taxco's silver was made into bars and exported overseas. No one even considered developing a local jewelry industry. Journeying to a nearby town, Spratling hired a couple of goldsmiths and commissioned them to create jewelry, flatware, trays, and goblets from his own designs.

Ever the artist with a keen mind for drawing, design, and aesthetics, Spratling decided to experiment with silver using his designs. Shortly afterward, he set up his own workshop and began producing highly innovative pieces. By the 1940s Spratling's designs were gracing the necks of celebrities and being sold in high-end stores abroad.

Spratling also started a program to train local silversmiths; they were soon joined by foreigners interested in learning the craft. It wasn't long before there were thousands of silversmiths in the town, and Spratling was its wealthiest resident. He moved freely in Mexico's lively art scene, befriending muralists Diego Rivera (Rivera's wife, Frida Kahlo, wore Spratling necklaces) and David Alfaro Siqueiros as well as architect Miguel Covarrubios.

The U.S. ambassador to Mexico, Dwight Morrow, father of Anne Morrow, who married Charles Lindbergh, hired Spratling to help with the architectural details of his house in Cuernavaca. American movie stars were frequent guests at Spratling's home; once, he even designed furniture for Marilyn Monroe. Indeed, when his business failed in 1946, relief came in the form of an offer from the U. S. Department of the Interior: Spratling was asked to create a program of native crafts for Alaska. This work influenced his later designs.

Although he never regained the wealth he once had, he operated the workshop at his ranch and trained apprentices until he died in a car accident in 1969. A friend, Italian engineer Alberto Ulrich, took over the business and replicated Spratling's designs using his original molds. Ulrich died in 2002, and his children now operate the business.

Each summer PV shop owners travel to Taxco to procure silver jewelry.

6

MALLS

Plaza Marina. One long block north of Plaza Neptuno, this mall has several banks with ATMs, a dry cleaner, a photo-developing shop, a pharmacy, a café, Internet café, and several bars and shops. The whole place is anchored by the Comercial Mexicana supermarket. ⊠ *Carretera al Aeropuerto, Km 8, Marina Vallarta* ☏ *322/221–0490.*

Plaza Neptuno. This small mall in the heart of the marina district is home to a number of fine-home-furnishing shops, several classy clothing boutiques, and just behind it, a few good, casual restaurants. ⊠ *Carretera al Aeropuerto, Km 7.5, Marina Vallarta* ☏ No phone.

NAYARIT

NUEVO VALLARTA

BOOKS

★ **NV Bookstore.** It may be small, but it has the area's best-distilled selection of English-language books. There are guidebooks; books about Mexican culture, history, and arts; and best-selling titles to read around the pool. ⊠ *Paradise Plaza, 2nd fl., Nuevo Vallarta* ☏ *322/297–2274.*

CLOTHING

★ **Ruly's Boutique.** The owner designs the men's clothing sold here and supervises its construction. Look for nice trousers, shirts, and shorts in a wide selection of handsome yet vibrant colors, as well as accessories, underwear, hats, and so on. ⊠ *Paradise Plaza, Local 10, Paseo de los Cocoteros 85 Sur, Nuevo Vallarta* ☏ *322/297–1724.*

FOLK ART

La Aldaba. The interesting gift and decorative items and housewares here include Bustamante-inspired cat and moon candles, subtly painted sheet-metal candleholders and wall art, and glass vases. ⊠ *Paradise Plaza, 2nd fl., Nuevo Vallarta* ☏ *322/297–0903.*

GROCERIES

Mega Comercial Nuevo Vallarta. The area's first large supermarket is almost as convenient for people in Bucerías as for those in Nuevo Vallarta. It has the full range of grocery, liquor, deli items, and more. ⊠ *Hwy. 200, Fracc. Flamingos, just south of Flamingos Country Club, Nuevo Vallarta* .

MALL

Paradise Plaza. It's the most comprehensive plaza north of Marina Vallarta, with a food court, grocery store, several coffee and juice shops, Internet café, clothing and handicraft boutiques, and a bank. ⊠ *Paseo de los Cocoteros 85 Sur, Nuevo Vallarta* ☏ *322/226–3732.*

BUCERÍAS

BOOKS AND PERIODICALS

Gringo's Books & Coffee. This is a great place to pick up novels a-go-go, including lots of beach reading. ⊠ *Calle Morelos 7-A, Bucerías* ☎ *329/298–1767* ⊙ *Closed Sun.*

FOLK ART

Jan Marie's Boutique. The gift items here include small housewares and tin frames sporting Botero-style fat ladies. The classy selection of Talavera pottery is both decorative and utilitarian. This isn't the place for bargain hunters. ⊠ *Lázaro Cárdenas 56, Bucerías* ☎ *329/298–0303.*

GROCERY STORES

Frutería Chabacano. Chabacano has the reputation of selling the freshest fruits and vegetables in town. ⊠ *Calle Hidalgo 15, Bucerías* ☎ *329/298–0692* ⊙ *Closed after 3 PM Mon.–Sat., after 1 PM Sun.*

Super La Peque. There's a little bit of everything here: wine, liquor, cleaning supplies, junk food, and fresh fruit. ⊠ *Morelos 7, Bucerías* ☎ *329/298–0598.*

SAYULITA

FOLK ART

Fodor'sChoice **Galería Tanana.** The beauty of its glistening glass-bead (Czech) jewelry in iridescent and earth colors may leave you weak in the knees. Sometimes a Huichol artisan at the front of the store works on traditional yarn paintings, pressing the fine filaments into a base of beeswax and pine resin to create colorful and symbolic pictures. Money from sales supports the owner's nonprofit organization to promote cultural sustainability for the Huichol people. ⊠ *Av. del Palmar 8, Sayulita* ☎ *329/291–3889* ⊕ *www.huicholcenter.org* ⊙ *Closed Sun.*

★ **La Hamaca.** The inventory of folk art and utilitarian handicrafts is large, and each piece is unique. Scoop up masks and pottery from Michoacán, textiles and shawls from Guatemala, hammocks from the Yucatán, and lacquered boxes from Olinalá. The store is open daily 9 to 9. ⊠ *Calle Revolución 110, Sayulita* ☎ *329/291–3039.*

Mexica Teahui. It smells of incense and seems to have the usual shell-and-bead bric-a-brac. Closer investigation reveals inventive jewelry in 0.950 silver, obsidian statuettes of modern design, and freshwater pearl necklaces, among other treasures. The surfer-girl cotton Ts and gauzy blouses, shorts, and skirts are cute. ⊠ *Av. Revolución 53, Centro* ⊕ *329/291–3764* ⊙ *Closed Aug. and Sept.*

GROCERY STORE

Mi Tiendita. Deli sandwiches, wine and beer, and various sundries make up the stock here. ⊠ *Calle Marlin 44–A, Sayulita* ☎ *329/291–3145.*

SAN FRANCISCO

FOLK ART

Galería Corazón. The emphasis here is on high-end Mexican arts and crafts. Note that the shop doesn't open until noon. ⊠ *Av. América Latina 1, at Av. Tercer Mundo, San Pancho* ☎*311/258–4170* ⊗ *Closed Sun., Mon., and mid-May–Oct.*

GROCERY STORE

El Indio. You can't beat the convenience of this San Pancho shop for picking up liquor, wine, milk, water, and other necessities. ⊠ *Av. América Latina 23 at Av. Mexico, San Pancho* ☎*311/258–4010.*

HOME FURNISHINGS

Anthony Chetwynd Collection. The flamboyant, displaced British owner travels to estates and villages all over Mexico to stock his antiques shop. About half the inventory is antique masks, chandeliers, reliquaries. The rest are copies of the same, and some furnishings and housewares imported from Asia. ⊠ *Calle Las Palmas 130, Col. Costa Azul, San Francisco* ☎*311/258–4407.*

After Dark

Mariachi

WORD OF MOUTH

"We strolled up the malécon at sunset. Vallarta is famous for its sunsets, with the red orb sinking into the sea at the far end of the opening of the bay—the second-largest bay in the Americas, I'm told, after Hudson Bay in Canada. The whole time we were there, the late afternoons were uncharacteristically low and overcast, which made the sunsets even more dramatic. . . . and the crowds and street vendors and pleasant air of leisure made for a wonderful picture.

—fnarf999

Outdoorsy Vallarta switches gears after dark and rocks into the wee hours. When the beachgoers and sightseers have been showered and fed, Vallarta kicks up its heels and puts the baby to bed. Happy hour in martini lounges sets the stage for an evening that might include a show, live music, or just hobnobbing under the stars at a rooftop bar.

Many hotels have Mexican fiesta dinner shows, which can be lavish affairs with buffet dinners, folk dances, and even fireworks. Tour groups and individuals—mainly middle-age and older Americans and Canadians—make up the audience at the Saturday night buffet dinner show at Playa Los Arcos and other hotels. *Vaqueros* (cowboys) do rope tricks and dancers perform Mexican regional or pseudo-Aztec dances. The late-late crowd gets down after midnight at dance clubs, some of which stay open until 6 AM.

The scene mellows as you head north and south of Puerto Vallarta. In Punta Mita (aka Punta de Mita), Bucerías, Sayulita, and San Francisco (aka San Pancho), local restaurants provide live music; the owners usually scare up someone good once or twice a week in high season. Along the Costalegre, tranquillity reigns. Most people head here for relaxation, and nightlife generally takes the form of stargazing, drink in hand. If you're visiting June through October (low season), attend live performances whenever offered, as they are few and far between.

Although there's definitely crossover, many Mexicans favor the upscale bars and clubs of the Hotel Zone and Marina Vallarta hotels, while foreigners tend to like the Mexican flavor of places downtown and the south side (the Zona Romántica), where dress is decidedly more casual.

NIGHTLIFE OPTIONS

BARS AND PUBS

Like any resort destination worth its salt—the salt on the rim of the margarita glass, that is—PV has an enormous variety of watering holes. Bars on or overlooking the beach sell the view along with buckets of beer. Martini bars go to great lengths to impress with signature drinks, and sports bars serve up Canadian hockey and Monday-night football. Hotels have swim-up bars and lobby lounges, and these, as well as restaurant bars, are the main options in places like Nuevo Vallarta, Marina Vallarta, and most of the small towns to the north and south.

DANCE CLUBS

You can dance salsa with the locals, groove to rock in English or *en español,* or even tango. Things slow down in the off-season, but during school vacations and the winter clubs stay open until 3, 5, or even 6 AM. Except those that double as restaurants, clubs don't open until 10 PM. ■TIP➔ If you care about looking hip, don't show up at a club before midnight—it will most likely be dead. Arriving around 10 PM, however, could save you a cover charge.

Have a late and leisurely dinner, take a walk on the beach and get some coffee, then stroll into the club cool as a cucumber at 12:30 AM or so.

MUSIC CLUBS

Most of Puerto Vallarta's live music is performed in restaurants and bars, often on or overlooking the beach.
■ **TIP→** Musical events happening anywhere in Vallarta are listed in *Bay Vallarta* (⊕*www.bayvallarta.com*). This twice-monthly rag is an excellent source of detailed information for who's playing around Old Vallarta, the Zona Hotelera Norte, Marina Vallarta, and even as far north as Bucerías and La Cruz. More detail-oriented than most similar publications, *Bay Vallarta* lists showtimes, venues, genres, and cover charges. Live music is much less frequent in the smaller towns to the north and south of PV; to find out what's happening there, ask in tourist-oriented bars, restaurants, or hotels.

MOVIES

Movie tickets here are less than half what they are in the United States and Canada. Many theaters have discounted prices on Wednesday. See theater Web sites or ⊕*www.vallartaonline.com/cinema*.

SHOWS

Most hotels have lounge music, and many hotels have buffet dinners with mariachis, folkloric dancers and *charros* (elegantly dressed horsemen, who, in this case, perform mostly roping tricks, as horses are a bit too messy for the stage and most of their feats on horseback involve running at top speed in a specially designed arena called a *lienzo charro*). All-inclusive hotels generally include nightly entertainment in the room price. Drag shows are crowd pleasers—whether the crowd is straight or gay.

> ### HANGOVER CURES
>
> For a hangover, menudo (tripe stew) and pozole are recommended, both with the addition of chopped fresh onions and cilantro, a generous squeeze of lime and as much chili as one can handle. Ceviche is another popular cure, with the same key ingredients: lime and chili.

PUERTO VALLARTA

ZONA ROMÁNTICA

BARS, PUBS, AND LOUNGES

Andale. Most nights, crowds spill out onto the sidewalk as party-hearty men and women shimmy out of the narrow saloon, drinks in hand, to the strains of Chubby Checker and other vintage tunes. For a laugh, intoxicated or less inhibited patrons sometimes take a bumpy ride on the burro just outside Andale's door (a handler escorts the burro). ⊠*Av. Olas Altas 425, Col. E. Zapata* ☎*322/222–1054.*

★ **Apaches.** It's gay friendly, lesbian friendly, *people* friendly. Heck, superwomen Mariann and her partner Endra would probably welcome you

Continued on page 184

A cross-section of la piña (the heart) of the blue agave plant

¡TEQUILA!

If God were Mexican, tequila would surely be our heavenly reward, flowing in lieu of milk and honey. Local lore asserts that it was born when lightning hit a tall blue agave, cooking its heart.

Historians maintain that, following Spanish conquest and the introduction of the distillation process, tequila was developed from the ancient Aztec drink *pulque*. Whatever the true origin, Mexico's national drink long predated the Spanish, and is considered North America's oldest intoxicating spirit.

Conjuring up tequila, what might come to mind is late-night teary-eyed confessions or spaghetti-Western-style bar brawls. But tequila is more complex and worldly than many presume. By some accounts it's a digestive that reduces cholesterol and stress. Shots of the finest tequilas can cost upward of $100 each, and are meant to be savored as ardently as fine cognacs or single-malt scotches.

Just one of several agaves fermented and bottled in Mexico, tequila rose to fame during the Mexican Revolution when it became synonymous with national heritage and pride. Since the 1990s tequila has enjoyed a soaring popularity around the globe, and people the world over are starting to realize that tequila is more than a one-way ticket to a hangover.

The Blue Agave

Tequila is made from the blue agave plant, a member of the lily family. Nearly 100,000 acres of blue agave are grown in Mexico; the plant is native to the Sierra Madre region, still the center for tequila production.

After the blue agave plant matures (which takes 8–12 years), its spiky leaves are removed and the heart cooked up to three days in a traditional pit oven (or convection oven) to concentrate the sugars. Seeping blood-red juice, the hearts are then ground and strained, then fermented and distilled at least two or three times.

Workers harvest *Agave tequilana Weber azul*

Mezcal

Mezcal is liquor distilled from any maguey (agave) plant *except* the blue agave from which tequila is made. Originally hailing from Oaxaca, mezcal is as popular as tequila in Mexico, if not more so. Like tequila, quality varies widely from cheap firewater to smooth (and expensive) varieties with complex flavors. The type of maguey used influences the quality greatly.

Effortless Education

You can chat with your local bartender about the blue agave revolution, but the information you get may be flawed. You can learn a lot at **La Casa del Tequila** (✉ Calle Morelos 589, Centro ☎322/222–2000.) Ask the bartender to educate you as you taste a few of the 80 tequilas on hand.

At the fermentation stage, the agave is added to water.

TEQUILA TOURS

Near Boca de Tomatlán, **Agave Don Crispín** (✉ Las Juntas y Los Veranos, 10 mi south of PV ☎ 322/223–6002) is a small but proud producer of 100% agave tequila. Learn the basics of tequila production, and see the pit ovens and old-fashioned stills. Ask for René, who will give you a short tour and tasting at no charge (they usually only cater to groups). One of the most complete tequila country tours is with **Hacienda San José del Refugio** (✉ Calle Comercio 172, about 400 km [250 mi] east of PV, ☎ 33/3942–3900 ⊕ www.herradura.com), producer of the Herradura brand. It offers 90-minute tours weekdays 9–3. The 60 peso price includes a sip of three tequilas, all of which are for sale in the adjacent gift shop. On the 9-hour **Tequila Express** (☎ 33/3880–9090; Ticketmaster ☎ 33/3818–3800 ⊕ www.tequilaexpress.com.mx) train ride, blue agave fields zip by as you sip tequila and listen to roving mariachis. After a distillery tour, there's lunch, folk dancing, and *charro* (cowboy) demonstrations.

An assembly-line worker fills tequila bottles

José Cuervo is Mexico's largest tequila maker

CHOOSING A TEQUILA

Line 'em up!

Connoisseurs recommend imbibing nothing but 100% pure agave—with no added sugar or chemicals—even for mixed drinks. A tequila's quality is most directly related to the concentration of blue agave, and a higher agave content adds significantly to the price. This fact will be clearly marked on the label as TEQUILA 100% DE AGAVE or TEQUILA 100% PURO DE AGAVE. The cheapest varieties have 49% of their alcohol derived from sugars other than blue agave. (The max allowed by law.)

Aging tequila changes the flavor, but doesn't necessarily improve it. Whiskey and scotch inspired the aging process in oak barrels, which instills a smoky taste or imparts one of many other subtle bouquets. Some experts consider the unmitigated flavor of *blanco* (silver) superior to, or at least less influenced by Yankee and European tastes than that of *reposado* (aged) or *añejo* (mature).

Distinctions you should know (from—generally speaking—least to most expensive) are:

BLANCO (SILVER): Also known as white tequila (though "silver" is the official name), tequila blanco is clear as water. It is unaged—bottled immediately after distillation—and therefore has the purest agave taste of the tequila varieties.

ORO (GOLD): Also called *joven* (young) tequila, this is tequila blanco to which colorants or flavorings have been added, or that has been mixed with tequila aged in oak barrels, giving it a golden hue. Additives (all strictly regulated) such as caramel, oak tree extract, glycerin, and sugar syrup simulate the flavor of tequila aged in oak barrels.

REPOSADO (AGED): Aged in oak barrels 2 to 11 months, reposado is smoother and more flavorful than blanco, as it has acquired some of the oak flavor.

AÑEJO (EXTRA-AGED): Tequila aged more than one year in oak barrels; may also be called "mature tequila." This is the smoothest tequila variety, and the one that most resembles cognac or whiskey—ideal for sipping. Some feel that the agave taste is less noticeable.

CREAM OF THE CROP

In the tequila business, innovation and young energy aren't as successful as age and experience. Traditional *tequilera* families like those behind Don Julio, Sauza, and José Cuervo tend to get the most outstanding results, having pursued perfection for generations. All of our top picks are 100% blue agave.

El Tesoro de Don Felipe Platinum: Triple distilled, and produced the old-fashioned way, the agave hearts crushed with a stone grinder and baked in a brick oven

Don Eduardo: Youthful, crisp, and jubilant, with herby notes; triple distilled

Sauza's Tres Generaciones Blanco: Clean and balanced with hints of cinnamon

Chinaco Blanco: International World Spirits Competition judges proclaimed it "the epitome of tequila character, . . . with a lively finish"

Amatitlán Reposado: A complex spirit with a suggestion of nutmeg and spice; awarded best in class at the 2005 International World Spirits Competition

Penacho Azteca Reposado: Another award winner by the same distillery as Amatitlán Reposado

Three faces of tequila.

Chinaco Reposado: Medium-dry rested tequila with an oak-spice bite and subtle fruit and flower aromas

Don Julio 1942: Exquisite, complex tequila with the aroma of toffee and vanilla

José Cuervo's Reserva de la Familia: Aged for three years in new oak barrels; rich flavor with touches of vanilla and herbs, and a long, graceful finish

Arette Gran Clase Añejo: Ultrasmooth, one of the suavest tequilas anywhere; aged for a full three years, it goes for $100 – $150 a bottle

A TEQUILA BY ANY OTHER NAME ISN'T TEQUILA

To be called "tequila" a drink must meet the following strict requirements, as put forth by Consejo Regulador de Tequila (Tequila Regulatory Council; CRT):

- made entirely in Mexico, and from blue agave grown in certain regions of Mexico (though it can be bottled elsewhere)
- distilled twice; some varieties are distilled three times
- contains at least 51% alcohol derived from Weber blue agave plant
- bears the official stamp of the CRT on the label
- if it is 100% blue agave, it must be bottled in Mexico at the plant at which it was made

and your pet python with open arms—give you both a squeeze. PV's original martini bar, Apaches is the landing zone for expats reconnoitering after a long day, and a warm-up for late-night types. When the outside tables get jam-packed in high season, the overflow heads into the narrow bar and the adjacent, equally narrow bistro. It opens at 5 PM; happy hour is 5 to 7. If you're alone, this is the place to make friends of all ages. ⊠ *Olas Altas 439, Col. E. Zapata* ☎ *322/222–5235.*

Burro's Bar. Right on the sand across from Parque Lázaro Cárdenas, this restaurant-bar has bargain brewskis and equally inexpensive fruity margaritas by the pitcher. The seafood is less than inspired, but nachos and other munchies are good accompaniments to the drinks. Watch the waves and listen to Bob Marley and the Gypsy Kings among lots of gringo couples and a few middle-age Mexican vacationers. It opens daily at 10 AM. ⊠ *Av. Olas Altas at Calle Lázaro Cárdenas, Col. E. Zapata* ☎ *No phone.*

★ **Encuentros.** At this darkly atmospheric lounge, which is open from 6 PM to 1 AM, comfortable, suedelike barstools surround the horseshoe-shape bar; small tables face equally comfortable banquets. The small pizzas are a perfect snack, maybe during the 8 to 10 PM happy hour. ⊠ *Lázaro Cárdenas 312, Col. E. Zapata* ☎ *322/222–0643.*

Garbo. This isn't the kind of place where you'll strike up a conversation; rather it's an upscale place to go with friends for a sophisticated, air-conditioned drink or two. Cigarette smoke perfumes the air, and a musician plays piano or gentle electric guitar music weekend nights during high season, less often the rest of the year. Garbo's is open nightly after 6. ⊠ *Pulpito 142, Olas Altas, Col. E. Zapata* ☎ *322/223–5753.*

Kit Kat Club. Both straights and gays are drawn to this elegant lounge, which has full meals as well as millions of great martinis. Among the most popular are the Peggy Lee (vodka, orange, and cranberry juices, and banana liqueur) and the Queen of Hearts (vodka, amaretto, cranberry juice, and 7UP). There's a drag-queen fashion show Tuesday at 10:30. ⊠ *Calle Púlpito 120, Col. E. Zapata* ☎ *322/223–0093.*

Steve's Sports Bar. With NASCAR on Sunday morning, NFL on Monday night, hockey, indispensable motocross, and welterweight fights, Steve's is a sports mecca. Five feeds and nine television sets guarantee broadcasts of many sporting events from various continents, simultaneously. There are piles of board games, too, and the burgers and fries couldn't be better. ⊠ *Basilio Badillo 286, Col. E. Zapata* ☎ *322/222–0256.*

Uncommon Ground Chill Out Lounge. This lesbian-owned spot is painted purple, decorated with an Asian theme, and promises great pizza and free aromatherapy. Other offerings include appetizers, salads, desserts, specialty coffee drinks, and liqueurs. Hours are between approximately 5 PM and 2 AM. ⊠ *Lázaro Cárdenas 625, Col. E. Zapata* ☎ *322/223–3834* ⊕ *www.uncommon-grounds.com* ⊙ *Closed Mon., Tues., and July–Sept.*

GAY BARS
Blue Chairs. In addition to its famous beach scene, Blue Chairs has the popular **Blue Sunset Rooftop Bar,** which is the perfect place to watch

the sun set. Nightly late-afternoon and evening entertainment ranges from "Blue Balls" Bingo to the biweekly drag show and the Saturday night "Blue Hombre Review." The place has good snacks, and a small swimming pool. Monday is karaoke night, beginning at 8 PM. ✉*Almendro 4 at the malecón, south end of Los Muertos Beach, Col. E. Zapata* ☎322/222–5040.

> ### MUSIC ALFRESCO
>
> The outdoor Los Arcos amphitheater frequently has some sort of live entertainment on weekends and evenings. It's as likely to be mimes or magicians as musicians, but always worth stopping for the camaraderie with local people.

Frida. We've heard this place described as "the gay Cheers of Mexico." It's a friendly neighborhood cantina where you'll meet middle-aged to older queens, many Mexicans, a few foreigners, and maybe even some straights. Show up a few times for $1 beers (served daily between 1 and 7 PM) and everyone is sure to know your name. ✉*Lázaro Cárdenas 361, between Insurgentes and Aguacate, Col. E. Zapata* ☎No phone.

La Noche. This charming martini lounge has red walls and a huge, eye-catching chandelier. Gringo-owned, it attracts a crowd of gay 20- to 40-year-old men (a mix of foreigners and Mexicans). Electronica and house music are the favorites; speaking of which, the house makes excellent cocktails, and not too expensive, either. There's usually happy hour between 7 and 9 PM. ✉*Lázaro Cárdenas 257, Col. E. Zapata* ☎322/222–3364.

COFFEEHOUSES

Café San Angel. It's moody, romantic, and a favorite with locals and the gay crowd. It has tables along the sidewalk and comfortable couches and chairs inside. The menu holds soups, sandwiches, salads, and a great frappuccino. ✉*Av. Olas Altas 449, at Calle Francisca Rodriguez, Col. E. Zapata* ☎322/223–1273.

Pie in the Sky Vallarta. Come for the excellent coffee as well as *the* most scrumptious pies, cookies, and cakes. There's free Wi-Fi for those with their trusty laptops. ✉*Lázaro Cárdenas 247, Col. E. Zapata* ☎322/223–8183.

SHOWS

La Iguana. Enjoy Vallarta's original dinner show Thursday or Sunday. Large troops of professional mariachis entertain, beautiful women dance in colorful costumes, couples dance, kids whack piñatas, and fireworks light up the sky. The simulated cockfight is supposed to be painless for the roosters, and nearly so for alarmed foreign visitors. There's an open bar (national beer and well drinks only), and the buffet has 40 selections. Most folks deem this party worth the price of $55 per person. ✉*Calle Lázaro Cárdenas 311, Col. E. Zapata* ☎322/222–0105.

Playa Los Arcos. This place has a theme dinner show Monday, Wednesday, and Saturday 8–9 PM. The show, which costs $16, includes a buffet and one cocktail. The most popular theme night is Saturday's Mexico Night, with mariachis, rope tricks, and folkloric dance. ✉*Av. Olas Altas 380, Col. E. Zapata* ☎322/226–7100.

7

Mexican Rhythms and Roots

Salsa, merengue, *cumbia*. Do they leave you spinning, even off the dance floor? This primer is designed to help you wrap your mind around Latin beats popular in Pacific Mexico. Unfortunately, it can't cure two left feet.

These and other popular Latin dance rhythms were born of African drumming brought to the Caribbean by slaves. Dancing was vital to West African religious ceremonies; these rhythms spread with importation of slaves to the New World. Evolving regional tastes and additional instruments have produced the Latin music enjoyed today from Tierra del Fuego to Toronto, and beyond.

While the steps in most dances can be reduced to some basics, these flat-footed styles of dancing are completely foreign to most non-Latins. Dance classes can definitely help your self-esteem as well as your performance. In Puerto Vallarta, the dance club J.B. is the place to go for lessons.

From Colombia, wildly popular **cumbia** combines vocals, wind, and percussion instruments. With a marked rhythm (usually 4/4 time), the sensual music is relatively easy to dance to. Hip-hop and reggae influences have produced urban cumbia, with uptempo, accordion-driven melodies. Listen to Kumbia Kings, La Onda, Control, and Big Circo to get into the cumbia groove.

Fast-paced and with short, precise rhythms, **merengue** originated in the Dominican Republic. Although the music sounds almost frantic, the feet aren't meant to keep pace with the melody. Check out Elvis Crespo's 2004 album *Saboréalo*.

Born in Cuba of Spanish and African antecedents, **son** is played on accordion, guitar, and drums. The folkloric music was translated to various dialects in different parts of Mexico. "La Bamba" is a good example of *son jarrocho* (from Veracruz).

American Prohibition sent high rollers sailing down Cuba way, and they came back swinging to son, mambo, and rumba played by full orchestras—think Desi Arnaz and his famous song "Babalou." In New York these styles morphed into **salsa**, popularized by such luminaries as Tito Puente and Celia Cruz and carried on today by superstars like Marc Anthony. Wind instruments (trumpet, trombone), piano, guitar, and plenty of percussion make up this highly spiced music.

Mexicans love these African-inspired beats, but are especially proud of homegrown genres, like **música norteña**, which has its roots in rural, northern Mexico (in Texas, it's called *conjunto*). The traditional instruments are the *bajo sexto* (a 12-string guitar), bass, and accordion; modern groups add the trap drums for a distinctive rhythmic pulse. It's danced like a very lively polka, which is one of its main influences. Norteña is the music of choice for working-class Mexicans and Mexican-Americans in the United States. A subset of música norteña is the **corrido**, popularized during the Mexican Revolution. Like the ballads sung by wandering European minstrels, corridos informed isolated Mexican communities of the adventures of Emiliano Zapata, Pancho Villa, and their compatriots. Today's "narco-corridos" portray dubious characters: the drug lords who run Mexico's infamous cartels. Popular norteño artists include

Michael Salgado and the pioneering Los Tigres del Norte, whose album *Americas Sin Fronteras* was terrifically popular way back in 1987.

But the quintessential Mexican music is **mariachi**, a marriage of European instruments and native sensibilities born right here in Jalisco, Mexico. Guitars, violins, and trumpets are accompanied by the *vihuela* (a small, round-backed guitar) and the larger, deep-throated *guitarrón*. Professional mariachis perform at birthdays and funerals, engagements, anniversaries, and life's other milestones. You won't find mariachi music at nightclubs, however; the huapango, jarocho, and other dances the music accompanies are folk dances. ⇨ *For more about mariachi, see* "Mariachi: Born in Jalisco" *in Chapter 8.*

For concerts, clubbing, and dancing, Mexicans look to the contemporary music scene. Latin jazz was born when legendary Cuban musician Chano Pozo teamed up with the great bebop trumpeter Dizzy Gillespie. Current Latin jazz acts worth applauding are Puerto Ricans Eddie Palmieri and David Sanchez; representing pop, Obie Bermúdez also hails from that Caribbean mecca of music. Check out Latin pop by Cuba's Bebo Valdez, and rock en español by multi-Grammy winner Juanes, of Colombia, as well as Mexico's own los Jaguares, El Tri, Ely Guerra, Molotov, and the veteran band Maná.

7

CENTRO AND ENVIRONS

BARS, PUBS, AND LOUNGES

Constantini Wine Bar. Bon vivants should head for the latest innovation of hotshot restaurant Café des Artistes. Order one of 50 wines by the glass (more than 300 by the bottle, from 10 countries) and snack on caviar, bruschetta, and carpaccio—or go directly to dessert. Wine tastings are scheduled from time to time. There's live music most every night of the week. ⊠ *Café des Artistes, Av. Guadalupe Sánchez 740, Centro* ☎ 322/222–3229.

La Cantina. Although La Cantina isn't especially hip, it has a good view of Banderas Bay and the boardwalk from its second floor. It also has canned (and sometimes live) Mexican tunes, especially *ranchera, norteño, grupera,* and *cumbia.* ⊠ *Morelos 709, at J.O. de Dominguez, Centro* ☎ 322/222–1734.

★ **Le Bistro Jazz Café.** It's a mellow, grown-up venue with a good restaurant. There's usually bossa nova or jazz Wednesday or Thursday through Saturday after 7 PM in high season. ⊠ *Isla Río Cuale 16-A, Centro* ☎ 322/222–0283 ⊕ *www.lebistro.com.mx.*

Party Lounge. This place is open daily after 1 PM for stop-and-go drinks: mainly *litros,* that is, 32-ounce tequila sunrises, Long Island ice teas, piña coladas, and the like. The upstairs bar is open 8 PM to 4 AM and plays '70s, '80s, and lounge music, making it popular with an older set, foreign and domestic. ⊠ *Av. Mexico 993, across from Parque Hidalgo, Centro* ☎ No phone.

Regadera. Talent at this karaoke spot varies; it's open nightly (except during low season, when the schedule is less consistent) after 9 PM. Come practice your standard Beatles tunes or hip-hop before your next official recording session. ⊠ *Morelos 666, Centro* ☎ 322/221–3970.

Señor Frog's. What's called simply "Frog's" by the locals, is a good old-fashioned free-for-all for the young and the restless. There are black lights on the walls, bar stools shaped like thong-clad women's butts, and a giant-screen TV above the dance floor. Expect foam parties; ladies'-night Fridays; or, in the high season, beach parties with bikini contests and other shenanigans. ⊠ *Calle Morelos 518, Centro48300* ☎ 322/222–5171.

The Shamrock. At this Irish-owned pub, open daily after 11 AM, the Wi-Fi flows freely throughout the chummy bar, and the chips, batter-fried cod, cottage pies, and burgers are great. When the number of customers warrants it during busy season, the more sophisticated

> ### DRINKS ON THE BEACH
>
> Playa Los Muertos is the destination of choice for a sunset cocktail and dinner on the beach. Strolling mariachi bands serenade diners overlooking the sand; at some tables the waves kiss your toes under the table. Candles and torches light the scene, along with the moon. After dinner you can take a stroll or sit on the beach, or head to another restaurant bar for a coffee or after-dinner digestif to the tunes of marimba, folk music, or jazz.

(and peaceful) upstairs lounge is opened. ⊠*Av. México 22, Centro* ☎*329/298–3073.*

Ztai. Beyond its garden restaurant, multilevel Ztai offers curtained poster beds, supersoft bar stools, and backless sofas in addition to more standard club seating. The minimalist bar is imbued with a peachy glow and overlooks the

ocean: très cool! There's no cover except on ladies' night (currently Friday), when the gals can spend less than $5 and then attempt to maintain their decorum over unlimited drinks between 11 PM and 3 AM; guys pay four times that much. ⊠*Calle Morelos 737, Centro* ☎*322/222–0364.*

DANCE AND MUSIC CLUBS

Fodor's Choice ★ **Bebotero.** This upscale, second-story nightclub has live rock. Although it opens nightly after 7, music doesn't start until 10 or 11; closing time is 4 AM. ⊠ *Paseo Diaz Ordáz 522, Centro* ☎ *322/113–0099.*

Blanco y Negro. Here's a wonderful place for a quiet drink. The intimate café-bar is comfortable yet rustic, with *equipale* (leather-and-wood) love seats and traditional round cocktail tables. It's a wonderful place for a quiet drink. At least until the music starts. At around 10:30, *trova* (think Mexican Cat Stevens) by Latino legends Silvio Rodríguez and Pablo Milanés begins; songs composed and sung by the owner are thrown in. There's never a cover. It opens after 8 PM every night but Sunday and Monday. ⊠*Calle Lucerna at Calle Niza, behind Blockbuster Video store, Zona Hotelera* ☎*322/293–2556.*

La Bodeguita del Medio. It's a wonderful Cuban bar and restaurant with a friendly vibe. People of all ages come to salsa and drink mojitos made with Cuban rum. The small dance floor fills up as soon as the house sextet starts playing around 9:30 PM. There's no cover. ⊠*Paseo Díaz Ordaz 858, Centro* ☎*322/223–1585.*

★ **Christine.** Christine's has a spectacular light shows set to bass-thumping music that ranges from techno and house to disco, rock, and Mexican pop. Most people (young boomers and Gen-Xers) come for the duration (it doesn't close until 6 AM), as this is the top of the food chain for the PV dancing experience. The dance club is open Wednesday through Sunday after 10 PM, and the cover is typically $20. Exceptions include ladies' nights (no set night), when women get in free. On open-bar nights, the $36-per-person cover gets you unlimited drinks. ⊠ *Krystal Vallarta, Av. de las Garzas s/n, Zona Hotelera* ☎*322/224–6990 or 322/224–0202.*

Fodor's Choice ★ **de Santos.** In addition to having a pretty good Mediterranean dinner in the ground-floor restaurant, you can start an evening here with chill-out and lounge music that appeals to a mixed, though slightly older, crowd. Later, local and guest DJs spin the more danceable, beat-driven disco and house tunes that appeal to slightly younger folks. If the smoke and noise get to you, head upstairs to the rooftop bar, where you and your friends can fling yourselves on the giant futons for some stargazing. This is a see-and-be-seen place for locals, and the kitchen is generally open 'til 2 AM; the whole place shuts down at 4 AM. ⊠ *Calle Morelos 771, at Leona Vicario, Centro* ☎ *322/223–3052.*

> **ROCK ON**
>
> The sound system at de Santos is top-notch, not surprising since one of the principal partners is Alex González, the drummer from Mexico's venerable rock band Maná.

Hilo. Popular with young, hip *vallartenses,* Hilo attracts a mix of locals and visitors. It's mainly a young crowd, serving up house, techno, hip-hop, electronic, and Top 40. The ceiling is several stories high, and enormous bronze-color statues give an epic feeling. It's open from 4 PM to 6 AM, but doesn't get rolling until midnight. The cover is $7–$10, or $30 with open bar. ⊠ *Paseo Díaz Ordaz 588, Centro* ☎ *322/223–5361.*

★ **J.B.** It's pronounced "Hota Bay," and it's the best club in town for salsa. The age of the crowd varies, but tends toward thirty- and fortysomethings. J.B. is serious about dancing, so it feels young at heart. There's usually a band Friday and Saturday nights, DJ music the rest of the week. Those with *dos patas zurdas* (two left feet) can attend salsa lessons Thursday and Friday 8 to 10 PM (50 pesos); or take tango lessons for the same price on Monday at 8 PM. The dance club's cover is $8 when there's live music, otherwise about $4 and free on Monday and Tuesday. ⊠ *Blvd. Federico M. Ascencio 2043, Zona Hotelera* ☎ *322/224–4616.*

> **LET'S GET PHYSICAL**
>
> Tango aficionados since 1985, **Al and Barbara Garvey** (☎ *322/222–8895, 415/513–4497 in U.S.* ⊕ *www.tangobar-productions.com*) of San Francisco teach the Argentine dance for beginner through advanced levels. They also give private lessons and meet up with fellow dancers for practice at Vallarta's Latin dance club, J.B. The Garveys are around most of the year, but call or check their Web site for schedules.

La Paloma. This institution for Mexican breakfast has otherwise average food but is recommended for sunset cocktails with live marimba and, later, mariachi music. ⊠ *Paseo Diaz Ordaz, at Aldama, Centro* ☎ *322/222–3675.*

The Zoo. Ready to party? Then head here for DJ-spun techno, Latin, reggae, and hip-hop. The adventurous can dance in the cage. It attracts a mixed crowd of mainly young locals and travelers, though after midnight the median age plunges. It's open until 6 AM when things are hopping. The restaurant fills with cruise-ship passengers early in the evening. ⊠ *Paseo Díaz Ordaz 630, Centro* ☎ *322/222–4945.*

MOVIES

Cinemark. This easy-to-access cinema is in the heart of the Hotel Zone, on the second floor at the south end of the Plaza Caracol mall. The latest films are shown on its 10 screens. Tickets are about $4. ⊠ *Av. de los Tules 178, Plaza Caracol, Zona Hotelera* ☎ *322/224–8927* ⊕ *www.cinemark.com.mx.*

Cinépolis. Until Cinemark showed up, this was PV's newest theater. Next to Soriana department stores at the south entrance to El Pitillal, it has 15 screens and shows in English and Spanish. Tickets are about $4. ⊠ *Plaza Soriana, Av. Francisco Villa 1642–A, Pitillal* ☎ *322/225–1251* ⊕ *www.cinepolis.com.mx.*

Versalles. Tickets for a show one of the six screens here are $4. ⊠ *Av. Francisco Villa 799, Col. Versalles* ☎ *322/225–8766.*

SHOW

El Mariachi Loco. It's the place to see mariachi musicians and dance to Latin tunes—all at a price that locals can afford (and it's geared to them, not so much to foreign tourists). The schedule changes frequently, but on a typical night you'll hear mariachis at 11 PM followed by a comedian (in Spanish, of course). A ranchera group then takes over, and couples dance until the wee wee hours. The days most likely to have limited or no live entertainment are Sunday and Monday. The cover is $5. ⊠ *Lázaro Cárdenas 254, at Calle I. Vallarta, Centro* ☎ *322/223–2205.*

7

MARINA VALLARTA

BARS, PUBS, AND LOUNGES

El Faro. Here you can admire the bay and marina from atop a 110-foot lighthouse. It's mainly a baby-boomer crowd, with lots of yachties. ⊠ *Royal Pacific Yacht Club, Marina Vallarta* ☎ *322/221–0541.*

Tribu Bar Lounge. Locals decided that this was a bit out-of-the-way to become a serious hot spot, but Mexicans and foreigners in the Marina district find it atmospheric. DJ-spun music pulses house, lounge, techno, disco, or '80s music—whatever the crowd demands. Wednesday is usually salsa night, though the salsa is canned. There are also two billiard tables. In high season it's open every day but Monday from 5 PM to 1 AM, and there's no cover. In low season (generally August through mid-November) it's open Thursday and Friday only. ⊠ *Paseo de la Marina 220, Mayan Palace Marina, Marina Vallarta* ☎ *322/226–6000 Ext. 4786.*

Victor's Place (Café Tacuba). It's an excellent, inexpensive restaurant that doubles as a bar, well tended by the owner. Beer for a buck-fifty (or less, depending on the peso's fluctuations) and inexpensive tequila with beer chasers are practically a house rule. You can check it out nightly until 11 PM, a bit later on weekends. ⊠ *Condominios Las Palmas, Local 9, Marina Vallarta* ☎ *322/221–2808.*

MOVIES

MMCinema. Across from the cruise ship pier in the Liverpool shopping complex, is the newest Puerto Vallarta's cinemas. It has 10 screens and a $4.50 ticket price. ⊠*Blvd. Francisco M. Ascencio 2920, Col. Educación* ☏*322/221–0095* ⊕*www.mmcinema.com.*

NAYARIT

BARS, PUBS, AND LOUNGES

★ **The Bar Above.** It's difficult to categorize this little place above Tapas del Mundo. It's a martini bar without a bar: the owner, Buddy, prefers that people come to converse with friends at tables rather than hang out at a bar. It also serves dessert. Molten chocolate soufflé—the signature dish—or charred-pineapple-bourbon shortcake may be on the menu. Lights are dim, the music is romantic, and there's an eagle's view of the ocean from the rooftop crow's nest. It's closed every Sunday and June through October. At other times, it's open 6 PM–11 PM. ⊠*Av. México at Av. Hidalgo, 2 blocks north of central plaza, Bucerías* ☏*329/298–1194.*

Geckos Pub (⊠*Calle Morelos, between Calles Madero and Av. Cárdenas, Bucerías* ☏*329/298–1861*) is an unassuming local watering hole with a billiards table. It's the kind of place a single woman can enter without feeling weird or being hassled as bartenders tend to keep an eye out for them in the small venue.

Route 200 Bar & Grill. It calls itself a "good old-fashioned biker bar," and there are hogs and other impressive-looking bikes out front most any time during between noon and its 1 AM closing. You'll find burgers, hot dogs, and other bar food and two pool tables as well as live heavy metal music after 10:30 Wednesday through Saturday. ⊠*Carretera 200 (Vallarta a Tepic) 993, Nuevo Vallarta* ☏*322/297–1054* ⊕*www. route200.com* ☉*Closed Sun.*

MUSIC CLUBS

Claudio's Meson Bay. Every day, marimba musicians or romantic duos tap out lighthearted melodies at this casual, open-sided, ocean-facing restaurant. The show runs from 6:30 to 10 PM (less often in low season), which coincides with the excellent all-you-can-eat buffets Monday, Wednesday, and Friday. A branch in Nuevo Vallarta offers the same fare. ⊠*Lázaro Cárdenas 17, by footbridge, Bucerías* ☏*329/298–1634.*

Philo's. It's the unofficial cultural center and meeting place of La Cruz, with music, food, a large-screen TV, and pool table. The namesake owner, a former record producer, also has a small recording studio here. The space is plain but there's excellent live music after 8:30 PM Thursday through Saturday year-round. Get down with rhythm and blues, country, and rock; or chow down on good pizza or barbecue. ⊠*Calle Delfín 15, La Cruz de Huanacaxtle* ☏*329/295–5068.*

Overnight Excursions

Guadalajara

WORD OF MOUTH

"PV [has] this fun malécon to stroll down in the evening, the food is great, and if you want a getaway, Guadalajara is four hours by bus [and] the marshes of San Blas (you can see lots of birds, crocodiles, and turtles there) is about three hours away."

—junejuly

EXCURSIONS FROM PUERTO VALLARTA

Lake Chapala, Jalisco

TOP REASONS TO GO

★ **Alchemic atmosphere:** San Blas's basic but charismatic attractions—beaches, markets, churches, and boat trips—combine like magic for a destination that's greater than the sum of its parts.

★ **Highland rambles:** Drop-dead-gorgeous hills and river valleys from Talpa de Allende to San Sebastián get you out into nature and away from coastal humidity.

★ **Amazing photography:** In the mountain towns like San Sebastián, Mascota, and Talpa, even amateurs can capture excellent small-town and nature photos.

★ **Palpable history:** Soak up Mexican history and culture in Guadalajara's churches, museums, and political murals.

★ **Getting the goods:** Guadalajara has excellent housewares and handicrafts at great prices for sale in its megamalls as well as in nearby pre-Hispanic townships.

1 San Blas. Change happens slowly in San Blas, which has yet to experience a tourism boom. Cruise wide dirt streets on one-speed bikes, read books in the shade, dig your toes in the sand, and just enjoy life—one lazy day at a time. Blue mountains and green hills provide a beautiful backdrop.

Sand sculpture on the Beach

2 The Mountain Towns.

The former mining and supply towns within the Sierra Madre—Talpa de Allende, Mascota, and tiny San Sebastián—were isolated for centuries by narrow roads and dangerous drop-offs and remain postcards of the past. Soak up the small-town atmosphere and alpine air.

3 Greater Guadalajara.

Home to cherished archetypes like mariachi, charrería (elegant "rodeos"), and tequila, Guadalajara is often called "the Mexican's Mexico." The metropolitan area includes former farming community Zapopan, and two districts known for crafts: Tlaquepaque and neighboring Tonalá. Outside the city are unique archaeological digs at Teuchitlán, lakeside retreat Chapala, artists' and expats' enclave Ajijic, and Tequila, famous for . . . do we even need to say it?

GETTING ORIENTED

About 156 km (95 mi) north of PV, mountain-backed San Blas has beaches and birding. Inland 340 km (211 mi) or so from PV, Jalisco capital Guadalajara (pop. 4 million) sits in the Atemajac Valley, circled by Sierra Madre peaks. Sleepy mountain towns Talpa de Allende, Mascota, and San Sebastián lie about halfway between PV and Guadalajara; each offers a glimpse of rural life from centuries long gone.

8

San Cristóbal de la Barranca
Magdalena
Toll
23
54
Antonio Escobedo
15D
Tequila
Amatitán
3 Ixtlahuacán del Río
El Arenal
Zapopan
Ahualuco
Area de Protección de Flora y Fauna la Primavera
Guadalajara
80D
Jesús María
Teuchitlán
Zapotlanejo
Tlaquepaque
Tonalá
70
Ameca
Acatlán de Juárez
54
El Salto
15D
44
Area de Protección de Flora y Fauna
Cocula
Ajijic
Chapala
Jocotepec
80
Zacoalco de Torres
Lake Chapala
Ayutla
Tecolotlán
Tuxcueca
Juchitlán
Chiquilistlán
Unión de Tula
Amacueca
Sayula
54D
El Grullo
110
Autlán de Navarro
San Gabriel
Ciudad Guzman
Tamazula de Gordiano
Parque Nacional Nevado de Colima
Tuxpan
Reserva de la Biosfera Sierra de Manantlán
Atenquique
Tecalitlan
JALISCO COLIMA
Queseria
54
Colima
TO MANZANILLO, IXTAPA, ZIHUATANEJO

Tonalá Ceramics

EXCURSIONS PLANNER

Coming and Going

If you plan to visit both Puerto Vallarta and Guadalajara, consider flying into one and out of the other. Some open-jaw trips cost even less than a round-trip flight to/from PV. If you plan your trip right, travel between PV and Guadalajara by bus is $32–$37. One-way drop-off charges for rental cars are steep. Access to Mascota and Talpa from Guadalajara is more direct than from PV, although the latter road is now paved, with new bridges in place. Nonetheless, this windy mountain route is occasionally impassable in rainy season. Buses take you directly from PV to San Blas, or you can get off at nearby beaches. That said, a car is handier for exploring the coast. The mostly two-lane PV–San Blas road is curvy but otherwise fine.

■ **TIP→** **Most small towns that don't have official stations sell gas from a home or store. Ask around before heading out on the highway if you're low on gas.**

Day Trips versus Extended Stays

The San Blas area is best as an overnight unless you go with an organized tour, though you could easily drive to Platanitos, south of San Blas, for a day at the beach.

If busing or driving to the mountain towns, plan to overnight unless you take the day tour with Vallarta Adventures or another PV tour company. Alternatively, you can fly on your own with Aerotaxis de la Bahía (☎ *322/221–1990*) for a day trip or an overnight stay.

Guadalajara is too far to go for the day from Vallarta or San Blas; we recommend at least two days.

How Much Can You Do?

What you can (physically) do and what you should do are very different things. To get the most out of your excursion from Puerto Vallarta, don't overdo it. It's a vacation—it's supposed to be fun, and possibly even relaxing! If you'll be in the Sayulita, San Francisco, and Chacala areas in Nayarit, it's easy to do an overnight jaunt up to San Blas, enjoying the myriad beaches and small towns as you travel up and back. Or make San Blas your base and explore from there.

You could also feasibly spend one night in San Blas and two in Guadalajara, about 4 to 4½ hours by rental car and 5 hours by bus. For lovers of the road less traveled, two to three nights gives you ample time to explore the mountain towns of San Sebastián, Mascota, and Talpa as well as the surrounding countryside. Or you could spend one night in the mountains and continue to Guadalajara the next day. To fully appreciate Guadalajara, plan to spend at least two nights.

Driving Times from Puerto Vallarta	
San Blas	3–3.5 hours
San Sebastián	1.5–2 hours
Mascota	2.5–3 hours
Talpa de Allende	3–3.5 hours
Guadalajara	4–5 hours

Tour Companies

TB Tours (⊠*Calle Cisne 129, Fracc. Los Sauces* ☎*322/ 209–1655*) leads tours to San Blas, with a visit to the old fort and the town, and to La Tovara mangroves and the crocodile farm. It's a full-day tour including breakfast en route, the boat tour, guide, lunch, and hotel pick-up and return. The cost is about $100 per person. There are tours year-round, but only on Thursday. TB also has a San Sebastián tour, at about $75, Tuesday through Thursday.

Contact the **Cámera de Comercio** (Chamber of Commerce ⊠*Av. Vallarta 4095, Zona Minerva, Guadalajara* ☎*33/3880–9099 or 01800/503–9720 toll-free in Mexico* ⊕*www.tequilaexpress.com.mx*) for information about the all-day tour aboard the **Tequila Express Train**. The cost is about $80, including lunch, factory tour, mariachi serenades, and tequila.

Highly recommended **Vallarta Adventures** (⊠*Edifício Marina Golf, Local 13–C, Calle Mástil, Marina Vallarta, Puerto Vallarta* ☎*322/297–1212 or 322/221– 0657, 888/303–2653 in U.S. and Canada* ⊕*www. vallarta-adventures.com*) has daily, seven-hour jeep tours to San Sebastián ($80).

The bilingual guides of Ajijic's **Charter Club Tours** (⊠*Carretera Chapala–Jocotepec at Calle Colón, Plaza Montana mall, Ajijic* ☎*376/766–1777* ⊕*www.charterclubtours. com.mx*) lead tours of Guadalajara, shopping and factory trips in Tlaquepaque and Tonalá, Tequila, the Teuchitlán archaeological site, and treks to Jalisco's lesser-known towns.

WHAT IT COSTS IN U.S. DOLLARS

¢	$	$$	$$$	$$$$
Restaurants				
under $5	$5–$10	$10–$15	$15–$25	over $25
Hotels				
under $50	$50–$75	$75–$150	$150–$250	over $250

Restaurant prices are for a median main course at dinner, excluding tax, drinks, and service. Hotel prices are for a standard room, generally excluding taxes and service charges.

When to Go

Thanks to a springlike climate, Guadalajara is pleasant at any time of year, though in winter pollution can cause raw throats, sore eyes, and sinus irritation. Book well in advance to visit during the October Festival or other holidays. Roads can be dangerous during summer rains; June through October aren't the best time to visit the mountain towns by land.

San Blas and the coast begin to heat up in May; during the late June through October rainy season both the ambient and ocean temps are highest.

Festivals and Special Events

Guadalajara's major events include a May cultural festival; suburb Tlaquepaque celebrates the June ceramics festival. The International Mariachi and Tequila Festival, in September, teams mariachi bands with the philharmonic orchestra. Also in Guadalajara, the entire month of October is given up to mariachis, *charreadas* (rodeos), soccer matches, and theater.

At the San Blas Festival (February 3), a statue of the town's patron saint gets a boat ride around the bay and the town invests in a major fireworks show. In the Sierra Madre, Talpa's equally admired icon brings the faithful en masse four times a year for street dances and mariachi serenades.

Puerto Vallarta's location means lots of variety. You can explore little-visited beaches and miles of mangrove canals in San Blas. You can shop and "get culture" in historic Guadalajara. Or you can head to the mountains for a look at mining towns and long walks down country lanes.

Although San Blas is now the northern terminus of the so-called Riviera Nayarit (the new term for the stretch of coast from San Blas to the southern Nayarit State border at Nuevo Vallarta), thus far it's changed little. Things here are low-key and friendly—a nice change from bustling Vallarta and environs, where traffic sometimes snarls. There are no supermarkets; everyone shops at mom-and-pop groceries or the daily market for tropical fruits and vegetables, tortillas, and hot or cold snacks. Many of the restaurants around the plaza are relatively simple and inexpensive.

Founded by the Spanish but soon all but abandoned for busier ports, San Blas has several historic structures to visit, including the old customs and counting houses, and original churches. But more of a draw are its miles of sandy beaches and La Tobara, a serpentine series of mangrove-lined channels leading to a freshwater spring.

Even less sophisticated than San Blas are a handful of former silver-mining towns and supply centers in the hills behind Puerto Vallarta. Until a 21st-century road improvement, Mascota, Talpa de Allende, San Sebastián, and other villages en route to Guadalajara were accessible only by narrow, treacherous, snaky mountain road or small plane. Today sunny, unpolluted days and crisp nights lure people out of the fray and into a more relaxed milieu, where lingering over coffee or watching kids play in the town plaza are the activities of choice. If this sounds too tame, there's horseback riding, hiking, and fishing at Presa Coriches, among other activities.

Guadalajara—Mexico's second-largest city—makes an excellent add-on to a Vallarta beach vacation. You can shop in megamalls or in surrounding towns, where artisans were producing pottery centuries before the Spanish invasion. You can take in modern Russian ballet or Mexican folkloric dances; see a fast-paced charrería, with men and women on well-groomed Arabian horses; listen to a 12-piece mariachi band; or visit one of a dozen museums. Although at times overwhelming, this modern city provides an excellent overview of all Mexico has to offer. For a foray outside the metropolis, head for Lago de Chapala, Mexico's largest natural lake, or to Tequila, land of the blue agave, where the country's national drink is produced and bottled.

SAN BLAS AND ENVIRONS

The cool thing about San Blas and the surrounding beaches is that they're untouristy and authentic. Sure, there's an expat community, but it's minuscule compared to that of Puerto Vallarta. Parts of San Blas itself are deliciously disheveled, or should we say, ungentrified. The lively square is a nice place to polish off an ice-cream cone and watch the world. If you're looking for posh restaurants and perfect English speakers, this isn't the place for you.

Most people come to the San Blas area for basic R&R, to enjoy the long beaches and seafood shanties. The town's sights can be seen in a day, but stay for a few days at least to catch up on your reading, visit the beaches, and savor the town as it deserves. La Tovara jungle cruise through the mangroves should not be missed.

SAN BLAS

Many travelers come here looking for Old Mexico, or the "real Mexico," or the Mexico they remember from the 1960s. New Spain's first official Pacific port has experienced a long, slow slide into obscurity since losing out to better-equipped ports in the late 19th century. But there's something to be said for

> **CAUTION**
>
> The fierce biting *jejenes* (no-see-ums) of San Blas are legendary, but not everyone reacts to their sting.

being a bit player rather than a superstar. Industrious but not overworked, residents of this drowsy seaside city hit the beaches on weekends and celebrate their good fortune during numerous saints' days and civic festivals. You can, too.

GETTING HERE AND AROUND

If you want to head directly to San Blas from outside Mexico, fly to Mexico City and on to Tepic (69 km [43 mi] from San Blas), capital of the state of Nayarit, on Aeromar (affiliated with Mexicana de Aviación). To get to San Blas by road from Tepic, head north on Highway 15D, then west on Highway 11. Most visitors, however, make San Blas a road trip from PV.

The Puerto Vallarta bus station is less than 5 km (3 mi) north of the PV airport; there are usually four daily departures for San Blas ($10; 3 hours). These buses generally don't stop, and most don't have bathrooms. Departure times vary throughout the year, but at this writing, there are no departures after 4:30 PM. To get to Platanitos Beach, about an hour south of San Blas, take the Puerto Vallarta bus. ■ TIP→ Always check the return schedule with the driver when taking an out-of-town bus. A taxi from Puerto Vallarta or from the airport costs about $100.

A car is handy for more extensive explorations of the coast between PV and around San Blas. Within San Blas, the streets are wide, traffic is almost nonexistent, and, with the exception of the streets immediately surrounding the main plaza, parking is easy. From Puerto Vallarta,

San Blas

TO
LA TOVARA,
SINGAYTA

54

Tickets to
La Tovara

Embarcadero
La Tovara

Cerro de
San Basilio

El Templo de
Virgen del Rosario

54

◆ Contaduría

Zacatecas

Aviación

Bravo

Gómez ◆

Farías

Echeverría

Yucatán

Canalizo

Sonora

Sinaloa

Juárez

Zapata

Templo de San Blas ◆

◆ Tourism Office

◆ Plaza Principal

Mercado ◆
José María

Michoacán

Querétaro

Oaxaca

Restaurant La Isla ◆

Batallón de San Blas

Paredes

Del Puerto

Hotel Hacienda
◆ Flamingos

Matanchen

Aduana ◆

Arista

Comonfort

◆ Hotel Casa Roxanna

◆ Hotel Garza Canela

Campeche

Virgilio Uribe

TO
TEPIC

Playa Borrego

0   1 mi

0   1 km

abandon Highway 200 just past Las Varas in favor of the coast road (follow the sign toward Zacualpan, where you must go around the main plaza to continue on the unsigned road. Ask locals "¿San Blas?," and they'll point you in the right direction). The distance of about 160 km (100 mi) takes 3 to 3½ hours.

From Guadalajara, you can take 15D (the toll road, about $40) to the Miramar turnoff to San Blas. It's actually much faster and less congested, however, to take Highway 15 at Tequepexpan and head west through Compostela on Highway 68 (toll about US$5); merge with Highway 200 until Las Varas, then head north on the coastal route (Highway 66) to San Blas.

> ### BIRDER'S PARADISE
>
> More than 500 species of birds settle in the San Blas area; 23 are endemic. Organize a birding tour through Hotel Garza Canela (⇨ *below*). In late January, you can attend the **International Festival of Migratory Birds** for bird-watching tours and conferences with experts and fellow enthusiasts.

To really go native, rent a bike from Wala Restaurant, a half block up from the plaza on Calle Juárez, and cruise to your heart's content. To get to the beaches south of town, to Matanchén Bay, and to the village of Santa Cruz, take a bus (they usually leave on the hour) from the bus station across the street from the church on the main plaza. To come back, just stand by the side of the road and flag down a passing bus.

ESSENTIALS

Air Contacts Aeromar (☎ *55/5133–1111 in Mexico* ⊕ *www.aeromar.com.mx*). **Mexicana** (☎ *800/531–7921 in U.S., 866/281–3049 in Canada, 01800/502–2000 in Mexico* ⊕ *www.mexicana.com*).

Bank Banamex (✉ *Calle Juárez 26, 1 block east of plaza, San Blas* ☎ *323/285–0031*).

Bus Contact Transportes Norte de Sonora (☎ *323/285–0043 in San Blas, 322/290–0110 in Puerto Vallarta*).

Medical Assistance Centro de Salud San Blas (✉ *Calle H. Batallón at Calle Yucatán, San Blas* ☎ *323/285–0232*). **Emergency Hotline** (☎ *066*). **Farmacia Económica** (✉ *Calle H. Batallón at Calle Mercado, San Blas* ☎ *323/285–0111*) closes between 2 and 4:30 PM and for the night at 9 PM.

Tourist Board Oficina de Turismo de San Blas (✉ *Calles Canalizo and Sinaloa in Municipal Palace, 2nd fl., on main plaza, San Blas* ☎ *323/285–0221 or 323/285–0005*).

EXPLORING

San Blas has a few fun places to visit, but don't expect to be bowled over.

Check out the outside of the chaste little **Templo de San Blas**, called *La Iglesia Vieja* (the Old Church) by residents, on the town's busy plaza. It's rarely open these days, but you can admire its diminutive beauty and look for the words to Henry Wadsworth Longfellow's poem "The Bells of San Blas," inscribed on a brass plaque. (The long-gone bells were actually at the church dedicated to the Virgin of the Rosary, on Cerro de San Basilio.)

Browse for fruits or good photo-ops at the market, **Mercado José María** (⊠ *Calle H. Battalón de San Blas, between Calles Sonora and Sinaloa*), where you can take a load off at Chito's for a milk shake or fresh fruit juice.

The old **Aduana** (*Customs House* ⊠ *Calle Juárez, near Calle del Puerto*) has been partially restored and is now a cultural center with sporadic art or photography shows and theatrical productions.

For a bird's-eye view of town and the coast, hike or drive up Calle Juárez, the main drag, to **Cerro de San Basilio.** Cannons protect the ruined **Contaduría** (*Counting House* ⊠ *Cerro de San Basilio*), built during colonial times when San Blas was New Spain's first official port.

Continuing down the road from the Contaduría brings you to **El Templo de la Virgen del Rosario.** Note the new floor in the otherwise ruined structure; the governor's daughter didn't want to soil the hem of her gown when she married here in 2005. A bit farther on, San Blas's little cemetery is backed by the sea and the mountains.

WHERE TO EAT AND STAY

$ ✕**La Isla.** Shell lamps; pictures made entirely of scallops, bivalves, and
SEAFOOD   starfish; shell-drenched chandeliers; every inch of wall space is decorated in different denizens of the sea. Service isn't particularly brisk (pretty much par for the course in laid-back San Blas), but the seafood, filet mignon, and fajitas are all quite good. Afterward stroll over to the main plaza a few blocks away. ⊠ *Calle Mercado at Calle Paredes* ☎ *323/285–0407* ⊟ *No credit cards* ☾ *Closed Mon.*

$ ▦**Casa Roxanna.** This is an attractive little enclave of cozy and clean (albeit basic) cottages with screened windows. Full kitchens with lots of pots and pans invite cooking, but the real draws are the lovingly tended gardens surrounding the lodgings, the covered patio, and the sparkling, three-lane lap pool. If you love it, settle in a while; monthly rates are usually available. **Pros:** personable staff, great lap pool. **Cons:** so-so a/c units, lackluster interior decor. ⊠ *Callejón El Rey 1, San Blas* ☎ *323/285–0573* ⊕ *www.casaroxanna.com* ↪ *6 cottages* ♿ *In-room: no phone, kitchen (some), refrigerator (some). In-hotel: pool, laundry facilities, Wi-Fi, parking (free)* ⊟ *No credit cards* ❘○❘ *EP.*

$$ ▦**Hacienda Flamingos.** Built in 1882, this restored mansion-turned-hotel was once part of a large hacienda. The restoration is stunning: surrounding a pretty, plant-filled courtyard is a covered veranda of lovely floor tiles, with lazily rotating ceiling fans, antique furniture, and groupings of chairs for a casual conversation. Opening off the veranda, elegant suites have also been restored to their original glory. It's right across from the cultural center and near the market and town plaza. **Pros:** lovely decor, close to town center. **Cons:** sometimes eerily

devoid of other guests, staff can be chilly. ⊠*Calle Juárez 105, San Blas* ☎*323/285–0485* ⊕*www.sanblas.com.mx* ↪*20 rooms* ♿*In-room: no phone, DVD (some). In-hotel: pool, gym, laundry facilities, Wi-Fi, parking (free)* ▭*MC, V* ⦿*EP.*

$$ 🏨**Hotel Garza Canela.** Opened decades ago by a family of dedicated
★ bird-watchers, this meandering, three-story hotel with expansive grounds is the home base of choice for birding groups. Rooms have small balconies and polished limestone floors; junior suites have large whirlpool tubs. Betty Vasquez, who runs El Delfín French restaurant here, studied at Le Cordón Bleu in France; she prepares elegant and very tasty meals. **Pros:** very good French restaurant, suites have Jacuzzi tub. **Cons:** estuary location means there are some biting bugs, one shared computer for checking Internet in lobby, no Internet access, including Wi-Fi, after 8 PM. ⊠*Calle Paredes 106 Sur, San Blas* ☎*323/285–0112, 01800/713–2313 toll-free in Mexico* ⊕*www.garzacanela.com* ↪*44 rooms, 6 suites* ♿*In-room: no phone. In-hotel: restaurant, pool, Wi-Fi, parking (free)* ▭*AE, MC, V* ⦿*EP.*

SPORTS AND THE OUTDOORS

🕐 A series of narrow waterways wends through the mangroves to **La**
★ **Tovara**, San Blas's most famous attraction. Turtles on logs, crocs that *look* like logs, birds, iguanas, and exotic orchids make this maze of mud-brown canals a magical place. Begin the tranquil ride ($8 per person; four-person minimum or $27 [360 pesos] total for fewer than four) at the El Conchal Bridge, at the entrance-exit to San Blas, or the village of Matanchén. Boats depart when there are enough customers, which isn't usually a problem. Either way you'll end up, after a 45-minute boat ride, at the freshwater pool fed by a natural spring. Rest at the snack shop overlooking the water or jump in using the rope swing, keeping an eye out for the allegedly benign resident croc. There's an optional trip to a crocodile farm for a few dollars more, making it a three-hour instead of a two-hour tour.

ECOTOUR **Singayta** (⊠*8 km [5 mi] from San Blas on road to Tepic* ⊕*www.sin gayta.com*) is a typical Nayarit village that is attempting to support itself through simple and un-gimmicky ecotours. The basic tour includes a look around the town, where original adobe structures compete with more practical but less picturesque structures with corrugated tin roofs. Take a short guided hike through the surrounding jungle, and a boat ride around the estuary ($6 per person). This is primo birding territory. The townspeople are most geared up for tours on weekends and during school holidays and vacations: Christmas, Easter, and July, and August. The easiest way to book a tour is to look for English-speaking Juan Bananas, who sells banana bread from a shop called Tumba de Yako (look for the sign on the unmarked road Avenida H. Batallón between Calles Comonfort and Canalizo, en route to Playa Borrego). He can set up a visit and/or guide you there. Groups of five or more can call ahead to make a reservation with Juan (☎*323/285–0462* ✎*ecomanglar@ yahoo.com*) or with Santos (☎*323/100–4191*); call at least a day ahead if you want to have a meal.

8

THE BEACHES NEAR SAN BLAS

Like San Blas itself, the surrounding beaches attract mostly local people and travelers fleeing glitzier resort scenes. Beaches here are almost uniformly long, flat, and walkable, with light brown sand, moderate waves, and seriously bothersome no-see-ums, especially around sunrise and sunset (and during the waxing and waning moons). Almost as ubiquitous as these biting bugs are simple *ramadas* (open-sided, palm-thatch-roof eateries) on the beach whose owners don't mind if you hang out all day, jumping in the ocean and then back in your shaded hammock to continue devouring John Grisham or leafing through magazines. Order a cold lemonade or a beer, or have a meal of fillet of fish, ceviche, or chips and guacamole. Don't expect a full menu, rather what's fresh and available. All these beaches are accessible by bus from San Blas's centrally located bus station.

> ### BEST BEACH BITE
>
> For a marvelous albeit simple barbecue fish feast, visit **Enramada Ruiz**, a sinfully simple yet sublime seafood shanty on Playa Platanitos.

You can walk or ride a bike to long, lovely **Playa Borrego**, 1 km (½ mi) south of town. Rent a surfboard at Stoners' or Mar y Sol restaurant to attack the year-round (but sporadic) shore or jetty breaks here, or stroll down to the southern end to admire the lovely, palm-fringed estuary.

Fodor's Choice ★

About 6 km (4 mi) south of Playa Borrego, at the northern edge of Bahía de Matanchén, **Playa Las Islitas** used to be legendary among surfers for its long wave, but this has diminished in recent years; the beach is now suitable for swimming, bodysurfing, and boogie boarding.

★ At the south end of the Matanchén Bay, **Playa Los Cocos and Playa Miramar** are both great for long walks and for hanging out at ramadas.

Adjacent to Miramar Beach is the well-kept fishing village of **Santa Cruz**. Take a walk on the beach or around the town; buy a soft drink, find the bakery and pick up some banana bread. Outdoor dances are occasionally held on the diminutive central plaza.

★ Beyond Matanchén Bay the road heads inland and reemerges about 8 km (5 mi) later at **Playa Platanitos**, a lovely little beach in a sheltered cove. Fishermen park their skiffs here, and simple shacks cook up the catch of the day.

WHERE TO STAY

Casa Mañana. Some of the pleasant rooms overlook the beach from a balcony or terrace, but most people stay here for easy access to the good burgers, guacamole, and seafood platter for two ($13) at the adjoining El Alebrije restaurant. The bar, with its cool, brick-floor interior open to the beach, is also popular. Other perks: the long beach, large pool, and hiking and other outdoor activities. **Pros:** good burgers, nice beachfront location. **Cons:** must take a bus or taxi to and from San Blas. ⊠*South end of Playa Los Cocos, 13 km (8 mi) south of San Blas* ☎*323/254–9080 or 323/254–9070* ⊕*www.casa-manana.*

GREAT ITINERARIES

If you're not joining an organized day tour, there are many possible itineraries, depending on whether you leave from PV or from Guadalajara, your tolerance for driving mountain roads, and your desire to explore (i.e., either to see lots or just relax and enjoy the tranquillity, mountain-and-valley views, and quaint lifestyle).

From Puerto Vallarta, consider a two-day trip to the area beginning in San Sebastián and returning to PV (or Guadalajara) from Talpa de Allende. There are many ways to go; keys are not driving at night and enjoying the slow pace. Drive to San Sebastián, enjoying the mountain scenery en route. After a look around the quaint old mining village and an early lunch, continue to Mascota, the

area's largest town and a good base. Spend the night in Mascota. The Sierra Lodge on Lake Juanacatlán, which serves excellent food, can be added as an overnight trip, but it doesn't take day-trippers. If you prefer, take a day trip from Mascota to Talpa de Allende, whose raison d'être is the tiny, beloved Virgin statue in the town's ornate basilica.

Each of the three towns has hills to be climbed for excellent vistas and photos. Otherwise, activities include wandering the streets, visiting small museums and Catholic churches, tasting regional food, and drinking in the mountain air and old-fashioned ambience. Make sure you get where you're going before dark, as mountain roads are unlighted, narrow, and in many cases have sheer drop-offs.

com ➯*26 rooms* ⌂*In-hotel: restaurant, bar, pool, beachfront, parking (free)* ⊟*MC, V* ⏹*EP.*

8

THE MOUNTAIN TOWNS

A trip into the Sierra Madre is an excellent way to escape the coastal heat and the hordes of vacationers. The Spanish arrived to extract ore from these mountains at the end of the 16th century; after the Mexican Revolution the mines were largely abandoned in favor of richer veins. The isolation of these tiny towns has kept them old-fashioned.

The air is crisp and clean and scented of pine, the valley and mountain views are spectacular, and the highland towns earthy, unassuming, and charming. Whitewashed adobe homes radiate from plazas where old gents remember youthful exploits. Saturday night boys and girls court each other alfresco while oompah bands entertain their parents from the bandstand. Although most of the hotels in the region have only basic amenities (construction on a massively improved road from PV is encouraging entrepreneurs, however), the chill mountain air and kilos of blankets can produce a delicious night's sleep.

GETTING HERE AND AROUND

For an effortless excursion, go on a tour through Vallarta Adventures. It has excellent day trips ($80) to San Sebastián by bus or jeep, depending on the number of passengers.

For more flexibility or to spend the night in a cozy, no-frills hotel or a refurbished hacienda, charter a twin-engine Cessna through Aerotaxis de la Bahía in PV. For one to seven passengers the rate is about US$700 split among them to San Sebastián, US$750 to Mascota or Talpa de Allende. Add to these fares 15% sales tax and US$20 per person air travelers' tax. ■**TIP→** The return flight is usually free if you fly back with the pilot within three hours of arrival.

ATM (Autotransportes Talpa–Mascota) buses depart from their bus station in PV (Calle Lucerna 128, Col. Versalles) three times a day around 9 AM, 2:30, and 6:30 PM, stopping at La Estancia (11 km [7 mi] from San Sebastián; 1½ hours), then Mascota (2 to 2½ hours) and Talpa (3 to 3½ hours). Cost is about $5 one way to San Sebastián (La Estancia); $9 to Mascota; and $10 to Talpa.

Buses also depart several times a day from Guadalajara's new bus station (Entronque Carretera Libre a Zapotlanejo, Modules 3 and 4). Note that the bus doesn't enter San Sebastián; you'll be dropped at a small rest area, where taxis usually are available to transport you to town. The cost for the short drive is a bit steep at about $12. Share the cab with others on the bus to split the cost; or get a lift with a local and offer to pay, although many will decline or ask just a small amount to help out with gas.

From Puerto the road to San Sebastián is paved now, but those going to San Sebastián still have to get off the bus at La Estancia and take a taxi those last few miles. A suspension bridge was inaugurated in early 2007 to cover the last 8 km (5 mi) of the road to Mascota, which used to get washed out regularly in the rainy season. (Note: this road still may become dangerous or at least frightening during the rainy season, when landslides can occur.) Lago Juanacatlán is an hour from Mascota on a rough one-lane road of dirt and rock.

Taxis hang out near the main square in Talpa, Mascota, and San Sebastián.

ESSENTIALS
Air Contact Aerotaxis de la Bahia (☎ *322/221–1990*).

Banks Bancomer (✉ *Calle Constitución at Calle Hidalgo, Mascota* ☎ *388/386–0387*). Banco HSBC (✉ *Calle Independencia, across from la presidencia [town hall], Talpa* ☎ *388/385–0197*).

Bus Contact Autotransportes Talpa–Mascota (*ATM* ☎ *322/222–4816 in Puerto Vallarta, 388/386–0093 in Mascota, 388/385–0015 in Talpa, 33/3600–0588 or 33/3619–7549 in Guadalajara*).

Medical Assistance Centro de Salud de Mascota (✉ *Calle Dávalos 70, Mascota* ☎ *388/386–0174*). Farmacia Estrella (✉, *Calle 5 de Mayo, at Calle Ayuntamiento, Mascota* ☎ *388/386–0285*). Farmacia del Oeste (✉ *Calle Cuauhtemoc at Calle López Mateos, across from plaza, San Sebastián* ☎ *322/297–2833*). Farmacia San Miguel (✉ *Calle Independencia, at Calle Anahuac, across from square, Talpa* ☎ *388/385–0085*).

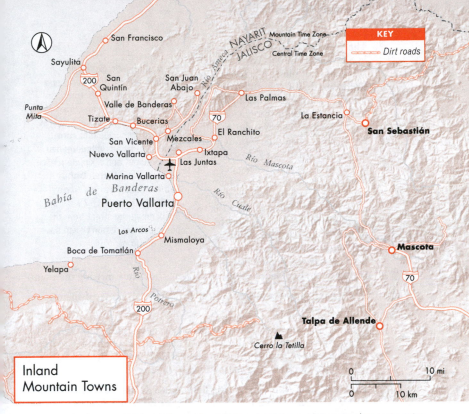

Inland
Mountain Towns

Tour and Visitor Information Oficina de Turismo de Mascota (✉ *La Presidencia [Town Hall], Calle Ayuntamiento, at Calle Constitución, facing plaza, Mascota* ☎ 388/386–1179). Oficina de Turismo de San Sebastián (✉ *Calle López Mateos, around corner from la presidencia [town hall], San Sebastián* ☎ 322/297–2938). **Oficina de Turismo de Talpa** (✉ *La Presidencia [Town Hall], Calle Independencia s/n, 2 blocks north of plaza, Talpa de Allende* ☎ 388/385–0009 or 388/385–0287). **Vallarta Adventures** (☎ 322/297–1212 ⊕ *www.vallarta-adventures.com*).

SAN SEBASTIÁN

If, physically, there are only about 80 km (50 mi) between Puerto Vallarta and San Sebastián, metaphorically they're as far apart as the Earth and the moon. Sleepy San Sebastián is the Mayberry of Mexico, but a little less lively. It's the kind of place where you feel weird walking past people without saying hello, even though you don't know them from Adam. The miners who built the town have long gone, and more recently, younger folks are drifting away in search of opportunity. Most of the 800 or so people who have stayed seem perfectly content with life as it is, although rat-race dropouts and entrepreneurs are making their way here along improved roads.

EXPLORING

The most interesting thing to see in San Sebastián is the town itself. Walk the cobblestone streets and handsome brick sidewalks, admiring the white-faced adobe structures surrounding the plaza. Take any side street and wander at will. Enjoy the enormous walnut trees lining the road into town, and diminutive peach trees peaking over garden walls. The reason to go to this cozy, lazy, beautiful town at 5,250 feet above sea level is to look inward, reflecting on life, or outward, greeting or chatting as best you can with those you meet. Look anywhere, in fact, except at a laptop or if possible, a television screen. That's just missing the point.

> ### WARM CUPPA CORN?
>
> For an authentic experience, pop into any *fonda* or *lonchería* (simple eateries, the former usually in someone's home, the latter open for lunch only) for a typical *atole con piloncillo* (hot corn drink sweetened with unrefined brown sugar) and a simple meal. Some, like the **Fonda Doña Leo** (⊠ *Calle Paso del Norte* 🕾 *322/297-2909* 🕘 *7 AM-4 or 5 PM*), down the street from the basketball court, don't even have signs out front.

San Sebastián has a few things to do, although none of them is the reason to visit.

Stop in the *abarrotes* (general store) on the north side of the square for a beverage or a spool of thread; then head directly behind it to **Iglesia de San Sebastián** a typically restored 1800's-era church that comes to life in the days preceding its saint's day, January 20.

You're welcome any time at the **Casa Museo de Doña Conchita** (⊠ *Calle Juárez 2* 🕾 *322/297-2860* 🖃 *$1*). The aged but affable lady loves to show visitors photos of her venerable family—which she traces back six generations. See bank notes from the mining days, bloomers, shirts made by hand by the lady for her many children, and other old memorabilia. If you speak Spanish, ask Doña Conchita to tell you about the ghosts that haunt her house, which is right on the square between the basketball court and *la presidencia,* or town hall. Hours are somewhat flexible, but stated hours are Monday through Saturday 10 AM to 3 PM and 5 PM to 7 PM; Sunday 11:30 to 3.

WHERE TO EAT AND STAY

$ ✗**Fonda de Doña Lupita**. Typical food of the countryside—enchiladas,
MEXICAN tamales, pozole, beefsteak with beans and tortillas, and so on—is served in an equally typical family home. The house has been enlarged to welcome guests, and the friendly owner does her part. Straw-bottom chairs are comfortable enough, and the oilcloths shiny and new. The small bar is at the back behind the large, open kitchen. It's open for breakfast, too. ⊠ *Calle Cuauhtemoc 89* 🕾 *322/297-2803* 🖃 *No credit cards*.

$$ 🛏 **La Galerita de San Sebastián**. A pair of displaced *tapatíos* (Guadalajarans) has created a cluster of pretty cabins on their property about four blocks from the plaza. Comfortable futons in each room provide a place to sleep, nap, or watch TV. The double-sided fireplace heats the bedroom and adjoining sitting room. Bed coverings and matching drapes

of earthy, muted colors are all good quality. This is the most modern place to stay in San Sebastián, and is geared to adults but accepts children, too, for an additional charge of about $20 per child. **Pros:** stylish, has in-room fireplaces. **Cons:** pricey compared to other area digs, extra charge for each child. ✉*Camino a Las Galeritas 62, Barrio La Otra Banda* ☎*322/297–3040* ⊕*www.lagalerita.com.mx* ⬎*3 bungalows* ⚲*In-room: no a/c, no phone, refrigerator, Wi-Fi. In-hotel: restaurant, parking (free), Wi-Fi* ▭*MC, V* ⦿*BP.*

$ 🏠**Real de San Sebastián.** Small rooms are dominated by snug king beds in curtained alcoves in this interesting B&B. It has a (somewhat cramped) shared main living space with a cushy plush couch facing a large-screen satellite TV, and more formal round tables where hot drinks like tea or cocoa may be served in the afternoon. In the morning, you get complimentary coffee or hot chocolate and rolls in bed, served through a small service window. The manager, Margarito Salcedo, is friendly and solicitous. **Pros:** friendly, helpful hosts, good value. **Cons:** living room is dated, guest rooms are dominated by the bed and don't have phones, credit cards aren't accepted. ✉*Calle Zaragoza 41* ☎*322/297–3224* ⊕*www.sansebastiandeloeste.com* ⬎*6 rooms* ⚲*In-room: no a/c, no phone, no TV. In-hotel: restaurant* ▭*No credit cards* ⦿*CP.*

SPORTS AND THE OUTDOORS

Local men can be hired for a truck ride up to **La Bufa**, a half-dome visible from the town square. One such man is **Obed Dueña** (☎*322/297–2864*), who charges about $46 for the trip, whether for two or eight passengers; it's about $62 for up to 15 people in a larger vehicle. It's the same price if you ride with him or hike back. The truck will wait while you climb—about 15 minutes to the top—and enjoy the wonderful view of the town, surrounding valleys, and, on a clear day, Puerto Vallarta. San Sebastián was founded as a silver- and gold-mining town; ask the driver to stop for a quick visit to a mine en route. The excursion takes about three hours all told. Or you can hike both ways; it takes most folks 2 to 2½ hours to reach the top, and half to two-thirds that time to return. A great destination for a walk is **Hacienda Jalisco** (⇨ *above*), a 20-minute walk from San Sebastián's plaza; for about $2 you can have a look around the beautiful property and the common areas. With 24 hours' notice, you can arrange to have lunch at this traditionally decorated country inn.

MASCOTA

Mascota's cool but sunny climate is perfect for growing citrus, avocados, nuts, wheat, corn, and other crops. Fed by the Mascota and Ameca rivers and many springs and year-round streams, the blue-green hills and valleys surrounding town are lusciously forested; beyond them rise indigo mountains to form a painterly tableau. This former mining town and municipal seat is home to some 13,000 people. Its banks, shops, and a hospital serve surrounding villages. On its coat of arms are a pine tree, deer, and rattlesnake. The town's name derives from the Nahuatl words for deer and snake.

8

EXPLORING

★ Mascota's pride is **La Iglesia de la Preciosa Sangre** (Church of the Precious Blood), started in 1909 but unfinished due to the revolution and the ensuing Cristero Revolt. Weddings, concerts, and plays are sometimes held here under the ruins of Gothic arches. Note the 3-D blood squirting from Jesus's wound in the chapel—you could hardly miss it.

Walk around the **plaza**, where old gents share stories and kids chase balloons. Couples dance the stately *danzón* on Thursday and Saturday evenings as the band plays in the wrought-iron bandstand. The town produces ceramics, saddles, and *raicilla*, a relative of tequila made from the green agave plant (tequila comes from the blue one).

> ### MASCOTA'S MARTYR
>
> In 1927, during the anticlerical Cristero movement, Mascota's young priest refused to abandon his post. Soldiers peeled the skin from his hands and feet before forcing him to walk to a large oak tree, where he was hanged. Mascota's hero, José María Robles was canonized in 2000 by Pope John Paul II.

On one corner of the plaza is the town's white-spire **Iglesia de la Virgen de los Dolores**. The Virgin of Sorrow is feted on September 15, which segues into Mexican Independence Day on the 16th.

A block beyond the other end of the plaza, the **Museo de Mascota** (⊠ *Calle Morelos, near Calle Allende*) is worth a look. It's open Monday through Saturday 10–3 and 5–8.

Around the corner from the Mascota Museum, the **Casa de la Cultura** (⊠ *Calle Allende 115*) has rotating exhibits of photography and art. It's open 10–2 and 4–7 Monday through Saturday.

WHERE TO EAT

$ ✕ **Café Napolés.** Originally a coffee-and-dessert stop and fashionable
CAFÉ hangout for Mascotans, this snug little eatery serves big breakfasts and now main dishes at lunch and dinner, too. Sit on the small, street-facing patio, in the diminutive dining room, or facing the glass case featuring fantastic-looking cakes, pies, and tarts. You can now get wine and beer as well as pizza, barbecue, spaghetti, and other Italian food. ⊠ *Calle Hidalgo 105, Centro* ☎ 388/386–0051 ▭ *No credit cards.*

$ ✕ **La Casa de Mi Abuela.** Everyone and his mother likes "Grandma's
MEXICAN House," which is conveniently open all day (and evening), every day, starting at around 8 AM with breakfast. In addition to beans, rice, carne asada, and other recognizable Mexican food, there are backcountry recipes that are much less familiar to the average traveler. ⊠ *Calle Corona, at Calle Zaragoza* ☎ *No phone.*

¢ ✕ **Navidad.** It is named for the small town 14 km (9 mi) from Mas-
MEXICAN cota, not the Christmas holiday, which is the only day this restaurant closes. The cavernous space, lined in red brick, makes the restaurant look rather generic, but it's actually family-owned and -run and oh-so-personable. Best yet, it's open 7 AM to nearly midnight. Try the regional dishes like goat stew and enchiladas, as well as pizza, or a daily special

such as beef tongue, *jocoque*, or perhaps another mystery dish. ⊠*Calle Juan Díaz de Sandi 28, Centro* ☎*388/386–0469* ⊟*MC, V.*

WHERE TO STAY

$ ★ **Mesón de Santa Elena.** Beautiful rooms in this converted 19th-century house have lovely old tile floors, beige cotton drapes covering huge windows, rag-rolled walls, and wonderful tile floors and sinks. The dining room has old-fashioned cupboards, and there are dining tables inside and out on two patios festooned with flowers and large potted plants. Second-floor rooms have views of fields and mountains to the west. **Pros:** two blocks from the town square, feels like you're a guest in someone's home, Internet café about a block away. **Cons:** Internet intermittent in some rooms, feels like you're a guest in someone's home. ⊠*Hidalgo 155* ☎*388/386–0313* ⊕*www.mesondesantaelena. com* ✎*10 rooms, 2 suites* △*In-room: no a/c, no phone, no TV. In-hotel: restaurant (breakfast only), Wi-Fi* ⊟*MC, V* ⏧ *BP, EP.*

$$ **Rancho La Esmeralda.** Catering to small groups and father-and-son outings, this ranch-style lodging near the entrance to town also accepts individual travelers. All interiors are pine-wood simple, with ceiling beams and tile roofs, and plain furnishings. The villas have kitchens, and most have a porch and fireplace; many sport a king-size bed. This working ranch offers horseback riding and also rents bicycles and ATVs. Because most guests are Guadalajarans on weekends, prices are discounted 20% Sunday through Thursday. **Pros:** newer construction, fireplaces and king-size beds, midweek discount. **Cons:** 10-minute drive from town center, bumpy cobblestone entry road. ⊠*Calle Salvador Chavez 47* ☎*388/386–0953* ⊕*www.rancholaesmeralda.com.mx* ✎*10 rooms, 7 cabins* △*In-room: kitchen (some), refrigerator (some), Wi-Fi (some). In-hotel: Wi-Fi, parking (free)* ⊟*MC, V.*

$$$ **Sierra Lago Resort & Spa.** An hour north of Mascota, this lodge of knotty pine is a tranquil lakeside retreat. Sail or kayak or just read a book in the steamy hot tub. The spa isn't as expansive as those in some of Sierra Lago's Villa Group sister properties, but it does have massage, a steam room, and an outdoor Jacuzzi. If you choose the all-inclusive plan, drinks are included, as are activities like horseback riding, kayaking, and mountain biking. There's also fishing, and, if he has time, the chef will cook up your freshly caught fish. **Pros:** beautiful scenery and mountain air, activities included in all-inclusive room rate. **Cons:** no phone in room, no Internet access. ⊠*Domicilio Conocido, Lago Juanacatlán* ☎*877/845–5247 in U.S. and Canada, 01800/823–4488 toll-free in Mexico* ⊕*www.sierralago.com* ✎*24 suites* △*In-room: no phone. In-hotel: restaurant, bar, tennis court, pool, spa, bicycles, parking (free)* ⊟*MC, V* ⏧*AI, EP.*

SPORTS AND THE OUTDOORS

★ The countryside just outside town is ideal for hikes and drives. From Mascota's plaza you can walk up Calle Morelos out of town to **Cerro de la Cruz.** The hike to the summit takes about a half hour and rewards with great valley views. **Presa Corinches**, a dam about 5 km (3 mi) south of town, has bass fishing, picnic spots (for cars and RVs), and a restaurant where locals go for fish feasts on holidays and weekend afternoons. To get to the dam,

8

head east on Calle Juárez (a block south of the plaza) and follow the signs to the reservoir. Take a walk along the shore or set up a tent near the fringe of pine-oak forest coming down to meet the cool blue water, which is fine for swimming when the weather is warm. **Lago Juanacatlán** is a lovely lake in a volcanic crater at 7,000 feet above sea level. Nestled in the Galope River valley, the pristine lake is surrounded by alpine woods, and the trip from Mascota past fields of flowers and self-sufficient *ranchos* is bucolic.

> **HOLY CITY**
>
> During several major annual fiestas, the town swells with visitors. The Fiesta de la Candelaria culminates in Candlemass, February 2. The town's patron saint, St. Joseph, is honored March 19. May 12, September 10, September 19, and October 7 mark rituals devoted to the Virgen del Rosario de Talpa.

SHOPPING

Stores in town sell homemade preserves, locally grown coffee, raicilla (an alcoholic drink made of green agave), and sweets. A good place to shop for local products and produce is the **Mercado municipal** (⊠ *Calle P. Sánchez, at Hidalgo, 1 block west of plaza*).

TALPA DE ALLENDE

Another tranquil town surrounded by pine-oak forests, Talpa, as it's called, has just over 7,000 inhabitants but welcomes 4 million visitors a year. They come to pay homage or ask favors of the diminutive Virgen del Rosario de Talpa, one of Jalisco's most revered Virgins. Some people walk three days from Puerto Vallarta as penance or a sign of devotion; others come by car, horse, bicycle or truck but return annually to show their faith.

WHAT TO SEE

★ On the large plaza, the **Basilica de Talpa** is the main show in town. The twin-spire limestone temple is Gothic with neoclassic elements. After visiting the diminutive, royally clad Virgin in her side chapel, stroll around the surrounding square. Shops and stalls sell sweets, miniature icons of the Virgin in every possible presentation, T-shirts, and other souvenirs. *Chicle* (gum) is harvested in the area, and you'll find small keepsakes in the shapes of shoes, flowers, and animals made of the (nonsticky) raw material.

WHERE TO EAT

$$ ✗ **Casa Grande**. This steak house also serves grilled chicken and seafood.
STEAKHOUSE   Under a roof but open on all sides and with an incredible view, it's highly recommended by visitors and locals. In fact, it's a popular place for locals' reunions and family parties. Lunch is served after 2 PM, and the kitchen stays open until 10:30. ⊠ *Calle Juárez 53* ☎ *388/385–0709* ▤ *MC, V* ☾ *Closed Tues.*

$ ✗ **El Herradero**. "The Blacksmith" will win no awards for cuisine, or, for
MEXICAN   that matter, decoration. But it's often filled with families of pilgrims, and the locals recommend it, too. The menu offers mainly meat dishes, including burgers with fries, plus *antojitos, gorditas,* and *sopes* (all cornmeal

based, fried concoctions stuffed with meat or beans and, in the case of the latter, topped with beans and salsa), pozole (hominy soup), and quesadillas. The tortillas are made fresh at the back of the restaurant. Half orders are available, and there's a bar serving national booze and beer. ⊠*Calle 23 de Junio #8* ☎*388/385–0376* ⊟*No credit cards.*

WHERE TO STAY

$ ⛩**Hacienda Jacarandas.** The charming, two-story building has high ceilings, wide corridors, and comfortable guest rooms with fine and folk art. Bougainvillea in shades of purple and pink climb up the cream-color exterior walls, and the rooftop terrace—with a terrific view—is a nice place to laze away a morning or afternoon, in the sun or under the covered portion. The 62-acre property has a small lake. **Pros:** you get to stay in a restored hacienda, savvy hoteliers who know how to treat foreign guests. **Cons:** has been for sale for some years, no elevator, credit cards not accepted. ⊠ *Rancho Portrellos, just over bridge at southeast end of town* ☎*388/102–7078* ⊕*www.haciendajacarandas.com* ⇆*5 rooms, 1 casita* ⚡*In-hotel: restaurant, bar, pool, Wi-Fi* ⊟*No credit cards* ⊘*Closed Easter–June* ⦿*BP.*

¢ ⛩**Renovación.** Basic yet comfortable rooms in this three-story hotel (opened in 2007) have king-size beds with dark blue, hunting-theme spreads and desks of shiny lacquered wood. The property is on the main road into town, just a few short blocks from the plaza and town hall. The price goes up slightly on weekends, although only January through May. **Pros:** newer property, a couple of blocks from the main plaza. **Cons:** no elevator, no credit cards accepted. ⊠*Calle Independencia 45, Centro* ☎*388/385–1412* ⇆*18 rooms* ⊟*No credit cards.*

THE GUADALAJARA REGION

Guadalajara rests on a mile-high plain of the Sierra Madre Occidental, surrounded on three sides by rugged hills and on the fourth by the spectacular Oblatos Canyon. Mexico's second-largest city has a population of 4 million and is the capital of Jalisco State. This cosmopolitan if traditional and quintessentially Mexican city offers a range of activities. Shop for handicrafts, housewares, and especially fine ceramics in smart shops or family-owned factories. Dress up for drinks, dinner, and dancing in smart Zona Minerva, in downtown Guadalajara, or put on your comfy walking shoes to visit satellite neighborhoods of indigenous origin. For shoppers and metropolis lovers, this is a great complement to a Puerto Vallarta vacation.

An hour's drive in just about any direction from Guadalajara will bring you out of the fray and into the countryside. Due south is Lake Chapala, Mexico's largest natural lake. Bordering it are several villages with large expat communities, including Chapala and Ajijic, a village of bougainvillea and cobblestone roads. Tequila, where the famous firewater is brewed, is northwest of Guadalajara. Teuchitlán, south of Tequila, has the Guachimontones ruins. The placid lakeside area around Chapala makes for a weeklong (expats would say lifelong) getaway, while Tequila and Teuchitlán are great for day-trippers.

8

GUADALAJARA

Metropolitan Guadalajara's sights are divided into four major areas: Guadalajara, Zapopan, Tlaquepaque, and Tonalá. Within Guadalajara are many districts and neighborhoods. Of most interest to visitors is the Centro Histórico (Historic District), a rather small section of town that's part of the larger downtown area (El Centro). Outside the Centro Histórico, Guadalajara resembles any large, sometimes polluted city with gnarly traffic. On the west side are Zona Minerva, the most modern section of the city and the place to go for dining, dancing, shopping in large malls, and high-rise hotels. The Centro Histórico, Tlaquepaque, and Tonalá can each be navigated on foot in a few hours, though they deserve at least half a day. Zapopan's high-end hotels, bars, shops, and cafés are spread out, but historic Zapopan, around the church, is reasonably compact. Likewise, Tonalá is a lot more spread out than more tourist-oriented, walkable Tlaquepaque.

GETTING HERE AND AROUND

BY AIR Many major airlines fly nonstop from the United States to Guadalajara. Aeropuerto Internacional Libertador Miguel Hidalgo is 16½ km (10 mi) south of the city, en route to Chapala. Autotransportaciones Aeropuerto operates a 24-hour taxi stand with service to any place in the Guadalajara area; buy tickets at the counters at the national and international exits. Some hotels also offer airport pickup shuttles; these need to be arranged in advance.

BY BUS AND SUBWAY Although flying from your hometown to Guadalajara, then back home from PV can be a good deal, flying round-trip to Guadalajara from Puerto Vallarta is not. The bus is much cheaper, scenic, and efficient. Luxury buses between PV and Guadalajara take 4½ hours and cost $30–$35. With one wide seat on one side of the aisle and only two on the other, ETN is the most upscale line, and has about nine trips a day to and from PV, except Sunday, with only one. Within Mexico, it accepts advance reservations with a credit card. Estrella Blanca is an umbrella of different bus lines, many of which head straight for Guadalajara. TAP (Transportes al Pacífico) is a first-class line that serves major Pacific coast destinations between Ixtapa/Zihuatanejo and the U.S. border, including service to Guadalajara, Puerto Vallarta, and Tepic. ■TIP➜ **Many bus lines do not accept credit cards.** Guadalajara's Nueva Central Camionera (New Central Bus Station) is 10 km (6 mi) southeast of downtown.

Most city buses (45¢) run from every few minutes to every half hour between 6 AM and 9 PM; some run until 11 PM. ⚠ **The city's public transit buses are infamously fatal; drivers killed more than 100 pedestrians annually in the late 1990s before the government intervened. These poorly designed, noisy, noxious buses are still driven ruthlessly and cause at least a dozen deaths per year.**

Large mint-green Tur and red Cardinal buses are the safest, quickest, and least crowded and go to Zapopan, Tlaquepaque, and Tonalá for around 70 cents. Wait for these along Avenida 16 de Septiembre.

ITINERARY: 2 OR 3 DAYS IN GUADALAJARA

The four primary municipalities of metropolitan Guadalajara are Guadalajara, Zapopan, Tlaquepaque, and Tonalá. Aside from Zapopan, areas of interest to visitors can be navigated on foot in a few hours, though each deserves at least half a day. Zapopan requires more time since it's a sprawling suburb with lots of shopping. Due west of Guadalajara's Centro Histórico, Zona Minerva is the place to go for great restaurants and after-dark action. Plan on a third day if you want to visit outlying areas like Lake Chapala and Teuchitlán.

On the morning of Day 1, visit historic Guadalajara, checking out the cathedral and other landmarks on the interconnecting plazas. Mercado Libertad (aka Mercado San Juan de Dios) is several long blocks east of Plaza Fundadores; you can walk or take the subway two blocks south of the cathedral on Avenida Juárez. If it's Sunday, see a charreada; otherwise head to Zapopan to see the basilica, the Huichol Museum, and the Art Museum of Zapopan, and spend 15 minutes at *la presidencia municipal* (city hall) to admire the mural inside. If you have more time, check out the market, two blocks west at Calles Eva Briseño and Hidalgo, and some surrounding churches before grabbing a drink or a bite on Paseo Teopinztle, two blocks south. Freshen up at your hotel, then dine in downtown Guadalajara or the Zona Minerva.

Spend the second day shopping and visiting churches and museums in the old towns of Tonalá and in more compact, walkable Tlaquepaque. If you're here on Thursday or Sunday, don't miss the Tonalá crafts market. El Parián in Tlaquepaque is a great place to enjoy a mariachi serenade and refreshments. Have lunch or dinner in one of Tlaquepaque's charming restaurants. If you don't want to shop, consider spending an afternoon listening to mariachi music, seeing a charrería, or visiting the gardens at Parque Azul.

If you have three days, you'll have time to visit Tequila or Lake Chapala. It's refreshing to get out of the city and admire the relatively dry hills and valleys, noting the fields of blue agave that are Tequila's reason for being. Tequila is en route to San Blas and Puerto Vallarta. Lake Chapala and the towns on the shore work well as a day excursion, especially if you have a car.

LOGISTICS AND TIPS

You need at least three hours for the Centro Histórico, longer if you really want to enjoy the sculptures and street scene. Mornings are the least crowded time of day, although the light is particularly beautiful in the afternoon, when the jugglers, street musicians, and other informal entertainers emerge. Take advantage of free walking tours in the historical district. Accompanied by mariachis or other musicians, the two-hour tours meet most evenings around dusk in front of city hall. Show up at about 7 PM (an hour earlier during winter) to register.

Beware of heavy traffic and *topes* (speed bumps). Traffic circles are common at busy intersections.

Tonalá's crafts market and Mercado Libertad are the region's top marketplaces. El Trocadero is a weekly antiques market at the north end of Avenida Chapultepec. Feel free to drive a hard bargain at all three.

8

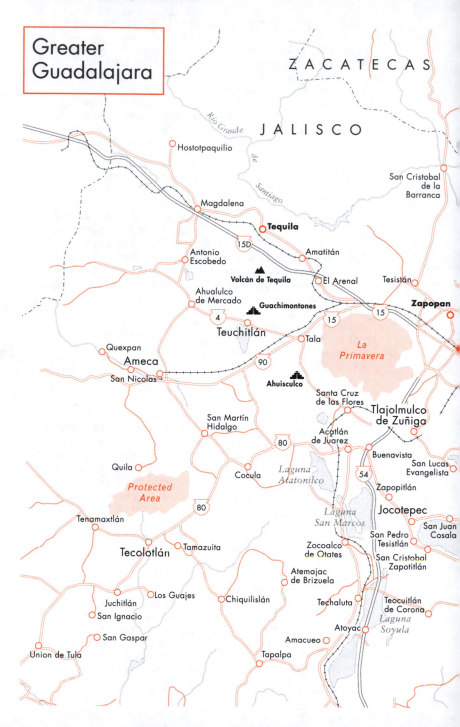

Greater Guadalajara

Z A C A T E C A S

J A L I S C O

Río Grande de Santiago

Hostotpaquilio

San Cristobal de la Barranca

Magdalena

Tequila

15D

Amatitán

Antonio Escobedo

Volcán de Tequila

El Arenal

Tesistán

Ahualulco de Mercado

Guachimontones

15

Zapopan

4

Teuchitlán

Tala

La Primavera

Quexpan

Ameca

90

San Nicolas

Ahuisculco

Santa Cruz de las Flores

Tlajolmulco de Zuñiga

San Martín Hidalgo

Acatlán de Juarez

Buenavista

San Lucas Evangelista

80

Quila

Cocula

Laguna Atatonilco

54

Zapopitlán

Protected Area

80

Laguna San Marcos

Jocotepec

Tenamaxtlán

Tamazuita

Zocoalco de Otates

San Pedro Tesistlán

San Juan Cosala

Tecolotlán

Atemajac de Brizuela

San Cristobal Zapotitlán

Juchitlán

Los Guajes

Chiquilislán

Techaluta

Teocuitlán de Corona

San Ignacio

Laguna Soyula

San Gaspar

Amacueo

Atoyac

Union de Tula

Tapalpa

0   10 miles
0   15 km

Moyahua de Estrada

Yahualica

Cañadas de Obregón

Las Cruces

Manalisco

J A L I S C O

Ixcatán

Barranca de Oblatos

Río Verde

Acatic

Tepatitlán de Morelos

80

80D

El Refugio

Río Prieto

La Arena

Guadalajara

Tonalá

Zapotlanejo

San José

Tlaquepaque

90D

Zorillos

San Augustín

San Francisco de Asís

La Laja

Coyotes

Tecematlán

Puente Espinoza

Tototlán

Juanacatlán

15D

Nuevo Refugio

El Nacimiento

Cajititlán

Río Grande de Santiago

Suchitlán

San Juan Evangelista

San Vicente

11

Ixtlahuacán Membrillos

Poncitlán

Ajijic

El Mirto

Chapala

San Nicolás de Ibarra

Ocotlán

San Pedro

Jamay

San Luis Soyitlán

Laguna de Chapala

23

La Barca

15

Tuxcueca

Tizapán el Alto

Cojumatlán de Régules

110

Sahuayo

La Manzanilla de la Paz

110

M I C H O A C Á N

Concepción de Buenos Aires

Jiquilpan

15

Mazamitla

8

Autotransportes Guadalajara–Chapala serves the lakeside towns from Guadalajara's new bus station (Central Camionera Nueva) and from the old bus station (Antigua Central Camionera); cost is around $4. It's 45 minutes to Chapala and another 15 minutes to Ajijic; there are departures every half hour from 6 AM to 9:30 PM. Make sure you ask for the *directo* (direct) as opposed to *clase segunda* (second-class) bus, which stops at every little pueblo en route.

Guadalajara's underground *tren ligero* (light train) system is clean and efficient. Trains run every 10 minutes from 5 AM to midnight; a token for one trip costs about 40 cents.

BY CAR Metropolitan Guadalajara's traffic gets intense, especially at rush hour; parking can be scarce. Streets shoot off at diagonals from roundabouts (called *glorietas*), and on main arteries, turns (including U-turns and left turns) are usually made from right-side lateral roads (called *laterales*)—which can be confusing for drivers unfamiliar with big city traffic. ■**TIP→** Ubiquitous and inexpensive, taxis are the best way to go in Guadalajara.

BY TAXI Taxis are easily hailed on the street in the Centro Histórico, Zapopan, Tlaquepaque, and most other areas of Guadalajara. All cabs are supposed to use meters (in Spanish, *taxímetro*)—you can insist the driver use it or else agree on a fixed price at the outset. Many hotels have rate sheets showing the fare to major destinations and parts of town.

Taxi is the best way to get to Tonalá or Tlaquepaque (about $7). To continue from Tlaquepaque to Tonalá, take a taxi from Avenida Río Nilo southeast directly into town and the intersection of Avenida de los Tonaltecas ($4–$6; 5–10 minutes depending on traffic).

ESSENTIALS

Air Contacts **Aeroméxico** (☎01800/021–4000, 01800/021–4010 toll-free in Mexico, 800/237–6639 toll-free in U.S. or Canada ⊕www.aeromexico.com). **American Airlines** (☎33/3616–4090, 33/3688–5518 (airport), 01800/904–6000, 800/443–7300 in U.S. and Canada ⊕www.aa.com). **Continental** (☎33/3647–4251, 33/3688–5141 airport, 01800/900–5000, 800/523–3273 in U.S. and Canada ⊕www.continental.com). **Mexicana** (☎55/2881–0000 in Mexico City, 01800/801–2030 toll-free in Mexico, 800/531–7921 in U.S. and Canada ⊕www.mexicana.com).

Airport Transfers **Autotransportaciones Aeropuerto** (☎33/3688–5293).

Bus Contacts **Autotransportes Guadalajara Chapala** (☎33/3619–5675). **ETN** (☎33/3600–0477 or 01800/360–4200 ⊕www.etn.com.mx). **Estrella Blanca** (☎55/5729–0807 in Mexico City). **TAP** (☎33/3668–5920).

Taxis **Taxi Plaza del Sol** (☎33/3631–5262). **Taxi Sitio Miverva no. 22** (☎33/3630–0050).

Medical Assistance **Emergency Hotlines** (☎066; 065 for Red Cross ambulance). **Farmacias Guadalajara** (⊠Av. Javier Mina 221, between Calle Cabañas and Vicente Guerrero, Centro Histórico, Guadalajara ☎33/3617–8555). **Hospital México-Americano** (⊠Calle Colomos 2110, Ladrón de Ybarra, Centro, Guadalajara ☎33/3641–3141).

Tour and Visitor Information Guadalajara Municipal Tourist Office (✉ *Monumento Los Arcos, Pedro Morelos 1596, 1 block east of Minerva Fountain, Zona Minerva, Guadalajara* ☎ *33/3818–3600*). **Jalisco State Tourist Office** (✉ *Plaza Tapatia, Calle Morelos 102, Centro Histórico, Guadalajara* ☎ *33/3668–1600 or 33/3668–1607*). **Tlaquepaque Municipal Tourist Office** (✉ *Calle Morelos 288, Tlaquepaque* ☎ *33/3562–7050 Ext. 2318*). **Tonalá Municipal Tourist Office** (✉ *Av. de los Tonaltecas Sur 140, in La Casa de los Artesanos, Tonalá* ☎ *33/3284–3092 or 33/3284–3093*).

EXPLORING

EL CENTRO AND THE CENTRO HISTÓRICO

Guadalajara's historical center is a blend of modern and old buildings connected by a series of large plazas radiating from the Cathedral.

> ### TOURS: BY HORSE OR HORSE POWER
>
> *Calandrias* (horse-drawn carriages) take in the Centro Histórico; it's about $17 for a tour of 45 minutes to one hour. They depart from the three streets skirting the cathedral (for example, on Calle Corona between Prisciliano Sánchez and Juárez). Tapatío Tour, an open-top, double-decker bus, loops Zona Rosa (☎ *33/3605–2335* 🎟 *$11* 🕙 *Daily 10 AM–8 PM every 30 minutes*). Get on and off as much as you like to explore the sights. The bus departs from the Rotunda, a plaza on the Cathedral's north side.

Many colonial-era structures were razed; others stand crumbling, as there's no money for restoration. But overall there are many colonial- and Republican-era buildings with impressive carved limestone facades, tiled steeples and domes, magnificent wooden doors, and wrought-iron grills. The surrounding parks, plazas, and fountains have Corinthian columns and a great sense of community.

★ **Catedral.** Construction was begun in 1561 on the cathedral, a downtown focal point and an intriguing mélange of baroque, Gothic, and other styles. Exquisite altarpieces line the walls. In a loft above the main entrance is a magnificent late-19th-century French organ. ✉ *Av. Alcalde, between Av. Hidalgo and Calle Morelos, Centro Histórico* ☎ *33/3614–5504* 🕙 *Daily 8–8.*

☻ **Instituto Cultural Cabañas.** Originally a shelter for the elderly and orphans, this neoclassical-style building has 106 rooms and 23 flower-filled patios that now house art exhibitions. Kids love the murals by Orozco, as well as his smaller paintings and cartoons and the labyrinthine compound in general. Large-scale theater, dance, and musical performances occasionally take place on one of the patios. The Tolsá Chapel hosts more-intimate events. ✉ *Calle Cabañas 8, Centro Histórico* ☎ *33/3668–1647* 🎟 *$7 foreigners, $3.50 nationals; free Tues.* 🕙 *Tues.–Sat. 10–6, Sun. 10–3; occasionally closed for maintenance.*

FodorśChoice
★

★ **Museo Regional de Guadalajara.** Artifacts from prehistoric times through the Spanish conquest and an impressive collection of European and Mexican paintings make this museum, in a grand former seminary, worth a visit. ✉ *Calle Liceo 60, Centro Histórico* ☎ *33/3614–5257* 🎟 *$3.50; free Sun.* 🕙 *Tues.–Sat. 9–5:30, Sun. 9–4:30.*

8

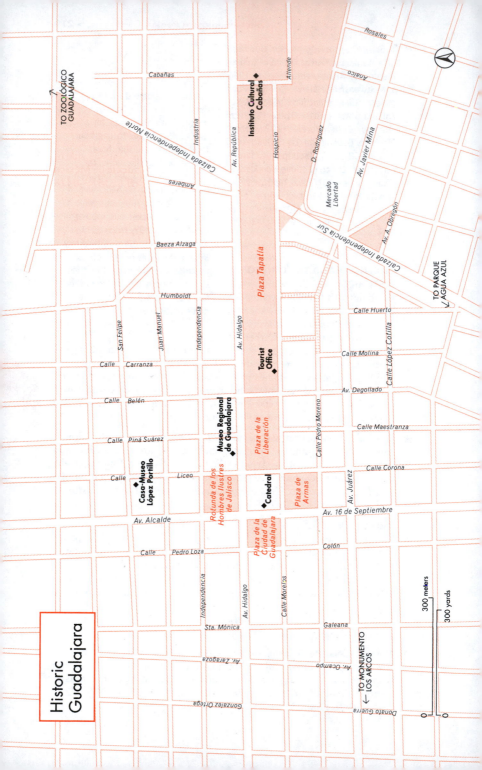

Historic Guadalajara

TO ZOOLÓGICO GUADALAJARA

Cabañas

Instituto Cultural Cabañas

Rosales

Analco

Altende

Hospicio

D. Rodríguez

Av. Javier Mina

Av. República

Industria

Calzada Independencia Norte

Amberes

Mercado Libertad

Av. A. Obregón

Calzada Independencia Sur

TO PARQUE AGUA AZUL

Baeza Alzaga

Plaza Tapatía

Humboldt

Independencia

Av. Hidalgo

Calle Huerto

Calle López Cotilla

San Felipe

Juan Manuel

Tourist Office

Calle Molina

Calle   Carranza

Av. Degollado

Calle   Belén

Av. Pedro Moreno

Calle Maestranza

Museo Regional de Guadalajara

Plaza de la Liberación

Calle   Piña Suárez

Calle Corona

Casa-Museo López Portillo

Liceo

Rotunda de los Hombres Ilustres de Jalisco

Catedral

Plaza de Armas

Av. Juárez

Calle

Av. Alcalde

Plaza de la Ciudad de Guadalajara

Av. 16 de Septiembre

Calle   Pedro Loza

Colón

Independencia

Sta. Mónica

Av. Hidalgo

Calle Morelos

Galeana

Av. Ocampo

TO MONUMENTO LOS ARCOS

300 meters

300 yards

Av. Zaragoza

Donato Guerra

González Ortega

☺ **Parque Agua Azul.** Walking paths crisscross this park's acres of trees and grass. Playgrounds and an orchid house are among the draws. There aren't many butterflies visible in the huge, geodesic sanctuary, but the semitropical garden inside still merits a visit. **The Museo de la Paleontología** (⊠ *Av. Dr. R. Michel 520, Centro* ☎ *33/3619–7043*), on the park's east side, has fossils as well as exhibits on the origin of the planet. Admission is less than $1, and the museum is open Tuesday through Saturday 10–6 and Sunday 11–4. (There's no museum entrance inside Agua Azul; walk to the park's north side.) On the opposite side of Parque Agua Azul, the **Museo de Arqueología del Occidente de México** (⊠ *Calz. Independencia Sur at Av. del Campesino* ☎ *33/3619–0328* 🎫 *50¢* ☉ *Daily 10–6*) specializes in West Coast cultures' shaft tombs (ritual burial sites) and pre-Hispanic ceramics.

WORTH
NOTING **Casa-Museo López Portillo.** For a taste of how the wealthy once lived, visit this mansion with a stunning collection of 17th- through 20th-century furniture and accessories. ⊠ *Calle Liceo 177, at Calle San Felipe, Centro Histórico* ☎ *33/1201–8720* 🎫 *Free* ☉ *Tues.–Sat. 10–5, Sun. 10–3.*

☺ **Zoológico Guadalajara.** The city's zoo, on the edge of the jagged Barranca de Huetitán, has more than 1,500 animals representing 360 species. There are two aviaries, a kids' zoo, and a herpetarium with 130 species of reptiles, amphibians, and fish. Admission is about $4, or a little more than twice that if you want to take a train tour of the grounds. ⊠ *Paseo del Zoológico 600, off Calz. Independencia, Zona Huentitán* ☎ *33/3674–4488* ⊕ *www.zooguadalajara.com.mx* ☉ *Wed.–Sun. 10–5; daily during school vacations.*

TLAQUEPAQUE
Another ancient pueblo that's gone upscale is crafts-crazy Tlaquepaque. Fabulous shopping for fine ceramics coupled with the attractive town's compact size make it appealing to Guadalajarans and visitors. Along its cobblestone streets are a wealth of old homes converted to shops and restaurants. B&Bs with jungly gardens, warming fires, and reasonable prices easily convince many travelers to make this their base.

Fodor's Choice **Museo del Premio Nacional de la Cerámica Pantaleon Panduro.** On display
★ here are prize-winning pieces from the museum's annual June ceramics competition. You can request an English-speaking guide at possibly the best collection of modern Mexican pottery anywhere. ⊠ *Calle Priciliano Sánchez at Calle Flórida, Tlaquepaque* ☎ *33/3562–7036* 🎫 *Free* ☉ *Mon.–Sat. 10–6, Sun. 10–3.*

Museo Regional de la Cerámica. In a colonial mansion, this ceramics museum has displays (in Spanish) explaining common processes used by local ceramics artisans; presentation isn't always strong. ⊠ *Calle Independencia 37, Tlaquepaque* ☎ *33/3635–5404* 🎫 *Free* ☉ *Tues.– Sat. 10–6.*

ZAPOPAN
Expanding over the years, Guadalajara's population of about 4 million now encompasses pre-Hispanic towns like Zapopan, which appears to blend seamlessly with the rest of the metropolis. The country's former

8

LIVE PERFORMANCE

The State Band of Jalisco and the municipal band usually play at the bandstand Tuesday through Friday at around 6:30 PM. Small, triangular Plaza de los Mariachis, south of the Mercado Libertad, was once the ideal place to tip up a beer and experience mariachi, the most Mexican of music, at about $15 a pop. Now boxed in by a busy street, a market, and a run-down neighborhood, it's safest to visit in the day or late afternoon.

For about the same amount of money but a more tourist-friendly atmosphere, mariachis at El Parián, in Tlaquepaque, will treat you to a song or two as you sip margaritas at this enormous, partly covered conglomeration of 17 cantinas diagonal from the town's main plaza. Once a marketplace dating from 1883, it has traditional *cazuela* drinks, which are made of fruit and tequila and served in ceramic pots.

After a brief transfer of affection to the newer Teatro Diana, the internationally acclaimed **Ballet Folclórico of the University of Guadalajara** (⊕ *www.ballet.udg.mx*) has returned to perform its traditional Mexican folkloric dances and music in the Teatro Degollado (⊠ *Calle Belén s/n 44630* ☎ *33/3614–4773*) most Sundays at 12:30 PM; tickets are $5–$25. The state-funded **Orquesta Filarmónica de Jalisco** (*Philharmonic Orchestra of Jalisco* ⊕ *www. ofj.com.mx*) performs pieces by Mexican composers mixed with standard orchestral fare. When in season (it varies), the OFJ usually performs Sunday afternoons or weeknights (usually Wednesday and Friday at 8:30 PM) at Teatro Degollado; tickets are $8–$35.

corn-producing capital, Zapopan is now a wealthy enclave of modern hotels and malls. Beyond, some farming communities remain, but the central district is now home to two interesting museums and one of Mexico's most revered religious icons.

★ **Basílica de la Virgen de Zapopan.** The vast basilica, with an ornate plateresque facade and *mudéjar* (Moorish) tile dome, is home to Our Lady of Zapopan: a 10-inch-high, corn-paste statue venerated for miraculous healings and answered prayers. Every October 12, more than a million people pack the streets around the basilica for an all-night fiesta capped by an early-morning procession. Don't miss the adjoining **Huichol Museum** (⇨ *below*), which has Huichol art for sale. ⊠ *Zona Zapopan Norte.*

★ **Museo de Arte de Zapopan.** Guadalajara's top contemporary art gallery is better known by its initials: MAZ. It regularly holds expositions of distinguished Latin American painters, photographers, and sculptors. ⊠ *Andador 20 de Noviembre 166, Zapopan* ☎ *33/3818–2575* 🖾 *$2.30; free Tues.* ☉ *Tues.–Sun. 10–6.*

Museo Huichol Wixarica de Zapopan. The Huichol Indians are famed for their independence, their spirituality, the use of peyote in religious ceremonies, and their exquisite beadwork and yarn "paintings" (⇨ *"The Art of the Huichol," in Chapter 6*). At this museum, bilingual placards explain the fascinating Huichol religion and worldview while somewhat

Continued on page 228

MARIACHI: BORN IN JALISCO

By Sean Mattson

It's 4 AM and you're sound asleep somewhere in Mexico. Suddenly you're jolted awake by trumpets blasting in rapid succession. Before you can mutter a groggy protest, ten men with booming voices break into song. Nearby, a woman stirs from her slumber. The man who brought her the serenade peeks toward her window from behind the lead singer's sombrero, hoping his sign of devotion is appreciated—and doesn't launch his girlfriend's father into a shoe-throwing fury.

At the heart of Mexican popular culture, mariachi is the music of love and heartache, of the daily travails of life, and nationalistic pride. This soundtrack of Mexican tradition was born in the same region as tequila, the Mexican hat dance, and *charrería* (Mexican rodeo), whose culture largely defines Mexican chivalry and machismo.

Today, mariachi bands are the life of the party. They perform at weddings, birthdays, public festivals, restaurants, and city plazas. The most famous bands perform across the globe. Guadalajara's annual mariachi festival draws mariachis from around the world.

The origin of the word *mariachi* is a source of some controversy. The legend is that it evolved from the French word *mariage* (marriage), stemming from the French occupation in the mid-1800s. But leading mariachi historians now debunk that myth, citing evidence that the word has its origins in the Nahuatl language of the Coca Indians.

THE RISE OF MARIACHI

Historians trace the roots of mariachi to Cocula, a small agricultural town south of Guadalajara. There, in the 17th century, Franciscan monks trained the local indigenous populations in the use of stringed instruments, teaching them the religious songs to help win their conversion.

The aristocracy, who preferred the more refined contemporary European music, held early mariachi groups in disdain. But by the late 19th century, mariachi had become enormously popular among peasants and indigenous people in Cocula, eventually spreading throughout southern Jalisco and into neighboring states.

MODERN MARIACHI INSTRUMENTS

Traditional mariachi groups consisted of two violins (the melody), and a vihuela and guitarrón (the harmony). Some long-gone groups used a *tambor* or drum, not used in modern mariachi. All members of the group shared singing responsibilities.

TRUMPETS
Added to the traditional mariachi lineup in the 1930s when mariachis hit the big screen, at the insistence of a pioneer in Mexican radio and television

VIOLINS
Essential to any mariachi group

THE FOLK HARP
Longstanding mariachi instrument, used today by large ensembles and by some traditional troupes

THE GUITARRÓN
A large-bellied bass guitar

GUITARS
The round-backed vihuela is smaller and higher-pitched than the standard guitar

5-string Vihuela   6-string guitar

In 1905, Mexican dictator Porfirio Díaz visited Cocula and was received with a performance of a mariachi group. Impressed with the performance, Diaz invited the group to Mexico City where, after a few years and a revolution, mariachi flourished. Over the next two decades, more groups followed to Mexico City. Mariachi groups gained wide popularity by the 1930s, when movie stars as Jorge Negrete and Pedro Infante began portraying mariachi musicians in their films.

MARIACHI STYLE

■ The mariachi *traje* (suit) consists of matching vest, *chaleco* (short jacket), and form-fitting pants, and a complementary *moño* (large bow tie). Simple *trajes* have soutache trim or embroidery; finer versions have suede patterns on the jacket with metal buttons down the pants legs. Trajes come in all colors, but formal costumes are black.

■ Sombreros made from pressed rabbit fur are the highest quality.

■ The modern mariachi's dress is an adaptation of *charro*, or Mexican cowboy, attire, first worn by the members of an early mariachi group led by Cirilo Marmolejo and adopted for Mexican movies of the 1930s–50s. A complete formal outfit can cost as much as US$3,000.

■ *Botonaduras* (decorative buttons on the pants legs) can be simple, or ornate, made of silver or gold. A brooch on the front of the jacket often matches the botonadura.

■ Black leather *botínes* (half-boots) are standard mariachi footwear.

WHERE AND HOW TO HEAR MARIACHI

HIRE A MARIACHI GROUP

There may be no better way to thoroughly surprise (or embarrass) your significant other, than with a mariachi serenade. Hiring a band is easy. Just go to Plaza de los Mariachis, beside Mercado Libertad in downtown Guadalajara. Pablo Garcia, whose Mariachi Atotonilco has been working the plaza for almost 40 years, says a serenade runs about 2,000 pesos, or just under US$155. Alternatively, you can ask for a recommendation at Casa Bariachi (⊠ *Av. Vallarta 2221 at Calderon de la Barca, ☎33/3616–9900*) Negotiate price and either leave a deposit (ask for a business card and a receipt) and have the band meet you at a determined location, or, as Mexicans usually do, accompany the band to the unexpecting lady.

HIT THE INTERNATIONAL MARIACHI FESTIVAL

The last weekend of every August, some 700 mariachi groups from around the world descend upon Guadalajara for this event. Mexico's most famous mariachi groups—Mariachi Vargas de Tecalitlán, Mariachi los Camperos, and Mariachi de América—play huge concerts in the Degollado Theater, accompanied by the Jalisco Philharmonic Orchestra. The weeklong annual charro championship is held simultaneously, bringing together the nation's top cowboys and mariachis.

THE WORLD'S BEST MARIACHI BAND

At least, the world's most *famous* mariachi band, Mariachi Vargas de Tecalitlán was founded in 1897, when the norm was four-man groups with simple stringed instruments. Started by Gaspar Vargas in Tecalitlán, Jalisco, the mariachi troupe shot to fame in the 1930s after winning a regional mariachi contest, which earned them the favor of Mexican president Lázaro Cárdenas. The group quickly became an icon of Mexican cinema, performing in and recording music for films. Now in its fifth generation, Mariachi Vargas performs the world over and has recorded more than 50 albums, and music for more than 200 films.

The *gabán* (poncho) was worn traditionally for warmth.

CATCH YEAR-ROUND PERFORMANCES

If you miss Guadalajara's mariachi festival you can still get your fill of high- quality mariachi performances on street corners, in city plazas, and at many restaurants. An estimated 150 mariachi groups are currently active in the City of Roses.

Restaurants, most notably Guadalajara's Casa Bariachi chain, hire mariachi groups, whose performance is generally included with your table (though tips won't be refused). On occasion, mariachis perform free nighttime concerts in Guadalajara's Plaza de Armas. Another venue, the Plaza de Mariachi, beside Guadalajara's landmark Mercado Libertad, is a longstanding attraction, albeit during the day—at night it's better known for crime than mariachi.

Tlaquepaque's El Parían, a former market turned series of bars around a tree-filled central patio, is a fantastic intimate setting for mariachi music. Between free performances in the central kiosk, you can request serenades at about $15–18 per song or negotiate deals for longer performances for your table.

ALL ABOARD THE TEQUILA TRAIN!

To experience the Jalisco quartet of traditions—mariachi, charrería, folkloric dance, and tequila—in one adventure, take the Tequila Express. It includes a train ride from Guadalajara through fields of blue agave to a tequila-making hacienda, live mariachi music, all the food and drink you can handle, and a charro and folkloric dance performance.

WORKING HARD FOR THE MONEY

It is becoming harder for mariachi groups to make a living at the trade. The increasing cost of living has made nighttime serenades, once a staple of a mariachi's diet of work, expensive ($200 and up) and out of the reach of many locals. Performers generally work day jobs to make ends meet.

THE COWBOY CONNECTION

Mariachi and Mexican rodeo, or *charreada* (Mexico's official sport), go together like hot dogs and baseball. Both charreada and mariachi music evolved in the western Mexican countryside, where daily ranching chores like branding bulls eventually took on a competitive edge. The first of Mexico's 800 charro associations was founded in Guadalajara in 1920, and to this day holds a two-hour rodeo every Sunday. Throughout the competition, mariachi music is heard from the stands, but the key mariachi performance is at the end of a competition when female riders called *escaramuzas* perform synchronized moves, riding side-saddle in traditional ribboned and brightly colored western Mexican dresses.

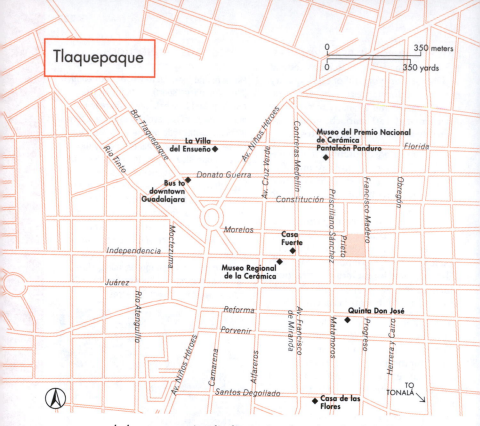

Tlaquepaque

hokey mannequins display intricately embroidered clothing. The gift shop sells a small inventory of beaded items, prayer arrows, and god's eyes. ✉ *Av. Hidalgo, 152, Zona Zapopan Norte* ☎ *33/3636–4430* 💰 *50¢* 🕐 *Mon.–Sat. 9:30–1:30 and 3–6, Sun. 10–2.*

WHERE TO EAT

Tapatíos love foreign food, but homegrown dishes won't ever lose their flavor. The trademark local dish is *torta ahogada*, a "drowned pork sandwich" soaked in tomato sauce and topped with onions and hot sauce. If you're not a fan of soggy bread, other favorites are *carne en su jugo* (beef stew with bacon bits and beans), *birria* (hearty goat or lamb stew), and pozole (hominy and pork in seasoned tomato broth). Seafood is popular and is available in trendy restaurants as well as at stands. The best Mexican food is in Tlaquepaque and near the main attractions downtown. The most popular non-Mexican restaurants are scattered about western Guadalajara, in Zona Minerva.

CENTRO HISTÓRICO

$$$ ✕ **La Fonda de San Miguel.** In a former convent, La Fonda is one of
MEXICAN Centro's most exceptional restaurants. Innovative Mexican eats are
★ presented in a soaring courtyard centered on a stone fountain and hung with an array of shining tin stars and folk art from Tlaquepaque and Tonalá. Relish the freshly made tortillas and the shrimp in tasty mole

sauce. Live performances are offered most days 2 to 4:30 PM and 9 to 11 PM: perhaps mandolin, piano, or guitar. There's a more complete folkloric show Saturday 9 to 11 PM. ⊠*Donato Guerra 25, Centro Histórico* ☎*33/3613–0809* ⊕*www.lafondadesanmiguel.com* ▭*AE, MC, V.*

$

MEXICAN

✗**Tacos Providencia del Centro.** This is the place for traditional Guadalajara street stand–style fare with a chair. Tacos *al pastor* top the clean restaurant's menu, and they come with every possible filling, including *trompa* (pig snout). Quesadillas and *gringas* (tortillas filled with cheese and meat) are also available. ⊠*Calle Morelos 84-A, at Plaza Tapatía, Centro Histórico* ☎*33/3613–9914* ▭*No credit cards.*

ZONA MINERVA

$

MEXICAN

✗**Karne Garibaldi.** Lightning service is made possible by the menu's single item: *carne en su jugo,* a combination of finely diced beef and bacon simmered in rich beef broth and served with grilled onions, tortillas, and refried beans mixed with corn. ⊠*Calle Garibaldi 1306, Zona Minerva* ☎*33/3826–1286* ▭*AE, MC, V* ⊠*Mariano Otero 3019, Zona Plaza del Sol* ☎*33/3133–2607* ▭*AE, MC, V.*

$

ITALIAN

★

✗**La Trattoria.** Guadalajara's top Italian restaurant is a bustling family place. The menu's highlights include spaghetti *frutti di mare* (with seafood), *scaloppine alla Marsala* (beef medallions with Marsala sauce and mushrooms), and fresh garlic bread. All meals include a trip to the salad bar. Make a reservation if you're eating after 8 PM. The restaurant opens daily at 1 PM and closes at midnight every night but Sunday, when things go dark at 9 PM. ⊠*Av. Niños Héroes 3051, Zona Minerva* ☎*33/3122–1817* ▭*AE, MC, V.*

$$

FRENCH

★

✗**Pierrot.** Nose through this hushed French dining room's extensive wine list for a drink to accompany the trout amandine or pâté-stuffed chicken breast in tarragon sauce. Wall-mounted lamps and flowers on each table are among the gracious touches. In business since the early 1980s, it is still popular with the locals, and plenty busy with business types in suits throughout the week. ⊠*Calle Justo Sierra 2355, Zona Minerva* ☎*33/3630–2087* ▭*AE, MC, V* ⊙*Closed Sun.*

$$$

MEXICAN

★

✗**Sacromonte.** Come here for creative haute–Mexican cuisine, superior service, and warm ambience. You're surrounded by *artesanías* in the dining area, and there's live music every afternoon from about 2 (when the restaurant opens) to 5, and some evenings after 9, light jazz. Try a juicy steak or *La Corona de Reina Isabel*—a crown of intertwined shrimp in lobster sauce. ⊠*Pedro Moreno 1398, Zona Minerva* ☎*33/3825–5447* ⌂*Reservations essential* ▭*MC, V* ⊙*No dinner Sun.*

TLAQUEPAQUE

$$

MEXICAN

★

✗**Casa Fuerte.** Relax with tasty Mexican dishes at the tables along the sidewalk or under the palms and by the fountain in the patio. You'll be tempted by the sidewalk tables facing the pedestrian street, but duck inside before you decide: the oversize garden patio surrounding a huge old tree is magnificent. Try the house specialties: chicken stuffed with *huitlacoche* (a corn fungus that's Mexico's answer to the truffle) and shrimp in tamarind sauce. Live, romantic music accompanies *comida* (2:30 to 6 PM, approximately) every day except Monday. Come early for dinner: the restaurant closes at 9 PM. ⊠*Calle Independencia 224, Tlaquepaque* ☎*33/3639–6481* ▭*AE, MC, V.*

8

TONALÁ

$ ✗ **El Rincón del Sol.** A covered patio invites you to sip margaritas while
MEXICAN   listening to live trova. The romantic ballads are presented Tuesday to
Friday evenings between around 7 and 9, and on weekends during
the leisurely lunch hour, about 3 to 5. Try one of the steak or chicken
dishes or the classic *chiles en nogada* (in walnut sauce) in the colors of
the Mexican flag. The waitstaff is helpful, as is the owner, who is right
on-site to supervise. It's open daily for breakfast after 8 AM. ⊠ *Av. 16 de
Septiembre 61, Tonalá* ☎ *33/3683–1989 or 33/3683–1940* ▤ *MC, V.*

WHERE TO STAY

People are often drawn to the Centro Histórico, where colonial-style
hotels are convenient to entertainment and historical sights, or to
Tlaquepaque's genial B&Bs. Businesspeople head for the Zona Minerva, specifically around Avenida López Mateos Sur, a 16-km (10-mi)
strip extending from the Minerva Fountain to the Plaza del Sol shopping center, where they can take advantage of modern office facilities
and four-star comforts.

CENTRO HISTÓRICO

$$ ▥ **Holiday Inn Centro Histórico.** Here's a spiffy, reliable international chain
in the heart of historic Guadalajara. Rooms have gold-and-white color
schemes, a workstation and plasma TV; in the bath is a glassed-in
shower but no tub. An inexpensive breakfast buffet is offered daily, and
the restaurant serves national and international dishes. **Pros:** free Wi-Fi,
free airport shuttle. **Cons:** no heat, small gym, no pool. ⊠ *Av. Juárez
211, Centro* ☎ *33/3560–1200, 800/465–4329 in U.S. and Europe*
⊕ *www.holidaycentrogdl.com* ⤴ *45 rooms, 45 suites* ♿ *In-room: safe,
Wi-Fi. In-hotel: restaurant, room service, bar, laundry facilities, laundry
service, Wi-Fi, parking (free), no-smoking rooms* ▤ *AE, MC, V.*

$$ ▥ **Hotel de Mendoza.** This refined hotel with postcolonial architecture
★   and hand-carved furniture is on a calm side street a block from Teatro
Degollado. Suites are worth the extra cost: standard rooms are comfortable but small. Some rooms have balconies overlooking a courtyard
pool. **Pros:** free Wi-Fi and use of hotel computers, package for about
$90 gets you a room plus breakfast, paid parking reasonable at less
than $4 per day. **Cons:** standard rooms have shower only, can't reserve
rooms with balconies ahead. ⊠ *Calle Venustiano Carranza 16, Centro Histórico* ☎ *33/3942–5151, 01800/361–2600 in Mexico* ⊕ *www.
demendoza.com.mx* ⤴ *86 rooms, 18 suites* ♿ *In-room: Wi-Fi. In-hotel:
restaurant, pool, gym, Wi-Fi, parking (paid)* ▤ *AE, MC, V* ▥*EP.*

$ ▥ **Hotel Morales.** This downtown hotel, originally a 19th-century room-
★   ing house, is elegant and quiet. Demure guest rooms have crown mold-
ing, blond-wood floors, and satiny gold-and-beige furnishings. Café
tables on the roof provide an escape from the more formal lobby with
its international restaurant. Among the distinguished guests who have
stayed here are the bullfighter El Cordobéz; cinema star Cantinflas;
and the Brazilian soccer hero Pelé. **Pros:** downtown elegance on the
cheap, free in-room coffee, double-paned windows. **Cons:** no Wi-Fi in
rooms. ⊠ *Av. Ramón Corona 243, Centro* ☎ *33/3658–5232* ⊕ *www.
hotelmorales.com.mx* ⤴ *59 rooms, 7 suites* ♿ *In-room: safe. In-hotel:
restaurant, Wi-Fi, parking (free)* ▤ *AE, MC, V.*

ZONA MINERVA

$$$ ⊞**Crowne Plaza Guadalajara.** Gardens encircling the pool add a bit of nature to this family-friendly hotel. A mix of antiques and reproductions fills public spaces. Rooms have very little in the way of decor, but they do offer marble baths with small tub, hair dryer, iron and ironing board, and natural lighting; those in the tower have city views. (Ask for a room near the back; those near the playground can be noisy.) Packages including breakfast are available. **Pros:** free coffee in rooms, pets accepted, car rental and travel agency on-site, La Fuente Restaurant opens at 6:30 AM. **Cons:** uninspired room decor. ⊠*Av. López Mateos Sur 2500, Zapopan* ☎*33/3634–1034 or 01800/009–9900* ⊕*www. cpguadalajara.com.mx* ⇆*297 rooms, 5 suites* ⚲*In-room: safe, Wi-Fi. In-hotel: restaurant, room service, bar, pool, gym, laundry service, Wi-Fi, parking (paid), no-smoking rooms* ▭*AE, DC, MC, V* �*IOIEP.*

$$ ⊞**Fiesta Americana.** The dramatic glass facade of this high-rise faces the Minerva Fountain and Los Arcos monument. Four glass-enclosed elevators ascend dizzyingly above a 14-story atrium lobby to the guest rooms, which have dignified, modern furnishings, small marble bathrooms with bathtub, and, for the most part, arresting views (rooms 1211 through 1217 have the very best). The lobby bar has live music every night. Executive-floor rooms come with continental breakfast and canapés, and there's a fully equipped business center. **Pros:** airport shuttle (fee), 24-hour room service, ample parking, nice bathroom amenities, AAA discount. **Cons:** some rooms have unattractive views of roof and generators, no pool. ⊠*Av. Aurelio Aceves 225, Col. Vallarta Poniente, Zona Minerva* ☎*33/3818–1400, 01800/fiesta1 in Mexico* ⊕*www.fiestamericana.com.mx* ⇆*387 rooms, 4 suites* ⚲*In-room: Wi-Fi. In-hotel: restaurant, bar, gym, laundry service, Internet terminal, Wi-Fi, parking (paid), no-smoking rooms* ▭*AE, DC, MC, V.*

$$ ⊞**Hotel Plaza Diana.** At this modest hotel two blocks from the Minerva
★ Fountain, the standard-size rooms are smallish and have white walls and bright, patterned fabrics; windows don't open. One suite has a sauna. The large, open, café-restaurant specializes in Argentine-style cuts of beef and there's a piano in the adjacent lounge. The huge, rectangular, indoor pool is good for laps. **Pros:** heated indoor pool, free Internet, free airport shuttle. **Cons:** basic rooms, small gym. ⊠*Av. Agustín Yáñez 2760, Zona Minerva* ☎*33/3540–9700, 01800/248–1001 in Mexico* ⊕*www.hoteldiana.com.mx* ⇆*127 rooms, 24 suites* ⚲*In-room: safe, Wi-Fi. In-hotel: restaurant, room service, bar, pool, gym, Internet terminal, Wi-Fi* ▭*AE, DC, MC, V* ⊡*IOIEP.*

$$$$ ⊞**Quinta Real.** Stone-and-brick walls, colonial arches, and objets d'art
★ fill public areas. Suites are plush, though small, with elegant neocolonial-style furnishings and faux fireplaces. Master suites have a separate seating area with love seat and marble-top desk. It's a small price upgrade to get the Gran Class suite with round Jacuzzi tub and CD player. You can get in-room spa treatments. The wood-floored gym boasts LifeFitness and FlexDeck brand equipment and has plasma-screen TVs, cold towels, water in a small fridge, and bouncy music. **Pros:** no charge for in-room dial-up, forced-air heating (many Guadalajara hotels aren't heated), stately, quiet grounds. **Cons:** pricey, no on-site spa. ⊠*Av. México 2727, at Av. López Mateos Norte, Col. Vallarta Norte,*

Zona Minerva ☎33/3669–0600, 01800/500–4000 in Mexico, 866/621–9288 in U.S. and Canada ⊕*www.quintareal.com* ↦*76 suites* ₺*In-room: safe, Internet. In-hotel: restaurant, bar, pool, gym, laundry service, Internet terminal, Wi-Fi, parking (free), no-smoking rooms* ▭*AE, D, MC, V.*

TLAQUEPAQUE

$$ 🏨 **Casa de las Flores.** A favorite with
★ those traveling for business as well as pleasure, this B&B is charismatic and inviting, with lovely art and wonderful food. Owners Stan and José, from the United States and

Mexico, respectively, enjoy directing you to the best shops and markets for purchasing handicrafts. Guests meet and socialize over breakfast; by the fireplace in the cozy living room; and out in the garden, which is packed with trees, shrubs, and flowering plants **Pros:** yummy, inventive breakfasts made by the owner, the inn is filled with local folk art and a brief tour is included, one computer for checking e-mail, no charge. **Cons:** some might consider the garden fussy, promised discounts not always delivered when owners off-site. ✉*Calle Santos Degollado 175, Tlaquepaque* ☎33/3659–3186 ⊕*www.casadelasflores.com* ↦*7 rooms* ₺*In-room: no a/c (some), no TV (some), Wi-Fi (some). In-hotel: laundry service, Wi-Fi, parking (free)* ▭*MC, V* ⦿*BP.*

$$ 🏨 **La Villa del Ensueño.** Even with the 10-minute walk from Tlaquepaque's center, this intimate B&B is near the town's shops. The restored 19th-century hacienda has thick, white adobe walls, exposed-beam ceilings, and plants in huge unglazed pots. Smokers should request a room with private balcony, as smoking isn't allowed inside. **Pros:** Jacuzzi, takeout available from adjacent Mexican restaurant, friendly staff. **Cons:** only junior suites have bathtubs, for smokers, no smoking inside. ✉*Florida 305* ☎33/3635–8792 ⊕*www.villadelensueno.com* ↦*16 rooms, 4 suites* ₺*In-room: refrigerator (some), Internet, Wi-Fi (some). In-hotel: restaurant, bar, pools, parking (free), no-smoking rooms* ▭*AE, MC, V* ⦿*BP.*

$$ 🏨 **Quinta Don José.** This B&B one block from Tlaquepaque's main plaza and shopping area feels more like a small hotel. Natural lighting and room size vary; suites face the pool, and are spacious but a bit dark. There's remarkable tile work in the master suite. Hearty continental breakfasts—with fruit, cereal, toast, breads, juice, and coffee—are served in an inner courtyard, and good pizza is produced in the brick oven during the evening meal in the on-site Italian restaurant (closed Monday). Inexpensive area tours are offered here, too. **Pros:** centrally located in downtown Tlaquepaque, friendly staff speaks excellent English, free coffee and fruit in reception, free phone calls worldwide, free Wi-Fi. **Cons:** more hotelish (which is fine unless you're craving a B&B), chilly pool. ✉*Calle Reforma 139, Tlaquepaque* ☎33/3635–7522,

01800/700–2223 in Mexico, 866/629–3753 in U.S. and Canada ⊕www.quintadonjose.com ↩8 rooms, 7 suites ♿In-room: Wi-Fi (some). In hotel: restaurant, bar, pool, laundry service, Internet terminal, Wi-Fi ☐AE, MC, V ⏹BP.

> **TIP**
>
> For the latest listings, grab a *Público* newspaper on Friday and pull out the weekly Ocio cultural guide.

NIGHTLIFE

With the exception of a few well-established nightspots like La Maestranza, downtown Guadalajara goes to bed relatively early. The existing nightlife centers around Avenida Vallarta, favored by the well-to-do, under-thirty set; Avenida Patria (full of bars for teenagers and young adults who party until early in the morning on weekend nights); and the somewhat seedy Plaza del Sol. Bars in these spots usually close by 3 AM. Dance clubs may charge a $15–$20 cover, and many are open on Friday and Saturday nights only. Dress up for nightclubs; highly subjective admission policies hinge on who you know or how you look. The local music scene is less formal and centers on more intimate digs.

Guadalajara has a decent arts and culture scene. You can catch the University of Guadalajara's Ballet Folclórico, the philharmonic orchestra, or an opera at Teatro Degollado or the newer Teatro Diana. International exhibitions are sometimes shown at the Instituto Cultural Cabañas or the Arts Museum of Zapopan.

★ Open since 1921, **La Fuente** (⊠ *Calle Pino Suarez at Hidalgo, Centro Histórico* ☎*No phone*) draws business types, intellectuals, and blue-collar workers, all seeking cheap drinks, animated conversation, and live music. To avoid crowds, arrive soon after it opens (8 PM every night but Monday, when it's closed). Restaurant by day, Guadalajara hot spot by night, **I Latina** (⊠*Av. Inglaterra 3128 at López Mateos,Col. Vallarta Poniente, Centro* ☎*33/3647–7774*) is where a cool upscale local and international crowd has cocktails.

For some local color, stop at **La Maestranza** (⊠*Calle Maestranza 179, Centro Histórico* ☎*33/3613–5878*), a renovated 1940s cantina full of bullfighting memorabilia. It's open daily between noon and 3 in the morning.

DANCE CLUBS **El Gran Mexicano** (⊠*Av. Mariano Otero 5850, Zapopan* ☎*33/3180–4012 or 33/3180–4013*) is the place to listen to or dance to some very typical Mexican music, including mariachi and banda groups. Cover is $10 per person; it's open on Friday and Saturday only between 9 PM and 3 AM.

Salón Astoria (⊠*Prisciliano Sánchez 345, Centro* ☎*33/3614–6570*) opens lots earlier than most clubs and offers live tropical tunes until about 4 AM. The dance hall opens Thursday and Sunday at 6 PM and Friday and Saturday at 8. Cover charge is $3 for the ladies and $4 for gents.

Salón Veracruz (⊠*Calle Manzano 486, behind Hotel Misión Carlton, Centro Histórico* ☎*33/3613–4422*) is a spartan, old-style dance hall where a 15-piece band keeps hoofers moving to *cumbia*, merengue, and the waltzlike *danzón*. It's closed Monday and Tuesday; cover is around $6 per person.

SPORTS AND THE OUTDOORS

These "rodeos" of elegant equestrian maneuvers and rope tricks are the epitome of upper-class rural Mexican culture. Men in tight, elegant suits with wide-brimmed felt hats perform *suertes* in which they subdue young bulls or jump from one galloping horse to another in *el paso de la muerte* (the pass of death). Teams of women in flowing dresses perform audacious (yet less dangerous) synchronized movements on horseback. Mariachi or brass bands play between acts. Charreadas run year-round at the **Lienzo Charros de Jalisco** (⊠ *Av. Dr. R. Michel 577, Centro Histórico* ☎ *33/3619–3232*), next to Parque Agua Azul, usually Sunday at noon. Admission is $3–$5.

SOCCER   *Futbol* (soccer) is a national obsession. Guadalajara's two main teams nurse a healthy rivalry—as do their fans. Atlas appeals more to the middle and upper classes; working-class Tapatíos and students prefer Las Chivas. In fact the Chivas seem to be the working-class heroes of much of Mexico. Both teams play at Guadalajara's **Estadio Jalisco** (⊠ *Av. Siete Colinas 1772, Col. Independencia* ☎ *33/3637–0301*) on weekends or Wednesday night July–May. Tickets are $5–$45.

SHOPPING

Guadalajara is shopping central for people from all over Nayarit, Jalisco, and surrounding states. The labyrinthine Mercado Libertad is one of Latin America's largest markets; modern malls are gathering spots with restaurants and theaters. Tlaquepaque and Tonalá have the most extensive selection of Mexican art and handicrafts (mainly pottery). In Tlaquepaque, stroll along Independencia and Juárez streets for dozens of artsy shops. In less touristy Tonalá most shops and factories are spread out, with the exception of a concentration of shops on Avenida de los Tonaltecas, the main drag into town. On Thursday and Sunday, bargain-price merchandise is sold at a terrific street market there packed with vendors from 8 to 4.

★ Better known as Mercado San Juan de Dios, **Mercado Libertad** (⊠ *Calz. Independencia Sur; use pedestrian bridge from Plaza Tapatía's south side, Centro Histórico*) has shops that are organized thematically on three expansive floors. Be wary of fakes in the jewelry stores. Most shops are open Monday–Saturday 10–8, and 10–3 on Sunday.

★ **Tonalá crafts market** (⊠ *Av. Tonaltecas, north of Av. Tonalá, Tonalá*) is *the* place for Mexican arts and crafts. Vendors set up ceramics, carved wood, candles, glassware, furniture, metal crafts, and more each Thursday and Sunday (roughly 9–5). Look for everything from red clay pots and simple plates to elaborately decorated ceramic *vajilla* (place settings). Antiquers come out of the woodwork every Sunday 10–5 to sell their antique European flatware and Mexican pottery at **El Trocadero** (⊠ *Av. Mexico at Av. Chapultepec, Zona Minerva*) market in the antiques district.

MALLS Sprawling, tri-level **La Gran Plaza** (⊠ *Av. Vallarta 3959, Zona Minerva* ☎ *33/3563–2900*) has nearly 330 shops and a big cinema. The food court is Guadalajara's best. Guadalajara's first mall, **Plaza del Sol** (⊠ *Av. López Mateos Sur 2375, at Mariano Otero, Zona Minerva* ☎ *33/3121–5950*) has 270 commercial spaces scattered around an outdoor atrium and wacky sculpture-fountains by Alejandro Colunga. It's got everything the more modern malls have in a more low-key environment.

> **CAUTION**
>
> Mercado Libertad has silver at great prices, but not everything that glitters there is certifiably silver. A safer, albeit pricier, bet are the shops along Avenida República in downtown Guadalajara, where there are more than 400 jewelers.

TEQUILA

56 km (35 mi) northwest of Guadalajara.

For an in-depth look at how Mexico's most famous liquor is derived from the spiny blue agave plant that grows in fields alongside the highway, stop by this tidy village.

GETTING HERE AND AROUND

Head west from Guadalajara along Avenida Vallarta for about 25 minutes until you reach the toll road junction (Puerto Vallarta Cuota). Choose the toll road (faster, safer, and about $10) or the free road (*libre*) toward Puerto Vallarta. Or catch a bus to Tequila from the Antigua Central Camionera (Old Central Bus Station), northeast of the Parque Agua Azul on Avenida Dr. R. Michel, between Calle Los Angeles and Calle 5 de Febrero. Buses marked Amatitán–Tequila are easy to spot from the entrance on Calle Los Angeles.

Another option for taking in "tequila country" is the *Tequila Express*, a daylong train ride with mariachis, a distillery tour, food, and plenty of tequila. There's no stop in the town of Tequila itself, but this is a great way to soak up Jalisco's tequila-making region. Tours depart from the Guadalajara train station at 10:30 AM. Purchase tickets ahead of time through TicketMaster, area hotels or tour operators, or the Guadalajara Chamber of Commerce (open weekdays 9–2:30 and 3:30–4:30). The cost is 950 pesos for adults (about $73), a little more than half that for children 6 to 11; younger kids are free. You'll return to the Guadalajara train station at about 8 PM.

ESSENTIALS

Tequila Express Contacts Guadalajara Chamber of Commerce (⊠ *Av. Vallarta 4095 at Niño Obrero, Guadalajara* ☎ *33/3880–9099 or 33/3122–7920*). **Guadalajara Train Station** (⊠ *Av. Washington at Calzada Independencia, Guadalajara* ☎ *33/3641–3141*). **TicketMaster** (*www.ticketmaster.com.mx*).

8

EXPLORING

The **Sauza Museum** (✉ *Calle Albino Rojas 22* ☎*374/742–0247*) has memorabilia from the Sauza family, a tequila-making dynasty second only to the Cuervos. The museum costs less than $1 and is open daily 10–3 (or until 5 PM during major holidays). Tours, which are included in the admission fee, are in English as well as Spanish, depending on the needs of the crowd.

Opened in 1795, the **José Cuervo Distillery** (✉ *Calle José Cuervo 73* ☎*374/742–2442*) is the world's oldest tequila distillery. Tours are offered daily every hour from 10 to 4. The tours at noon and 3 PM are in English, but English-speakers can often be accommodated at other times. The basic tour, which includes one margarita cocktail, costs $8. It's $12 for tours with a few additional tastings as well as an educational catalog; $20 gets you all this and special reserve tequilas. Tours including round-trip transportation, several tequila tastings, a complimentary margarita, and free time for lunch cost about $22. You can arrange them through the major hotels and travel agencies in Guadalajara. Call ☎*33/3343–4481* at least a day in advance to make arrangements. ■**TIP→** Make sure to ask the guide for coupons for an additional margarita as well as discounts at an area restaurant and in the gift shop.

> ### DEDICATED TO ITS CRAFT
>
> Like Tlaquepaque, neighboring **Tonalá** was in the crafts business long before the Spanish conquistadors arrived. Independent and industrious, less touristy Tonalá remains dedicated to traditional pursuits: brilliant blown glass, gold jewelry, and goofy piñatas. But it's the exquisitely stylized *petatillo*-style ceramics that are the town's best-known handcraft. The distinctively Mexican earthenware is decorated with placid-looking birds and beasts and glazed in subtle tans and blues. Thursday and Sunday markets are the source of terrific bargains.

TEUCHITLÁN

50 km (28 mi) west of Guadalajara.

For decades, residents in this sleepy village of sugarcane farmers had a name for the funny-looking mounds in the hills above town, but they never considered the Guachimontones to be more than a convenient source of rocks for local construction. Then in the early 1970s an American archaeologist asserted that the mounds were the remnants of a long-vanished, 2,000-year-old state. It took Phil Weigand nearly three decades to convince authorities in far-off Mexico City that he wasn't crazy. Before he was allowed to start excavating and restoring this monumental site in the late 1990s, plenty more houses and roads were produced with Guachimonton rock—and countless tombs were looted of priceless art.

The spot is most distinctive for its sophisticated concentric architecture—a circular pyramid surrounded by a ring of flat ground, surrounded by a series of smaller platforms arranged in a circle. The "Teuchitlán Tradition," as the concentric circle structures are called, is unique in world architecture. Weigand believes the formations suggest the existence of a pre-Hispanic state in the region, whereas it was previously held that only socially disorganized nomads inhabited the region at the time. Similar ruins are spread throughout the foothills of the extinct Tequila Volcano, but this is the biggest site yet detected.

GETTING HERE AND AROUND

To get to Teuchitlán from Guadalajara, drive west out along Avenida Vallarta for 25 minutes to the toll road junction to Puerto Vallarta: choose the free road 70 (*libre*) toward Vallarta. Head west along Route 15 for a couple of miles, then turn left onto Route 70 and continue until you reach the town of Tala. One-and-a-half kilometers (1 mi) past the sugar mill, turn right onto Route 27. Teuchitlán is 15 minutes from the last junction. The ruins are up a dirt road from town—just ask for directions when you arrive. There's a small museum off the main square. Plans to build greater infrastructure around the site continue. If you visit during the dry season, you may score a look at a dig or restoration project.

LAKE CHAPALA

Lake Chapala is Mexico's largest natural lake and just an hour's drive south of Guadalajara. Surrounded by jagged hills and serene towns, it is a favorite Tapatío getaway and a haven for thousands of North American retirees.

The area's main town, Chapala, is flooded with weekend visitors, and the pier is packed shoulder-to-shoulder most Sundays. An improved malecón has invigorated the area, attracting more strollers, fishermen, and craftspeople to the lake there. Neighboring Ajijic, 8 km (5 mi) west, has narrow cobblestone streets and vibrantly colored buildings. Its mild climate and gentle pace has attracted a large colony of English-speaking expats, including many artists.

8

CHAPALA

45 km (28 mi) south of Guadalajara.

When elitist president Porfirio Díaz bought a retreat in lakeside Chapala in 1904, his aristocratic pals followed suit. Today, some of these residences on the shore of Mexico's largest natural lake have been converted to cozy lodges, many geared to families. About an hour south of downtown Guadalajara, the diminutive town is a retreat for the middle and upper classes, although there aren't as many restaurants, shops, and cafés as one might expect.

Three blocks north of the promenade, the plaza at the corner of López Cotilla is a relaxing spot to read a paper or succumb to sweets from surrounding shops. The Iglesia de San Francisco (built in 1528), easily recognized by its blue neon crosses on twin steeples, is two blocks south of the plaza.

On weekends the town is energized by Mexican families who flock to the shores of the rejuvenated lake. Vendors sell refreshments and souvenirs, while lakeside watering holes fill to capacity.

WHERE TO EAT AND STAY

$$ ✕ **Cozumel.** Ajijic residents regularly drive to Chapala on Wednesday
SEAFOOD and Friday for live mariachi music (from 7 PM to closing at 8:30 PM) and inexpensive, well-prepared specials, which includes, in addition to a main course, a margarita cocktail, dessert, coffee, and a digestive after-dinner drink called "el beso." Wednesday is chicken cordon bleu night, and Friday it's surf-n-turf; on other days, choose from trout, breaded shrimp, and other seafood and international dishes. Reservations are essential for Wednesday and Friday. ✉ *Paseo Corona 22–A* ☎ *376/765–4606* ▭ *MC, V* ☉ *Closed Mon.*

$$ ✕ **Mariscos Guicho's.** Bright orange walls and checkerboard tablecloths
SEAFOOD lend the best of the waterfront seafood joints an authentic Mexican flair. Dig into savory caviar tostadas, frogs' legs, garlic shrimp, and spicy seafood soup. Hours are 11 AM to 7:30 PM. ✉ *Paseo Ramón Corona 20* ☎ *376/765–3232* ▭ *No credit cards* ☉ *Closed Tues.*

$ ▥ **Hotel Villa Montecarlo.** The hotel's simple, clean rooms are in three-story contiguous units, all with patios or terraces. The nearly 100-year-old Mediterranean-style villa is surrounded by grounds with several picnic and play areas. One of the two swimming pools is filled with natural thermal water; it's drained regularly and usually only open on weekends and holidays. At the current exchange rate, less than 10 bucks upgrades you from a standard room to a suite with terrace or balcony, dining room, mini-refrigerator and sink, extra half bath, and king bed. **Pros:** huge pools and extensive grounds, outdoor dining under enormous, flowering Indian laurel tree. **Cons:** can be noisy with student groups. ✉ *Av. Hidalgo 296, about 1 km (½ mi) west of Av. Madero* ☎ *376/765–2216 or 376/765–2120* ⇨ *46 rooms, 2 suites* ⌂ *In-hotel: restaurant, bar, tennis courts, pools, laundry service, parking (free)* ▭ *AE, MC, V.*

$$ ▥ **Lake Chapala Inn.** This lakeside European-style inn is an especially
★ appealing place to stay. Three of the four rooms in this restored mansion face the shore; all have high ceilings and whitewashed oak furniture. Rates include an English-style breakfast (with a continental breakfast on Sunday). **Pros:** deep green, solar-heated lap pool, English-speaking host, big sunny reading room. **Cons:** dated, 1970s-style furniture, square, tiled bathtubs not conducive to comfortable soaks. ✉ *Paseo Ramón Corona 23* ☎ *376/765–4786* ⊕ *www.chapalainn.com* ⇨ *4 rooms* ⌂ *In-room: no a/c, Wi-Fi. In-hotel: restaurant, pool, laundry service, Wi-Fi, parking (free)* ▭ *No credit cards* ⃝ *BP.*

AJIJIC

8 km (5 mi) west of Chapala.

Ajijic has narrow cobblestone streets, vibrantly colored buildings, and a gentle pace—with the exception of the very trafficky main highway through the town's southern end. The foreign influence is unmistakable: English is widely (though not exclusively) spoken and license plates come from far-flung places like British Columbia and Texas.

The Plaza Principal (aka El Jardín) is a tree- and flower-filled central square at the corner of Avenidas Colón and Hidalgo. In late November the plaza and its surrounding streets fill for the nine-day fiesta of the town's patron, St. Andrew. From the plaza, walk down Calle Morelos (the continuation of Avenida Colón) toward the lake and peruse the boutiques on Ajijic's main shopping strip. (There are also many galleries and shops east of Morelos, on Avenida 16 de Septiembre and Calle Constitución.) Turn left onto Avenida 16 de Septiembre or Avenida Constitución for art galleries and studios. Northeast of the plaza, along the highway, activity centers on the soccer field, which doubles as a venue for bullfights and concerts.

> ### HEALING WATERS
>
> ⚘ San Juan Cosalá, 2 km (1 mi) west of Ajijic, is known for its natural thermal-water spas along Lago de Chapala. **Hotel Balneario San Juan Cosalá** (✉ *Calle La Paz Oriente 420, at Carretera Chapala–Jocotepec, Km 13* ☎ 387/761-0302 ⊕ *www. hotelspacosala.com*) has a spa offering massage and other services at reasonable prices. The water park has a picnic area as well as several mineral-spring-fed swimming pools and two wading pools; admission is about $10. The park also has barbecue grills and Wi-Fi; weekends are crowded with tapatío (Guadalajaran) families.

WHERE TO EAT AND STAY

$$
GERMAN
✗**Johanna's.** Come to this intimate bit of Bavaria on the lake for German cuisine like sausages and goose or duck pâté. Main dishes come with soup or salad, applesauce, and cooked red cabbage. For dessert indulge in plum strudel or blackberry-topped torte. ✉ *Carretera Chapala-Jocotepec, Km 6.5* ☎ 376/766–0437 ▭ *No credit cards* ⊗ *No dinner Sun.; closed Mon.*

$$
ECLECTIC
✗**La Bodega de Ajijic.** Eat in a covered patio overlooking a grassy lawn and a small pool at this low-key restaurant. The menu has Italian and Mexican dishes, which are a bit small and overpriced. Still, service is friendly, and there's live music—ranging from Mexican pop and rock to blues, jazz, guitar, and harp—most nights. It opens at 8 AM daily except Thursday. ✉ *Av. 16 de Septiembre 124* ☎ 376/766–1002 ▭ *AE, MC, V* ⊗ *Closed Thurs.*

$
AMERICAN
✗**Salvador's.** An old mainstay of the expat community, this cafeteria-like eatery has a well-kept salad bar and specialties from both sides of the border. On Friday and Saturday people flock here for the fish-and-chips lunch special. Reasonable breakfasts are offered daily after 7:30 AM; some include juice and coffee along with main dish for $4 to $5. ✉ *Carretera Chapala–Jocotepec Oriente 58* ☎ 376/766–2301 ▭ *No credit cards* ⊗ *No dinner Sun.*

$–$$$
▥ **Casa Blanca.** The "white house" has gracious gardens, tinkling fountains, and rooms that are cheerful and tastefully decorated, if compact. Most have a king bed, microwave, coffeemaker, and pleasant, shared outdoor patio. Despite their diminutive size, rooms are decorated in pretty blond furnishings with pleasingly clean lines. Each room has plenty of free drinking water. The on-site Internet center offers inexpensive access to guests and others. **Pros:** charming and inexpensive,

manicurist and massage therapist by reservation, free shoe shine. **Cons:** small rooms. ✉*Calle 16 de Septiembre 29, Centro* ☎*376/766–4440, 800/436–0759 from U.S. and Canada* ⊕*www.casablancaajijic.com* ↩*8 rooms* ⟐*In-room: kitchen (some), Wi-Fi (some). In-hotel: Wi-Fi* ▤*AE, MC, V* ⦿|*CP.*

$$
★ 🏨 **La Nueva Posada**. The gardens framed in bougainvillea define this inviting inn. Rooms are large, with carpets, high ceilings, and local crafts. Villas share a courtyard and have tile kitchenettes. The bar has jazz or Caribbean music some weekend evenings. In the garden restaurant ($$), strands of tiny white lights set the mood for an evening meal. **Pros:** unique and lively decor, airy rooms, on-site restaurant with entertainment. **Cons:** small room TV. ✉*Calle Donato Guerra 9* ☎*376/766–1344* ↩*19 rooms, 4 villas* ⟐*In-hotel: restaurant, bar, pool, laundry service* ▤*MC, V* ⦿|*BP.*

SPORTS AND THE OUTDOORS
The **Rojas family** (✉*Paseo Del Lago and Camino Real, 4 blocks east of Los Artistas B&B* ☎*376/766–4261*) has been leading horseback trips for more than 30 years. A ride along the lakeshore or in the surrounding hills costs around $10 an hour.

UNDERSTANDING
PUERTO VALLARTA

History

Chronology

Books and Movies

Spanish Vocabulary

HISTORY

PRE-COLUMBIAN MEXICO

The first nomadic hunters crossed the Bering Straight during the Late Pleistocene Era, some 30,000 or 40,000 years ago, fanning out and finding niches in the varied landscape of North America. In the hot and arid "Great Chichimeca," as the vast area that included the Sonora and Chihuahua deserts and the Great Plains of the United States was known, lived far-flung tribes whose circumstances favored a nomadic lifestyle. Even the unassailable Aztecs were unable to dominate this harsh wilderness and its resilient people.

Mesoamerica, the name given posthumously to the great civilizations of mainland Mexico, spanned as far south of the Great Chichimeca as Honduras and El Salvador. Here, trade routes were established, strategic alliances were formed through warfare or marriage, and enormous temples and palaces were erected on the backs of men, without the aid of beasts of burden or the wheel. Some cultures mysteriously disappeared, others were conquered but not absorbed.

It was in northern Mesoamerica that the continent's first major metropolis, Teotihuacán—which predated the Aztec capital of Tenochtitlán by more than half a century—was built. The gleaming city with beautifully decorated pyramids, palaces, homes, and administrative buildings covered miles and administered to some 175,000 souls; it was abandoned for unknown reasons around AD 700. On the Yucatán Peninsula, great and powerful Maya cities rose up, but like Teotihuacán were abandoned one by one, seemingly at the height of civilization.

During the rise and fall of these great cities, small, loosely organized bands of individuals occupied Mesoamerica's western Pacific coast. By 1200 BC, the culture that archaeologists call Capacha occupied river valleys north and south of what would later be named Bahía de Banderas. From well-positioned settlements, they planted gardens and took advantage of animal and mineral resources from the sea and the surrounding foothills.

These cultures—centered primarily in the present-day states of Nayarit, Jalisco, and Colima—built no large, permanent structures and left few clues about their society. Some of the most compelling evidence comes from artifacts found in tombs. Unlike their more advanced neighbors, the Pacific coast people housed these burial chambers not in magnificent pyramids but in the bottom of vertical shafts deep within the earth. Lifelike dog sculptures were sometimes left to help their deceased owners cross to the other side; servants, too, were buried with their masters for the same purpose. Realistically depicted figures involved in myriad rituals of daily and ceremonial life, most of them excavated only since the 1970s, have given more clues about pre-Hispanic civilizations of western Mexico.

Only so much information can be gleaned, however, especially since the majority of tombs were looted before archaeological research began. North and south of Banderas Bay, the Aztatlán people seem to have established themselves primarily in river valleys between Tomatlán, in southern Jalisco, and northern Nayarit. In addition to creating utilitarian and ceremonial pottery, they appear to have been skilled in at least rudimentary metallurgy. Aside from the Purépecha of Michoacán, to whom the Aztatlán (or Aztlán) are related, no other Mesoamerican societies were skilled in making or using metal of any kind.

The Colonial Period

History favors those who write it, and the soldier-priest-scribe who documented the discovery of Banderas Bay in 1525 gave it a decidedly European spin. According to Padre Tello, four years after the Spanish demolished the Aztec capital at Tenochtit-lán, about 100 Spanish troops met 10,000 to 20,000 Aztatlán at Punta Mita (aka Punta de Mita), the bay's northernmost point. Then, by Tello's fantastic account, the sun's sudden illumination of a Spanish battle standard (a large pennant) bearing the image of the Virgin of the Immaculate Conception caused the armed indigenous peoples to give up without a fight. When they lay their colorful battle flags at the feet of Francisco Cortés de Buenaventura, the Spanish commander named the site Bahía de Banderas, or Bay of Flags.

Subsequent adventurers and explorers rediscovered and used the region around the bay, but it wasn't colonized until three centuries later. The name Bahía de Banderas is seen on maps from the 1600s, although whalers in the 1800s called it Humpback Bay, after their principal prey. Boats were built on the beach in today's Mismaloya for a missionary expedition to Baja California, and the long, deep bay was used as a pit stop on other long sailing voyages.

To a lesser extent, Banderas Bay was a place of refuge and refueling for pirates. Around the end of the 16th century, Sir Francis Drake lay in wait here for the Manila galleon—sailing south along the coast laden with wares from the Orient. He sent the booty to his patron, Queen Elizabeth of England.

The Formative Years

Although adventurers made use of the area's magnificent bay, Puerto Vallarta's story started inland and made its way to the coast. Mining in this part of the Sierra Madre wasn't as profitable as in Zacatecas and Guanajuato, but there was plenty of gold and silver to draw the Spaniards' attention. At the vanguard of Spanish exploration in 1530, the infamous conquistador Nuño Beltrán de Guzmán arrived in the region with a contingent of Spanish soldiers and indigenous allies.

During his tenure in Nueva Galicia (which included today's Jalisco, Zacatecas, and Durango states), de Guzmán seized land that was settled by native peoples and parceled out *encomiendas* (huge grants of land) to lucky *encomendados* (landholders) in return for loyalty and favors to the Crown. The landholders were entitled to the land and everything on it: the birds of the trees; beasts of the forest; and the unlucky indigenous people who lived there, who were consequently enslaved. De Guzmán's behavior was so outrageous that by 1536 he had been stripped of authority and sent to prison.

In exchange for their forced labor, the native population received the "protection" of the encomendado, meaning food and shelter, that they had enjoyed previously without any help from the Spanish. Abuse was inevitable, and many overworked natives died of famine. Epidemics of smallpox, diphtheria, scarlet fever, influenza, measles, and other imported diseases had a disastrous effect. The region's native population was reduced by about 90% within the first 100 years of Spanish occupation.

By the early 17th century, gold and silver were being mined throughout the region; there were bases of operation at San Sebastián del Oeste, Cuale, and Talpa. After the War for Independence (1810–21), Mexican entrepreneurs began to extract gold, silver, and zinc previously claimed by the Spanish. In the mid-1800s, the coast around today's Vallarta was under the jurisdiction of the mountain municipalities.

Independence from Spain brought little contentment to average people, who were as disenfranchised and poor as ever. A prime topic of the day among the moneyed elite was the growing conflict between Liberals and Conservatives. Liberals, like the lawyer Benito Juárez, favored curtailing the Church's vast power. When the Liberals prevailed and Juárez became Mexico's first indigenous president (he was a Zapotec from Oaxaca), a host of controversial reforms were enacted. Those regarding separation of church and state had immediate and lasting effects.

Settlers on the Bay

The power struggles of the first half of the 19th century had little real impact on relatively unpopulated coastal areas like Banderas Bay. In 1849, a few men from the fishing hamlet of Yelapa camped out at the mouth of the Cuale River, in present-day Puerto Vallarta. A few years later, young Guadalupe Sánchez, his wife, and a few friends were the first official settlers. This entrepreneur made his money by importing salt, vital for extracting mineral from rock. From this business grew the tiny town Las Peñas de Santa María de Guadalupe.

When silver prices dipped between the two World Wars, some of the mountain-based miners returned to their farming roots, relocating to the productive lands of the Ameca River basin (today, Nuevo Vallarta) at the southern border of Nayarit. The fecund land between the mountains and the bay produced ample corn crops, and the growing town of Las Peñas—renamed Puerto Vallarta in honor of a former Jalisco governor—became the seat of its own municipality in 1918.

Development came slowly. By the 1930s there was limited electricity; a small airstrip was built in the 1950s, when Mexicana Airlines initiated the first flights and electricity was finally available around the clock. Retaining the close-knit society and values brought down from the mining towns, each family seemed to know the others' joys and failures. They sat outside their adobe homes to discuss the latest gossip and the international news of the day.

THE MODERN ERA

Honoring a promise made to the Mexican government by John F. Kennedy, President Richard Nixon flew into an improved PV airport in 1970 to sign a treaty settling boundary disputes surrounding the Rio Grande, meeting with his Mexican counterpart, Gustavo Díaz Ordaz. Upon asking for an armored car, he was cheerfully told that the convertible that had been arranged would do just fine. After riding parade-style along the roadway lined with cheering citizens and burros garlanded in flowers, the American leader is said to have asked why, if he was a Republican, the road was lined with donkeys. To which his host sensibly responded, "Well, where in the world would we get all those elephants?"

It took about 500 years for Puerto Vallarta to transition from discovery to major destination, but the city is making up for lost time. "When I was a child here, in the 1950s, Puerto Vallarta was like a big family," the town's official chronicler, the late don Carlos Munguía, said. "When I married, in 1964, there were about 12,000 people." By the early '70s the population had jumped to 35,000 and continued to grow steadily.

Today the greater Puerto Vallarta area has some 220,368, a significant number of them expat Americans and Canadians who vacationed here and never left. The metropolitan area has three universities and a vast marina harboring yachts, tour boats, and the Mexican navy. In 2005 the harbor was expanded to accommodate three cruise ships; the overflow has to anchor offshore. While many folks lament the loss of the good old days before tourism took off, some things haven't changed: Most *vallartenses* (Puerto Vallarta natives) are still intimately acquainted with their neighbors and the man or woman who owns the corner taco stand, which is likely to have been there for years, maybe even generations.

CHRONOLOGY

ca. 350 BC Oldest evidence of civilization—a ceramic piece from Ixtapa (northwest of Puerto Vallarta)—dates to this time

ca. 1100 Indigenous Aztatlán people dominate region from present-day Sinaloa to Colima states; create first-known settlement in area

1525 First Spanish–Indian confrontation in the region, at Punta Mita. By Spanish accounts, 100 Spanish soldiers prevailed over tens of thousands armed native peoples. Bahía de Banderas (Bay of Flags) was named for the battle flags of the indigenous army that were (or so claimed the Spanish) thrown down in defeat

1587 Pirate Thomas Cavendish attacks Punta Mita, looting pearls gathered from Mismaloya and the Marietas Islands

1664 Mismaloya serves as a shipyard for vessels bound for exploration and conquest of Baja California

1849 Yelapa fishermen are said to have found excellent fishing at the mouth of the Cuale River, making them the first unofficial settlers

1851 Puerto Vallarta founded, under the name Las Peñas de Santa María de Guadalupe, by the salt merchant Guadalupe Sánchez

1918 The small but growing seaside town becomes county seat and is renamed Puerto Vallarta in honor of former Jalisco State governor Ignacio Luis Vallarta (1871–75)

1922 Yellow fever kills some 150 people

1925 Flood and landslides during a great storm form narrow Cuale Island in the middle of the Cuale River in downtown PV

1931 Puerto Vallarta gets electricity (7–10 PM only)

1951 Reporters covering centennial celebrations—marked with a 21-gun naval salute and a wealthy wedding—capture the small-town charm, exposing this isolated coastal gem to their countrymen

1963 Hollywood film *The Night of the Iguana,* directed by John Huston and starring Richard Burton and Ava Gardner, puts PV on the world map, due to the much-publicized affair between Burton and Elizabeth Taylor (who was not in the movie) during the filming here

1970 Vallarta builds a new airport, and improves the electrical and highway systems for Richard Nixon's official visit with President Díaz Ordaz

2000 Census reports the city's population as 159,080

2005 Population rapidly increases to 220,368 in greater metropolitan area

2006 Ground is broken for the 385-slip luxury-yacht marina at La Cruz de Huanacaxtle, north of Bucerías, continuing the trend of converting quiet fishing villages into big-bucks vacation destinations

2007   The "Riviera Nayarit," referring to the real estate between San Blas and Nuevo Vallarta, is officially launched as a newly branded destination

2008   On May 31, Puerto Vallarta celebrates its 40th anniversary as a full-fledged city. Although Puerto Vallarta is largely unaffected, in 2008 gang-related violence escalates on both sides of the U.S.–Mexican border, with the fatality count reaching into the thousands by year's end.

2009   In April, U.S. President Barack Obama and Mexican President Felipe Calderon meet to discuss ways to curb gang violence on both sides of the border. Late April also sees outbreaks of H1N1 influenza (swine flu), with Mexico City as the epicenter. Health clubs, nightclubs, stadiums, and many businesses in the Distrito Federal and elsewhere go dark for days, and several international air carriers temporarily suspend service in an effort to prevent the spread of the virus.

BOOKS AND MOVIES

Books

Those interested in Mexican culture and society have a wealth of books from which to choose. *The Mexicans: A Personal Portrait of a People,* by Patrick Oster, is a brilliant nonfiction study of Mexican persona and personality. Like Patrick Oster, Alan Riding, author of *Distant Neighbors: A Portrait of the Mexicans,* was a journalist for many years in Mexico City whose insight, investigative journalism skills, and cogent writing skills produced an insightful look into the Mexican mind and culture.

Written by poet, essayist, and statesman Octavio Paz, *The Labyrinth of Solitude,* is classic, required reading for those who love Mexico or want to know it better. *The True Story of the Conquest of Mexico,* by Bernal Diaz de Castillo, is a fascinating account of the conquest by one of Cortés's own soldiers.

There are few recommended books specifically about Puerto Vallarta. These are available mainly in PV.

La Magia de Puerto Vallarta, by Marilú Suárez-Murias, is a bilingual (English and Spanish) coffee-table book discussing beaches, history, people, and places of Puerto Vallarta. The information is interesting, but the photographs are terribly grainy. For a lighthearted look at life in PV through the eyes of an expat, read *Puerto Vallarta on 49 Brain Cells a Day* and *Refried Brains,* both by Gil Gevins. Along these same lines is *Gringos in Paradise,* by Barry Golson, which evolved out of an assignment for AARP magazine and provides a lighthearted look at building the author's dream house in Sayulita, Nayarit. Those interested in Huichol art and culture might read *People of the Peyote: Huichol Indian History, Religion and Survival,* by Stacy Shaefer and Peter Furst. If you can get past the first couple of chapters, it's smoother sailing. Also by Stacy Shaefer is *To Think With a Good Heart: Wixarica Women, Weavers and Shamans.*

Movies

The Night of the Iguana (1964), directed by John Huston, is the movie that alerted the world to Puerto Vallarta's existence. Set on the beach and bluffs of Mismaloya, the haunting movie with the jungle-beat soundtrack combines great directing with an excellent cast: Richard Burton as a cast-out preacher-turned-tour-guide, Sue Lyons and Deborah Kerr as his clients, and Ava Gardner as the sexy but lonely proprietress of the group's idyllic Mexican getaway. There's no better mood-setter for a trip to Vallarta.

Like Water for Chocolate (Como Agua Para Chocolate) (1992) is a magic-realism glance into rural Mexico during the Mexican Revolution. This visual banquet will make your mouth water for the rose-petal quail and other recipes that the female lead, Tita, prepares. It's based on the novel of the same name by Laura Esquivel, which is equally wonderful. Academy Award winner *The Treasure of the Sierra Madre* (1948), with Humphrey Bogart, is a classic with great mountain scenery. For more fantastic scenery and a great town fiesta, see *The Magnificent Seven* (1960), starring Yul Brynner and Eli Wallach. Set in Mexico City with Pierce Brosnan as a failing hit man, *The Matador* (2005) has some good scenes of the Camino Real in Mexico City, a great bullfighting sequence, and is a good drama.

SPANISH VOCABULARY

	ENGLISH	SPANISH	PRONUNCIATION
BASICS			
	Yes/no	Sí/no	see/no
	Please	Por favor	pore fah-**vore**
	May I?	¿Me permite?	may pair-**mee**-tay
	Thank you (very much)	(Muchas) gracias	(**moo**-chas) **grah**-see-as
	You're welcome	De nada	day **nah**-dah
	Excuse me	Con permiso	con pair-**mee**-so
	Pardon me	¿Perdón?	pair-**dohn**
	Could you tell me?	¿Podría decirme?	po-dree-ah deh-**seer**-meh
	I'm sorry	Lo siento	lo see-**en**-toh
	Good morning!	¡Buenos días!	**bway**-nohs **dee**-ahs
	Good afternoon!	¡Buenas tardes!	**bway**-nahs **tar**-dess
	Good evening!	¡Buenas noches!	**bway**-nahs **no**-chess
	Good-bye!	¡Adiós!/¡Hasta luego!	ah-dee-**ohss/ah** -stah **lwe**-go
	Mr./Mrs.	Señor/Señora	sen-**yor**/sen-**yohr**-ah
	Miss	Señorita	sen-yo-**ree**-tah
	Pleased to meet you	Mucho gusto	**moo**-cho **goose**-toh
	How are you?	¿Cómo está usted?	**ko**-mo es-**tah** oo-**sted**
	Very well, thank you.	Muy bien, gracias.	**moo**-ee bee-**en**, **grah**-see-as
	And you?	¿Y usted?	ee oos-**ted**
	Hello (on the telephone)	Diga	**dee**-gah
NUMBERS			
	1	un, uno	oon, **oo**-no
	2	dos	dos
	3	tres	tress
	4	cuatro	**kwah**-tro
	5	cinco	**sink**-oh

ENGLISH	SPANISH	PRONUNCIATION
6	seis	saice
7	siete	see-**et**-eh
8	ocho	**o**-cho
9	nueve	new-**eh**-vey
10	diez	dee-**es**
11	once	**ohn**-seh
12	doce	**doh**-seh
13	trece	**treh**-seh
14	catorce	ka-**tohr**-seh
15	quince	**keen**-seh
16	dieciséis	dee-**es**-ee-**saice**
17	diecisiete	dee-**es**-ee-see-**et**-eh
18	dieciocho	dee-**es**-ee-**o**-cho
19	diecinueve	**dee**-es-ee-new-**ev**-eh
20	veinte	**vain**-teh
21	veinte y uno/ veintiuno	**vain**-te-**oo**-noh
30	treinta	**train**-tah
32	treinta y dos	train-tay-**dohs**
40	cuarenta	kwah-**ren**-tah
43	cuarenta y tres	kwah-**ren**-tay-**tress**
50	cincuenta	seen-**kwen**-tah
54	cincuenta y cuatro	seen-**kwen**-tay **kwah**-tro
60	sesenta	sess-**en**-tah
65	sesenta y cinco	sess-**en**-tay **seen**-ko
70	setenta	set-**en**-tah
76	setenta y seis	set-**en**-tay **saice**
80	ochenta	oh-**chen**-tah
87	ochenta y siete	oh-**chen**-tay see-**yet**-eh
90	noventa	no-**ven**-tah

ENGLISH	SPANISH	PRONUNCIATION
98	noventa y ocho	no-**ven**-tah-o-choh
100	cien	see-**en**
101	ciento uno	see-**en**-toh **oo**-noh
200	doscientos	doh-see-**en**-tohss
500	quinientos	keen-**yen**-tohss
700	setecientos	set-eh-see-**en**-tohss
900	novecientos	no-veh-see-**en**-tohss
1,000	mil	meel
2,000	dos mil	dohs meel
1,000,000	un millón	oon meel-**yohn**

COLORS

black	negro	**neh**-groh
blue	azul	ah-**sool**
brown	café	kah-**feh**
green	verde	**ver**-deh
pink	rosa	**ro**-sah
purple	morado	mo-**rah**-doh
orange	naranja	na-**rahn**-hah
red	rojo	**roh**-hoh
white	blanco	**blahn**-koh
yellow	amarillo	ah-mah-**ree**-yoh

DAYS OF THE WEEK

Sunday	domingo	doe-**meen**-goh
Monday	lunes	**loo**-ness
Tuesday	martes	**mahr**-tess
Wednesday	miércoles	me-**air**-koh-less
Thursday	jueves	hoo-**ev**-ess
Friday	viernes	vee-**air**-ness
Saturday	sábado	**sah**-bah-doh

	ENGLISH	SPANISH	PRONUNCIATION
MONTHS			
	January	enero	eh-**neh**-roh
	February	febrero	feh-**breh**-roh
	March	marzo	**mahr**-soh
	April	abril	ah-**breel**
	May	mayo	**my**-oh
	June	junio	**hoo**-nee-oh
	July	julio	**hoo**-lee-yoh
	August	agosto	ah-**ghost**-toh
	September	septiembre	sep-tee-**em**-breh
	October	octubre	oak-**too**-breh
	November	noviembre	no-vee-**em**-breh
	December	diciembre	dee-see-**em**-breh
USEFUL PHRASES			
	Do you speak English?	¿Habla usted inglés?	**ah**-blah oos-**ted** in-**glehs**
	I don't speak Spanish	No hablo español	no **ah**-bloh es-pahn-**yol**
	I don't understand (you)	No entiendo	no en-tee-**en**-doh
	I understand (you)	Entiendo	en-tee-**en**-doh
	I don't know	No sé	no seh
	I am American/ British	Soy americano (americana)/ inglés(a)	soy ah-meh-ree- **kah**-no (ah-meh-ree- **kah**-nah)/in-**glehs(ah)**
	What's your name?	¿Cómo se llama usted?	koh-mo seh **yah**-mah oos-**ted**
	My name is . . .	Me llamo . . .	may **yah**-moh
	What time is it?	¿Qué hora es?	keh **o**-rah es
	It is one, two, three . . . o'clock.	Es la una./Son las dos, tres . . .	es la **oo**-nah/sohnahs dohs, tress
	Yes, please/No, thank you	Sí, por favor/ No, gracias	**see** pohr fah-**vor**/no **grah**-see-us
	How?	¿Cómo?	**koh**-mo

ENGLISH	SPANISH	PRONUNCIATION
When?	¿Cuándo?	**kwahn**-doh
This/Next week	Esta semana/ la semana que entra	**es**-teh seh-**mah**- nah/ lah seh-**mah**-nah keh **en**-trah
This/Next month	Este mes/el próximo mes	**es**-teh mehs/el **proke**-see-mo mehs
This/Next year	Este año/el año que viene	**es**-teh **ahn**-yo/el **ahn**-yo keh vee-**yen**-ay
Yesterday/today/ tomorrow	Ayer/hoy/mañana	ah-**yehr**/oy/mahn-**yah**-nah
This morning/ afternoon	Esta mañana/ tarde	**es**-tah mahn-**yah**- nah/ **tar**-deh
Tonight	Esta noche	**es**-tah **no**-cheh
What?	¿Qué?	keh
What is it?	¿Qué es esto?	keh es **es**-toh
Why?	¿Por qué?	pore **keh**
Who?	¿Quién?	kee-**yen**
Where is . . . ?	¿Dónde está . . . ?	**dohn**-deh es-**tah**
the train station?	la estación del tren?	la es-tah-see-on del trehn
the subway station?	la estación del tren subterráneo?	la es-ta-see-**on** del trehn la es-ta-see-**on** soob-teh-**rrahn**-eh-oh
the bus stop?	la parada del autobus?	la pah-**rah**-dah del ow-toh-**boos**
the post office?	la oficina de correos?	la oh-fee-**see**- nah deh koh-**rreh**-os
the bank?	el banco?	el **bahn**-koh
the hotel?	el hotel?	el oh-**tel**
the store?	la tienda?	la tee-**en**-dah
the cashier?	la caja?	la **kah**-hah
the museum?	el museo?	el moo-**seh**-oh
the hospital?	el hospital?	el ohss-pee-**tal**
the elevator?	el ascensor?	el ah-**sen**-sohr
the bathroom?	el baño?	el **bahn**-yoh

ENGLISH	SPANISH	PRONUNCIATION
Here/there	Aquí/allá	ah-**key**/ah-**yah**
Open/closed	Abierto/cerrado	ah-bee-**er**-toh/ ser-**ah**-doh
Left/right	Izquierda/derecha	iss-key-**er**-dah/ dare-**eh**-chah
Straight ahead	Derecho	dare-**eh**-choh
Is it near/far?	¿Está cerca/lejos?	es-**tah sehr**-kah/ **leh**-hoss
I'd like . . .	Quisiera . . .	kee-see-ehr-ah
a room	un cuarto/una habitación	oon **kwahr**-toh/ **oo**-nah ah-bee- tah-see-**on**
the key	la llave	lah **yah**-veh
a newspaper	un periódico	oon pehr-ee-**oh**- dee-koh
a stamp	un sello de correo	oon **seh**-yo deh korr-ee-oh
I'd like to buy . . .	Quisiera comprar . . .	kee-see-**ehr**-ah kohm-**prahr**
cigarettes	cigarrillos	ce-ga-**ree**-yohs
matches	cerillos	ser-**ee**-ohs
a dictionary	un diccionario	oon deek-see-oh- **nah**-ree-oh
soap	jabón	hah-**bohn**
sunglasses	gafas de sol	**ga**-fahs deh sohl
suntan lotion	Loción bronceadora	loh-see-**ohn** brohn- seh-ah-**do**-rah
a map	un mapa	oon **mah**-pah
a magazine	una revista	**oon**-ah reh-**veess**-tah
paper	papel	pah-**pel**
envelopes	sobres	**so**-brehs
a postcard	una tarjeta postal	**oon**-ah tar-**het**-ah post-**ahl**
How much is it?	¿Cuánto cuesta?	**kwahn**-toh **kwes**-tah
It's expensive/ cheap	Está caro/barato	es-**tah kah**-roh/ bah-**rah**-toh

ENGLISH	SPANISH	PRONUNCIATION
A little/a lot	Un poquito/ mucho	oon poh-**kee**-toh/ **moo**-choh
More/less	Más/menos	mahss/**men**-ohss
Enough/too much/too little	Suficiente/ demasiado/ muy poco	soo-fee-see-**en**-teh/ deh-mah-see-**ah**- doh/ **moo**-ee **poh**-koh
Telephone	Teléfono	tel-**ef**-oh-no
Telegram	Telegrama	teh-leh-**grah**-mah
I am ill	Estoy enfermo(a)	es-**toy** en-**fehr**- moh(mah)
Please call a doctor	Por favor llame a un medico	pohr fah-**vor ya**-meh ah oon **med**-ee-koh

ON THE ROAD

Avenue	Avenida	ah-ven-**ee**-dah
Broad, tree-lined boulevard	Bulevar	boo-leh-**var**
Fertile plain	Vega	**veh**-gah
Highway	Carretera	car-reh-**ter**-ah
Mountain pass	Puerto	poo-**ehr**-toh
Street	Calle	**cah**-yeh
Waterfront promenade	Rambla	**rahm**-blah
Wharf	Embarcadero	em-bar-cah-**deh**-ro

IN TOWN

Cathedral	Catedral	cah-teh-**dral**
Church	Templo/Iglesia	**tem**-plo/ ee-**glehs**- see-ah
City hall	Casa de gobierno	kah-sah deh go-bee-**ehr**-no
Door, gate	Puerta portón	poo-**ehr**-tah por-**ton**
Entrance/exit	Entrada/salida	en-**trah**-dah/sah-**lee**- dah
Inn, rustic bar, or restaurant	Taverna	tah-**vehr**-nah

ENGLISH	SPANISH	PRONUNCIATION
Main square	Plaza principal	plah-thah prin- see-**pahl**

DINING OUT

Can you recommend a good restaurant?	¿Puede recomendarme un buen restaurante?	**pweh**-deh rreh-koh-mehn-**dahr**-me oon bwehn rrehs-tow- **rahn**-teh?
Where is it located?	¿Dónde está situado?	**dohn**-deh ehs-**tah** see-**twah**-doh?
Do I need reservations?	¿Se necesita una reservación?	seh neh-seh-**see**-tah **oo**-nah rreh-sehr- bah-**syohn**?
I'd like to reserve a table . . .	Quisiera reservar una mesa . . .	kee-**syeh**-rah rreh-sehr-**bahr oo**-nah **meh**-sah . . .
for two people.	para dos personas.	**pah**-rah dohs pehr- **soh**-nahs
for this evening.	para esta noche.	**pah**-rah **ehs**-tah **noh**-cheh
for 8 PM	para las ocho de la noche.	**pah**-rah lahs **oh**-choh deh lah **noh**-cheh
A bottle of . . .	Una botella de . . .	**oo**-nah bo-**teh**-yah deh
A cup of . . .	Una taza de . . .	**oo**-nah **tah**-thah deh
A glass of . . .	Un vaso de . . .	oon **vah**-so deh
Ashtray	Un cenicero	oon sen-ee-**seh**-roh
Bill/check	La cuenta	lah **kwen**-tah
Bread	El pan	el pahn
Breakfast	El desayuno	el deh-sah-**yoon**-oh
Butter	La mantequilla	lah man-teh-**key**-yah
Cheers!	¡Salud!	sah-**lood**
Cocktail	Un aperitivo	oon ah-pehr-ee-**tee**-voh
Dinner	La cena	lah **seh**-nah
Dish	Un plato	oon **plah**-toh
Menu of the day	Menú del día	meh-**noo** del **dee**-ah
Enjoy!	¡Buen provecho!	bwehn pro-**veh**-cho

ENGLISH	SPANISH	PRONUNCIATION
Fixed-price menu	Menú fijo o turistico	meh-**noo fee**-hoh oh too-**ree**-stee-coh
Fork	El tenedor	el ten-eh-**dor**
Is the tip included?	¿Está incluida la propina?	es-**tah** in-cloo-**ee**-dah lah pro-**pee**-nah
Knife	El cuchillo	el koo-**chee**-yo
Large portion of savory snacks	Raciónes	rah-see-**oh**-nehs
Lunch	La comida	lah koh-**mee**-dah
Menu	La carta, el menú	lah **cart**-ah, el meh-**noo**
Napkin	La servilleta	lah sehr-vee-**yet**-ah
Pepper	La pimienta	lah pee-me-**en**-tah
Please give me	Por favor déme	pore fah-**vor deh**-meh
Salt	La sal	lah sahl
Savory snacks	Tapas	**tah**-pahs
Spoon	Una cuchara	**oo**-nah koo-**chah**-rah
Sugar	El azúcar	el ah-**thu**-kar
Waiter!/Waitress!	¡Por favor Señor/ Señorita!	pohr fah-**vor** sen- **yor**/ sen-yor-**ee**-tah

Travel Smart
Puerto Vallarta

WORD OF MOUTH

"Here's a tip for Puerto Vallarta. You can't walk five feet without someone trying to sell you a timeshare or get you to attend a sales pitch. . . . We prefer not to be bugged and our (Mexican native) friend suggests the best way is to ask the first couple of salesmen who approach you for a brochure. Stick the brochures in your shirt pocket so they're noticable. After you have a small collection, people will stop bugging you."

—bdjtbensen

GETTING HERE & AROUND

▌ BY AIR

Flights with stopovers in Mexico City tend to take the entire day. There are nonstop flights from a few U.S. cities, including Los Angeles (Alaska Air), San Francisco (United), Seattle (Alaska Air), Phoenix (US Airways), Houston (Continental), Dallas (American), Denver (Frontier Air, United), and Kansas City, Missouri (Frontier Air).

Air Canada has nonstop flights from Toronto, and connecting flights (via Toronto) from all major cities. Web-based Volaris is a Tijuana-based airline with reasonable fares. It flies to Colima (near the Costalegre), Tepic in Nayarit, and Guadalajara. You can fly to Manzanillo, just south of the Costalegre, via many airlines with a stop in Mexico City.

If you plan to include Guadalajara in your itinerary, consider an open-jaw flight to Puerto Vallarta with a return from Guadalajara (or vice versa). There's almost no difference in price when you fly a Mexican airline like Aeromexico, even when factoring in bus fare; sometimes the open jaw is even cheaper.

Flying times are about 2¾ hours from Houston, 3 hours from Los Angeles, 3½ hours from Denver, 4 hours from Chicago, and 8 hours from New York.

Airline and Airport Links Airline and Airport Links.com (⊕ *www.airlineandairportlinks. com*).

Airlines Aeroméxico (☎ *800/237–6639 in U.S. and Canada, 01800/021–4010 in Mexico, 322/221–1204 in PV* ⊕ *www.aeromexico.com*). **Air Canada** (☎ *888/247–2262 in Canada and U.S., 322/221–1823 in PV* ⊕ *www.aircanada. com*). **Alaska Airlines** (☎ *800/252–7522, 01800/426–0333 in Mexico, 322/221–1350 in PV* ⊕ *www.alaskaair.com*). **American Airlines** (☎ *800/433–7300, 800/904–6000 in Mexico, 322/221–1799 in PV* ⊕ *www.aa.com*).

Continental Airlines (☎ *800/523–3273 for U.S. and Mexico reservations, 800/900–5000 in Mexico, 322/221–1025 in PV* ⊕ *www.con tinental.com*). **Frontier** (☎ *800/432–1359 in U.S.* ⊕ *www.frontierairlines.com*). **Mexicana** (☎ *800/531–7921 in U.S., 866/281–3049 in Canada, 01800/801–2010 in Mexico, 322/221–1823 in PV* ⊕ *www.mexicana. com*). **US Airways** (☎ *800/428–4322 in U.S., 322/221–1333 in PV* ⊕ *www.usairways.com*). **Volaris** (☎ *No phone* ⊕ *www.volaris.com.mx*).

Airline Security Issues Transportation Security Administration (⊕ *www.tsa.gov*).

AIRPORTS

The main gateway, and where many PV-bound travelers change planes, is Mexico City's large, modern Aeropuerto Internacional Benito Juárez (airport code: MEX), infamous for pickpocketing and taxi scams; watch your stuff.

Puerto Vallarta's small international Aeropuerto Internacional Gustavo Díaz Ordáz (PVR) is 7½ km (4½ mi) north of downtown.

Airport Information Aeropuerto Internacional Benito Juárez (*MEX* ⊕ *www.aicm.com. mx*). **Aeropuerto Internacional Gustavo Díaz Ordáz** (*PVR* ☎ *322/221–1298* ⊕ *vallarta.aero puertosgap.com.mx*).

GROUND TRANSPORTATION

Vans provide transportation from the airport to PV hotels; there's a zone system with different prices for the Zona Hotelera (Hotel Zone), downtown PV, and so on. Outside the luggage collection area, vendors shout for your attention. It's a confusing scene. Purchase the taxi vouchers sold at the stands inside the terminal, and be sure to avoid the time-share vendors who trap you in their vans for a high-pressure sales pitch en route to your hotel. Avoid drivers who approach you, and head for an official taxi kiosk, which will have zone information clearly posted.

As in any busy airport, don't leave your luggage unattended for any reason.

Before you purchase your ticket, look for a taxi-zone map (it should be posted on or by the ticket stand), and make sure your taxi ticket is properly zoned; if you need a ticket only to Zone 3, don't pay for a ticket to Zone 4 or 5. Taxis or vans to the Costalegre resorts between PV and Manzanillo are generally arranged through the resort. If not, taxis charge about 200 pesos an hour—more if you're traveling beyond Jalisco State lines.

▌BY BUS

LONG-DISTANCE SERVICE

PV's Central Camionero, or Central Bus Station, is 1 km (½ mi) north of the airport, halfway between Nuevo Vallarta and downtown.

First-class Mexican buses (known as *primera clase*) are generally timely and comfortable, air-conditioned coaches with bathrooms, movies, and reclining seats—sometimes with seat belts. Deluxe (*de lujo* or *ejecutivo*) buses offer the same and usually have refreshments. Second-class (*segunda clase)* buses are used mainly for travel to smaller, secondary destinations.

A lower-class bus ride can be interesting if you're not in a hurry and want to experience local culture; these buses make frequent stops and keep less strictly to their timetables. Often they will wait until they fill up to leave, regardless of the scheduled time of departure. Fares are up to 15%–30% cheaper than first-class buses. The days of pigs and chickens among your bus mates are largely in the past. ▐TIP→ Unless you're writing a novel or your memoir, there's no reason to ride a second-class bus if a first-class or better is available. Daytime trips are safer.

Bring snacks, socks, and a sweater—the air-conditioning on first-class buses is often set on high—and toilet paper, as restrooms might not have any. Smoking is prohibited on all buses.

Estrella Blanca goes from Mexico City to Manzanillo, Mazatlán, Monterrey, Nuevo Laredo, and other central, Pacific coast, and northern-border points. ETN has the most luxurious service—with exclusively first-class buses that have roomy, totally reclining seats—to Guadalajara, Mexico City, Barra de Navidad, Chamela, and Manzanillo. Primera Plus connects Mexico City with Manzanillo and Puerto Vallarta along with other central and western cities.

TAP serves Mexico City, Guadalajara, Puerto Vallarta, Tepic, and Mazatlán. Basic service, including some buses with marginal or no air-conditioning, is the norm on Transportes Cihuatlán, which connects the Bahía de Banderas and PV with southern Jalisco towns such as Barra de Navidad.

You can buy tickets for first-class or better in advance; this is advisable during peak periods, although the most popular routes have buses on the hour. You can make reservations for many, though not all, of the first-class bus lines, through the Ticketbus central reservations agency. Rates average 40–67 pesos per hour of travel, depending on the level of luxury. Plan to pay in pesos, although most of the deluxe bus services accept Visa and MasterCard.

Bus Contacts Central Camionero (✉ *Puerto Vallarta–Tepic Hwy., Km 9, Las Mojoneras*). **Estrella Blanca** (☎ *01800/507–5500 toll-free in Mexico, 322/290–1001 in Puerto Vallarta* ⊕ *www.estrellablanca. mx*). **ETN** (☎ *01800/800–0386 toll-free in Mexico, 322/290–0996, 322/290–0997 in PV* ⊕ *www.etn.com.mx*). **Primera Plus** (☎ *322/290–0715 in PV*). **Transportes Cihuatlán** (☎ *322/290–0994 in PV*). **Transporte del Pacifico (TAP)** (☎ *322/290–0119, 322/290–0993 in PV*).

CITY BUSES

City buses (5.5 pesos) serve downtown, the Zona Hotelera Norte, and Marina Vallarta. Bus stops—marked by blue-and-white signs—are every two or three long blocks along the highway (Carretera Aeropuerto) and in downtown Puerto Vallarta. Green buses to Playa Mismaloya and Boca de Tomatlán (6 pesos) run about every 15 minutes from the corner of Avenida Insurgentes and Basilio Badillo downtown.

Gray ATM buses serving Nuevo Vallarta and Bucerías (20 pesos), Punta Mita (30 pesos), and Sayulita (50 pesos) depart from just two places: Plaza las Glorias, in front of the HSBC bank, and Wal-Mart, both of which are along Carretera Aeropuerto between downtown and the Zona Hotelera.

■ TIP➜ It's rare for inspectors to check tickets, but just when you've let yours flutter to the floor, a figure of authority is bound to appear. So hang on to your ticket and hat: PV bus drivers race from one stoplight to the next in jerky bursts of speed.

There's no problem with theft on city buses aside from perhaps an occasional pickpocket that might be at work anywhere in the world.

■ BY CAR

From December through April—peak season—traffic clogs the narrow downtown streets, and negotiating the steep hills in Old Vallarta (sometimes you have to drive in reverse to let another car pass) can be frightening. Avoid rush hour (7–9 AM and 6–8 PM) and when schools let out (2–3 PM). Travel with a companion and a good road map or atlas. Always lock your car, and never leave valuable items in the body of the car. The trunk is generally safe, although any thief can crack one open if he chooses.

■ TIP➜ It's absolutely essential that you carry Mexican auto insurance for liability, even if you have full coverage for collision,

damages, and theft. If you injure anyone in an accident, you could well be jailed—whether it was your fault or not—unless you have insurance.

GASOLINE

Pemex (the government petroleum monopoly) franchises all of Mexico's gas stations, which you can find at most junctions and in cities and towns. Gas is measured in liters, and stations usually don't accept U.S. or Canadian credit cards or dollars, but this is beginning to change.

Premium unleaded gas (called *premium,* the red pump) and regular unleaded gas (*magna,* the green pump) are available nationwide, but it's still best to fill up whenever you can and not let your tank get below half full. Fuel quality is generally lower than that in the United States, but it has improved enough so that your car will run acceptably. At this writing gas is about 7.5 pesos per liter (about $2.18 per gallon) for the cheap stuff and 10 pesos per liter ($2.91 per gallon) for super. Some people bring fuel additive and add every third tank or so.

Attendants pump the gas for you and may also wash your windshield and check your oil and tire air pressure. A small tip is customary (from just a few pesos for pumping the gas only to 5 or 10 for the whole enchilada of services). Keep an eye on the gas meter to make sure the attendant is starting it at "0" and that you're charged the correct price.

PARKING

A circle with a diagonal line superimposed on the letter *E* (for *estacionamiento*) means "no parking." Illegally parked cars are usually towed or have wheel blocks placed on the tires, which can require a trip to the traffic-police headquarters for payment of a fine.

When in doubt, park in a lot rather than on the street; your car will probably be safer there anyway. There are parking lots in PV at Parque Hidalgo (Av. México at Langarica, Col. 5 de Diciembre), in El

Centro (at Av. Juárez at Calle 31 de Octubre and another at Leona Vicario), just north of the Cuale River at the malecón and Calle A. Rodríguez, and in the Zona Romántica at Parque Lázaro Cárdenas. Fees are reasonable—as little as $4 for a day up to $1 or more an hour, depending on where you are. Sometimes you park your own car; more often, you hand the keys to an attendant.

ROAD CONDITIONS

Several well-kept toll roads head into and out of major cities like Guadalajara—most of them four lanes wide. However, these *carreteras* (major highways) don't go too far into the countryside. *Cuota* means toll road; *libre* means no toll, and such roads are often two lanes and not as well-maintained. A new 21-mi highway between Tepic and San Blas will shorten driving time to about 20 minutes.

Roads leading to, or in, Nayarit and Jalisco include highways connecting Nogales and Mazatlán; Guadalajara and Tepic; and Mexico City, Morelia, and Guadalajara. Tolls between Guadalajara to Puerto Vallarta (207 mi/334 km) total about $25.

In rural areas roads are sometimes poor; other times the two-lane, blacktop roads are perfectly fine. Be extra cautious during the rainy season, when rock slides and potholes are a problem.

Watch out for animals, especially untethered horses, cattle, and dogs, and for dangerous, unrailed curves. *Topes* (speed bumps) are ubiquitous; slow down when approaching any town or village and look for signs saying TOPES or VIBRADORES. Police officers often issue tickets to those speeding through populated areas.

Generally, driving times are longer than for comparable distances in the United States and Canada. Allow extra time for unforeseen occurrences as well as for traffic, particularly truck traffic.

ROADSIDE EMERGENCIES

To help motorists on major highways, the Mexican Tourism Ministry operates a fleet of more than 250 pickup trucks, known as the Angeles Verdes, or Green Angels, reachable by phone throughout Mexico by dialing 078 or, in some areas near Puerto Vallarta, 066. The bilingual drivers provide mechanical help, first aid, radio-telephone communication, basic supplies and small parts, towing, tourist information, and protection.

Services are free, and spare parts, fuel, and lubricants are provided at cost. Tips are always appreciated (figure a minimum of $5–$10 for big jobs and $3–$5 for minor stuff). The Green Angels patrol the major highways twice daily 8–8 (usually later on holiday weekends). If you break down, pull off the road as far as possible, lift the hood of your car. If you don't have a cell phone, hail a passing vehicle and ask the driver to notify the patrol. Most drivers will be quite helpful.

Emergency Services Angeles Verdes (☎ *078*).

RULES OF THE ROAD

When you sign up for Mexican car insurance, you may receive a booklet on Mexican rules of the road. It really is a good idea to read it to familiarize yourself with not only laws but also customs that differ from those of your home country. For instance: if an oncoming vehicle flicks its lights at you in daytime, slow down: it could mean trouble ahead; when approaching a narrow bridge, the first vehicle to flash its lights has right of way; right on red is not allowed; one-way traffic is indicated by an arrow; two-way, by a double-pointed arrow. (Other road signs follow the widespread system of international symbols.)

⚠ **On the highway, using your left turn signal to turn left is dangerous. Mexican drivers—especially truck drivers—use their left turn signal on the highway to signal the vehicle behind that it's safe to pass. Conversely they rarely use their signal** to actually make a turn. Foreigners signaling a left turn off the highway into a driveway or onto a side road have been killed by cars or trucks behind that mistook their turn signal for a signal to pass. To turn left from a highway when cars are behind you, it's best to pull over to the right and make the left turn when no cars are approaching, to avoid disaster.

Mileage and speed limits are given in kilometers: 100 kph and 80 kph (62 mph and 50 mph, respectively) are the most common maximums on the highway. A few of the toll roads allow 110 kph (68 mph). However, speed limits can change from curve to curve, so watch the signs carefully. In cities and small towns, observe the posted speed limits, which can be as low as 20 kph (12 mph).

Seat belts are required by law throughout Mexico. Drunk driving laws are fairly harsh in Mexico, and if you're caught you may go to jail immediately. It's difficult to say what the blood-alcohol limit is since everyone we asked gave a different answer, which means each case is probably handled in a discretionary manner. The best way to avoid any problems is simply to not drink and drive.

If you're stopped for speeding, the officer is supposed to take your license and hold it until you pay the fine at the local police station. But the officer will usually prefer a *mordida* (small bribe). Just take out a couple hundred pesos, hold it out discreetly while asking politely if the officer can "pay the fine for you." Conversely, a few cops might resent the offer of a bribe, but it's still common practice.

If you decide to dispute a charge that seems preposterous, do so with a smile, and tell the officer that you would like to talk to the police captain when you get to the station. The officer usually will let you go rather than go to the station.

SAFETY ON THE ROAD
Never drive at night in remote and rural areas. *Bandidos* are one concern, but so

are potholes, free-roaming animals, cars with no working lights, road-hogging trucks, drunk drivers, and difficulty in getting assistance. It's best to use toll roads whenever possible; although costly, they're safer, too.

Off the highway, driving in Mexico can be nerve-wracking for novices, with people sometimes paying little attention to marked lanes. Most drivers pay attention to safety rules, but be vigilant. Drunk driving skyrockets on holiday weekends.

A police officer may pull you over for something you didn't do; unfortunately a common scam. If you're pulled over for any reason, be polite—displays of anger will only make matters worse. Although efforts are being made to fight corruption, it's still a fact of life in Mexico, and for many people, it's worth the $10 to $100 it costs to get their license back to be on their way quickly. (The amount requested varies depending on what the officer assumes you can pay—the year, make, and model of the car you drive being one determining factor.) Others persevere long enough to be let off with a warning only. The key to success, in this case, is a combination of calm and patience.

RENTAL CARS
Mexico manufactures Chrysler, Ford, General Motors, Honda, Nissan, and Volkswagen vehicles. With the exception of Volkswagen, you can get the same kind of midsize and luxury cars in Mexico that you can rent in the United States and Canada. Economy usually refers to a Volkswagen Beetle or a Chevy Aveo or Joy, which may or may not come with air-conditioning or automatic transmission.

It can really pay to shop around: in Puerto Vallarta, rates for a compact car with air-conditioning, manual transmission, and unlimited mileage range from $18 a day and $120 a week to $50 or even $60 a day and $300–$400 a week. Full-coverage insurance varies greatly depending on whether it includes a deductible, but averages $25 a day. As a rule, stick with the major companies because they tend to be more reliable.

You can also hire a car with a driver (who generally doubles as a tour guide) through your hotel. The going rate is about $20 an hour within town. Limousine service runs about $65 an hour and up, with a three- to five-hour minimum.

In Mexico the minimum driving age is 18, but most rental-car agencies have a surcharge for drivers under 25. Your own country's driver's license is perfectly acceptable.

Surcharges for additional drivers are around $5 per day plus tax. Children's car seats run about the same, but not all companies have them.

CAR-RENTAL INSURANCE
You must carry Mexican auto insurance, at the very least liability as well coverage against physical damage to the vehicle and theft at your discretion, depending on what, if anything, your own auto insurance (or credit card, if you use it to rent a car) includes. For rental cars, all insurance will all be dealt with through the rental company.

Major Rental Agencies Alamo
(☎ 800/522–9696 ⊕ www.alamo.com).
Avis (☎ 800/331–1084 ⊕ www.avis.com).
Budget (☎ 800/472–3325 ⊕ www.budget.com). **Hertz** (☎ 800/654–3001 ⊕ www.hertz.com). **National Car Rental** (☎ 800/227–7368 ⊕ www.nationalcar.com).

▌ BY TAXI

PV taxis aren't metered, and instead charge by zones. Most of the larger hotels have rate sheets, and taxi drivers should produce them upon request. Tipping isn't necessary unless the driver helps you with your bags, in which case a few pesos are appropriate.

The minimum fare is 40 pesos (about $3), but if you don't ask, you'll probably be overcharged. Negotiate a price in advance for out-of-town and hourly services as well; many drivers will start by asking how much you want to pay or how much others have charged you to get a sense of your street-smarts. The usual hourly rate at this writing is $19 (200 pesos) per hour. In all cases, if you are unsure of what a fare should be, ask your hotel's front-desk personnel.

The ride from downtown to the airport or to Marina Vallarta costs about $8, it's $17 to Nuevo Vallarta, and $22 to Bucerías. From downtown south to Mismaloya it's about $4 to Conchas Chinas, $8 to $10 to the hotels of the Zona Hotelera, $10 to Mismaloya, and $14 to Boca de Tomatlán. You can easily hail a cab on the street. Radio Taxi PV provides 24-hour service.

Taxi Company Radio Taxi PV
(☎ 322/225–0716).

ESSENTIALS

■ COMMUNICATIONS

INTERNET

Internet cafés have sprung up all over Puerto Vallarta and even small surrounding towns and villages, making e-mail by far the easiest way to get in touch with people back home. At PV Café you can enjoy a sandwich or a salad and coffee while downloading digital photos, sending a fax, or surfing the Web (30 pesos per hour).

At less comfortable PV Net (computers lower than eye level promote slouching), which is open 24 hours a day, 365 days a year, you obtain an access code and use your minutes each time you visit. The cost for Internet access is 25 pesos per hour; there's also a room at the back for the kids and teens. For laptop connections you can pay by the day, week, or month.

If you're bringing a laptop with you, check with the manufacturer's technical support line to see what service and/or repair affiliates it has in the areas you plan to visit. Carry a spare battery to save yourself the expense and headache of having to hunt down a replacement on the spot. Memory sticks and other accessories are usually more expensive in Mexico than in the United States or Europe, but are available in megastores such as Sam's Club and Office Depot as well as mom-and-pop computer shops.

The younger generation of Mexicans are computer savvy and there are some excellent repair wizards and technicians to help you with problems; many are bilingual.

Contacts Cybercafes (⊕ *www.cybercafes. com*) lists more than 4,000 Internet cafés worldwide. **PV Café** (⊠ *Calle Olas Altas 246, Olas Altas* ☎ *322/222–0092*). **PV Net** (⊠ *Blvd. Francisco M. Ascencio 1692, across from Sheraton Buganvilias, Zona Hotelera Norte* ☎ *322/223–1127*).

PHONES

The area code for PV (and the northern Costalegre) and Nuevo Vallarta is 322; San Francisco has both 311 and 329 area codes, otherwise between Bucerías and San Francisco it's 329. Lo De Marcos and Rincón de Guayabitos: 327. The Costalegre from around Rancho Cuixmala to San Patricio–Melaque and Barra de Navidad has a 315 area code.

The country code for Mexico is 52. When calling a Mexico number from abroad, dial any necessary international access code, then the country code, and then all of the numbers listed for the entry. When calling a cell phone in Mexico from outside the country, dial 01152 (access and country codes) and then 1 and then the number.

Toll-free numbers in Mexico start with an 800 prefix. These numbers, however, are billed as local calls if you call one from a private phone. To reach them, you need to dial 01 before the number. In this guide, Mexico-only toll-free numbers appear as follows: 01800/123–4567. The toll-free numbers listed simply 800/123–4567 are U.S. or Canadian numbers, and generally work north of the border only (though some calling cards will allow you to dial them from Mexico, charging you minutes as for a toll call). Numbers listed as 001800/123–4567 are toll-free U.S. numbers; if you're calling from Mexico, you'll be charged for an international call.

INTERNATIONAL CALLS

To make an international call, dial 00 before the country code, area code, and number. The country code for the United States and Canada is 1. Avoid phones near tourist areas that advertise in English (e.g., "Call the U.S. or Canada here!"). They charge an outrageous fee per minute. If in doubt, dial the operator and ask for rates. AT&T, MCI, and Sprint calling cards are useful, although infrequently hotels block access to their service numbers.

CALLS WITHIN MEXICO

Directory assistance is 040 nationwide. For assistance in English, dial 090 first for an international operator; tell the operator in what city, state, and country you require directory assistance, and he or she will connect you.

A *caseta de larga distancia* is a long-distance/overseas telephone service usually operated out of a store such as a *papelería* (stationery store), pharmacy, restaurant, or other small business; look for the phone symbol on the door. Casetas may cost more to use than pay phones, but you tend to be shielded from street noise, as you get your own little booth. They also have the benefit of not forcing you to buy a prepaid phone card with a specific denomination—you pay in cash according to the calls you make. Tell the person on duty the number you'd like to call, and she or he will give you a rate and dial for you. Rates seem to vary widely, so shop around. Overall, they're higher than those of pay phones.

PHONE CARDS

Using a prepaid phone card is by far the most convenient way to call long distance within Mexico or abroad. Look for a phone *booth* away from traffic noise; these phones are tucked behind three sides of Plexiglas, but street noise can make hearing difficult. If you're calling long distance within Mexico, dial 01 before the area code and number. For local calls, just dial the seven-digit number; no other prefix is necessary. If calling abroad, buy the 100-peso card, the largest denomination available.

PAY PHONES

Most pay phones only accept prepaid cards, called Ladatel cards, sold in 30-, 50-, or 100-peso denominations at newsstands, pharmacies, or grocery stores. These Ladatel phones are all over the place—on street corners, in bus stations, and so on.

Older, coin-only pay phones are rarely encountered, those you do find are often broken or have poor connections. Still other phones have two unmarked slots, one for a Ladatel (a Spanish acronym for "long-distance direct dialing") card and the other for a credit card. These are primarily for Mexican bank cards, but some accept Visa or MasterCard, though *not* U.S. phone credit cards.

To use a Ladatel card, simply insert it in the appropriate slot with the computer chip insignia forward and right-side up, and dial. Credit is deleted from the card as you use it, and your balance is displayed on a small screen on the phone. You'll be charged about 3 pesos per minute for local calls, 4 pesos per minute for national long-distance, and 5 pesos for calls to the United States or Canada. Most pay phones display a price list and dialing instructions.

MOBILE PHONES

If you have a multiband phone (some countries use different frequencies from those used in the United States) and your service provider uses the world-standard GSM network (as do T-Mobile, Cingular, and Verizon), you can probably use your phone abroad. Roaming fees can be steep, however: 99 cents a minute is considered reasonable. And you normally pay the toll charges for incoming and outgoing calls. It's almost always cheaper to send a text message (or at least to receive one, which is sometimes substantially cheaper than to send).

If you just want to make local calls, consider buying a new SIM card (note that your provider may have to unlock your phone for you to use a different SIM card) and a prepaid service plan in the destination. You'll then have a local number and can make local calls at local rates. If your trip is extensive, you could also simply buy a new cell phone in your destination, as the initial cost will be offset over time.

■ **TIP →** **If you travel internationally frequently, save one of your old mobile phones or buy a cheap one on the Internet; ask your cell phone company to unlock it for you, and take it with you as a travel phone, buying a new SIM card with pay-as-you-go service in each destination.**

There are now companies that rent cell phones (with or without SIM cards) for the duration of your trip. You get the phone, charger, and carrying case in the mail and return them in the mailer. Daystar rents cell phones at $5 per day, with all incoming calls (national or international) at 33 cents a minute; outgoing cost 30 cents a minute to call within Mexico or $1.16 per minute to call the United States.

Contacts Daystar (☎ 888/908–4100 ⊕ www. daystarwireless.com).

■ CUSTOMS AND DUTIES

Upon entering Mexico, you'll be given a baggage declaration form and asked to itemize what you're bringing into the country. You are allowed to bring in 3 liters of spirits or wine for personal use; 400 cigarettes, 25 cigars, or 200 grams of tobacco; a reasonable amount of perfume for personal use; one video camera and one regular camera and 12 rolls of film for each; and gift items not to exceed a total of $300. If driving across the U.S. border, gift items shouldn't exceed $50, although foreigners aren't usually hassled about this. ⚠ **Although the much-publicized border violence doesn't affect travelers, it is real. To be safe don't linger long at the border.**

You aren't allowed to bring firearms, ammunition, meat, vegetables, plants, fruit, or flowers into the country. You can bring in one of each of the following items without paying taxes: a cell phone, a beeper, a radio or tape recorder, a musical instrument, a laptop computer, and

portable copier or printer. Compact discs and/or audio cassettes are limited to 20 total and DVDs to five.

Mexico also allows you to bring one cat or dog, if you have two things: (1) a pet health certificate signed by a registered veterinarian in the United States and issued not more than 72 hours before the animal enters Mexico; and (2) a pet vaccination certificate showing that the animal has been treated (as applicable) for rabies, hepatitis, distemper, and leptospirosis.

For more information or information on bringing other animals or more than one type of animal, contact the Mexican consulate, which has branches in many major American cities as well as border towns. To find the consulate nearest you, check the Ministry of Foreign Affairs Web site (go to the "Servicios Consulares" option).

Information in Mexico Mexican Embassy (☎ 202/728–1600 ⊕ www.embassyofmexico. org). **Ministry of Foreign Affairs** (⊕ portal.sre. gob.mx/eua).

U.S. Information U.S. Customs and Border Protection (⊕ www.cbp.gov).

■ ELECTRICITY

For U.S. and Canadian travelers, electrical converters aren't necessary because Mexico operates on the 60-cycle, 120-volt system; however, many Mexican outlets have not been updated to accommodate three-prong and polarized plugs (those with one larger prong), so to be safe bring an adapter.

Blackouts and brownouts—often lasting an hour or so—are not unheard of, particularly during the rainy season, so bring a surge protector.

Consider making a small investment in a universal adapter, which has several types of plugs in one lightweight, compact unit.

LOCAL DO'S AND TABOOS

CUSTOMS OF THE COUNTRY

In the United States and elsewhere in the world, being direct, efficient, and succinct is highly valued. But Mexican communication tends to be more subtle, and the direct style of Americans, Canadians, and Europeans is often perceived as curt and aggressive. Mexicans are extremely polite, so losing your temper over delays or complaining loudly will get you branded as rude and make people less inclined to help you. Remember that things move slowly here, and that there's little stigma attached to being late; be gracious about this and other local customs and attitudes.

You'll probably notice that local friends, relatives, and significant others show a fair amount of physical affection with each other, but you should be more retiring with people you don't know well.

GREETINGS

Learning basic phrases in Spanish such as "*por favor*" (please) and "*gracias*" (thank you) will make a big difference in how people respond to you. Also, being deferential to those who are older than you will earn you lots of points, as does addressing people as señor, señora, or señorita.

Also, saying "*Desculpe*" before asking a question of someone is a polite way of saying "Excuse me" before launching into a request for information or directions. Similarly, asking "*¿Habla inglés?*" is more polite than assuming every Mexican you meet speaks English.

SIGHTSEEING

In Puerto Vallarta, it is acceptable to wear shorts in houses of worship, but do avoid being blatantly immodest. Bathing suits and immodest clothing are also inappropriate for shopping and sightseeing in general. Mexican men don't generally wear shorts, even in extremely hot weather, although this rule is generally ignored by both Mexican and foreign men on vacation here and at other beach resorts.

OUT ON THE TOWN

Mexicans call waiters "*joven*" (literally, "young man") no matter how old they are (it's the equivalent of the word "maid" being used for the old woman who cleans rooms). Call a female waitress *señorita* ("miss") or *señora* ("ma'am"). Ask for "*la cuenta, por favor*" ("the check, please") when you want the bill; it's considered rude to bring it before the customer asks for it. Mexicans tend to dress nicely for a night out, but in tourist areas, dress codes are mainly upheld only at the more sophisticated discotheques. Some restaurants have separate smoking sections, but in smaller establishments people may smoke with abandon anywhere.

DOING BUSINESS

Personal relationships always come first here, so developing rapport and trust is essential. A handshake and personal greeting is appropriate along with a friendly inquiry about family, especially if you have met the family. In established business relationships, don't be surprised if you're greeted with a kiss on the cheek or a hug. Always be respectful toward colleagues in public and keep confrontations private.

Meetings may or may not start on time, but you should be patient. When invited to dinner at the home of a client or associate, it's not necessary to bring a gift; however, sending a thank-you note afterward scores points.

Your offers to pick up the tab at business lunches or dinners will be greatly appreciated but will probably be declined; as a guest in their country, most Mexicans will want to treat you to the meal. Be prepared to exchange business cards, and feel free to offer yours first. Professional attire tends to be on the conservative side. Mexicans are extremely well-groomed, so you'll do well if you follow suit.

■ EMERGENCIES

If you get into a scrape with the law, you can call your nearest consulate; U.S. citizens can also call the Overseas Citizens Services Center in the United States. The Mexican Ministry of Tourism has Infotur, a 24-hour toll-free hotline.

Consulate and Embassy United States Consul (✉ Local 4, Int. L-7, 2nd fl., Centro Comercial Paradise Plaza, Nuevo Vallarta, Puerto Vallarta ☎ 322/222–0069). U.S. Embassy (✉ Paseo de la Reforma 305, Col. Cuauhtémoc, Mexico City ☎ 55/5080–2000 ⊕ mexico. usembassy.gov).

General Emergency Contacts General Emergency (Police, Transit, Fire) (☎ 060 or 066). Infotur (☎ 01800/903–9200 toll-free in Mexico). U.S. Overseas Citizens Services Center (☎ 888/407–4747 or 202/501–4444 ⊕ www.travel.state.gov).

■ HEALTH

FOOD AND DRINK

Despite concerns raised by the H1N1 influenza outbreak of early 2009, in Mexico the biggest health risk is *turista* (traveler's diarrhea) caused by consuming contaminated fruit, vegetables, or water. To minimize risks, avoid questionable-looking street stands and bad-smelling food even in the toniest establishments; and if you're not sure of a restaurant's standards, pass up ceviche (raw fish cured in lemon juice) and raw vegetables that haven't been or can't be, peeled (e.g., lettuce and tomatoes).

Drink only bottled water or water that has been boiled for at least 20 minutes, even when you're brushing your teeth. *Agua mineral* or *agua con gas* means mineral or carbonated water, and *agua purificada* means purified water. Hotels with water-purification systems will post signs to that effect in the rooms; even then, it's best not to drink the stuff.

Despite these warnings, keep in mind that Puerto Vallarta, Nuevo Vallarta, and the Costalegre have virtually no industry beyond tourism and are unlikely to kill (or seriously distress) the geese that lay their golden egg. Some people choose to bend the rules about eating at street stands and fresh fruits and chopped lettuce or cabbage, as there's no guarantee that you won't get sick at a five-star resort and have a delicious, healthful meal at a shack by the sea. If fish or seafood smells or tastes bad, send it back and ask for something different.

Don't fret about ice: tourist-oriented hotels and restaurants, and even most of those geared toward the locals, use purified water for ice, drinks, and washing vegetables. Many alleged cases of food poisoning are due instead to hangovers or excessive drinking in the strong sun. But whenever you're in doubt, ask questions about the origins of food and water and if you feel unsure, err on the side of safety.

Mild cases of turista may respond to Imodium (known generically as loperamide), Lomotil, or Pepto-Bismol (not as strong), all of which you can buy over the counter; keep in mind, though, that these drugs can complicate more serious illnesses. You'll need to replace fluids, so drink plenty of purified water or tea; chamomile tea (*te de manzanilla*) is a good folk remedy, and it's readily available in restaurants throughout Mexico.

In severe cases, rehydrate yourself with Gatorade or a salt-sugar solution (½ teaspoon salt and 4 tablespoons sugar per quart of water). If your fever and diarrhea last longer than a day or two, see a doctor—you may have picked up a parasite or disease that requires prescription medication.

PESTS

Mosquitoes are most prevalent during the rainy season, when it's best to use mosquito repellent daily, even in the city; if you're in jungly or wet places and lack strong repellent, consider covering up well or going indoors at dusk (called the "mosquito hour" by locals).

An excellent brand of *repelente de insectos* (insect repellent) called Autan is readily available; do not use it on children under age two. Repellents that are not at least 10% DEET or picaridin are not effective here. If you're hiking in the jungle or boggy areas, wear repellent and long pants and sleeves; if you're camping in the jungle, use a mosquito net and invest in a package of *espirales contra mosquitos,* mosquito coils, which are sold in *farmacias,* or *tlalpalerías* (hardware stores).

OTHER ISSUES
According to the CDC, there's a limited risk of malaria, dengue fever, and other insect-carried or parasite-caused illnesses in certain areas of Mexico (largely but not exclusively rural and tropical coastal areas). In most urban or easily accessible areas you need not worry. If, however, you're traveling to remote areas or simply prefer to err on the side of caution, check with the CDC's International Travelers' Hotline. Malaria and dengue are both carried by mosquitoes; in areas where these illnesses are prevalent, use insect-repellant coiling, clothing, and sprays/lotion. Also consider taking antimalarial pills if you're doing serious adventure activities in tropical and subtropical areas.

Make sure polio and diphtheria–tetanus shots are up-to-date well before your trip. Hepatitis A and typhoid are transmitted through unclean food or water. Gamma-globulin shots prevent hepatitis; an inoculation is available for typhoid, although it's not 100% effective.

Caution is advised when venturing out in the Mexican sun. Sunbathers lulled by a slightly overcast sky or the sea breezes can be burned badly in just 20 minutes. To avoid overexposure, use strong sunscreens, sit under a shade umbrella, and avoid the peak sun hours of noon to 3 PM. Sunscreen, including many Ameri-can brands, can be found in pharmacies, supermarkets, and resort gift shops.

Health Information National Centers for Disease Control & Prevention (*CDC* ☎*800/232–4636 international travelers' health line* ⊕ *www.cdc.gov/travel*). **World Health Organization** (*WHO* ⊕ *www.who.int*).

MEDICAL CARE
Cornerstone Hospital accepts various types of foreign health insurance and traveler's insurance and is American owned. The other recommended, privately owned hospital is Hospital San Javier Marina. Although most small towns have at least a clinic, most travelers would be more comfortable traveling to the major hospitals than using these clinics.

Farmacias (pharmacies) are the most convenient place for such common medicines as *aspirina* (aspirin) or *jarabe para la tos* (cough syrup). You'll be able to find many U.S. brands (e.g., Tylenol, Pepto-Bismol), but don't plan on buying your favorite prescription or nonprescription sleep aid, for example. The same brands and even drugs aren't always available. The Sanborns chain stores also have pharmacies, as do the Cornerstone and San Javier Marina hospitals.

Pharmacies are usually open daily 9 AM to 10 PM; on Sunday and in some small towns they may close several hours earlier. In neighborhoods or smaller towns where there are no 24-hour drug stores, local pharmacies take turns staying open 24 hours so that there's usually at least one open on any given night—it's called the *farmacia de turno*. Information about late-night pharmacies is published in the daily newspaper, but the staff at your hotel should be able to help you find an all-night place.

Hospitals and Clinics **Cornerstone Hospital** (⊠*Av. Los Tules 136, next to Plaza Caracol, Zona Hotelera* ☎*322/226–3700* ⊕*www.hospitalcornerstone.com*). **Hospital San Javier Marina** (⊠*Blvd. Francisco M. Ascencio 2760,* at María Montessori, Zona Hotelera Norte (☎ 322/226–1010).

Pharmacy Farmacia CMQ (✉ Calle Basilio Badillo 36548350 ☎ 322/222–2941 ⊕ www. cmq.com.mx).

MEDICAL INSURANCE AND ASSISTANCE

Consider buying trip insurance with medical-only coverage. Neither Medicare nor some private insurers cover medical expenses anywhere outside of the United States. Medical-only policies typically reimburse you for medical care (excluding that related to pre-existing conditions) and hospitalization abroad, and provide for evacuation. You still have to pay the bills and await reimbursement from the insurer, though.

Another option is to sign up with a medical-evacuation assistance company. Membership gets you doctor referrals, emergency evacuation or repatriation, 24-hour hotlines for medical consultation, and other assistance. International SOS Assistance Emergency and AirMed International provide evacuation services and medical referrals. MedjetAssist offers medical evacuation.

Medical Assistance Companies AirMed International (⊕ www.airmed.com). **International SOS Assistance Emergency** (⊕ www. intsos.com). **MedjetAssist** (⊕ www.medjet assist.com).

Medical-Only Insurers International Medical Group (☎ 800/628–4664 ⊕ www. imglobal.com). **International SOS** (⊕ www. internationalsos.com). **Wallach & Company** (☎ 800/237–6615 or 540/687–3166 ⊕ www. wallach.com).

▮ HOURS OF OPERATION

Banks are generally open weekdays 9 to 3. In Puerto Vallarta most are open until 4, and some of the larger banks keep a few branches open Saturday from 9 or 10 to 1 or 2:30; however, the extended hours are often for deposits or check cashing only.

HSBC is the one chain that stays open for longer hours; on weekdays it is open 8 to 7 and on Saturday from 8 to 3. Government offices are usually open to the public weekdays 9 to 3; along with banks and most private offices, they're closed on national holidays.

Gas stations are normally open 7 AM– 10 PM daily. Those near major thoroughfares stay open 24 hours, including most holidays.

Stores are generally open weekdays and Saturday from 9 or 10 AM to 5 or 7 PM; in resort areas, those stores geared to tourists may stay open until 9 or 10 at night, all day on Saturday; some are open on Sunday as well, but it's good to call ahead before making a special trip. Some more traditional shops close for a two-hour lunch break, roughly 2–4. Airport shops are open seven days a week.

HOLIDAYS

Banks and government offices close on January 1, February 5 (Constitution Day), March 21 (Benito Juárez's birthday), May 1 (Labor Day), September 16 (Independence Day), November 20 (Revolution Day), and December 25. They may also close on unofficial holidays, such as Day of the Dead (November 1–2), Virgin of Guadalupe Day (December 12), and during Holy Week (the days leading to Easter Sunday). Government offices usually have reduced hours and staff from Christmas through New Year's Day.

▮ MAIL

The Mexican postal system is notoriously slow and unreliable; never send packages through the postal service or expect to receive them, as they may be stolen. (For emergencies, use a courier service.)

Post offices (oficinas de correos) are found in even the smallest villages. International postal service is all airmail, but even so your letter will take anywhere from 10 days to six weeks to arrive. Service within

Mexico can be equally slow. It costs 10.5 pesos (about 70 cents) to send a postcard or letter weighing under 20 grams to the United States or Canada; it's 13 pesos ($1.17) to Europe and 14.5 pesos ($1.30) to Australia and New Zealand.

Contacts Correos (⊠ *Calle Mina 188, El Centro* ☎ *322/222–1888*).

SHIPPING PACKAGES

Federal Express, DHL, Estafeta, and United Parcel Service are available in major cities and many resort areas (though PV doesn't have a FedEx office). It's best to send all packages using one of these services. These companies offer office or hotel pickup with 24-hour advance notice (sometimes less, depending on when you call) and are very reliable. FedEx's Web site is especially easy to navigate. From Puerto Vallarta to large U.S. cities, for example, the minimum charge is around $30 for an envelope weighing about ½ pound.

Express Services DHL (⊠ *Blvd. Francisco M. Ascencio 1834, across from Sheraton, Col. Olímpica* ☎ *322/222–4720 or 01800/765–6345* ⊕ *www.dhl.com*). **Estafeta** (⊠ *Blvd. Francisco M. Ascencio 1834, across from Mega grocery store, Col. Olímpica* ☎ *322/223–2700 or 322/223–2898* ⊕ *www.estafeta.com*). **Mail Boxes Etc.** (⊠ *Edifício Andrea Mar, Blvd. Francisco M. Ascencio 2180, Local 7, Zona Hotelera Norte (Col. Versalles)* ✛ *Across from Hotel Los Tules* ☎ *322/224–9434*).

▌ MONEY

Prices in this book are quoted most often in U.S. dollars. Some services in Mexico quote prices in dollars, others in pesos. Because of the current fluctuation in the dollar/peso market, prices may be different than those listed here, but we've done our best at this writing to give accurate rates.

A stay in one of Puerto Vallarta's top hotels can cost more than $350, but if you aren't wedded to standard creature

comforts, you can spend as little as $40 a day on room, board, and local transportation. Lodgings are less expensive in the less developed spots north and south of Puerto Vallarta as well as the charming but unsophisticated mountain towns like San Sebastián del Oeste.

You can get away with a tab of $50 for two at a wonderful restaurant (although it's also easy to pay much more). The good news is that there are hotels and eateries for every budget, and inexpensive doesn't necessarily mean bargain basement. This guide will clue you in to some excellent places to stay, eat, and play for extremely reasonable prices.

ITEM	AVERAGE COST
Cup of Coffee	80¢ to $2.50
Glass of Wine	$3.50–$8
Bottle of Beer	$1.50–$3
Sandwich	$2.50–$4
One-Mile Taxi Ride	$3
Museum Admission	$1

Prices throughout this guide are given for adults. Substantially reduced fees are almost always available for children, students, and senior citizens.

ATMS AND BANKS

ATMs (*cajeros automáticos*) are widely available, with Cirrus and Plus the most frequently found networks. Your own bank will probably charge a fee for using ATMs abroad; the foreign bank you use may also charge a fee. You'll usually get a better rate of exchange at an ATM, however, than you will at a currency-exchange office or at a teller window. And extracting funds as you need them is a safer option than carrying around a large amount of cash.

Many Mexican ATMs cannot accept PINs with more than four digits. If yours is longer, change your PIN to four digits before you leave home. If your PIN is fine yet your transaction still can't be completed, chances are that the computer lines are busy or that the machine has run out of money or is being serviced. Don't give up.

For cash advances, plan to use Visa or MasterCard, as many Mexican ATMs don't accept American Express. Large banks with reliable ATMs include Banamex, HSBC, BBVA Bancomer, Santander Serfín, and Scotiabank Inverlat. Travelers must have their passport or other official identification in order to change traveler's checks.

Banks Banamex (✉ *Calle Juárez, at Calle Zaragoza, Centro* ☎ *322/226–6110* ✉ *Calle Emiliano Zapata 175, Pitillal* ☎ *322/224–8115* ✉ *Paseo de los Cocoteros s/n, Paradise Plaza, Nuevo Vallarta* ☎ *322/297–0688).* **Banorte** (✉ *Paseo Díaz Ordaz 690 at Calle L. Vicario, Centro* ☎ *322/222–4040* ✉ *Calle Olas Altas 246, at Calle Basilio Badillo, E. Zapata* ☎ *322/223–0481* ✉ *Blvd. Francisco M. Ascencio 500, Zona Hotelera Norte* ☎ *322/224–9744).*

CREDIT CARDS

Throughout this guide, the following abbreviations are used: **AE**, American Express; **D**, Discover; **DC**, Diners Club; **MC**, MasterCard; and **V**, Visa.

Credit cards are accepted in Puerto Vallarta and at major hotels and restaurants in outlying areas. Smaller, less expensive restaurants and shops tend to take only cash. In general, credit cards aren't accepted in small towns and villages, except in some hotels. The most widely accepted cards are MasterCard and Visa.

When shopping, you can often get better prices if you pay with cash, particularly in small shops. But you'll receive wholesale exchange rates when you make purchases with credit cards. These exchange rates are usually better than those that banks give you for changing money. The decision to pay cash or to use a credit card might depend on whether the establishment in which you are making a purchase finds bargaining for prices acceptable, and whether you want the safety net of

your card's purchase protection. To avoid fraud or errors, it's wise to make sure that "pesos" is clearly marked on all credit-card receipts.

Before you leave for Mexico, contact your credit-card company to get lost-card phone numbers that work in Mexico; the standard toll-free numbers often don't work abroad. Carry these numbers separately from your wallet so you'll have them if you need to call to report lost or stolen cards. American Express, MasterCard, and Visa note the international number for card-replacement calls on the back of their cards.

CURRENCY AND EXCHANGE

Mexican currency comes in denominations of 20-, 50-, 100-, 200-, and 500-peso bills. Coins come in denominations of 1, 2, 5, 10, and 20 pesos and 20 and 50 centavos. (Twenty-centavo coins are only rarely seen.) Many of the coins are very similar, so check carefully; bills, however, are different colors and easily distinguished.

U.S. dollar bills (but not coins) are widely accepted in tourist-oriented shops and restaurants in Puerto Vallarta. Pay in pesos where possible, however, for better prices. Although in larger hotels U.S. dollars are welcome as tips, it's generally better to tip in pesos so that service personnel aren't stuck going to the bank to exchange currency.

At this writing, the exchange rate was 15 pesos to the U.S. dollar. ATM transaction fees may be higher abroad than at home, but ATM exchange rates are the best because they're based on wholesale rates offered only by major banks. Most ATMs allow a maximum withdrawal of $300 to $400 per transaction. Banks and *casas de cambio* (money-exchange bureaus) have the second-best exchange rates. The difference from one place to another is usually only a few pesos.

Some banks change money on weekdays only until 1 or 3 PM (though they stay open until 4 or 5 or later). Casas de cambio generally stay open until 6 or later and often operate on weekends; they usually have competitive rates and much shorter lines. Some hotels exchange money, but they give a poor exchange rate.

You can do well at most airport exchange booths, though not as well as at the ATMs. You'll do even worse at bus stations, in hotels, in restaurants, or in stores.

When changing money, count your bills before leaving the window of the bank or casa de cambio, and don't accept any partially torn or taped-together notes: you won't be able to use them anywhere. Also, many shop and restaurant owners are unable to make change for large bills. Enough of these encounters may compel you to request *billetes chicos* (small bills) when you exchange money. It's wise to have a cache of smaller bills and coins to use at these more humble establishments to avoid having to wait around while the merchant runs off to seek change.

PACKING

High-style sportswear, cotton slacks and walking shorts, and plenty of colorful sundresses are the palette of clothing you'll see in PV. Bring lightweight sportswear, bathing suits, and cover-ups for the beach. In addition to shorts, pack at least a pair or two of lightweight long pants.

Men may want to bring a lightweight suit or slacks and blazers for fancier restaurants (although very few have dress codes). For women, dresses of cotton, linen, or other lightweight, breathable fabrics are recommended. Puerto Vallarta restaurants are extremely tolerant of casual dress, but it never hurts to exceed expectations.

The sun can be fierce; bring a sun hat and sunscreen for the beach and for sightseeing. You'll need a sweater or jacket to cope with hotel and restaurant air-conditioning, which can be glacial,

and for occasional cool spells. A lightweight jacket is a necessity in winter, and pack an umbrella for summer or unexpected rainstorms.

Bring along tissue packs in case you hit a place where the toilet paper has run out. You'll find familiar toiletries and hygiene products, as well as condoms, in shops in PV and in most rural areas.

PASSPORTS AND VISAS

In early 2007, the first part of the Western Hemisphere Travel Initiative (WHTI) went into effect, requiring air travelers to present a valid passport to reenter the United States from Mexico. Up until June 2009, you could re-enter the United States via land or sea simply by presenting a government-issued photo ID and another form of proof of citizenship, such as a birth certificate. *Nowadays it's all about the passport.* If, however, you travel frequently between Mexico and the United States by land—as many border-area residents do—or sea, the U.S. passport card is also acceptable. It's smaller (think wallet size) and cheaper than a passport and valid for just as long, but you can't use it for travel by air.

Upon entering Mexico all visitors must get a tourist card. If you're arriving by plane from the United States or Canada, the standard tourist card will be given to you on the plane. They're also available through travel agents and Mexican consulates and at the border if you're entering by land.

■TIP→ You're given a portion of the tourist card form upon entering Mexico. Keep track of this documentation throughout your trip: you will need it when you depart. You'll be asked to hand it, your ticket, and your passport to airline representatives at the gate when boarding for departure.

If you lose your tourist card, plan to spend some time (and about $60) sorting it out with Mexican officials at the airport on departure.

A tourist card costs about $20. The fee is generally tacked onto the price of your airline ticket; if you enter by land or boat you'll have to pay the fee separately. You're exempt from the fee if you enter by sea and stay less than 72 hours, or by land and do not stray past the 26- to 30-km (16- to 18-mi) checkpoint into the country's interior.

Tourist cards and visas are valid from 15 to 180 days, at the discretion of the immigration officer at your point of entry (90 days for Australians). Americans, Canadians, New Zealanders, and the British may request up to 180 days for a tourist card or visa extension. The extension fee is about $20, and the process can be time-consuming. There's no guarantee that you'll get the extension you're requesting. If you're planning an extended stay, plead with the immigration official for the maximum allowed days at the time of entry. It will save you time and money later.

■**TIP➜** Mexico has some of the strictest policies about children entering the country. Minors traveling with one parent need notarized permission from the absent parent. And all children, including infants, must have proof of citizenship (the same as adults; ➪*above*) for travel to Mexico.

If you're a single parent traveling with children up to age 18, you must have a notarized letter from the other parent stating that the child has his or her permission to leave his or her home country. The child must be carrying the original letter—not a facsimile or scanned copy—as well as proof of the parent/child relationship (usually a birth certificate or court document), and an original custody decree, if applicable. If the other parent is deceased or the child has only one legal parent, a notarized statement saying so must be obtained as proof. In addition, you must fill out a tourist card for each child over the age of 10 traveling with you.

Info Mexican Embassy (☎ 202/728–1600 ⊕ *portal.sre.gob.mx/usa/*).

U.S. Passport Information U.S. Department of State (☎ 877/487–2778 ⊕ *travel.state.gov/ passport*).

■ RESTROOMS

Expect to find reasonably clean flushing toilets and cold running water at public restrooms in the major tourist destinations and attractions; toilet paper, soap, hot water, and paper towels aren't always available, though. Keep a packet of tissues with you at all times.

At many markets, bus stations, and the like you usually have to pay 5 pesos to use the facilities.

■**TIP➜** Remember that unless otherwise indicated you should put your used toilet paper in the wastebasket next to the toilet; many plumbing systems in Mexico still can't handle toilet paper.

Gas stations have public bathrooms—some tidy and others not so tidy. You're better off popping into a restaurant, buying a little something (or not), and using its restroom, which will probably be simple but clean and adequately equipped.

Find a Loo The Bathroom Diaries (⊕ *www. thebathroomdiaries.com*) is flush with unsanitized info on restrooms the world over—each one located, reviewed, and rated.

■ SAFETY

Horror stories about drug-cartel killings and border violence are making big news these days, but Puerto Vallarta is many hundreds of miles away. Imagine not going to visit the Florida Keys because of reports of violence in a bad section of New York City. Still, Puerto Vallarta is no longer the innocent of years gone by; pickpocketing and the occasional mugging can be a concern, and precaution is in order here as elsewhere. Store only enough money in your wallet or bag to cover the day's spending. And don't flash big wads of money or leave valuables like cameras unattended. Leave your passport and other valuables you don't need in your hotel's safe.

Bear in mind that reporting a crime to the police is often a frustrating experience unless you speak good Spanish and have a great deal of patience. If you're victimized, contact your local consulate or your embassy in Mexico City.

One of the most serious threats to your safety is local drivers. Although pedestrians have the right-of-way, drivers disregard this law. And more often than not, drivers who hit pedestrians drive away as fast as they can without stopping, to avoid jail. Many Mexican drivers don't carry auto insurance, so you'll have to shoulder your own medical expenses. Pedestrians should be extremely cautious of all traffic, especially city bus drivers, who often drive with truly reckless abandon.

If you're on your own, consider using only your first initial and last name when registering at your hotel. Solo travelers, or women traveling with other women rather than men, may be subjected to *piropos* (flirtatious compliments). Piropos are one thing, but more aggressive harassment is another. If the situation seems to be getting out of hand, don't hesitate to ask someone for help. If you express outrage, you should find no shortage of willing defenders.

General Information and Warnings Transportation Security Administration (*TSA* ⊕ *www.tsa.gov*). **U.S. Department of State** (⊕ *www.travel.state.gov*).

▌ TAXES

Mexico charges an airport departure tax of US$18 or the peso equivalent for international and domestic flights. This tax is usually included in the price of your ticket, but check to be certain. Traveler's checks and credit cards aren't accepted at the airport as payment for this, but U.S. dollars are. Jalisco and Nayarit charge a 2% tax on accommodations, the funds from which are being used for tourism promotion.

Puerto Vallarta and environs have a value-added tax of 15%, called IVA (*impuesto al valor agregado*). It's often waived for cash purchases, or it's incorporated into the price. When comparing hotel prices, it's important to know if yours includes or excludes IVA and any service charge. Other taxes and charges apply for phone calls made from your hotel room.

▌ TIME

Puerto Vallarta, Guadalajara, and the rest of Jalisco State fall into Central Standard Time (the same as Mexico City). Nayarit and other parts of the northwest coast are on Mountain Standard Time.

The fact that the state of Nayarit (including Nuevo Vallarta and points north) are in a different time zone from Puerto Vallarta and points east and south leads to confusion. And to add to this confusion, Mexico does observe daylight savings time, but not on the same schedule as the United States.

▌**TIP→** Businesses in Nuevo Vallarta and some tourism-related businesses in Bucerías run on Jalisco time.

Since tourism in these towns has traditionally been linked to that of Puerto Vallarta, hotels in the two areas almost always run on Jalisco time to avoid having their clients miss planes when returning home. However, as Nayarit exerts itself as a destination in its own right with development of the Riviera Nayarit, this is no longer a given. When asking the time, checking hours of operation, or making dinner reservations, double-check whether the place runs on *hora de Jalisco* (Jalisco time) or *hora de Nayarit*.

TIPPING GUIDELINES FOR PUERTO VALLARTA

Bartender	10% to 15% of the bill
Bellhop	10 to 30 pesos (roughly 80¢ to $2) per bag, depending on the level of the hotel
Hotel Concierge	30 pesos or more, if he or she performs a service for you
Hotel Doorman	10 to 20 pesos if he helps you get a cab
Hotel Maid	10 to 30 pesos a day (either daily or at the end of your stay); make sure the maid gets it, and not the guy who checks the minibar prior to your departure
Hotel Room-Service Waiter	10 to 20 pesos per delivery, even if a service charge has been added
Porter/Skycap at Airport	10 to 20 pesos per bag
Restroom Attendant	5 pesos
Taxi Driver	cab drivers aren't normally tipped; give them 5 to 10 pesos if they help with your bags
Tour Guide	10% of the cost of the tour
Valet Parking Attendant	10 to 20 pesos but only when you get your car
Waiter	10% to 15%; nothing additional if a service charge is added to the bill

▮ TIPPING

When tipping in Mexico, remember that the minimum wage—which is what those on the lowest rungs of the tourism industry earn—is just under $5 a day. Waiters and bellmen in international chain hotels think in dollars and know, for example, that in the United States porters are tipped about $2 a bag; they tend to expect the equivalent.

▮ TRIP INSURANCE

Comprehensive trip insurance is valuable if you're booking a very expensive or complicated trip (particularly to an isolated region) or if you're booking far in advance. Comprehensive policies typically cover trip cancellation and interruption, letting you cancel or cut your trip short because of a personal emergency, illness, or, in some cases, acts of terrorism in your destination. Such policies also cover evacuation and medical care. (For trips abroad you should at least have medical-only coverage). Some also cover you for trip delays because of bad weather or mechanical problems as well as for lost or delayed baggage.

Another type of coverage to look for is financial default—that is, when your trip is disrupted because a tour operator, airline, or cruise line goes out of business. Generally you must buy this when you book your trip or shortly thereafter, and it's only available to you if your operator isn't on a list of excluded companies.

Always read the fine print of your policy to make sure that you are covered for the risks that are of most concern to you. Compare several policies to make sure you're getting the best price and range of coverage available.

Insurance Comparison Sites Insure My Trip. com (☎ 800/487–4722 ⊕ www.insuremytrip. com). **Square Mouth.com** (☎ 800/240–0369 ⊕ www.squaremouth.com).

Comprehensive Travel Insurers Access America (☎ 800/284–8300 ⊕ www.accessamerica. com). **AIG Travel Guard** (☎ 800/826–4919 ⊕ www.travelguard.com). **CSA Travel Protection** (☎ 800/711–1197 ⊕ www.csatravelprotection. com). **Travelex Insurance** (☎ 800/228–9792 ⊕ www.travelex-insurance.com). **Travel Insured International** (☎ 800/243–3174 ⊕ www.travel insured.com).

▮ **TIP→ OK.** You know you can save a bundle on trips to warm-weather destinations by traveling in rainy season. But there's also a chance that a severe storm will disrupt your plans. The solution? Look for hotels and resorts that offer storm/hurricane guarantees. Although they rarely allow refunds, most guarantees do let you rebook later if a storm strikes.

▌ VISITOR INFORMATION

Contacts Abroad Mexican Ministry of Tourism (SECTUR) (☎ *55/3002–6300, 01800/006–8839 toll-free in Mexico* ⊕ *www. sectur.gob.mx*). **Mexican Tourism Board (U.S. and Canada)** (☎ *800/446–3942 [44-MEXICO] in U.S. and Canada* ⊕ *www.visitmexico.com*).

PV and Jalisco Contacts Jalisco State Tourism Office (✉ *Plaza Marina shopping center, Local 144, Planta Alta, Marina Vallarta* ☎ *322/221–2676*). **Municipal Tourist Office** (✉ *Av. Independencia 123, Centro* ☎ *322/223–2500 Ext. 131*). **Puerto Vallarta Tourism Board & Convention and Visitors Bureau** (✉ *Local 18 Planta Baja, Zona Comercial Hotel Canto del Sol, Zona Hotelera, Las Glorias* ☎ *322/224–1175, 888/384–6822 in U.S., 01800/719–3276 in Mexico* ⊕ *www.visit puertovallarta.com*).

NV and Nayarit Contacts Bay of Banderas/ Nuevo Vallarta Tourism Office (✉ *Paseo de los Cocoteros at Blvd. Nuevo Vallarta, between Gran Velas and Maribal hotels* ☎ *322/297–1006* ⊕ *www.visitnayarit.com*).

Riviera Nayarit Convention & Visitors Bureau (✉ *Paseo de los Cocoteros 85 Sur, Local Int. 6–A, Paradise Plaza* ☎ *322/297–2516* ⊕ *www. rivieranayarit.com*).

ONLINE RESOURCES

The best of the private-enterprise Web sites are PV Mirror and Virtual Vallarta, which have tons of good info and short articles about life in PV. Bucerías, Sayulita, and Punta Mita have their own Web sites, as does the Costalegre region as a whole.

Excellent English-language sites for general history, travel information, facts, and news stories about Mexico are Mexico Online and Mexico Connect. Mexico Guru has news about PV and nearby destinations, and interactive maps.

The nonprofit site Ancient Mexico has information about western Mexico as well as more comprehensive information about the Maya and Aztecs.

Contacts Ancient Mexico (⊕ *www.ancient mexico.com*). **Bucerías** (⊕ *www.bucerias mexico.com*). **Costalegre** (⊕ *www.costalegre. ca*). **Mexico Connect** (⊕ *www.mexconnect. com*). **Mexico Guru** (⊕ *www.mexicoguru. com*). **Mexico Online** (⊕ *www.mexonline. com*). **Punta Mita** (⊕ *www.puntamita.com*). **PV Mirror** (⊕ *www.pvmirror.com*). **Sayulita Life** (⊕ *www.sayulitalife.com*). **Virtual Vallarta** (⊕ *www.virtualvallarta.com*).

INDEX

NOTES

NOTES

NOTES

NOTES

ABOUT OUR WRITER

Jane Onstott was primed for adventure travel in her late teens, when she wandered Central America for six months after being stood up at the Tegucigalpa airport up by an inattentive suitor. She has since survived a near plunge into a gorge in the highlands of Mexico, a knife-wielding robber in Madrid, and a financial shipwreck on one of the more remote Galapagos Islands. The last led to a position as director of communications and information at the Charles Darwin Research Station on the island of Santa Cruz, where she lectured on the ecology of Ecuador's unique Galapagos archipelago.

Jane's trip to rural Honduras became an unofficial total-language-immersion course, paving the way for a love of the Spanish language and of Hispanic culture. She studied for a year at la Universidad Complutense de Madrid, in Spain, and graduated from San Diego State University with a B.A. in Spanish language and literature.

But at age 17 this adventurer's first foray outside the United States—Southern California's concrete jungle—was to a small village in the tropical forest just a few hours north of Puerto Vallarta. The stick-and-thatch house where she stayed has since been replaced by a more modern one of cement and bright stucco, but the warm hearts of its owners have changed little in the ensuing three decades. Mexico is Jane's favorite country, and the surrounding coast is one of her more frequent destinations, whether she's traveling for business or pleasure.

In the 1990s Jane spent several years studying painting, sculpting, and the fine art of loafing in Oaxaca—ancient capital of the Zapotec nation—where she was inspired by landscape, the people, and the culture. Today Jane continues to edit and write mainly about travel and mostly about Mexico. She has a home in San Diego county, a short hop north of the border—and of the Tijuana airport.